David Austin **The Rose**

# DAVID AUSTIN

# THE ROSE

GARDEN
•ART•
PRESS

## Acknowledgements

I would like to thank all those who have assisted me in the writing and production of this book; in particular:

Michael Marriott, for his help in describing many of the Hybrid Teas and Floribunda Roses and some of the Climbers—also, for much other assistance.

Erica Hunningher, for her diligent editing and other valuable advice; also for making a major contribution, together with Tony Lord, on the subject of plants for association with roses.

My Publisher, Diana Steel of the Antique Collectors' Club, for her encouragement and help.

Ken Wilson, for his beautiful design work.

Finally, I would particularly like to thank Diane Ratcliff for typing the manuscript and for making many helpful suggestions on the use of the English language.

## Author's note

I should like to make a suggestion as to how my book might be used, since few people read a book of this kind in its entirety. My advice to readers using it to find roses for a specific purpose is to start with the short introductory sections to each group of roses. These will give an overall picture of the various classes of roses that are available to us today and readers can then choose the most suitable.

To my wife Pat

# CONTENTS

Frontispiece
*A mass of roses in one corner of
the Long Garden at David Austin Roses
with CAPITAINE JOHN INGRAM
in the foreground and, from left to right,
the ramblers MARY WALLACE,
ALEXANDRE GIRAULT
and PAUL'S HIMALAYAN MUSK
at the back.*

This page, left to right
*Top row, 1 MRS OAKLEY FISHER;
2 MARGARET MERRIL; 3 × ALBA ALBA
SEMIPLENA; 4 MOUNTBATTEN;
5 COMTES DE CHAMPAGNE;
6 JULIA'S ROSE; 7 NATHALIE NYPELS;
8 BLYTHE SPIRIT; 9 GEORG ARENDS.
Second row, 1 FRAGRANT CLOUD;
2 VIOLACEA; 3 L'AIMANT;
4 LOUISE ODIER; 5 MUNSTEAD WOOD;
6 DUSKY MAIDEN; 7 PERLE D'OR;
8 TUSCANY SUPERB;
9 CROWN PRINCESS MARGARETA*

# *Introduction*

# THE ROSE

FOR CENTURIES the rose has been the most popular of all garden flowers in the Western world and it is still so today. More recently, its popularity has spread to most other parts of the world. Fortunately, the rose has a remarkable adaptability and will grow and thrive in a great variety of climates.

Why the rose should be so admired is easier to see than to explain in words. It is certainly very different in character from other flowers. The best explanation I can give is that, to me at least, the rose has a certain charm and humanity that we do not find in any other flower. There is also an informality about the flower that is unique to the rose and the growth tends to be rampant and almost out of control—though not quite. Both these are qualities that we might describe as very human. This would explain why it is that the rose, over its long history, has always been used as a symbol of love and beauty.

The history of the rose as a garden flower goes back further than any other, with the possible exception of the peony in China and Japan, the earliest known illustration being found on a north African tombstone in the 5th century AD. Since that period, the rose has spread all over the Middle East and Europe until, today, it is known and loved world wide. It is not too much to say that since almost the beginning of civilisation, the rose has never been far from humankind.

Throughout the history of western civilization, from the earliest times to the present day, the rose has been the

*Right,* UT ROSA FLOS FLORUM SIC EST DOMUS ISTA DOMORUM: *'As the rose is the flower of flowers so this is the house of houses.' This 13th century panel is from the Chapter House at York Minster. The same inscription can be found in the floor tiles at Westminster Abbey in London*

*Facing page, royal lovers in a rose garden:* The Persian Prince Humay meeting the Chinese Princess Humayun in a Garden, c.1450

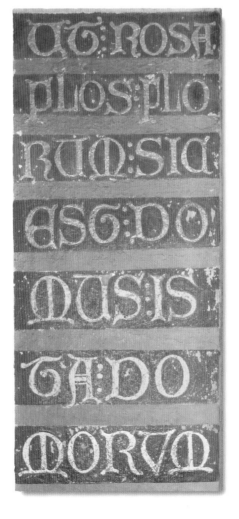

flower closest to the heart of man. During this time the rose has never stood still—it has always been changing and evolving —first by chance hybridization and more recently, by the hand of man; each new period building on the work of the past.

In Greek mythology Aphrodite, goddess of love, was regarded as the creator of the rose, which was supposed to have arisen from a mixture of her tears and the blood of her wounded lover Adonis. In Roman legend it was said to have sprung from the blood of Venus. Again and again, we find it appearing in ancient history as a symbol of love and beauty, and sometimes of licentiousness and excess.

With the rise of Christianity the rose was at first looked upon with disapproval due to its pagan past, but this attitude soon changed, and we find the rose becoming intertwined with the Christian faith; for example, the rosary and the idea of the five petals of the rose representing the five wounds of Christ. Indeed, it was the church which was in a large degree responsible for carrying the rose across Europe to many lands.

Although we in the West, and in Britain in particular, like to think of the rose as being very much our own, this is

by no means entirely true. Roses appear at one time or another in association with Brahma, Buddha, Mahomet, Vishnu and Confucius, and the origins of the roses we enjoy today lie in a large degree in the lands of the Middle and Far East. This is perhaps best summed up in the following extract from Vita Sackville-West's long poem *The Garden* (1946):

> June of the iris and the rose,
> The rose not English as we fondly think,
> Anacreon and Bion sang the rose;
> And Rhodes the isle whose very name means rose
> Struck roses on her coins;
> Pliny made lists and Roman libertines
> Made wreaths to war among the flutes and wines;
> The young Crusaders found the Syrian rose
> Springing from Saracenic quoins,
> And China opened her shut gate
> To let her roses through, and Persian shrines
> Of poetry and painting gave the rose.

Throughout history the rose has appeared in painting and sculpture, on pottery and fabrics, and as a decoration of all kinds, in all ages and in many lands.

It is, however, in poetry and literature that this affection is most vividly proclaimed, both for the beauty of the rose itself and as a symbol of all that is best and most beautiful in human nature. As early as the 5th century BC what is probably the first poem to the rose was written by the poet Anacreon:

> I sing of Spring, flower crowned
> I sing the praises of the Rose
> Friend aid me in my song.
> The rose is the perfume of the Gods,
>     the joy of men,
> It adorns the Graces at the blossoming
>     of Love,
> It is the favoured flower of Venus,
> It is the chief care of the Nymphs,
> It is the joy of the Muses,
> In spite of its many thorns
> We gather it with delight.

The Bible mentions the rose on frequent occasions, as for example in *Isaiah* Chapter 35:

> The wilderness and the solitary place shall be glad for them;
> and the desert shall rejoice and blossom as the rose.

Nearer to our own time, Shakespeare, in his plays and

*Roses in a Dish, 1882, by Henri Fantin-Latour, who is best known for his flower paintings, especially of roses*

sonnets, mentions the rose more than sixty times, as for example, in 'My mistress' eyes are nothing like the sun':

> I have seen roses damask'd, red and white
> But no such roses see I in her cheeks.
> …
> And yet, by heaven, I think my love as rare
> As any she belied with false compare.

The great herbalist, Gerard, writing in 1596 in the beautiful language of the time, says of the rose:

> The plant of Roses, though it be a shrub full of prickles, yet is has been more fit and convenient to have placed it with the most glorious of flowers of the worlde, than to insert the same here among base and thornie shrubs; for the rose doth deserve the chiefest and most principall place among all flowers whatsoever, being not only esteemed for his beautie, vertues, and his flagrant [*sic*] and odiferous smell; but also because it is the honour and ornament of our English Scepter, as by the conjunction apeereth in the uniting of these two most royall houses of Lancaster and York.

John Keats, in the 19th century, wrote in his sonnet 'To a friend who sent me some roses':

> But when, O wells, thy roses came to me
> My sense with their deliciousness was
>     spell'd:
> Soft voices had they, that with tender plea
> Whisper'd of peace, and truth, and
>     friendliness unquell'd.

In our own time we have Walter de la Mare's much-quoted lines from his poem 'All that's past':

> Through what wild centuries
> Roves back the rose.

In more sombre mood, from T.S. Eliot's *Little Gidding*, are the lines:

> Ash on an old man's sleeve
> Is all the ash the burnt roses leave.
> Dust in the air suspended
> Marks the place where a story ended.

It would not be difficult to compile a small book of such poems and quotations.

*La France* (*see page 79*), one of the earliest Hybrid Teas, bred by Guillot in 1867, in a lithograph from the March 1879 edition of the Journal des Roses

In painting, too, the rose has been much in evidence, particularly from the Renaissance onwards, although it seems to be less so today, due, perhaps, to the less sympathetic nature of the various modern schools and also perhaps to the less sympathetic nature of the modern rose. In painting, the rose is more often used as an embellishment rather than as a main subject, but time and again it is chosen by the artist for this purpose.

At times we find the rose painted for its own sake, particularly in the paintings of the Dutch school of the late sixteenth and seventeenth centuries. Works by Jan Brueghel, Jan

*Roses from
the* Nassau
Florilegium,
*a volume of
flower paintings
by the 17th-
century artist
Johann Walther,
commissioned
by the Count
of Nassau*

Davidsz de Heem, Rachel Ruysch, Jan van Huysum and Daniel Seghers include many paintings of roses.

As decoration, the rose stands supreme above all other flowers. Indeed it is unusual to walk into any house in the West without finding some representation of a rose. This, I think, illustrates better than anything else the very special place the rose holds in our lives. I remember talking to the chief designer from one of our largest firms of pottery manufacturers who told me that the rose is by far the most popular decoration for china and pottery, the demand for rose designs exceeding those of all other flowers put together.

The rose also appeals to us not simply for its visual beauty, but for its wonderful fragrance or, should I say, fragrances—for these take on many beautiful shades. Indeed, among roses we can find nearly all the fragrances to be found in flowers. The rose fragrance is, in fact, the basis of most manufactured perfumes.

The rose, as a garden plant, has many practical advantages. Foremost among these is the fact that it is alone amongst major garden flowers—or at least, nearly all roses introduced over the past one hundred and fifty years—in being able to bloom throughout the summer.

The rose is also the most adaptable of flowers. There seems to be a rose for every part of the garden. There are Shrub Roses that are excellent for growing with other plants in the flower border; there are roses for formal beds and roses that are suitable for the wilder areas of the garden—the Wild Species from which all roses sprang are themselves beautiful garden flowers. There are also Climbing Roses that are ideal for growing on a wall, or on trellis work. The Rambler Roses are perhaps better for growing on a pergola than any other plant. There are giant rambling roses that will, with a little encouragement, grow up to 12m/40ft into trees or creep along the ground and over other shrubs. At the other end of the spectrum we have tiny miniatures that fit into the smallest gardens.

As if all this were not enough, the rose is one of the few flowers that can successfully be grown in a border of its own and be filled with interest and beauty throughout the summer. Indeed, it is perhaps the only flower that can fill a whole garden. Finally, but by no means least, the rose is the most beautiful of cut flowers. No flower lends itself more to arrangement in the house than the rose.

In this book I endeavour to describe the roses that are available today, from the past to the most recent, which I regard as being worthy of growing in our gardens. Inevitably, these are largely drawn from the last two hundred years or so and most are from the past one hundred years. As I write, I become conscious that I am not only describing the best roses for our garden, but telling the story of a flower that, down the ages, has given countless millions of people pleasure and brought a little happiness into their lives—and never more so than the present day.

*Left, EMPRESS JOSEPHINE (see page 22), a watercolour by Susan Williams-Ellis (1918–2007) for a set of Portmeirion Pottery*

# 1

# THE OLD ROSES

INCLUDED IN THIS CHAPTER are those classes which were established prior to the introduction of the repeat-flowering China Rose at the end of the eighteenth century, that is to say the Gallicas, the Damasks, the Albas, the Centifolias and the Moss Roses. As most readers will be aware these are not

small upright bushes, as are Modern Hybrid Teas, but genuine shrubs like any other shrub in the garden. Their growth will reach somewhere in the region of 90cm–1.8m/3–6ft according to variety, although there are among them many shorter shrubs that fit nicely into a small garden.

The formation of the flowers of the Old Roses is quite different to that with which we have become accustomed today. In the Modern Rose the ideal lies in the bud with its high-pointed centre, and this is indeed often beautiful, but the disadvantage is that the mature flower tends to be muddled and almost completely lacking in form. Old Roses are quite different; their buds, though often charming, are likely to open as small cups, with little petals developing within, but it is as the flower gradually expands into the full bloom that its true beauty is revealed. At this later stage it can take on many forms: it may remain cupped, it may become flat with many petals, or it may reflex at the edges to form an almost domed flower. Between these shapes there are many gradations. The flower may also, of course, be semi-double, exposing an airy bunch of stamens at the centre. Thus we have a bloom that is beautiful at all stages, from the opening of the bud to the eventual fall of the petals. It is this variety of form that makes these roses so worthwhile. Fine as the Hybrid Tea may be, the Old Roses offer so much more scope, and for this reason we have, at our nursery, thought it worthwhile to proceed further with the breeding of roses of the old type. I shall be discussing the role of Old Roses in the development of English Roses in Chapter 5.

It has to be admitted that Old Roses are rather limited in their colour range. We have white through pink all the way to

a maroon-crimson, mauve and purple—all colours often of exceptional purity and softness of tone. Susan Williams-Ellis (who spent many weeks at our nursery painting roses for her Portmeirion Pottery) speaking in terms of fabrics has suggested that these are like vegetable dyes in comparison with the harsher 'chemical' colours of Modern Roses. I think this puts it rather well. There are, unfortunately, only one or two yellows and not many whites, although 'Madame Hardy' and 'Madame Legras de Saint Germain' can produce some of the most perfect blooms. Pink is the true colour of the rose, and in the Old Roses it often has a clarity rarely found elsewhere. The colour crimson is seldom pure in these early roses, but it does have the great virtue of turning to wonderful shades of purple, violet and mauve.

The Old Roses of this section do have one disadvantage, if in fact it can be truly described as a disadvantage; they flower only once in a season, whereas their successors are repeat flowering. It should, however, be borne in mind that we expect no more of any other shrub. We do not, for example, expect repeat flowering of the lilac or the rhododendron. If your garden is reasonably large, you may not wish to have all your roses in flower throughout the summer, even though you will probably like to have at least some in bloom later in the season. You may prefer that they should take their place in due season, like any other flower. It should also be remembered that a rose which flowers but once tends to give a better show for that limited period, during which it is able to devote all its energy to one glorious burst of flowers. It will also usually form a more shapely shrub for, unlike bush roses, shrub roses produce long growth from the base of the plant. This

16

*MADAME
LEGRAS
DE SAINT
GERMAIN
is a rose of
exceptional
beauty with
a strong and
delicious
fragrance*

It is my personal opinion that we are today much too obsessed with the past, and often too little concerned with the creations of our own time. If we consider the devotion that we put into the preservation of old buildings and how little concern we show for new ones, it sometimes seems a little unhealthy. Having said this, there is a certain satisfaction to be gained from the sheer permanence of the Old Roses; we have had time to get to know them and to love them, something that cannot be said for Modern Roses that come and go with bewildering speed. In spite of this, it cannot be stressed too strongly that Old Roses are not mere curiosities but first-class shrubs in their own right, and their gentle colours and more natural growth melt perfectly into the garden scheme. Finally, but by no means least, it is hardly necessary to say that, with the exception of the English Roses, their fragrance excels that of the majority of those which have come after them.

The naming of Old Roses is always a source of controversy and many Old Rose enthusiasts like to show their knowledge on the subject. These roses suffered a long period of neglect before re-emerging in our time, and inevitably many names were lost. Although a great deal of research has gone into finding the correct names, this has not always been possible. A description we find in an old book or catalogue may have been adequate for the gardeners of that time, but is frequently insufficient for us to give a name to a particular rose. It has often been necessary simply to do the best that we can, and, in fact, this does not matter very much, for as we all know, a rose by any other name will smell as sweet. The important thing is to agree on a name so that we all know what we are talking about.

does not flower in the first season but subsequently sends out flowering branches. It is this strong growth that forms the basic structure of a well-shaped shrub which is not only more pleasing to the eye, but which also displays its flowers in a more natural and satisfactory manner.

Almost all these roses are over one hundred years old, and one or two may well be over a thousand years old. There must have been many more of their brethren who have fallen by the wayside. Those that remain really are great survivors. It is, therefore, not surprising that they are extremely tough and hardy. It is our experience that they are also more disease resistant than most Hybrid Teas and Floribundas, mildew being their worst fault, though this is not difficult to control. They are easy to grow and will do well with minimal care, although a little extra attention can yield rich rewards.

The rose has received far more attention from the plant breeder than any other flower, so it may seem strange that so many gardeners should turn back to the beginning and start growing varieties from the distant past. There is little doubt this has something to do with the attractions of the antique, and I see no reason to decry this. There is, however, much more to the Old Roses than this, for they possess a very special charm that is not always to be found in roses of more recent date.

Now that we have the English Roses, the question arises, 'Do we any longer need the Old Roses?' English Roses are hybrids between the Old Roses and the Modern. They have much of the particular kind of beauty of an Old Rose and similar shrubby growth, and yet are regularly repeat flowering and have a much wider range of colour. I, for one, would not like to be without the Old Roses or, indeed, any others. The rose changes in mood over the generations. We never quite regain that particular kind of beauty that belongs to roses of another age. The beauty of a rose is not something that can ever be repeated, any more than an artist can ever repeat a picture from the past.

# Gallica Roses

*ROSA GALLICA* is a native of central and southern Europe. It forms an upright shrub of 1m/3ft in height which suckers freely, with slender stems and many small thorns. It bears deep pink flowers of 5–7cm/2–3in across, followed by round, red hips. Our garden Gallicas have been developed over the centuries from this species.

Although so much of the history of Old Roses is shrouded in mystery, it is safe to assume that the Gallicas are the oldest of garden roses and have been involved, to a greater or lesser extent, in the development of all the four other classes of Old Roses. Their influence is present, at least in some small degree, in nearly all our garden roses of today. Long before they received their name, their predecessors were grown by both the Greeks and Romans and almost certainly by others before them. Although they are the oldest of the truly Old Roses, they also became the most highly developed. In 1629 the great English botanist and gardener John Parkinson listed twelve varieties. A little later the Dutch began raising seedlings to produce new varieties. It was not long before the French started breeding them on a large scale and they became known as Gallicas. Soon after 1800 there were said to be over one thousand varieties. Most of these have long since been lost, but we still have more of them than any other group of the truly 'old' roses, and these include some of the most beautiful roses that can be grown today.

Not surprisingly, all this work led to highly developed flowers in a variety of colours. These tend to be in the stronger shades: deep pinks and near crimsons, as well as rich mixtures of purple, violet and mauve. There are a number of good striped varieties as well as others that are attractively mottled, marbled or flecked, and there are also a few soft pinks, though these are probably hybrids of other classes. No other Old Rose produces such subtle and fascinating mixtures of colour. They are nearly all very fragrant.

The Gallica Rose or, as it is sometimes called, the 'Rose of Provins', is not difficult to recognise. It usually forms a small shrub, generally not more than 1.2m/4ft in height, with strong rather upright growth and numerous small, bristly thorns. The leaves are oval, pointed at the tip, of rather rough texture and often dark green in colour. The flowers are usually held either singly or in threes, and the buds are typically of spherical shape.

These roses are excellent garden subjects, with low, easily managed growth that is ideal for the smaller garden. They will, if required, grow in poor, even gravelly soil, and demand a minimum of attention. If grown on their own roots they will sucker freely and quickly spread across a border. Although they are often effective when grown in this manner they can become a problem, and for this reason it is usually better to plant budded stock and not to plant too deeply.

*BEAU NARCISSE is a beautiful, and in many ways typical Gallica, whose crimson flowers are speckled with purple*

The origin of
*BELLE ISIS is
something of
a mystery as it is
unusual to find so
delicate a pink, a
myrrh fragrance
and such a short,
neat shrub
amongst the
Gallicas*

**Alain Blanchard** This variety has almost single flowers of deep purple-crimson, with contrasting golden stamens, the colour later turning to a purple which is attractively dotted and mottled with pink. Its growth is thorny, about 1.2m/4ft in height, with pale green foliage. Fragrant. Probably a Gallica/Centifolia cross. Bred by Vibert (France), introduced 1839.

**Anaïs Ségalas** This rose has perfectly shaped flowers which open flat and are well filled with petals, showing a green eye at the centre. The colour is a rich mauve-crimson, turning with age to a pale lilac-pink. It forms a low-growing, branching and free-flowering bush with light green foliage. Strong fragrance. Height 1m/3ft. Vibert (France), introduced 1837.

**Assemblages des Beautés** ('Rouge Éblouissante') Very double flowers of a vivid cherry-red, unusual amongst Gallicas; later becoming tinged with mauve, the petals reflexing almost to a ball, with a button eye at the centre. Very fragrant. Height 1.2m/4ft. Introduced by Delaage 1823.

**Beau Narcisse** A rather short and unassuming rose but beautiful in detail. The flowers are medium sized, no more than about 5cm/2in across and crimson, speckled with purple, the reverse of the petals being paler. It has bushy, quite wiry growth about 1.2m/4ft tall. There is a good fragrance. Bred by Miellez (France) before 1828.

**Belle de Crécy** One of the finest, most free-flowering and reliable of Gallica Roses. On opening the flowers are a cerise-pink mixed with mauve, later turning to soft parma-violet and ultimately to lavender-grey; a wonderful succession of tints. They are shapely in form, the petals opening wide and reflexing to expose a button centre. A very rich fragrance. This variety will grow to about 1.2m/4ft in height and about 1m/3ft across. Bred by Roeser (?) prior to 1848.

**Belle Isis** A charming little rose of short growth that is ideal for the small garden. The flowers are not large but are full petalled, opening flat, neatly formed and of a delicate flesh-pink colour. It has tough, sturdy growth, with many prickles and small light green leaves. Its origins are something of a mystery as it is unusual to find so delicate a pink among the Gallicas, but it is probable that one of its parents was a Centifolia. It has the unusual fragrance of myrrh, and this would seem to indicate there is also Ayrshire 'Splendens' in its make up, for this scent was unique to those roses. Height 1m/3ft. Bred by Parmentier (Belgium), introduced 1845.

**Burgundiaca** (Burgundy Rose, 'Parviflora', 'Pompon de Bourgogne') A charming miniature Gallica which forms a dense, very short jointed shrub, with very small dark green pointed leaves and tiny claret-coloured pompon flowers made up of numerous small petals. It is as though a large shrub had shrunk in all its parts, resulting in something quite unlike any other rose. The growth is about 1m/3ft in height. It can become rather too narrowly upright, but careful clipping will enable it to maintain its shape. In existence before 1664.

**Camayeux** One of the most pleasing of the striped roses. Its flowers are only loosely double but of shapely formation. They are white and heavily striped and splashed with a crimson that soon turns to purple, later becoming pale lilac and remaining attractive at all stages. There is a sweet and spicy fragrance. It forms a small shrub of about 1m/3ft in height. Introduced by Gendron in 1826.

**Cardinal de Richelieu** One of the darkest of all roses. The flowers are mauvish-pink in the bud, becoming mauve, and ending in the richest pure purple. They are quite small and as they develop the petals reflex back almost forming a ball. This is an excellent garden shrub, developing into an arching mound of growth with dark green leaves and few thorns. It requires good cultivation and fairly severe pruning if it is to attain its full potential, otherwise the flowers may be rather insignificant. It is advisable to thin out the shrub by the annual removal of some of its older growth. The height is 1.5m/5ft. Fragrant. Bred by Parmentier prior to 1847. (Illustrated overleaf)

**Charles de Mills** The largest flowered and most spectacular of the Old Roses. Each bloom has numerous evenly placed petals which open so flat that they give the impression of having been sliced off with a sharp knife. The colour is rich purple-crimson gradually turning to pure purple. It is an erect grower but forms a rather floppy shrub of 1.2m/4ft in height and may require some support. Unfortunately there is no more than a slight fragrance. Introduced about 1790. (Illustrated overleaf)

*BELLE DE CRÉCY is one of the most free-flowering and reliable of Gallica Roses, with petals that open wide to reveal a button centre*

*CAMAYEUX bears striped flowers that are loosely double but of shapely formation*

*CHARLES DE MILLS is the largest-flowered and most spectacular of the Old Roses*

*Right, CARDINAL DE RICHELIEU is one of the darkest of all roses. The flowers are mauvish-pink in the bud, becoming mauve, and ending in the richest purple*

*Facing page, DUCHESSE DE MONTEBELLO bears sprays of soft pink full-petalled flowers of open-cupped formation*

**Cramoisi Picotée** A pretty and unusual little rose with small, full, almost pompon flowers which are crimson in the bud, opening to a deep pink with crimson at the edges. The growth is short and compact with small dark green leaves. Little fragrance. Height 1 m / 3 ft. Bred by Vibert (France), introduced 1834.

**D'Aguesseau** This rose has the brightest red colouring to be found among the Gallicas. For this reason we find it is in great demand – perhaps greater demand than its qualities warrant. Its colour is a bright cerise-scarlet although this soon fades to cerise-pink. The flowers are full petalled and fragrant, the growth strong with ample foliage. Height 1.5 m / 5 ft. Bred by Vibert (France), introduced 1837.

**Duc de Guiche** A magnificent Gallica with large flowers of a rich wine-crimson shaded with purple. They have many petals and are beautifully formed, opening at first to a cup and gradually reflexing. It is one of the finest of its class, but in a dry season the colour can become dull and altogether less pleasing, particularly in light soils. Height about 1.2 m / 4 ft. Fragrant. Bred by Prévost, introduced 1829.

**Duchesse d'Angoulême** This little charmer is probably not wholly Gallica. The delicacy of its transparent blush-pink globular flowers, which hang so gracefully from its arching growth, strongly suggests some other influence — *Rosa centifolia* has been suggested, but it is difficult to be sure. It has few thorns, light green foliage and a spreading growth to about 1 m / 3 ft in height and as much across. It was, at one time, also known as the 'Wax Rose'. Bred by Vibert (France), prior to 1821.

**Duchesse de Buccleugh** A variety with unusually large flowers that open flat and quartered with a button eye. Their colour is an intense magenta-pink which does not appeal to everyone. The growth is very strong and upright, to 1.8m / 6ft in height, with fine luxurious foliage. One of the latest of the Gallicas to flower. Bred by Vibert (France), introduced 1837.

**Duchesse de Montebello** A rather loose-growing shrub bearing sprays of soft pink full-petalled flowers of open-cupped formation. These have a delicate charm and blend nicely with its grey-green foliage. It is unlikely that it is a true Gallica. I have used it for breeding purposes crossing it with repeat-flowering English Roses and, much to my surprise, obtained a proportion of repeat-flowering seedlings. This would suggest that it was itself the result of a cross with a repeat-flowering rose. Such mysteries contribute much to the interest of Old Roses. A beautiful rose with a sweet fragrance. Height 1.2m / 4ft. Bred by Laffay (France), introduced prior to 1829.

**Du Maître d'École** ('De La Maître d'École') A variety producing some of the largest flowers found among Gallicas. They are full petalled and open flat and quartered, later reflexing to reveal a button centre. Their colour is a deep pink, gradually turning to lilac-pink and taking on mauve and coppery shading as the flowers age. The growth is lax, about 1–1.2m / 3–4ft in height, arching under the weight of its heavy, fragrant blooms. Coquereau (France) 1831.

**Empress Josephine** (Impératrice Joséphine) An entirely appropriate name for one of the most beautiful Old Roses. Josephine perhaps did more than anyone else to establish and encourage interest in roses throughout Europe, gathering together at Malmaison the largest collection of roses ever established up to her time. This variety is far removed from the typical Gallica and is classed as *Rosa × franco-furtana*. It is probably a hybrid of *R. cinnamomea*. The flowers are semi-double with wavy petals of an unusual papery appearance. Their colour is a rich Tyrian rose veined with a deeper shade. Unlike the majority of Old Roses, the flowers are followed by a fine crop of large turbinate hips. 'Empress Josephine' forms a low, shapely, rather

flat growing bush some 1 m / 3 ft in height, with very coarse textured grey-green foliage and few thorns. Excellent in every way, the only possible complaint being that it has no more than a faint fragrance. It has one close relative, 'Agatha', which is of the same class, but which is an altogether taller and coarser rose with, rather surprisingly, an intense fragrance. Bred by Descemet 1815.

***gallica* var. *officinalis*** (the Apothecary's Rose) This historic rose is said to be the 'Red Rose of Lancaster', the emblem chosen by the House of Lancaster at the time of the Wars of the Roses, and there is little doubt it is the oldest cultivated form of the Gallica Rose that we have. It seems to have first appeared in Europe in the town of Provins, south east of Paris, where it was used in the making of perfume. It was said to have been brought there by Thibault Le Chansonnier on his return from the Crusades. Thibault IV, King of Navarre, wrote the poem *Le Roman de la Rose* in about 1260, and in it he refers to this rose as the rose from the 'Land of the Saracens'. Whatever the truth may be, this is a rose of great antiquity. For centuries it was grown for its medicinal qualities, and for this reason it is known as the Apothecary's Rose. Today we appreciate it for its excellent garden qualities, for it certainly deserves a place among the very finest of garden shrubs of any kind. It forms low branching growth, carries its semi-double light crimson fragrant flowers (with golden stamens) nicely poised above ample dark green foliage, blooms very freely, and provides a most satisfactory effect in the border. If grown on its own roots it will quickly spread by suckering and might well be used on banks and in other areas where ground cover is required. Budded on a stock it will grow to about 1.2 m / 4 ft in height and about the same across. The colour varies widely according to climate and season and is much paler under hot conditions. In autumn it produces small round hips which are not without ornamental value. (Illustrated, p. 17)

*Right and far right, EMPRESS JOSEPHINE is far removed from the typical Gallica. The flowers are semi-double with wavy petals of an unusual papery appearance and, unlike the majority of Old Roses, they are followed by a fine crop of large red hips*

**gallica Versicolor** (Rosa Mundi) This is a striped sport of *R. g.* var. *officinalis*, having all the virtues of that excellent rose, to which it is similar in every respect except colour. This is palest blush-pink, clearly striped and splashed with light crimson which provides an attractively fresh appearance. Occasionally a flower will revert to the colour of its parent. It has the same strong bushy growth, and flowers in the same happy profusion, providing a wonderful massed effect. Both roses make fine low hedges – indeed it would be hard to find better roses for this purpose. The date of this rose is not known, but it certainly goes back to the sixteenth century and earlier. Like its parent it will make a 1.2 x 1.2m / 4 x 4ft shrub.

**Georges Vibert** Rather small flowers which open flat, with narrow quilled petals of blush pink striped with light crimson. The growth is narrow and upright, about 1.5m / 5ft in height, with many thorns and unusually small leaves. Bred by Bizard (France) 1828.

**Gloire de France** A small shrub with somewhat spreading growth of 1m / 3ft in height and rather more across. It bears beautifully shaped full lilac-pink flowers with reflexing petals which hold their colour at the centre while paling with age towards the edges. Strongly fragrant. Bred prior to 1819.

**Hyppolyte** A tall, vigorous shrub of 1.5m / 5ft in height, with few thorns and small dark green leaves. The flowers, too, are small, flat at first, later reflexing into a ball-like formation. The colour is mauve-violet. Bred by Parmentier prior to 1842.

**Ipsilante** ('Ypsilante') A most beautiful rose, producing some of the finest blooms in this group. They are large, of a lustrous warm pink colouring, cupped at first, opening flat and quartered. The growth is shapely with fine foliage, and in my garden it is more disease resistant than any other Old Rose. Rich fragrance. Height 1.2m / 4ft. Bred by Vibert in 1821.

**Nestor** Lilac-pink flowers, deepening towards the centre, opening cupped, later becoming flat and quartered and gradually taking on

mauve and grey tints. It has almost thornless growth of 1.2m / 4ft in height. Slightly fragrant. Introduced by Vibert 1834.

**Pompon Panaché** A pretty little miniature-flowered rose with neatly-formed blooms that have deep pink stripes on a cream ground. They are held in ones and twos on wiry upright stems with small leaves. Erect growth of 1–1.2m / 3–4ft in height. It has a strong and positively delicious fragrance. Bred by Moreau & Robert (France).

**Président de Sèze** ('Jenny Duval') A perfect bloom of this rose can be more beautiful than any other to be found among the Gallicas. Its attractive lilac buds open to magnificent large full-petalled flowers that display a bewildering array of tints. Graham Thomas mentions cerise, magenta, purple, violet, lilac-grey, soft brown and lilac-white, and all these colours are to be found, depending on the stage of development of the flower and the prevailing weather conditions. Perhaps it is simpler to say the overall colour effect is lilac, violet and silvery grey. It forms a sturdy shrub with ample foliage, and will grow to about 1.2m / 4ft in height. For some years a rose named 'Jenny Duval' was distributed by nurserymen, including ourselves, but it is now generally agreed that this is the same as 'Président de Sèze'. To those who have known this rose under both names, it may seem strange that we have taken so long to arrive at this conclusion. My only defence is that this rose is so various and ever-changing in its colour that the confusion between the two was understandable. I have had more than one experienced rose enthusiast come to me with what they thought was yet another entirely different sport, and this too has turned out to be the same variety. The truth is that 'Président de Sèze' differs so widely according to the conditions under which it is grown that it seldom looks the same on any two occasions. There is a pleasing fragrance. Hébert (France) 1828.

**Sissinghurst Castle** ('Rose des Maures') It is said that Vita Sackville-West and Harold Nicolson found this rose when they were

*Tuscany
Superb is
a larger version
of 'Tuscany',
with taller more
vigorous growth,
larger, more
rounded leaves
and larger
flowers with more
numerous petals*

clearing the garden of Sissinghurst Castle. The petals are a beautiful rich plum colour, edged and flecked with light magenta-crimson, and contrast strongly with the golden yellow stamens in the centre. It is a particularly tough rose and a great survivor and, when planted deeply, will sucker freely and form a thicket of upright stems. Lightly fragrant. Height 1.2m/4ft. Reintroduced by V. Sackville-West (UK) 1947.

**Surpasse Tout**  Large full, tightly packed flowers of light rose-crimson, turning with age to cerise-pink. The petals reflex and there is a button eye at the centre. The growth is strong and bushy, the height about 1.2m/4ft. Strong fragrance. Bred by Hardy (France) 1823.

**Tricolore de Flandre**  Large, fairly full white flowers heavily striped with shades of lilac, purple and crimson. The growth is short, about 1m/3ft in height, but vigorous with plentiful smooth foliage. Fragrant. Bred by Van Houtte (Belgium) 1846.

**Tuscany**  A rose which can be compared with *R. gallica* var. *officinalis* and *Rosa Mundi*, both in its habit of growth and for its excellence as a garden shrub. It has fairly large semi-double flowers of the darkest maroon-crimson; these open wide, with bright golden stamens lighting up the centre. It forms a sturdy bush of 1.2m/4ft and, on its own roots, will spread freely if permitted. The foliage is dark green. We do not know the age of this beautiful variety, but it probably goes back a very long way. There is only a slight fragrance. It was once known as the 'Old Velvet Rose' – the herbalist Gerard, writing in 1597, mentions a 'Velvet Rose', and it is likely that this is the same variety.

**Tuscany Superb**  A larger version of 'Tuscany', with taller more vigorous growth to about 1.5m/5ft, larger, more rounded leaves and larger flowers with more numerous petals. It is in fact 'more' everything, while remaining at the same time very similar in its general character and colouring; the stamens are partially obscured, as these tend to be hidden by the extra petals. It must have been either a sport or a seedling from 'Tuscany' – probably the latter. Bred by Rivers in 1837, it was one of the few Gallicas bred in Britain.

**Violacea** ('La Belle Sultane') With its almost single flowers, this has the appearance of a very old rose, although it is thought to originate from France about 1810. The flowers are of the most wonderful rich darkest crimson, darker towards the edges and redder towards the centre. In the middle there is a big, bold group of golden stamens. It is a rather tall and wiry shrub and, while not particularly free flowering, it is well worth planting especially with perennials in a mixed border. It is lightly fragrant. Height 1.5–2m/5–7ft. Introduced by Du Pont (France) before 1811.

*Surpasse Tout has large full, tightly packed flowers of light rose-crimson, turning with age to cerise-pink*

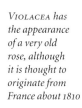

*Violacea has the appearance of a very old rose, although it is thought to originate from France about 1810*

# Damask Roses

THE DAMASK ROSE, like the Gallica, dates back to ancient times. It is said to have been widely grown by the Persians, from whose country it spread to the Holy Land and other areas of the Middle East, eventually being brought to Europe by the Crusaders. S.F. Hamble gives the credit for this to a Robert de Brie who, he says, brought it to his castle in Champagne at some time between 1254 and 1276, whence it was distributed throughout France and later brought to the British Isles.

According to Dr Hurst, the Damask Rose originated from a natural hybrid of the Gallica Rose and a wild species known as *Rosa phoenicea*. However, DNA analysis now strongly suggests that the original seed parent was a cross between *R. moschata* and *R. fedtschenkoana*, while the pollen parent was *R. gallica*. We thus have two widely differing parents, and it is therefore not surprising that this family is itself somewhat diverse in its nature.

In general Damask Roses are taller than Gallicas, perhaps 1.5 m / 5 ft in height, more lax in growth, with more and larger thorns. The leaves are elongated and pointed, of a greyish-green colour and downy on the underside. Where there are hips these will usually be long and thin. The flowers are nearly always a lovely clear pink and are often held in nicely poised sprays. They are usually strongly fragrant, the very name being synonymous with this quality. The Damasks bring elegance to the rose, both in leaf and general habit of growth.

Closely related to these roses is the Autumn Damask— *Rosa × damascena* var. *semperflorens*. This is a rose of great antiquity. It is not, perhaps, of the highest value for the garden, but is of great interest to those who study roses because it was the only rose to have the ability to repeat flower prior to the introduction of the China Rose late in the eighteenth century. It is of equal interest for its very long history. Dr Hurst tells us that it is first noted in the Greek island of Samos towards the end of the tenth century BC, where it was used in the cult of Aphrodite. It was later introduced to mainland Greece and then to Rome where it continued to play a part in ceremonies connected with Venus. In the first century BC Virgil in *The Georgics* mentions the rose which flowers twice a year, and this was no doubt the Autumn Damask. This is a rather prickly shrub, with the leaves running right up to and clustering around the flowers. It has an unsophisticated charm and the typical Damask fragrance. It eventually led to the Portland Roses, through which it played an important part in the development of repeat-flowering roses about which I write in the next chapter.

---

*Right,*
× DAMASCENA
VAR. SEMPER-
FLORENS
*AUTUMN*
*DAMASK is an*
*ancient and most*
*historic rose*

*Facing page,*
CELSIANA, *is a*
*typical Damask*
*Rose, its soft pink*
*flowers are large,*
*opening wide,*
*semi-double, and*
*held in delicately*
*poised sprays*

**Celsiana** A typical Damask Rose, with fine, graceful grey-green foliage. The flowers are large, opening wide, semi-double, and of a soft pink colour that later fades to blush, with a central boss of golden stamens. They are held in delicately poised sprays, and the petals have the appearance of crumpled silk. There is a strong fragrance. Height approximately 1.5 m / 5 ft. I place this rose high on any list of Old Roses. Known to have been in existence before 1750.

**× *damascena* var. *semperflorens*** (Autumn Damask, *Rosa damascena bifera*, 'Quatre Saisons', 'Rose of the Four Seasons') This is the repeat-flowering Autumn Damask I mentioned above. The flowers are clear pink, loosely double, with long sepals and a powerful and most delicious fragrance. It has rather spreading growth and greyish-green foliage. An ancient and most historic rose. Interestingly it sometimes sports to 'Quatre Saisons Blanc Mousseux' which, as the name suggests, is pure white with abundant mossy growth and repeat-flowers just as well as its parent. Height 1.5 m / 5 ft.

**× *damascena* var. *versicolor*** ('York and Lancaster') A tall shrub, with clear, downy grey-green foliage, which carries its flowers with elegance in dainty, open sprays. These are unusual in that they may be pink or almost white, or a mixture of both, the white being flecked with pink and vice versa, all these variations being found on one shrub at the same time. The individual flowers are informal and semi-double, usually exposing their stamens. It is not a dramatic shrub, but it does have a certain airy elegance. The story that the two

*ISPAHAN
flowers early and
continues over
a long period,
bearing blooms
that are large and
very full, opening
flat, and of a rich
warm pink that
does not fade*

factions in the Wars of the Roses each took a bloom from a bush of this rose—a red and a white—is probably not true. The roses of the two houses were more likely to have been *R. gallica* var. *officinalis* and *R. alba semi-plena*, but there is no firm historical evidence for this. It is important to obtain bushes from correct stock, as the flowers can revert to pink. Strongly fragrant. Height 1.5m/5ft. Known to be in existence before 1550.

**Gloire de Guilan**  In 1949 this rose was collected by Nancy Lindsay from Iran, where it is used for the making of attar of roses. It forms a loose sprawling shrub with apple-green leaves. The flowers are cupped at first, later becoming flat and quartered. Their colour is a pink of unusual clarity and purity, and they are very fragrant although always much stronger in warmer climates. I have found it to be particularly resistant to disease. Height 1.2m/4ft.

**Hebe's Lip**  (Rubrotincta) A modest rose but not without its attractions. It has cupped, semi-double flowers, with red-tipped petals that give it its name. A strong and myrrh-like fragrance. The growth is short and thorny with fresh green foliage. Height 1.2m/4ft. It is probably of hybrid origin, perhaps Damask × *Rosa arvensis*. Bred by Lee (UK) 1846.

**Ispahan**  ('Pompon des Princes') A very fine shrub which begins to flower early and continues over a long period. The flowers are large and very full, opening flat, and of a rich warm pink that does not fade. A good cut flower, lasting well in water. It has a glorious fragrance. Height 1.5m/5ft. In cultivation before 1832.

**La Ville de Bruxelles**  ('Ville de Bruxelles') Exceptionally large full-petalled  blooms of a clear rich pink. When fully open the petals reflex at the edges, leaving a slightly domed centre filled with small petals. A truly luxurious flower of fine quality. The foliage is large and plentiful, pale green in colour and of typical Damask shapeliness. Its growth is upright but often weighed down by the heavy blooms, particularly in moist weather. Rich fragrance. Height 1.2m/4ft or more if lightly pruned. Vibert (France) 1836.

**Leda**  Milk-white flowers with the slightest suggestion of pink. As they open they develop a picot effect, the rim of the petals becoming stained with crimson, so giving rise to its other name the 'Painted Damask'. The blooms are full petalled, reflexing to reveal a button centre. Although not perhaps quite so exciting as the description implies, it is a pretty rose with good foliage. Slight fragrance. Height 1m/3ft. Prior to 1827.

**Madame Hardy**  One of the classic Old Roses—few others approach the perfection of its flowers. They are not very large, of pretty cupped formation at first, later becoming flat and finally reflexing. There is the slightest hint of blush in the early stages, but later they become a pure glistening white, while at the centre a small green eye adds to the attraction. They are held in nicely poised clusters, and are fragrant with just a hint of lemon. It will grow to about 1.5m/5ft and is reasonably strong, but it will repay generous treatment with manure. The foliage is pale green. We cannot be sure of its origin,

× DAMASCENA VAR. VERSICOLOR *carries its semi-double flowers with elegance in dainty, open sprays*

*LA VILLE DE BRUXELLES bears exceptionally large full-petalled blooms of a clear rich pink. When fully open the petals reflex at the edges, leaving a slightly domed centre filled with small petals*

*MADAME HARDY
is one of the
classic Old Roses
—few others
approach the
perfection of its
compact flowers*

*PETITE LISETTE
is a miniature-
flowered Damask
carrying small
bunches of perfect
little flowers, each
well filled with
clear pink petals*

though it is obviously not pure Damask, the leaves
and growth showing signs of Centifolia influence.
It is strongly fragrant. Bred in 1832 by Hardy (who
had charge of the Empress Josephine's famous rose
collection at Malmaison) and named after his wife.

**Madame Zöetmans** A charming rose not often seen
but gaining in popularity. Its flowers are of medium
size, fully double, of cupped formation at first, opening
to reveal a button eye. Their colour is white, tinted with
blush at the centre, and they are borne on graceful
growth on a nice bushy plant with fresh green foliage.
Strongly fragrant. Height 1.2m/4ft. Bred by Marest
(France) 1830.

**Marie Louise** A lax-growing shrub vying with 'La
Ville de Bruxelles' for the splendour of its flowers.
These are unusually large and full, of deep pink with
the petals reflexing, and very fragrant. The sheer
weight and quantity of the flowers often bows down
the branches to the ground. The height is about 1.2m/
4ft with plentiful large foliage. Here we have a rose that
might well be encouraged to flop over a low retaining
wall. Raised at Malmaison, 1813.

**Oeillet Parfait** A compact, twiggy shrub of 1–1.2m/
3–4ft, with small pale green leaves. The flowers open
flat with numerous petals of warm pink colouring,
later reflexing almost to a ball. There is also a striped
Gallica of the same name.

**Omar Khayyám** This rose is perhaps of more historic interest than garden value. It is the rose that
grows on the poet Edward Fitzgerald's grave at Boulge,
Suffolk, and which was itself first raised from seed
from a rose on Omar Khayyam's grave at Nishapur in
Iran. The flowers are soft pink, fragrant, of medium
size, and quartered, with a button eye. The foliage is
grey-green and downy. Height 1m/3ft. About 1893.

**Petite Lisette** A miniature-flowered Damask carrying
small bunches of perfect little flowers, each well filled
with clear pink petals. It has small, neat, downy grey-
green foliage, and forms an excellent well-rounded
shrub of 1–1.2m/3–4ft in height. Fragrant. Bred and
introduced by Vibert (France) 1817.

**Professeur Emile Perrot** ('Kazanlik', *Rosa damascena* 'Trigintipetala') With 'Trigintipetala' and 'Gloire
de Guilan', this is one of several roses traditionally sold
under the single name of 'Kazanlik'. They are all grown
at Kazanlik in Bulgaria for the production of attar of
roses. The blooms of 'Professeur Emile Perrot' are pink
and of no great merit, but it does form a graceful and
typical Damask shrub, and has, as might be expected,
a rich fragrance, especially in hot summers. Height 1.5–
1.8m/5–6ft. Probably of great antiquity.

**Quatre Saisons** see × *damascena* var. *semperflorens*.

**Saint Nicholas** A recent addition to this very old
class, which occurred as a chance seedling, in 1950, in
the garden of The Hon. Robert James, at Richmond,
Yorkshire. The flowers are semi-double, opening flat,
and of a rich pink colour with yellow stamens. It forms
a short prickly bush of 1.5m/5ft in height, with good,
dark green foliage.

*MARIE LOUISE*
*is a lax-growing*
*shrub with*
*unusually large*
*deep pink flowers,*
*the petals*
*reflexing, and*
*very fragrant.*
*The sheer weight*
*and quantity of*
*the flowers often*
*bows the*
*branches to the*
*ground*

35

# Alba Roses

THE ALBA ROSES form another very old group. In existence in classical times and probably brought to Britain by the Romans, they were widely grown in the Middle Ages, no doubt mainly for medicinal purposes, and appear in many paintings of that period. The other classes of ancient roses have a great deal in common and a casual observer might see them as all of one type, but this is not the case with the Albas which are quite distinct. It is generally agreed that they are the result of natural hybridization between the Damask Rose and *Rosa canina*, the Dog Rose of our hedgerows, or at least a species closely allied to it. A cursory inspection of the growth of the Dog Rose will show its close affinity to Alba Roses. As with other Old Roses many of its varieties appear to be the result of further hybridization with roses of other classes.

The Albas form a small but important group which includes some of the best and most beautiful of the Old Roses. Their growth is larger than that of the other old classes, often 1.8m/6ft or more in height, and it is no doubt for this reason that they were formerly known as Tree Roses. The flowers, as the name suggests, are rather limited in their colour range, being restricted to white, blush and pink, but they have a delicacy and refinement that is hard to match elsewhere. Their foliage is frequently grey-green in colour, and this tones well with their soft tints and provides an excellent contrast with other roses and plants. They are generally extremely healthy although some varieties suffer from rust; this doesn't seem to worry them much. They nearly all have a pleasing and characteristic fragrance.

The delicate appearance of the flowers is in sharp contrast to the undoubted toughness of the plant which will grow under difficult conditions. Albas are, in fact, among the most easily grown of all roses, and even in partial shade will do better than most others, although no roses really like such conditions. Whenever we are asked at our Nursery for roses that will grow in partial shade, it is always to these we first turn. They are ideal for the border or as individual specimens, or for planting in the more wild areas of the garden. They also make perfect hosts for the late-flowering varieties of *Clematis viticella*. They will also form a particularly fine hedge, different varieties of similar stature mingling together most satisfactorily. The taller varieties may be trained as climbers and they are quite happy when grown on a north wall.

*Right, × ALBA ALBA MAXIMA is an ancient rose known to have existed in classical times, with fully double flowers that are blush-pink at first but soon turn to creamy-white*

*Facing page, × ALBA ALBA SEMIPLENA bears large flowers, almost single, with a large boss of stamens, followed in the autumn by large, orange Dog Rose hips*

× *alba* **Alba Maxima** ('Great Double White', 'Cheshire Rose', 'Jacobite Rose') An ancient rose known to have existed in classical times, it has been grown in cottage gardens in Britain for many centuries, where it lives on almost indefinitely, continually renewing its growth. It is not uncommon to see this variety growing, apparently wild, in hedgerows, such plants marking the place where a cottage once stood but long since gone. There can be no better testimony to its durability. Surely this must be one of the longest lived of all roses? It forms a tall if rather top-heavy shrub of 1.8m/6ft, and although the individual flowers are not particularly distinguished they are most effective in the mass. Fully double, they are blush-pink at first but soon turn to creamy-white. Strong fragrance.

× *alba* **Alba Semiplena** Said to have been the 'White Rose of York', this is a luxuriant shrub with fine grey-green foliage and elegant shapely growth. The flowers are large, almost single, symmetrical in outline and milky-white in colour, with a large boss of stamens. They are followed in the autumn by large, orange Dog Rose hips. This is one of the roses cultivated at Kazanlik, Bulgaria, for the production of attar of roses. In every way a first class garden shrub. Very fragrant. Height 1.8m/6ft. A very ancient rose which can be traced back to the fourteenth century.

**Amélia** Here we have a smaller shrub than is usual among Albas. It bears large strongly fragrant pure pink semi-double flowers with pronounced golden stamens. Its height is about 1.2m/4ft. Bred by Vibert (France) 1823.

**Belle Amour** A strong shrub, 1.8m/6ft in height, bearing clusters of semi-double slightly cupped flowers of a soft salmon-pink – a

*Right,* CÉLESTE *is much treasured for its exquisitely scrolled buds and semi-double, soft pink flowers*

*Far right top,* FÉLICITÉ PARMENTIER *bears perfect quartered flowers tightly packed with petals of clear fresh pink; these later reflex and fade to cream at the edges*

*Far right bottom,* MAIDEN'S BLUSH *is an old rose, in existence since the 15th century, with loosely double flowers that have a wonderful fragrance*

shade almost unique among Old Roses. These have a myrrh fragrance which suggests this rose may have some Ayrshire 'Splendens' in its make up. It was originally discovered growing on the wall of a convent at Elboeuf, Normandy.

**Céleste** ('Celestial') A modest rose, much treasured for the charm and delicacy of its exquisitely scrolled buds and semi-double flowers of lovely soft pink colouring. These are not large and have yellow stamens. The blooms are beautiful against the grey-green of the typically Alba foliage, and have a sweet fragrance. However the growth is anything but delicate, forming a robust shrub which, in our experience, should not be pruned too severely, otherwise it tends to make growth at the expense of flowers. It forms a shrub of 1.5m/5ft in height by 1.2m/4ft across. It is said to have been bred in Holland towards the end of the eighteenth century.

**Félicité Parmentier** At its best this is a most beautiful rose, with perfect quartered flowers very tightly packed with petals of clear fresh pink; these later reflex and fade to cream at the edges. The

growth is quite short, about 1.2m/4ft in height, but bushy, with many thorns and pale green leaves. It is an excellent rose, but in dry seasons on sandy soil the flowers sometimes fail to open properly; with good management this should not be a problem. Very fragrant. Bred by Parmentier in 1834.

**Madame Legras de Saint Germain** A rose of exceptional beauty. Starting as a prettily cupped bud, it opens to form a perfectly shaped slightly domed flower with many petals. The colour is a glowing white with just a tinge of yellow, and this gives us a hint as to its origins – there has to have been a Noisette somewhere in its breeding. It would be hard to think of a more perfect marriage than Alba and Noisette, although in this case it has led to one weakness: the flowers can be damaged by wet weather. Otherwise it is sheer perfection. The growth is tall and lax, forming a graceful shrub of 1.8m/6ft in height, with very few thorns and pale green leaves. Strong and delicious fragrance. It can equally well be grown as a Climber. Introduced prior to 1848.

**Madame Plantier**  This is an Alba/Noisette hybrid and, in fact, is sometimes classified as a Noisette. It forms a sprawling mound of graceful growth covered with large clusters of rather small pompon-like blooms against pale green foliage. The colour is creamy-white, lightly tinged with yellow at first, later turning to pure white, and there is a pointed green eye at the centre of each flower. Its sweet and powerful fragrance fills the air. It is equally effective when trained as a Climber, and I have vivid memories of a visit to Sissinghurst Castle and being shown this rose climbing up the trunks of fruit trees where they made a wonderful sight like billowing dresses. The height is 1.8m/6ft spreading to 1.8m/6ft across. Bred and introduced by Plantier (France) 1835.

**Maiden's Blush**  ('Great Maiden's Blush', known in France as 'Cuisse de Nymphe Émue' and at other times and in various countries as 'La Royale', 'La Seduisante', 'Virginale', 'Incarnata') This forms a graceful arching shrub of 1.5m/5ft in height with typical grey-green Alba foliage. The flowers are loosely double, of soft blush-pink, the petals reflexing slightly with age and paling towards the edges. They have a wonderful fragrance. An old and much loved rose and certainly in existence before the beginning of the sixteenth century.

**Maiden's Blush**  (small) This has smaller flowers than the above rose and grows to only 1.2m/4ft in height. I do not know whether it was a sport or a seedling from 'Maiden's Blush', but it is similar in every respect except size. Raised at Kew in 1797.

**Pompon Blanc Parfait**  An unusual rose and difficult to compare with any other. It has little round buds which open to small, flat, tightly-packed pompon flowers on short thin stems. The flowers are pale lilac-pink in colour and of very neat formation. They appear late in the season and are then produced a few at a time in long succession. The growth tends to be slow to develop, with small grey-green leaves and twiggy, rather stiff, almost reluctant growth, of perhaps 1.2m/4ft in height. Slight fragrance. Introduced 1876.

**Queen of Denmark**  ('Königin von Dänemark') Few old roses can equal this for the perfection of its individual blooms. These are prettily cupped in the bud and later develop into a full perfectly quartered, slightly reflexing flower with a button eye at the centre. The colour is a warm rose-pink. A particularly strong and delicious Old Rose fragrance. The growth is comparatively short, perhaps 1.2 or 1.5m/4 or 5ft in height, with typical grey-green foliage. Like all Albas it is easily grown, but superb blooms can be obtained with good cultivation. Raised in 1816 by John Booth, who recorded it as a seedling from 'Maiden's Blush', and introduced it in 1826.

*QUEEN OF DENMARK bears full, perfectly quartered flowers with a button eye and a particularly strong Old Rose fragrance*

# Centifolia Roses

THE CENTIFOLIAS were for a long time thought to be the most ancient of all roses, but subsequent research has proved this to be far from the truth. They are mere children by comparison with the three classes discussed so far. It seems that they evolved over a period extending from early in the seventeenth century to the beginning of the eighteenth century, that they were largely the result of the work of Dutch breeders, and that during this period some two hundred varieties were known to have been introduced. It is not easy to say exactly how they arose, but Dr Hurst's work shows that *Rosa gallica,*

*R. phoenicea, R. moschata* and *R. canina* all come into their make up. This would seem to indicate that a Damask / Alba cross might have occurred at some time, although it was probably rather more complex than that and preliminary DNA analysis suggests a close affinity with the Damasks but not the Albas. It is likely that a series of crosses took place over a long period, resulting in what came to be regarded as a distinct breed. Centifolias were great favourites with our forefathers who seem to have prized them above all others, and evidence of this is provided by the Dutch and Flemish flower painters who used them in their work more frequently than any other roses.

The typical Centifolia has lax, open, rather lanky growth with a mixture of large and small thorns; the leaves are large, rounded and broadly toothed; the flowers tend to be heavy and globular with numerous petals. In spite of all this Centifolias are seldom clumsy and their luxuriant blooms nod gracefully on their stems. Their colours are, in the main, warm clear shades of pink, which do not normally fade in the sun. There are also a number of varieties of hybrid origin which tend towards crimson and pleasing shades of purple and mauve, as well as one or two whites. They are rightly famous for their rich fragrance.

The Centifolias have a strong tendency to produce sports, and this has resulted in a number of unusual forms. Foremost amongst these are the Moss Roses, but there are also quaint and unusual varieties such as 'Chapeau de Napoléon', 'Bullata' and a number of charming miniatures.

It is sometimes worthwhile giving some of the more lax-growing varieties a little support to stop them bending too near the ground. Pruning can be rather more severe than with other Old Roses, and should be just enough to keep the bush in order, without losing the grace of their arching growth.

*CHAPEAU DE NAPOLÉON is very similar to* × centifolia, *but distinguished by the greatly enlarged calyx which gives the bud the appearance of a three-cornered cockade hat*

**Blanchefleur** Heavy, full-petalled, creamy-white flowers with a tinge of blush at the centre and red on the tips of the petals. It forms a vigorous 1.5 m / 5 ft bush with many thorns and apple-green foliage, and shows signs of hybrid origin. Perhaps a little coarse in appearance for my taste, but as a white Centifolia it is valuable. Fragrant. Raised by Vibert (France) 1835.

**Bullata** ( 'Lettuce-leaved Rose') This is probably a sport of 'Centifolia' to which it is similar, with the same cupped flowers and rich fragrance. The difference lies in the leaves, which are excessively enlarged and deeply crinkled, like the leaves of a lettuce. It is perhaps due to the effort of producing such foliage that the flowers tend to be rather inferior to 'Centifolia' and do not always open well. The height is 1.2 m / 4ft. An interesting curiosity that seems to have originated in 1801.

**× *centifolia*** ('Cabbage Rose', 'Rose of a Hundred Leaves', 'Rose des Peintres', 'Provence Rose') The type from which this group derives its name. Even those who know little or nothing about Old Roses will usually have heard of it by its name of 'Old Cabbage Rose'. To the old herbalists it was the 'Queen of Roses', and indeed it is the most beautiful of the Centifolia Roses with its heavy nodding blooms of warm glowing pink and rich Old Rose fragrance. It has strong, nicely arching growth of about 1.5 m / 5 ft. The flowers are at their best in warm, dry weather. Prior to 1600.

**× *centifolia* Spong** A miniature Centifolia of bushy, branching growth, about 1.2 m / 4ft in height, with typical Centifolia leaves. Its flowers are rich pink, paling a little towards the edges. It is rather less formal than 'De Meaux' and 'Petite de Hollande', and has the bad habit of holding its petals long after the flower has died, which is rather unsightly. This is a pretty little rose, but the least effective of the miniatures. Raised by Spong (England), introduced 1805.

**× *centifolia* Unique** ('Unique Blanche', 'White Provence Unique') Creamy-white flowers which are nicely cupped at first, later opening rather untidily with a button eye. At their best they can be most beautiful, the petals having a lovely silky texture. It has strong (if rather untidy) growth and there is a good fragrance. Height 1.2 m / 4ft. Discovered at Needham, Suffolk, 1775.

**Chapeau de Napoléon** (*Rosa centifolia* 'Cristata', 'Crested Moss') This rose is very similar to × *centifolia*, described above. It is distinguished by the fact that the calyx is greatly enlarged in much the same way as a Moss Rose, giving the bud the appearance of a three-cornered cockade hat. Closer observation will reveal that this is not the same as the 'moss' of a Moss Rose, but what Bunyard describes as 'an exaggerated development of the sepals'. However we describe it, the result is very attractive. Although the open flower is not quite so deep as × *centifolia*, it is otherwise indistinguishable, with the same clear pink colouring. It is said that it was originally found in 1820, growing in the crevice of an old wall at Fribourg in Switzerland. This suggests, rather surprisingly, that it was a seedling, not a sport. There is a rich fragrance. Height about 1.5 m / 5 ft. Introduced by Vibert (France) as 'Crested Moss', 1826.

**Cottage Maid** A rose which has had many names in its time: 'Belle des Jardins', 'La Rubanée', 'Village Maid', 'Panachée à Fleurs Doubles', 'La Belle Villageoise', 'Dometil Beccard' and 'Dominic Boccardo'. It is perhaps more properly known as 'Variegata', but we have chosen 'Cottage Maid' as being rather more picturesque. The flowers are quite large and globular in shape with numerous petals, the colour creamy-white, delicately striped with pale pink. It is a vigorous bushy shrub of 1.5 m / 5 ft in height, with dark green foliage and many thorns. Rich fragrance. Introduced by Vibert (France) 1845.

**De Meaux** ('Rose de Meaux') A miniature Centifolia which has to be compared with other miniatures of this class – 'Petite de Hollande' and 'Spong'. Each of these is charming in its own way, like the little roses we might expect to see decorating tea cups. They are ideal for very small gardens. In spite of some reports to the contrary, I suspect that they are all sports of larger Centifolias. 'De Meaux' forms a bushy, twiggy shrub of 1.1 m / 3 ½ft in height, with tiny flowers of only a little more than 25 mm / 1 in. across, and small light green foliage to match. The flowers open as little miniature cups and develop into small pompon flowers of typical Old Rose pink. It is in every way a charming little shrub. Said to have originated with a man named Sweet in 1789. (Illustrated, p. 42)

**Fantin-Latour** This rose turned up as a seedling in an English garden in 1940 and is clearly not of pure Centifolia descent. The leaves

and growth show signs of China Rose influence. The flowers, however, have much of the character of a Centifolia, being of a nicely cupped shape, the outer petals reflexing as the flower ages to reveal a button centre. The colour is a blush-pink which deepens towards the centre and there is a delicate and pleasing fragrance. It forms an excellent shrub with good broad growth of 1.5 m / 5 ft in height although it is rather susceptible to blackspot. Named, most appropriately, after the great French artist Henri Fantin-Latour, whose finest paintings were nearly all of flowers and whose favourite flower was the rose. In every way a fine shrub.

**Juno** Like 'Fantin-Latour', this rose has more modern affinities and is probably connected with the Bourbons. It bears fragrant globular flowers of soft blush pink, later opening flat to reveal a button eye. The growth is rather lax and about 1.2 m / 4ft in height. In cultivation before 1832.

**Paul Ricault** This is a 1.5 m / 5 ft shrub of medium vigour. The flowers are deep pink, very full petalled and rather globular, the outer petals later recurving. It has a strong fragrance and is free

*FANTIN-LATOUR bears flowers of a nicely cupped shape, the outer petals reflexing as the flower ages to reveal a button centre*

flowering, the blooms hanging gracefully upon the stem. It is sometimes classed as a Hybrid China and sometimes as a Hybrid Perpetual. Raised by Portemer (France) 1845.

**Petite de Hollande** ('Petite Junon de Hollande', 'Pompon des Dames', 'Normandica') This is another pretty miniature, with charming little Centifolia flowers of pure rose-pink. It forms a nice bushy little shrub of 1.2m/4ft with small leaves and tiny flowers all to scale. Although all are delightful, it is perhaps the best of the miniature-flowered Centifolias, and there is very little to choose between it and 'De Meaux'. Fragrant. First raised in Holland about 1800.

**Robert de Diable** A lax shrub with dark green leaves and thorny stems. The flowers are purple, shaded with slate-grey and splashed with carmine, providing a most pleasing mixture of colour, particularly in hot weather. Of neat rosette shape, the blooms are not large, the petals reflexing towards the edges. Both foliage and flowers show signs of Gallica influence. Late flowering. Introduced about 1831. Height 1.2m/4ft.

**The Bishop** ('Le Rosier Évêque') A very double flower of rosette formation and unique colouring: cerise-magenta with pale lilac on the reverse of the petals, later becoming slate-grey and parma-violet. In certain lights the blooms appear to be almost blue. Gallica influence is very much in evidence. Fragrant. It has rather erect growth of 1.8m/6ft in height. In cultivation about 1831.

**Tour de Malakoff** A most beautiful rose which will appeal to those who like the purple shades. The flowers are large, opening wide and slightly cupped and only loosely double, but it is the colouring which is their chief glory – a purplish-crimson tinted with magenta becoming violet and with a few stamens usually to be seen at the centre. It is magnificent at all stages. The growth is excellent, perhaps 1.8m/6ft in height, arching broadly to form a rather sprawling shrub although it is rather susceptible to blackspot. Given suitable support it might well be used as a climber. Raised by Soupert & Notting (Luxemburg) 1856.

**White de Meaux** This is a white sport from 'De Meaux', to which it is similar in every way except that the flowers are white tinged with pink. This may sound attractive, but unfortunately the pink is such that it gives the flowers a rather dirty appearance. It is, nonetheless, worthy of its place.

*Above left, PETITE DE HOLLANDE is a pretty miniature, with charming little Centifolia flowers of pure rose-pink.*

*Left, TOUR DE MALAKOFF has large flowers, but it is their colouring which is their chief glory —a purplish-crimson tinted with magenta becoming violet*

*Facing page, DE MEAUX is ideal for very small gardens: the flowers open as miniature cups and develop into small pompon flowers of typical Old Rose pink*

# Moss Roses

THE MOSS ROSES are Centifolias and Damasks which have developed moss-like growth on their sepals and, in some varieties, a little way down the flower stem. This peculiarity is the result of a sport, or fault, in the plant. Small glandular growth is always present to some extent on the sepals of the flower, and in the case of Moss Roses this has become greatly exaggerated. The result is that the bud is covered in this mossy material, giving a most charming effect. It is quite sticky to the touch and aromatic too. We do not know exactly when this curious phenomenon occurred, but Dr Hurst quotes various French sources which state that a rose of this nature existed in France at Carcassonne in 1696, where it had been for half a century, having been first brought there by one Freard Ducastrel. The earliest mention of it in England was in 1724, when it was listed in the catalogue of Robert Furber of Kensington. Mossing has probably occurred from time to time before and since; indeed it has been recorded subsequently on at least three other occasions. It has also occurred on an Autumn Damask, giving us the 'Perpetual White Moss'.

The majority of Moss Roses were bred over a short period of time, from approximately 1850 to 1870. Arriving, as they did, comparatively late on the rose scene, they show considerable signs of hybridity; in some varieties there are definite signs of China Rose ancestry and indeed some of them repeat flower really quite well. Here we have the first hint of the Modern Rose creeping in on the Old. The result is sometimes a loss of that charm which we so value in Old Roses, the first loss of innocence. Nonetheless, most Moss Roses have a beauty which is different from that of other roses. A Moss Rose bud just opening does have a certain charm that is all its own – in George Bunyard's words, 'a cosiness'; for, as he says, 'cosiness lay at the very centre of Victorian taste'. Indeed, I doubt that any other age would have taken them up quite so enthusiastically. They are often a little more stiff and upright than Centifolias, and there is more variation in quality. Disease resistance is often rather suspect. It is at this stage in the development of the rose that we have to become a little more selective in our choice of varieties.

Most Moss Roses have inherited the strong fragrance of their Centifolia ancestors and pruning should be as recommended for the Centifolias.

---

× CENTIFOLIA
*SHAILER'S
WHITE MOSS
bears cupped
white flowers
tinted blush at
the centre when
they first open*

**Blanche Moreau** Very double, paper-white flowers, starting as a cup and later becoming flat, with contrasting brown moss. This rose is said to be a cross between 'Comtesse de Murinais' and 'Quatre Saisons Blanc', and it does occasionally flower in the autumn. It is perhaps a little lacking in refinement. The growth is rather slender and tall, up to 1.8m/6ft. Raised by Moreau-Robert (France) 1880.

**Capitaine Basroger** Rather shapeless flowers of cerise-purple, and fairly coarse and ungainly growth which is tall and narrow, about 1.8m/6ft. Little moss. Raised by Moreau-Robert (France) 1890.

**Capitaine John Ingram** Full recurving flowers of dusky maroon-purple later becoming purple and showing a button eye. The buds are only sparsely covered with red moss. It forms a vigorous bushy shrub with dark foliage and many thorns. Fragrant. Height 1.5m/5ft. Bred by Laffay (France) 1854.

× *centifolia* **Muscosa** ('Old Pink Moss', 'Common Moss') It seems certain that this well-known rose was a sport from *Rosa centifolia*. It is a little smaller and less deep in the flower, probably due to the burden of producing moss. Otherwise it has the same warm, rich pink colouring and strong fragrance, as well as the elegance and poise and other good characteristics of its parent. This is probably the original Moss Rose from which the others are descended. Although many varieties have followed, none have excelled it, either for the beauty of its flowers or its value as a garden shrub. Height 1.2m/4ft. It probably dates back to 1700.

× *centifolia* **Shailer's White Moss** (*Rosa* × *centifolia* 'Muscosa Alba', 'Clifton Rose', also often known as 'White Bath') This is a

sport from 'Old Pink Moss', and is similar
except for its colour. As one might expect, it
is a most attractive rose, with cupped white
flowers tinted with blush at the centre when
they first open. It is certainly the best white
Moss Rose, and indeed one of the most
beautiful of the small band of white Old
Roses. It forms an excellent shrub of 1.2m/
4ft in height. Fragrant. Discovered by
Shailer, 1788.

**Comtesse de Murinais** Pretty blush-pink
buds enfolded in hard green moss, opening
to superb quartered blooms with a button
eye and fading to white. The growth is
vigorous, tall, and erect, its many thorns
and light green foliage suggesting a Damask
ancestry. Height 1.8m/6ft. Fragrant. A most
beautiful rose. Bred by Vibert (France) 1843.

**Duchesse de Verneuil** A charming rose
of delicate refinement, with flowers of a
clear fresh-pink colouring, the petals being
slightly paler on the reverse side. It has well
mossed buds, good foliage and forms a
shapely shrub of 1.2m/4ft in height. Bred
by Portemer (France), introduced 1856.

**Général Kléber** Pretty buds wrapped in
fresh green moss opening to form wide flat
flowers with silky petals of soft clear pink
and a button eye at the centre. It has good
bushy growth, about 1.2 × 1.2m/4 × 4ft,
with light green foliage. One of the most
beautiful of the Moss Roses. Fragrant. Bred
by Robert (France), introduced 1856.

**Gloire des Mousseuses** ('Madame
Alboni') This variety has the largest flowers
of the Moss Roses, and indeed some of the
largest flowers of all Old Roses. Its full-
petalled blooms open wide and flat, reflex at

× CENTIFOLIA
MUSCOSA is
probably the
original Moss
Rose from which
the others are
descended and
none have
excelled it

the edges and have a strong fragrance. Their colour is a soft pink
which pales with age. There is ample pale green moss on unusually
long sepals. A beautiful flower that may occasionally be damaged
by rain. It forms a strong, rather erect, but not unshapely shrub of
1.5m/5ft with thick stems and large, light green leaves. Bred by
Laffay (France) 1852.

**Henri Martin** ('Red Moss') Long crimson buds with contrasting
but rather sparse green moss. The open flower is not very full but of
attractive, neatly rounded form, and of an unusually pure crimson
for a Moss Rose, later becoming purple-crimson. The flowers, which
are held daintily on thin, wiry stems on a vigorous shrub of up to
1.8m/6ft in height, are followed by red hips. Fragrant. Bred by
Laffay (France) 1863.

**James Mitchell** A vigorous shrub with small magenta flowers that
fade to lilac-pink. The buds are dainty and wrapped in dark moss.
Height 1.5m/5ft. Bred by Verdier (France) 1861.

**Japonica** ('Moussu du Japon') This rose not only has mossy buds
but also moss spreading heavily well down the stem, and even on to
the leaves. The blooms are magenta-pink and not very impressive;
the foliage has purple and copper tints when young. Really only
valuable as a curiosity. Height 1m/3ft.

**Jeanne de Montfort** A tall and vigorous Moss Rose of 1.8–2m/6–
7ft in height. Its flowers are clear pink, not very full, have exposed
yellow stamens, and are sweetly scented. The buds have plenty of
brown moss on long sepals. Bred by Robert (France) 1851.

**Little Gem** A miniature variety which has small, flat, pompon
flowers of a uniform light crimson, but with very little moss. It
forms a low bush, no more than 0.6m/2ft in height, with small
leaves. Raised by Paul (England) 1880.

**Louis Gimard** Large cup-shaped flowers, tightly packed with petals
of light crimson. It has deep green foliage and the buds are enclosed
in dark moss. Height 1.5m/5ft. Raised by Pernet Père (France) 1877.

**Madame Delaroche-Lambert** Attractive crimson buds with
dark moss and long sepals, opening to form flat, shapely, full-
petalled flowers of crimson-purple. It makes a good bushy shrub of
1.2m/4ft in height and occasionally repeat flowers. Bred by Robert
(France) 1851.

**Maréchal Davoust** One of the most satisfactory Moss Roses, when
we consider it as a garden shrub. It flowers freely and has graceful,
shapely, rather arching growth, creating a most pleasing overall
effect. The buds are attractive, with green-brown moss, and open to
form shapely flowers of light crimson tinted with purple and mauve,

45

the petals reflexing to show a button centre and a green eye. Height about 1.2m/4ft. Fragrant. Raised by Robert (France) 1853.

**Mousseline** This rose is often found under the name 'Alfred de Dalmas'. No other Moss repeat flowers quite so well, except perhaps 'Salet', which is a much less attractive rose. The buds of 'Mousseline' are pretty and have green-brown moss, although this is not very plentiful. The open flowers are medium sized, cupped, of a soft flesh-pink and delicately scented. The growth is bushy, with pale green, peculiarly spoon-shaped leaves. It appears to be related to the Autumn Damask, probably 'Quatre Saisons Blanc'. A charming rose. Height 1.5m/5ft. Raised by Portemer (France), introduced 1855.

**Nuits de Young** ('Old Black') The darkest of all the Moss Roses, having small flowers of rich velvety maroon-purple lit by contrasting yellow stamens, with thin buds wrapped in very dark moss. Its growth is slender and wiry and it has small, dark leaves of an almost purple shade. Careful thinning at pruning time and some feeding will be worthwhile. Height 1.5m/5ft. Bred by Laffay (France) 1845.

**René d'Anjou** Pretty buds with brown-green moss opening to beautiful soft pink flowers with a delicious perfume. The foliage is tinted with bronze and it forms a bushy shrub of 1.2m/4ft in height. A charming rose. Bred by Robert (France) 1853.

**Salet** A repeat-flowering Moss Rose with blooms of a good clear

*Above left, NUITS
DE YOUNG, the
darkest of all the
Moss Roses, has
small flowers
of rich velvety
maroon-purple
lit by contrasting
yellow stamens,
with dark leaves
of an almost
purple shade*

*Left and far left,
WILLIAM LOBB
is a tall and
vigorous shrub.
The flowers are
dark crimson-
purple turning
to lavender and
eventually almost
to grey, held in
large, open sprays*

pink, and red moss. Unfortunately it is rather coarse both in flower and growth, although it is the most perpetual in this class. Height 1.2m/4ft. Bred by Lacharme (France) 1854.

**Soupert et Notting** A neat rose, which is rather different to other Mosses. The flowers are quite small, deep lilac-pink, neatly rounded and flat with closely packed petals, and have an attractive formality. The growth is short and bushy, to about 1m/3ft, and it repeat flowers well in the late summer. Although the moss is not very conspicuous, this is a charming rose. Bred by Pernet Père (France) 1874.

**William Lobb** ('Old Velvet Moss') A tall and vigorous shrub of rather straggly growth, 1.8–2.5m/6–8ft in height, with thorny stems

and leaden-green foliage. The flowers are of the most beautiful colouring: a dark crimson-purple turning to lavender and eventually almost to grey, the reverse of the petals being light magenta. They are held in large, open sprays, have plentiful green moss and a strong fragrance. This is an ideal rose for the back of the border, where it will look over the top of other smaller shrubs without showing its rather ungainly growth. It may even, as Graham Thomas suggests, be allowed to scramble into other shrubs, often combining with them to make pleasing colour effects. It is a tough and fairly healthy rose although it does sometimes succumb to powdery mildew. Raised by Laffay (France) 1855.

47

# 2

# THE REPEAT-FLOWERING OLD ROSES

TOWARDS THE END OF THE 18TH CENTURY something happened that was to change our garden roses for ever. As European travellers and traders began to throw just a little chink of light on the ancient mysteries of China, it was inevitable that plants of that massive land should be brought back to Europe. China is probably the finest source of plant material in the world, and is certainly the home of some of the most beautiful wild roses, having to its credit somewhere in the region of one hundred different species. Before Europeans had seen these in the wild, certain garden hybrids were brought to Britain. These were to be known as the China Roses. Although not particularly striking in appearance, they did have one very important characteristic: the ability to flower not just in early summer but throughout the growing season. They were, as we say, repeat flowering, perpetual flowering, remontant, or recurrent, according to which term you choose. It is interesting and rather surprising that China, in spite of her wealth of wild roses and the fact that she has a very long and honourable tradition of gardens and flowers, never rated the rose very highly. The Chinese were essentially gardeners and their interests centred around peonies, chrysanthemums and other flowers, but only to a small degree the rose, although we do from time to time find it depicted on old pottery and in pictures.

The repeat-flowering characteristic of the China Roses was not entirely new—as we have already seen the Autumn Damask Rose had the same ability which it owed to *Rosa moschata*, itself recurrent flowering from late summer onwards. The ability to flower repeatedly is a phenomenon which does not usually occur in nature and is the result of a sport or mutation in the mechanism of the plant. With one or two exceptions wild roses first of all send up tall non-flowering shoots, and it is only in the next season that the shorter flowering shoots appear on these. In the case of the China Rose something went wrong—or perhaps I should say, for us,

went right. A plant appeared which lost its ability to form its main non-flowering stems and produced only flowering stems, with the result that we had a bush on which every stem produced a flower. Having flowered, the rose would normally busy itself with the production of strong stems ready to bear next season's flowers and fruit, but in this case the plant continued to flower without thought for the future. This important fact was, no doubt, noted by some observant and long-forgotten Chinaman, who subsequently propagated the plant. Whoever he was, he made a most important contribution to our garden roses—greater perhaps than anyone has done since, for this discovery doubled or even trebled the period over which we can enjoy roses.

The China Rose originally arrived in the British Isles in four different varieties. These became known as 'Slater's Crimson China' (introduced 1792); 'Parsons' Pink China' (Old Blush China, brought to Europe 1751, introduced 1793); 'Hume's Blush China' (1809); and 'Parks' Yellow Tea-Scented China' (1824). The origin of these roses is difficult to trace. 'Parks' Yellow' can only have been the result of a cross between *R. gigantea*—which bears the largest flowers of all rose species—and a China Rose.

It may be thought that the arrival of these roses would have caused a great flurry of interest among plant breeders, but this was not the case. For one thing, the existing native roses were far more showy by comparison. Before long, however, hybrids with the European roses did appear, but the gene that provided the repeat-flowering characteristic was what is known as recessive, with the result that the first hybrids were once flowering. It was only when these hybrids

48

were again crossed with the China Roses that perpetual-flowering varieties began to appear and the revolution began. From then on things moved apace and the rose has never looked quite the same again.

This revolution was not confined to the repeat-flowering characteristic. The China Rose, with its connection with *R. gigantea*, was an entirely different rose. Whereas the European roses tended to have rough-textured leaves and many thorns, the China Roses had smooth leaves and few thorns. Moreover, their whole character was different. This provided great opportunities but, as is so often the case, also certain dangers. These we shall be discussing later.

'Slater's Crimson China' brought the richer and purer reds we now find in many roses. Previously the crimsons invariably turned to purple and mauves, though often with very pleasing effect. 'Parks' Yellow' gave us the larger, thicker, more waxy petals of *R. gigantea*. It also provided the Tea Rose scent and tints of yellow, though not yet a rich yellow.

As China blood became mingled with that of the Gallicas and Damasks a great variety of new roses appeared, most of them with the ability to flower repeatedly, if not well at least to some extent.

In this chapter we cover the various classes which, while showing signs of having a strong China influence, still bear flowers with much of the character of the truly Old Rose and can generally be described as shrubs rather than bushes. These include the Portland Roses, the Bourbons, the Hybrid Perpetuals and the Tea Roses, as well as the China Roses themselves, although there is some doubt as to the inclusion of China blood in the Portlands—at least in the early varieties. All these groups tend to have foliage nearer the China Roses than the European roses; they are, in fact, beginning to look more like the Modern Roses, but the flowers retain the full, open Old Rose formation.

This second part of the Old Rose history is rather in the nature of an unfinished story. The flower formation and shrub-like growth of the Old Roses were soon to be superseded by the pointed buds and low bush growth of the Hybrid Teas before breeders had brought Old Roses to their full potential. It was unfortunate that the development of the two types was not allowed to continue side by side, but it was not to be. Nonetheless, we have here some roses of real value which it would be a great shame to lose. Happily, as things stand at the moment, there is very little likelihood of this happening.

As regards cultivation, it must be borne in mind that these roses are repeat flowering and therefore require more careful attention due to their greater productivity. Soil conditions should be better and manuring more generous; spraying becomes more necessary. The older once-flowering roses can often be planted and more or less forgotten; this is not possible with repeat-flowering roses if we want to obtain worthwhile results.

Now that we are dealing with repeat-flowering shrubs, pruning takes on a greater significance. It is usual to recommend that pruning be done in spring (March in the UK), but there is a lot to be said for pruning in winter (from December to February). This has the advantage that the young shooting buds will not be cut away and thus force the plant to start again. The result of December pruning is that flowers appear earlier in the year, leaving the rose plenty of time to produce its second crop, and this before the soil may have dried out. Early pruning can be particularly important in more northerly areas where the seasons are shorter. These roses, being of a shrubby nature, are frequently slow in flowering again. Strong main shoots should be pruned by about one third of their length, while short side shoots should be pruned to two or three eyes. At the same time it is important to remove old and dying growth completely, while always trying to create a nice shapely shrub.

*Near right, ROSE DU ROI, a Portland, has had a great influence on our Modern Roses*

*Middle, BARON GIROD DE L'AIN is a Hybrid Perpetual with neatly edged petals (see page 68)*

*Far right, MADAME ISAAC PEREIRE, a Bourbon, is a sumptuous beauty bearing large, fragrant flowers (see pages 60–61)*

# China Roses

CHINA ROSES differ in character to most other garden roses, even to those unnumbered masses that are their heirs. They are altogether lighter in growth. This is perhaps because they are diploid, whereas the majority of garden roses are tetraploid; that is to say their cells contain two sets of chromosomes, whereas it is more usual to have four sets which result in larger cells and therefore heavier growth. China Roses have airy, twiggy growth, and rather sparse foliage, with pointed leaves, like a lighter version of a Hybrid Tea. Both growth and leaves are often tinted with red when young. The flowers are not showy, nor are they particularly shapely, but they do have a certain unassuming charm. They have an exceptional ability to repeat their flowering, and are seldom without blooms throughout the summer. Their colours are unusual in that they intensify with age, rather than pale, as is the case with European roses.

Until recently the origins of the China Rose remained a mystery. We know of the four original varieties described in the introduction to this chapter, but the wild form eluded us. It would appear that this rose was found by Mr Mikinori Ogisu of Tokyo in the Chinese Province of Sichuan. A photograph of this rose appeared in the Royal National Rose Society's Journal, *The Rose*, in September 1986, together with an article by Graham Thomas. Mr Ogisu describes it as growing into trees to a height of up to 3m/10ft, and bearing flowers of 5–6cm/2–2½in wide, which vary in colour from pink to crimson—the colour being darker in regions of higher altitude. Previously, this rose had been seen by Dr Augustine Henry in 1884, who described it in *The Gardener's Chronicle* in 1902, where it was illustrated with a drawing. The species is known as *R. chinensis* var. *spontanea*.

The China Roses of our gardens vary considerably according to the conditions under which they are grown. In an open position in the British Isles they will rarely reach much more than 60–90cm/2–3ft in height, although in more favourable areas they will grow much taller. In countries with warmer climates they will make quite large shrubs of 1.8m/6ft and more. As to position, it is best to select a sheltered corner of the garden, perhaps with the protection of a south-facing wall which is shielded from the wind. Here they will grow much nearer their full potential. Having said all this, China Roses are not really tender and can be relied on to withstand all but the very hardest winters in the British Isles.

The light growth and dainty flowers of China Roses make them particularly suitable for mixing with other plants, especially where something heavier and more robust might be out of place. They require fertile soil, or at least soil that has been well manured, but unlike other repeat-flowering Old Roses they dislike hard pruning, and this should usually be done only to maintain the shape of the shrub and to remove dead and ageing growth.

*HERMOSA, a China that has something of the appearance of a Bourbon Rose, is smaller in all its parts and more delicate in appearance*

*Old Blush China* is often the first rose to start flowering in spring and the last to finish in the winter

**Bengal Crimson** (*R.* × *odorata* 'Bengal Crimson', 'Sanguinea', 'Rose de Bengale') This rose is rarely seen and rarely available in the UK but well worth seeking out if you have a warm, sheltered spot. It much prefers warm climates where it has the advantage of flowering 12 months of the year. The flowers are truly single, about 9cm/3½in across and of the purest blood red that fades to a more crimson shade as they age. There is a light tea fragrance. Interestingly, although not a true species, it comes true from seed. In the British Isles it will make a rounded bushy plant about 1–1.2m/3–4ft tall but will grow twice that height in hotter climates. Introduced *c.*1824.

**Comtesse du Cayla** A dainty little shrub of 90cm/3ft in height with almost single flowers of varying shades of coppery-pink, eventually becoming salmon-pink with yellow tints at the base of the petal. The foliage is purplish-bronze when young. Tea Rose scent. Raised by P. Guillot (France) 1902.

**Cramoisi Supérieur** Small, cupped, fragrant flowers of a clear unfading crimson, produced in small clusters. The growth is short and twiggy, about 90cm/3ft in height in a warm situation. There is also a good climbing form, 'Cramoisi Supérieur Grimpante'. Bred and introduced by Coquereau, 1832.

**Fabvier** ('Madame Fabvier', 'Colonel Fabvier') A small low-growing plant of about 30cm/1ft in height, rather similar in habit to a Polyantha Rose. The flowers are small and bright scarlet with a white streak in their petals. It is constantly in bloom and the petals fall before they fade, giving an effect of continuing brilliance. Laffay (France) 1832.

**Hermosa** This shows all the signs of being a China Rose hybrid. We do not know what the other parent was, but certainly it is an excellent little rose. It has something of the appearance of a Bourbon Rose, but is smaller in all its parts and more delicate in appearance. The growth is branching and more sturdy than most China Roses, bearing small lilac-pink flowers of a pretty cupped formation. They are borne with admirable continuity throughout the summer. Slight fragrance. Bred and introduced by Marcheseau (France) 1834. (Illustrated, p. 51)

**Le Vésuve** ('Lemesle') Dainty scrolled buds of Tea Rose appearance, soft creamy-pink in colour, gradually deepening with age and finally taking on tints of carmine. The flowers have a Tea Rose fragrance and are produced continually on a branching twiggy bush which will, given a warm sheltered position, achieve 1.5m/5ft in height, although 90cm/3ft is more usual under average conditions. Introduced by Laffay (France) 1825.

**Madame Laurette Messimy** Long slender buds with only a few petals which open quickly. They are salmon-pink at first, shaded copper at the base of the petal, the open flower soon fading. It is the result of a cross between 'Rival de Paestum' and the Tea Rose 'Madame Falcot', and is, in fact, of somewhat Tea Rose appearance. It will grow to 1.2m/4ft in height in a warm position. Bred by Guillot Fils (France) 1887.

**Mutabilis** ('Tipo Ideale') Often incorrectly known as *Rosa turkestanica*, this variety rivals the 'Old Blush China' for its excellence

as a garden shrub. Its pointed copper-flame buds open to single copper-yellow flowers of butterfly daintiness, soon turning to pink and finally almost crimson. Given a warm sheltered position near a wall it will form a 2.5m/8ft shrub which will probably flower as constantly as any other rose. In more exposed positions it is often quite small and frail in appearance. Apart from knowing that it comes from Italy in around 1900, we know little of the origins of this rose. (Illustrated, p. 49)

**Old Blush China** ('Parsons' Pink China', × *odorata* 'Pallida') This is a very good garden shrub, with twiggy but quite robust growth and dainty flowers in small clusters. These are produced continually

*Sophie's Perpetual bears flowers of shapely cupped formation that are held in sprays against dark green foliage*

throughout the summer, starting early and finishing late, and for this reason it was formerly known as the Monthly Rose. The flowers are not large and of a loose informality. They are pale pink in colour, deepening with age. The bush usually grows to about 1.2m/4ft in height but may be considerably taller in favourable conditions. I have seen it growing as a 3m/10ft shrub near to a wall in the warm climate of Pembrokeshire. It has a pleasing fragrance which has been described as being similar to that of a Sweet Pea. Introduced to England in 1789.

**Rival de Paestum** Long, pointed buds, tinted blush, opening to semi-double ivory-white flowers elegantly poised on a shrub some 1.2m/4ft in height. Sometimes classified as a Tea Rose. Raised by Beluze 1841.

**Sophie's Perpetual** A beautiful rose found in an old garden, named by Humphrey Brooke and reintroduced in 1960. The flowers are quite small, of shapely cupped formation and held in small sprays. Their colour is a deep pink. Strong growth with few thorns and dark green foliage. The fragrance has been described as the closest to a perfume to be found in roses. It will grow into a 1.8m/6ft shrub and may be used as a Climber. Of obvious hybrid origin.

**Viridiflora** (the Green Rose) In this rose the petals are entirely missing and have been replaced by numerous green sepals giving the effect of a green rose. It is, no doubt, a sport from the 'Old Blush China' to which it is very similar in growth. It is of little value as a garden plant, except as a curiosity, although it may have its uses for inclusion in flower arrangements. Height 90cm/3ft. Introduced 1855.

# Portland Roses

THE
REPEAT-
FLOWERING
OLD ROSES
———
Portland
Roses

The Portland Roses were the first family in which the China Rose played a part by passing on its ability to repeat flower. They had only a short period of popularity, for they were soon overtaken, first by the Bourbons, and not long after by the Hybrid Perpetuals, but in 1848 there were eighty-four varieties growing at Kew. Today only a handful remain, but they form, nonetheless, a not unimportant class, both for their beauty and as one of the parents of the Hybrid Perpetuals.

The origins of the Portland Roses are shrouded in mystery and writers tend to step lightly over the subject, but we do know that around the year 1800 the Duchess of Portland obtained from Italy a rose known as *Rosa paestana* or 'Scarlet Four Seasons' Rose', and that it was from this rose that the group developed. The Portland Rose was repeat flowering and was thought to have been the result of a cross between *Rosa gallica* var. *officinalis* and the repeat-flowering Autumn Damask and certainly DNA analysis supports the presence of these two parents. Hurst seems to have had little to say on the subject, although he does note that Redouté's print of 1817 has the appearance of a China-Damask-French hybrid. I would thus assume Hurst had not seen the growing plant. One would expect there to be some China Rose influence

(probably 'Slater's Crimson China'), although there is not much evidence of this in the plant. If this is so, it may well have inherited the recurrent-flowering characteristic from two different sources. The Portland Rose was sent from England to France where André Dupont, gardener to the Empress Josephine, named it 'Duchess of Portland', and it was not very long before the French had raised numerous varieties.

Portland Roses are not difficult to recognise. They usually show a strong Damask influence, but they are shorter in growth, perhaps 1.2m/4ft in height. The flowers tend to have very little stem so that the leaves are packed closely around the flowers, forming what Graham Thomas describes as a rosette or shoulder of leaves.

Although they cannot be said to be graceful in growth, being rather upright, Portland Roses are well suited to smaller gardens as they form small, compact shrubs. Their virtue lies in the fact that, though repeat flowering, they retain much of the character of the truly Old Roses and have a strong Damask fragrance. Their ability to repeat is by no means unfailing and varies according to variety, but most of them can be relied on to provide flowers later in the year, many of them producing particularly beautiful Old Rose blooms.

---

**Arthur de Sansal** A compact, upright shrub with ample foliage, the attractive buds opening to form flat, neatly-shaped very double dark crimson-purple flowers, paler on the reverse side of the petals. There is usually a button eye at the centre of the flower. Richly fragrant. Height 90cm/3ft. Raised by Cochet (France) 1855.

**Blanc de Vibert** This variety bears prettily-cupped, many-petalled white flowers with a strong fragrance. It forms an upright bush with ample pale green Damask Rose foliage. Height 90cm/3ft. Raised by Vibert (France), introduced 1847.

**Comte de Chambord** Very full quartered flowers of rich clear pink with a powerful Damask Rose fragrance. The growth is strong and rather upright, about 1.2m/4ft in height, with ample foliage, the leaves coming all the way up to the flower in true Portland style. Here we have a rose that retains the true Old Rose character, while at the same time repeat flowering well. One of the best and most beautiful of this class. Raised by Moreau-Robert (France), introduced 1860.

**Delambre** A compact bush, bearing full-petalled deep pink flowers against ample dark green foliage. Height 90cm/3ft. Bred by Moreau-Robert (France) 1863. (Illustrated, p. 57)

**Indigo** The colour of this varies considerably according to climate and age of flower; it does include indigo although it may also be purple, crimson or deep mauve. The blooms and growth are typically Portland with fully double flowers and stiff stems. It repeat flowers and is relatively healthy. There is a delicious fragrance. Height 90cm/3ft. Bred by Laffay (France) 1830. (Illustrated, p. 57)

**Jacques Cartier** ('Marchesa Boccella') Very similar

*Right,* COMTE DE CHAMBORD *retains the true Old Rose character and repeat flowers well*

*Facing page,* JACQUES CARTIER *has some of the most perfectly formed blooms of any variety*

THE
REPEAT-
FLOWERING
OLD ROSES

Portland
Roses

*ROSE DE RESCHT,*
*an excellent*
*all-round variety,*
*has beautiful*
*blooms, a strong*
*fragrance, good*
*repeat flowering*
*and attractive,*
*healthy, rounded*
*growth*

to 'Comte de Chambord', but the shapely full-petalled flowers have, if anything, a little more refinement, although it is not such a good repeat flowerer. It has the same clear pink colouring, fading a little with age, and a button eye at the centre. The growth is compact and erect with light green Damask Rose foliage. Rich fragrance. Height 1.1 m/3½ft. Raised by Moreau-Robert (France), introduced 1868.

**Marbrée** Deep purple-pink flowers mottled with a paler pink and opening flat. The growth is strong and tall for a Portland, with plentiful dark green foliage. Slight fragrance. Height 1.2m/4ft. Raised by Robert et Moreau (France) 1858.

**Portland Rose** (the 'Scarlet Four Seasons' Rose', 'Duchess of Portland', 'Paestana', 'Portlandica') This forms an excellent bushy and rather spreading shrub of 90cm/3ft. in height with ample foliage. The flowers are semi-double opening wide and of light crimson colouring with conspicuous yellow stamens. A good garden shrub both in summer and autumn. Strong Damask fragrance.

**Rose de Rescht** A shapely, bushy shrub that has quite small neatly-formed very double flowers with closely-packed petals. The purplish-crimson blooms are nicely placed on short stems against ample rough-textured deep green foliage. There are signs of Gallica Rose influence both in flower and leaf, but the fact that it produces a second crop of flowers suggests its place is in this class. Delicious and strong fragrance. Height 90cm/3ft. Brought to England by Miss Nancy Lindsay in the 1940s, possibly from Rasht on the Caspian Sea, Iran.

**Rose du Roi** ('Lee's Crimson Perpetual') An interesting little rose which has had a great influence on our Modern Roses, being the channel through which we obtained the clear red colouring, first of all in the Hybrid Perpetuals, and from them in the Hybrid Teas of the present day. It is a short rather spreading bush and not particularly robust. The flowers are loosely double, crimson mottled with purple. Strong fragrance. It repeats well and is, all in all, a worthwhile rose in its own right. Raised by Lélieur (France), introduced by Souchet, 1815. (Illustrated, p. 50)

**Rose du Roi à Fleurs Pourpres** ('Roi des Pourpres', 'Mogador') Said to be a sport from 'Rose du Roi', its appearance casts some doubt on this. It is a pretty little rose with loosely formed purple flowers. Of spreading growth, it may achieve about 90cm/3ft under suitable conditions. Introduced 1819.

*Left,* DELAMBRE *bears full-petalled flowers against ample dark green foliage*

*Far left,* ROSE DU ROI À FLEURS POURPRES *bears flowers of a wonderful, rich colour*

*Left,* INDIGO *flowers vary considerably in colour, creating a most attractive mixed effect*

# Bourbon Roses

THE
REPEAT-
FLOWERING
OLD ROSES

Bourbon
Roses

The origins of the Bourbon Rose make a fascinating story and illustrate very well how the various developments of the early roses always happened by chance, and sometimes in what seem to be the most unlikely places. These roses take their name from l'Île de Bourbon, a small island near Mauritius in the Indian Ocean, now known as Réunion. It is said that farmers of this island were in the habit of planting both the Autumn Damask and the 'Old Blush China' together as hedges. With so many of these roses growing in close proximity there was always a chance that a hybrid would arise, and this is what happened. The Parisian botanist Nicolas Bréon found a rose growing in the garden of a man named A. M. Perchern. This rose was intermediate between the Autumn Damask and the 'Old Blush China' and had been grown in the island for some years under the name 'Rose Edward'. Bréon sent seed of this rose to his friend Jacques, gardener to King Louis-Philippe, from which a rose called 'Rosier de l'Île de Bourbon' was raised. It was distributed in France in 1823 and two years later in England. Not much is known about the early development of these roses, for breeding was then still confined to the chance collection of seed, but we can be sure that several other roses played a part in their development.

The Bourbons represent the first real step towards the Modern Roses. Their flowers retain the character of the Old Roses with their strong fragrance, and they still have shrubby growth, but their leaves and stems begin to look more like those of the Hybrid Tea, and they are nearly all repeat flowering. Thus we have something of the best of both worlds. They are usually of robust growth and some highly desirable roses are to be found among them, although, in general, their resistance to black spot is poor.

With Bourbons pruning becomes more important, particularly if we are to take advantage of their ability to flower a second time. Side shoots should be pruned back to three eyes, and strong main shoots reduced by one third. As the years go by, ageing and dead growth should also be removed. A liberal mulching with farmyard manure or compost, and an application of a rose fertilizer in spring (March in the UK) and again after the first crop of flowers will greatly improve the results. Immediate dead heading is also important.

---

**Adam Messerich** A late arrival on the scene. One of its parents was a Hybrid Tea, and this shows up in the rather modern appearance of its growth and foliage—it might be argued that it is not a Bourbon at all. However, this need not worry us as it is a good shrub which may also be grown as a Climber or pillar rose. It is very vigorous, sending up long slightly arching almost thornless growth from the base of the plant. The flowers are large, semi-double, slightly cupped in shape and of a deep warm pink. The fragrance is strong, with a somewhat fruity, some say raspberry, flavour. It flowers freely in early summer but there are only occasional blooms later. Height 1.5 m/5 ft. Bred by P. Lambert (Germany), introduced 1920.
**Blairii No.2** See Chapter 6.

*Bourbon Queen may be grown either as a tall rather open shrub or as a Climber*

**Boule de Neige** A slender upright shrub of perhaps 1.5 m/5 ft in height, its neat dark green foliage betraying its partly Tea Rose ancestry. The flowers are held in small clusters, and its small, round, crimson-tinted buds open to the most perfectly formed creamy-white blooms of posy freshness, the petals gradually turning back on themselves almost forming a ball. Add to this a strong fragrance and we have one of the most charming white Old Roses. Bourbon 'Blanche Lafitte' × the Tea Rose 'Sappho'. Bred by Lacharme (France) 1867. (Illustrated, p. 59)

**Bourbon Queen** ('Queen of the Bourbons', 'Reine des Îles Bourbon') A rose frequently found surviving in old gardens after many years. It may be grown either as a tall rather open shrub of up to 1.8 m/6 ft in height, or as a Climber; on a wall it can achieve 3–3.5 m/10–12 ft. The flowers are cupped and rather loosely formed with exposed stamens and crinkled petals. They are medium pink veined with deeper pink paling towards the edges. Strong fragrance. Raised by Mauget (France), introduced 1834.

**Commandant Beaurepaire** ('Panachée d'Angers') The three Bourbon Roses with striped flowers—'Commandant Beaurepaire', 'Honorine de Brabant' and 'Variegata di Bologna'—are all rather similar. This one is notable for the lovely mixture of colours in its flowers: carmine pink flecked and striped with mauve, purple, scarlet and pale pink, and this so variously that they might be described in a dozen different ways. These colours are at their best in cool weather, as they tend to be rather muddy in very hot sun. The flowers are shallowly cupped in shape, strongly fragrant and produced very freely. This rose forms a dense leafy bush of strong growth that requires some thinning at pruning time to maintain the quality of its flowers. The height is 1.5m/5ft and as much across. It flowers only in early summer. Raised by Moreau-Robert (France) 1874.

**Coupe d'Hébé** Cupped flowers of pale pink opening full and slightly quartered. The growth is tall, narrow and rather too upright, with light green foliage. It may be grown as a Climber. Bred from a Bourbon hybrid × a China hybrid. Laffay (France) 1840.

**Honorine de Brabant** A rose similar to 'Commandant Beaurepaire' but paler in colour—light pink splashed with shades of crimson and purple. It has the advantage over 'Commandant Beaurepaire' in that it repeat flowers quite well, the later flowers often being of better quality in the less intense sunlight of late summer. They are of shallow cupped-shape, opening quartered, with a strong fragrance. The growth is robust and bushy, to about 1.8m/6ft, with ample foliage. It may also be grown as a Climber.

**Kronprinzessin Viktoria** This is a sport from 'Souvenir de la Malmaison', see p. 65, and is similar to that rose except that the flowers are creamy white shaded with pale lemon-yellow. They can easily become discoloured in wet weather, and I have found it to be even less strong than its parent. Unless it is possible to give it exceptional care, it would probably be better not to grow this variety. It originated in 1887 and was introduced by Späth of Berlin.

**Louise Odier** A rose out of very much the same mould as 'Reine Victoria', having all

*BOULE DE NEIGE has small, crimson-tinted buds that open to perfectly formed blooms*

*HONORINE DE BRABANT is one of three Bourbon Roses with striped flowers*

its virtues but with more robust and bushy growth. The flowers are beautifully formed, cupped at first, opening flatter and neatly rounded, with each petal precisely in place. Their colour is a lovely warm pink and they have a rich fragrance. Like 'Reine Victoria' it repeats well throughout the summer, and for me it is the most desirable of the recurrent-flowering Old Roses. Height 1.5m/5ft. I have used this rose for breeding and the results suggest that it has some Noisette in its make up. Raised by Margottin (France), introduced 1851.

**Madame Ernst Calvat** A sport from 'Madame Isaac Pereire', described below. It is similar in every respect, except for the colour which is a medium pink. In my opinion the flowers are a little less happy in this colour than in the deeper shades of its parents, often appearing rather coarse, but as with so many roses we get the occasional perfect flower, particularly in autumn, that makes it all worth while. It has the same strong growth and rich fragrance as 'Madame Isaac Pereire'. Height 1.8m/6ft. Discovered by Vve Schwartz (France) 1888.

**Madame Isaac Pereire** A vigorous shrub some 2m/7ft in height with large, thick, deep green foliage. It bears huge flowers, perhaps 12cm/5in across. These are cupped at first and quartered on opening, the petals being rolled back at the edges. The colour is a very deep pink shaded with magenta, giving a rich effect, and there is an extremely powerful fragrance. It flowers well in the autumn when it often produces some of its best blooms. A sumptuous beauty, especially when well grown. The parentage is not recorded. Bred by Garçon (France) 1881. (Also illustrated p.50)

**Madame Lauriol de Barny** A most beautiful rose carrying silky, richly fragrant quartered blooms of silvery pink colouring. They are held in weighty, slightly drooping sprays on a vigorous 1.8m/6ft shrub, which may also be trained as a Climber. It has a good crop of flowers in early summer but there are rarely any blooms later. Raised by Trouillard (France) 1868.

**Madame Pierre Oger** A sport from 'Reine Victoria', see below, to which it is similar in every respect except for the colour of the flowers. This is a pale creamy blush, giving the flowers a refinement exceeding even that of its parent, the beautiful chaliced blooms taking on the appearance of the most delicate porcelain. In very hot weather the colour tends to deepen and harden on the sunny side of the blooms, and in the rain the petals become speckled. The growth is narrow and upright, about 1.5m/5ft in height. Fragrant. Discovered by A. Oger (France) 1878.

**Mrs Paul** Probably a seedling from 'Madame Isaac Pereire' with which it shares many characteristics. It has large blush-white flowers with a strong perfume. The growth is robust though rather floppy and may require a little support. Plentiful large leaves. Height 1.5m/5ft. Bred by George Paul (England), introduced by Paul & Sons 1891.

**Prince Charles** Dark purple-crimson flowers turning almost lilac as they age. They are large, flat when open and have petals of a veined and crimpled appearance. The growth is strong, about

THE
REPEAT-
FLOWERING
OLD ROSES

Bourbon
Roses

Facing page,
MADAME ISAAC
PEREIRE is a
vigorous shrub
that will hold its
own in a mixed
border, here with
a tall campanula
and Sambucus
nigra 'Marginata'

Far left, MADAME
PIERRE OGER
similar to 'Reine
Victoria' in every
respect except for
the colour of the
chaliced blooms

Left, LOUISE
ODIER is the
most desirable
of the recurrent-
flowering Old
Roses

Following pages,
REINE VICTORIA
has few rivals
among the Old
Roses in its
ability to flower
repeatedly
throughout the
summer

1.5 m/5 ft in height, with large leaves and few thorns. It has little fragrance and is not recurrent. One of the few dark-coloured roses in this class. A sport or seedling of 'Bourbon Queen', introduced 1842.

**Reine Victoria** In this rose and its sport, 'Madame Pierre Oger', see p. 61, we have two of the most beautiful and best loved roses of the late 19th century. They both form slender shrubs of about 1.5 m/5 ft in height, with the blooms elegantly poised above the foliage, indicating a close relationship with China Roses. The flowers are medium sized, chalice shaped rather than cupped, the petals incurving towards the centre to provide a charming enclosed effect and holding their form to the end. The colour is lilac-pink on the outside and paler within. This variety has few rivals among the Old Roses in its ability to flower repeatedly throughout the summer. Unfortunately, as so often happens, along with this goes a greater tendency to blackspot. Fragrant. Height 1.2 m/4 ft. Bred by J. Schwartz (France), introduced 1872. (Illustrated, p. 62–3)

**Sir Joseph Paxton** A vigorous, healthy and sturdy rose with very full cup-shaped flowers held in small clusters. The flowers are particularly strongly coloured and the petals have beautiful colour shadings, the base colour is bright rose-pink with crimson tints running through it. Unfortunately it doesn't repeat flower. There is a medium fragrance. Height 1.2 m/4 ft by the same across. Bred by Laffay (France) 1852.

**Souvenir de la Malmaison** This rose was named in memory of the Empress Josephine's famous garden at Malmaison and is one of the most popular of the Bourbon Roses. It is available both as a bush and a Climber, the bush being a short rather spreading shrub of about 90cm/3 ft in height. The flowers are a delicate blush-pink which pales a little with age. They are cup-shaped at first, later becoming flat and distinctly quartered to form a large and beautiful flower about 12cm/5 in across, with a fragrance similar to that of a Tea Rose. Raised in 1843 by J. Beluze of France, from a cross between the Bourbon Rose 'Madame Desprez' and a Tea Rose, it has, as we might expect, foliage of rather modern appearance, although the flowers are of truly Old Rose persuasion. It is a reliable repeat flowerer. The growth is rather too short for the flowers, and it is, perhaps, better in its climbing form (see Chapter 7).

**Souvenir de Saint Anne's** An almost single sport of 'Souvenir de la Malmaison', found by Graham Thomas in Lady Ardilaun's garden at St Anne's, near Dublin. With extra generous treatment, it is capable of forming a fine shrub of 2m/7 ft in height. The large flowers are a delicate blush-pink colouring and have a nice clean-cut appearance. Rather surprisingly, unlike 'Souvenir de la Malmaison', it has a strong fragrance. Graham Thomas told me that this stems from *Rosa moschata* in its parentage, in which the fragrance comes from the stamens rather than the petals. Of course, this rose does have stamens, whereas its parent does not. Introduced 1950.

**Variegata di Bologna** The last of our trio of striped Bourbon Roses, and of more recent origin, having been bred in Italy by A. Bonfiglioli as late as 1909. The flowers are white, clearly striped with dark crimson-purple, giving them a purity and freshness that is very appealing, particularly in cool weather. They are fully double, cupped in shape, globular at first and quartered when open, and have a strong perfume. This rose has ample foliage and forms a dense shrub of 1.5–1.8m/5–6 ft or will climb to 3 m /10 ft. A distinct and beautiful rose but susceptible to blackspot.

**Zépherine Drouhin.** See chapter 6.

*Left,* SOUVENIR DE LA MALMAISON *has flowers of truly Old Rose persuasion and foliage of somewhat modern appearance, seen here in the climbing form*

*Facing page,* VARIEGATA DI BOLOGNA, *arguably the most attractive of the striped Old Roses, has flowers of a wonderful freshness and purity*

# Tea Roses

THE TEA ROSES were the result of crossing two of the original China Roses, 'Hume's Blush China' (*Rosa × odorata* 'Odorata') and 'Parks' Yellow Tea-Scented China' (*Rosa × odorata* 'Ochroleuca', with various Bourbon and Noisette Roses. The first Tea Rose was introduced in 1835 and most appropriately named 'Adam', having been bred by an English nurseryman of that name. The class was originally known as Tea Scented China Roses, but this was soon abbreviated to Tea Roses. How they came to be known by this name is a mystery; there is, in fact, a range of fragrances to be found amongst them, but none of them, to my nose at least, has much in common with that of tea, although Graham Thomas insists that the scent of a typical Tea Rose is exactly like that of a freshly opened packet of China tea. However this may be, we still refer to certain roses as having a Tea Rose scent, and the name has now acquired a meaning of its own.

The Tea Rose was destined to become one of the parents of the Hybrid Tea, and could perhaps be best described as a rather slender version of that class while at the same time exhibiting a fairly close affinity to the twiggy, branching growth of the China Rose. Like the Chinas they are diploids. The popular, rather romanticised impression of a Tea Rose is of a long, slender and refined bud of the most delicate colouring, but this is only partly true; in fact they come in various forms and sometimes in quite harsh colours.

These roses cannot be recommended for general garden use in the UK; indeed I am not entirely sure that I would include them in this book were it not for the fact that they complete the historical picture. I have grown a number of them in my garden but have never found them satisfactory in our climate. If they survive the winter they are frequently cut back by frost and, although some are hardier than others, they often have the appearance of rather run-down Hybrid Teas. When grown in the warmer parts of the British Isles, such as Cornwall or Devon, it might be quite a different matter, and I have seen them growing as fine large shrubs in Mediterranean countries. If space can be found for them in a cold greenhouse, you may expect some very beautiful roses and the connoisseur may feel this worthwhile; after all, is it not true that many alpine plant enthusiasts go to equal lengths to grow their own particular treasures? Another less extreme method is to plant them against a warm and sheltered wall and treat them as short Climbers.

However, it is very worthwhile planting Tea Roses in countries with warm and frost-free climates—most of the survivors in this class have come from such regions. The Climbing Teas are usually much hardier and can be recommended for the average garden. Whether this is due to different breeding or to the fact that they are usually grown on walls, I cannot say—perhaps it is a bit of both. These are described in Chapter 7.

Tea Roses prefer a well-drained, fertile soil and, as the reader will have gathered, should be planted in a warm and sheltered position. Like their parents the China Roses, they object to too much pruning. This should consist only of the thinning out of old growth, the removal of dead wood, and general maintenance of the shape of the bush. Height will vary enormously according to climate. They seldom achieve more than 90cm/3ft in the United Kingdom, but I have no doubt that in more southerly countries they could form much larger bushes.

Included here is a short list of Tea Roses that are still obtainable and mainly those with flowers in softer shades as I think these are more appealing. As I have not grown many of them under garden conditions I have not had sufficient experience of some of the varieties to say which are the best.

---

**Archiduc Joseph** One of the hardiest of the Tea Roses, forming a strong bush or Climber, with plentiful dark green foliage. The flowers are of a purplish-pink, opening flat with many petals, gradually turning to blush at the centre. Height 1.5m/5ft. A seedling from 'Madame Lombard'. Bred by Nabonnand (France) 1892.

**Catherine Mermet** Once widely grown for the cut-flower trade. When well grown it has exquisitely formed buds, blush-pink at the centre and tinted lilac-pink at the edges. Only suitable for the greenhouse in the UK. Height 1.2m/4ft. Bred by Guillot Fils (France) 1869.

**Dr. Grill** (Docteur Grill) Pointed rose-pink buds shaded with copper, opening flat and full petalled. Branching growth. Fragrant. Height 90cm/3ft. 'Ophirie' × 'Souvenir de Victor Hugo'. Bred by Bonnaire (France) 1886.

**Homère** Nicely cupped soft pink flowers with red tints at the edges, paling almost to white at the centre. An early variety that is hardier than most. It has bushy, twiggy growth with dark green foliage. Height 90cm/3ft. Bred by Robert et Moreau (France) 1858.

**Lady Hillingdon** The only bush Tea Rose that can be said to be in anything like general circulation, and virtually as hardy as a Hybrid Tea. The recorded parentage is 'Papa Gontier' × 'Madame Hoste', both of which are Tea Roses, but this is doubtful due to the fact that the chromosome count indicates a cross with a Hybrid Tea. This illustrates very well that we should not place too much credence on early breeding records. 'Lady Hillingdon' has large petals, forming long slender buds of a lovely deep apricot-yellow which eventually open to rather shapeless flowers with a strong Tea Rose fragrance.

*CATHERINE
MERMET
has exquisitely
formed buds and
was once widely
grown for the cut-
flower trade*

It has fine contrasting dark green foliage which is coppery-mahogany when young. There is a particularly good climbing sport, better by far than the bush, and it is wiser to grow this form where space is available (see Chapter 7). Height 1.2m/4ft. Bred by Lowe & Shawyer (UK) 1910.

**Madame Bravy** ('Adele Pradel', 'Madame de Sertat') Large creamy-white flowers shaded buff, with a strong Tea Rose fragrance. Height 90cm/3ft. Guillot Père (France) 1846.

**Maman Cochet** Large globular blooms of pale pink, deepening towards the centre with lemon-yellow shades at the base. The growth is quite vigorous with dark green foliage. Once a famous exhibition rose. Height 90cm/3ft. 'Marie van Houtte' × 'Mme Lombard'. Bred by Cochet (France) 1893.

**Marie van Houtte** Large pointed buds of cream tinged carmine-pink, with buff at the base of the petals. Fragrant. Sprawling habit. Height 90cm/3ft. 'Madame de Tartas' × 'Madame Falcot'. Ducher (France) 1871.

**Papa Gontier** Long, pointed, deep pink buds, with the reverse side of the petals carmine-red, opening semi-double. Bushy growth. Height 90cm/3ft. Nabonnand (France) 1883.

**Perle des Jardins** Pointed buds developing into fragrant full-petalled flowers of a straw-yellow colour. These fail to open well in damp weather. The growth is slender but reasonably hardy. Fragrant. Height 90cm/3ft. 'Madame Falcot' × a seedling. Levet (France) 1874.

**Triomphe de Luxembourg** Full-petalled flowers borne in clusters. Salmon-pink becoming salmon-buff. Height 90cm/3ft. Hardy (France) 1839.

# Hybrid Perpetual Roses

THE
REPEAT-
FLOWERING
OLD ROSES

Hybrid
Perpetual
Roses

WE NOW REACH the final stage of development of the rose before arriving at the Hybrid Teas which are, of course, the predominant roses of the present day. None of the classes described so far can be said to be in any way pure or clearly defined in so far as their origins are concerned, although they may be quite distinct in their general character and appearance. When we come to the Hybrid Perpetuals this is more than ever true. They can best be described as an idea rather than as roses of any definite origins. They are, in fact, an amalgamation of various roses with certain objectives in view—for it is at this stage that large-scale breeding comes into its own—with breeders raising numerous seedlings in the hope of arriving at an ideal. William Paul tells us that the French breeder Laffay raised up to 200,000 seedlings annually—more than many large-scale breeders grow today.

It cannot be said that breeding on such a scale led to an all round improvement; indeed there is, to me, a decline in the beauty of the rose since Hybrid Perpetuals first appeared. It is true that, as their name suggests, the Hybrid Perpetuals are repeat flowering, but they are rather clumsy and their growth too tall, narrow and upright, to be suitable for use as shrubs in the garden. The nature of their development was in no small degree due to the advent of the rose show which was, during the latter half of the 19th century, at the height of its popularity. Roses were exhibited in boxes in which six or more blooms would be placed at equal distances in order to show each of them individually. So keen was the competition that it resulted in a tendency to breed for exhibition only, and the flower as a bud became the exhibitor's ideal. Unfortunately this led to the notion of a rose perfect in bud formation only, while the open bloom, so much appreciated by Old Rose enthusiasts today, was given little regard. At the same time, and equally unfortunately, the breeders' attention was centred on the flower and habit of growth was ignored often resulting in tall ungainly plants and poor resistance to disease. As garden plants they left much to be desired.

There are, however, some beautiful Hybrid Perpetuals still surviving, particularly those of earlier date, and many of them well worth a place in the garden. It is these I include here. A few may be a little ungainly, but they are beautiful as cut flowers and do have at least three virtues: they are nearly all very fragrant, they are recurrent flowering, and many have the Old Rose flower formation. In this class we also find varieties of a rich pure crimson colouring, something rarely found in roses before the latter half of the 19th century.

Hybrid Perpetuals are gross feeders and repay generous treatment. Some, if left to their own devices, become too tall, and it is best to prune them down by about half their height to maintain reasonable proportions and ensure quality and continuity of bloom.

---

**Arrillaga** A very late arrival with interesting parentage (*Rosa centifolia* × 'Mrs John Laing') × 'Frau Karl Druschki', and therefore by no means a pure Hybrid Perpetual, if indeed there is such a thing. It forms a tall shrub, often growing to a height of over 1.8m/6ft. The flowers are in the Old Rose tradition, soft pink in colour, with a light fragrance. The first flowering is very prolific, but there is only an occasional bloom later in the summer. Bred by Schoener (USA), introduced 1929.

**Baroness Rothschild** Large shallowly cupped flowers, frequently of the most perfect formation, the petals later recurving. They are of a soft pink colour, deepening towards the centre. The growth is erect, to 1.2m/4ft, and thorny, with greyish-green foliage coming close up to the flower in the manner of a Portland Rose to which it is probably closely related. It is free flowering and repeats quite well. This variety produces some of the most beautiful flowers in this section—it is unfortunate that it has little fragrance. A sport of 'Souvenir de la Reine d'Angleterre'. Discovered by Pernet Père (France) 1868.

**Baron Girod de l'Ain** A 'Eugène Fürst' sport, discovered by Reverchon of France in 1897. Unlike many Hybrid Perpetuals it forms a broad shapely shrub which grows strongly without being too upright. It has fine large foliage although disease resistance is poor. The flowers, like those of its parent, are a dark heavy crimson, but

THE
REPEAT-
FLOWERING
OLD ROSES

Hybrid
Perpetual
Roses

*BARONNE
PRÉVOST has
magnificent,
perfectly formed
blooms and strong
upright growth*

THE
REPEAT-
FLOWERING
OLD ROSES

Hybrid
Perpetual
Roses

*FERDINAND PICHARD is one of the best striped roses, as good as its Bourbon rivals, and the one to choose for the smaller garden* with the added and unusual attraction that the petals are neatly edged with a thin line of white. They are large and of shapely cupped formation, and their colour holds well, showing off the dual effect to perfection. It repeats quite well under good conditions and has a rich fragrance. Height 1.2m/4ft. (Illustrated, p. 50)

**Baronne Prévost** Large flowers in the Old Rose tradition, opening flat and quartered with a small button eye. The colour is pale rose-pink. Its growth is strong and very upright, about 1.2m/4ft in height. Fragrant. Bred by M. Desprez (France) 1841. (Illustrated, p. 69)

**Comtesse Cécile de Chabrillant** The Hybrid Perpetuals are not particularly known for their well formed blooms but Comtesse Cécile has most attractive, neat, rounded flowers. The overall colour is a rich pink but close examination reveals veining in many other shades of pink and a much paler pink on the reverse. It makes an attractive, reasonably compact shrub that flowers freely and, if dead headed, repeats well too. Like most in this group it can be grown as a short climber if lightly pruned. Strongly fragrant. A beautiful rose that should be more widely planted. Height and spread 1.2m/4ft. Bred by Marest (France) 1858.

**Duke of Edinburgh** One of the best of the bright red Hybrid Perpetuals, forming a strong erect bush of about 90cm/3ft in height. The flowers are full, of open incurved formation and fragrant, repeating quite well in the autumn. A hybrid of 'Général Jacqueminot'. Bred by George Paul (England) 1868. (Illustrated, p. 68)

**Empereur du Maroc** This variety is chiefly notable for the richness of its dark velvety maroon-crimson colouring. The flowers are not very large, opening flat, quartered, and well filled with petals which later reflex. Strong fragrance. Unfortunately the growth is rather weak, often resulting in poor flowers, and it requires a high standard of cultivation to produce worthwhile results. Its foliage is similar to that of a Hybrid Tea and is rather sparse. Only slightly recurrent. Height 90cm/3ft. A seedling from 'Géant des Batailles'. Bred by Guinoisseau (France) 1858.

**Ferdinand Pichard** A striped rose that can be compared to the striped Bourbon varieties such as 'Commandant Beaurepaire'. Its flowers are pink, striped and splashed with crimson, the pink gradually fading almost to white while the crimson intensifies. They are of medium size, cupped in shape, not very full and fragrant. This rose forms a bushy shrub by the standards of a Hybrid Perpetual and flowers intermittently in late summer after the first crop. One of the best striped roses, as good as its Bourbon rivals, and perhaps the most suitable one for the smaller garden. Height 1.5m/5ft. It was raised by R. Tanne of France as recently as 1921, and may well be a sport, but from which rose we do not know.

*Facing page, FERDINAND PICHARD is one of the best striped roses, as good as its Bourbon rivals, and the one to choose for the smaller garden*

*Left, FRAU KARL DRUSCHKI is a particularly tough and vigorous variety, although the flowers are very much like those of a Hybrid Tea*

**Fisher Holmes** Pointed buds of scarlet and crimson, in the manner of a Hybrid Tea, the colour soon fading. It flowers both in summer and autumn and forms a healthy bush of about 1.2m/4ft in height. Fragrant. Thought to be a seedling of 'Maurice Bernardin'. Bred by Verdier (France) 1865.

**Frau Karl Druschki** ('Snow Queen', 'Reine des Neiges', 'White American Beauty') This rose belongs theoretically to the Hybrid Teas, being a cross between the Hybrid Perpetual 'Merveille de Lyon' and the Hybrid Tea 'Madame Caroline Testout', but the growth is so tall, up to 1.8m/6ft in height, that it would be misleading to place it anywhere but here. The flowers, however, which are white with just a hint of lemon, are very close to those of a Hybrid Tea, and even today it is difficult to find a white Hybrid Tea flower that is better than this. It should be pruned as described in the introduction to this section, and will then form a tall, narrow, but slightly arching shrub, ideal for the back of the border. A group of two or three plants will knit together into a more shapely whole and give a more satisfactory effect. The foliage is light green. This is a tough old campaigner,

THE
REPEAT-
FLOWERING
OLD ROSES

Hybrid
Perpetual
Roses

*GEORG ARENDS*
*bears blooms*
*that have more*
*in common with*
*the typical Hybrid*
*Tea, although they*
*are produced on*
*an attractively*
*shaped shrub*

*MRS JOHN LAING*
*is a good reliable*
*rose, strongly*
*scented and*
*truly recurrent-*
*flowering*

although it may require spraying against mildew. Little or no fragrance. Raised by Lambert (Germany) 1901.

**Général Jacqueminot** ('General Jack', 'Jack Rose') An important variety in the development of the Modern Rose and perhaps of more interest for this than for any particular qualities of its own. In fact, most of the red roses of the present day relate back to this variety. It has rich crimson full-petalled flowers, opening rather untidily. The fragrance is particularly strong, and it was perhaps because of this rose and other similar Hybrid Perpetuals that the idea grew up that a red rose should have a strong rich fragrance— something that is sadly no longer always true today. Height 1.2m/ 4ft. A hybrid between 'Gloire des Rosomanes' and 'Géant des Batailles'. Bred by Roussel (France) 1852.

**Georg Arends** ('Fortuné Besson') The breeding of this rose was 'Frau Karl Druschki' × 'La France' and it should, therefore, technically be placed with the Hybrid Teas. In practice it conforms to neither the Hybrid Teas nor the Hybrid Perpetuals, forming as it does a fine shapely, slightly arching shrub of 1.5m/5ft in height with plentiful foliage. The flowers, on the other hand, are of distinctly Hybrid Tea persuasion, with large high-centered buds, the petals rolling back at the edges in the most attractive manner. Its colour is a clear rose-pink and it has a delicious fragrance. It is interesting to note that even a Hybrid Tea flower can be displayed to greater advantage on taller more shrubby growth. Raised by W. Hinner (Germany) 1910.

**Gloire de Ducher** No other Hybrid Perpetual can match this variety for the splendour and richness of its flowers. They form very large informal cups of a deep purple-crimson shaded with maroon and are very fragrant. The blooms are particularly fine in the cool of the autumn. The growth is strong and rather sprawly, up to 2m/7ft in height, with large dark green leaves, and it might well be grown on a pillar or some other form of support. Its only drawback is a susceptibility to mildew. The parentage is not known. Bred by Ducher (France), introduced 1865.

**Henry Nevard** The most recent variety on my list, this rose was bred by Cant's of Colchester as late as 1924 and may have some Hybrid Tea in its make up. Its large deep crimson flowers are of cupped formation, with a powerful fragrance. They are held on long stems and repeat well. It has the tall upright habit of growth of a Hybrid Perpetual, perhaps 1.5m/5ft in height. The leaves are large, leathery and deep green.

**Hugh Dickson** Introduced in 1905, this was one of the most popular roses of its day, but in spite of this it does not have very much to recommend it—perhaps an indication of a decline in taste at the time, at least in so far as the rose was concerned. The flowers are large, scarlet-crimson, of a globular formation and produced on long shoots. They tend to lack character, being unshapely and rather coarse. The growth is very tall and ungainly, 2m/7ft, and it is perhaps more effective as a Climber when it will easily achieve 3m/10ft. In its heyday it was frequently grown by pegging the long growth to the soil, so that it became effectively a climbing rose trailing along the ground. In this way numerous flower shoots are sent up along the stems, thus rendering it more suitable for bedding and providing an attractive 'Edwardian' effect. It flowers freely and recurrently and has a strong fragrance. The result of a cross between 'Lord Bacon' and 'Gruss an Teplitz', it was bred by H. Dickson (UK).

**John Hopper** Large fragrant lilac-pink flowers, deepening towards the centre. Vigorous, upright growth of 1.2m/4ft. 'Jules Margottin' × 'Madame Vidot'. Bred by Ward (UK) 1862.

THE
REPEAT-
FLOWERING
OLD ROSES

Hybrid
Perpetual
Roses

*PAUL NEYRON
is in every way
a large shrub,
the flowers being
some of the largest
in the rose world*

**Mabel Morrison** A white sport of 'Baroness Rothschild', see above, with the same Portland Rose characteristics and fine, shapely, shallowly cupped blooms. In autumn these will sometimes take on delicate blush tints. Very little scent. Discovered by Broughton (UK), introduced 1878.

**Mrs John Laing** Bred by Henry Bennett (UK), this may be regarded as his finest production. The flowers are large, deeply cupped, fully double and of a silvery-pink colouring. The growth is vigorous and upright, up to 1.2m/4ft in height, with greyish-green foliage. 'Mrs John Laing' is a good reliable rose, truly recurrent flowering and strongly scented. Introduced in 1887, and one of the most popular roses of its time, it was said that Bennett received $45,000 for the distribution rights in America, an unheard of sum in those days. It was a seedling from 'François Michelon'.

**Paul Neyron** In the past this rose was regarded as having the largest flowers of all roses, and I suspect this may not be far from true today. It is in every way a large shrub, with large leaves and strong upright growth. Unfortunately with size comes clumsiness, as is so often the case, but if the flowers are cut and mixed with an arrangement of other flowers they can be very effective. Their colour is deep rose-pink flushed with lilac; they are cupped in shape and have a light fragrance. A cross between 'Victor Verdier' and 'Anna de Diesbach'. Bred and introduced by A. Levet (France) 1869.

**Prince Camille de Rohan** ('La Rosière') This variety has long held the reputation of being the darkest of all roses, and for this reason it continues to be in demand. I often fear that our customers may sometimes be disappointed, as it is of very weak growth, except when well grown under favourable conditions. It will form a bushy plant of 90cm/3ft, bearing medium-sized very double flowers of the richest velvety crimson-maroon. These are carried on weak stems but have a powerful fragrance. Raised by R. Verdier (France) 1861.

THE
REPEAT-
FLOWERING
OLD ROSES

Hybrid
Perpetual
Roses

*REINE DES VIOLETTES is a beautiful rose that is closer to the Gallicas in appearance and very different from a typical Hybrid Perpetual*

**Reine des Violettes** ('Queen of the Violets') A unique and charming rose with flowers closer to the Gallica Rose than to a typical Hybrid Perpetual. These are of full-petalled rosette formation, opening flat and quartered, with a button eye at the centre. Their colour is a deep velvet purple, turning with time to soft parma-violet. The growth is upright, about 1.2–1.5 m/4–5 ft in height, with grey-green foliage and hardly any thorns. It is reliably repeat flowering which, combined with the Old Rose form of flower, makes it particularly valuable. This rose requires good cultivation if it is to give of its best. A seedling from 'Pius IX'. Bred by Millet-Malet (France), introduced 1860.

**Roger Lambelin** A sport from 'Prince Camille de Rohan', see p. 73, with all the failings of that rose, having very weak growth and poor flowers in all but the best of conditions. In appearance, too, it is similar to 'Prince Camille de Rohan', except that its deep crimson petals are prettily edged with white. Like its parent it can be beautiful if well grown, but for most gardens it might be better to grow 'Baron Girod de l'Ain' which is much stronger. Very fragrant. Height 90cm/3ft. Discovered by Schwartz (France), distributed 1890.

**Souvenir du Docteur Jamain** Not a typical Hybrid Perpetual, this rose is notable for its deep rich dark crimson colouring and its equally deep and rich perfume. The flowers are of medium size, shallow, showing just a hint of their yellow stamens. It is repeat flowering but, like so many crimson roses, does not make ideal growth, being rather lean and lanky, and about 1.5–1.8m/5–6ft in height. However, since there are few shrub roses with flowers of such colouring it is worth its place in the garden. It has for some years also been on sale under the name of 'Souvenir d' Alphonse Lavallée', though it is impossible to see any difference between the two roses. Introduced by Lacharme (France) 1865.

**Triomphe de l'Exposition** Full-petalled cherry-red flowers, opening almost flat and quartered, with a button eye. The growth is strong and bushy with recurrent blooms. Height 1.5m/5ft. Bred and introduced by Margottin (France) 1855.

**Ulrich Brünner** A tall, robust and durable shrub of narrow, ungainly and upright habit, about 1.8m/6ft in height. The flowers are cupped in form and of a rather crude pale crimson colour. Fine blooms are sometimes produced and it is a useful rose for cutting. Strong fragrance, recurrent flowering. It creates a spectacular display at Sissinghurst Castle in Kent, where its long shoots are pegged down. Bred by Levet (France) 1881.

**Vick's Caprice** Very large full-cupped flowers, their colouring of deep pink lightly striped with paler pink and white providing a delicate effect. It is very fragrant, recurrent flowering, with ample foliage that comes all the way up to the flower. Height 1.2m/4ft. A sport from the pure pink 'Archiduchesse Élisabeth d'Autriche' (to which it frequently reverts) found in the garden of a Mr Vick of Rochester, New York, introduced 1891.

*SOUVENIR DU DOCTEUR JAMAIN is notable for its dark colouring and rich perfume*

# 3

# THE HYBRID TEA
# & FLORIBUNDA
# ROSES

THE HYBRID TEAS and Floribundas are the two most widely grown classes of roses of the present day. They are to be found in almost every garden in the British Isles and are very popular in all other countries where roses will grow at all. The two groups have, over the years, become so interbred that it seems best to discuss them together. Indeed, it is often a matter of some debate as into which group a new variety should be placed. Both groups are short bushes of upright habit of growth. Both were originally bred to be grown in rose beds, although they can equally well be placed in narrow borders—perhaps along a fence or in front of the house. Their often garish colours and upright habit of growth render them less suitable for mixed borders or more general garden use, where they tend to jar with other plants.

Although we refer to Hybrid Teas and Floribundas as 'Modern Roses', the Hybrid Teas, at least, have been with us for a long time. As early as the middle of the 19th century, the stage was set for their arrival on the scene. No other garden plant of any kind has received so much attention from the plant breeder. There are at least ten large specialist rose breeders around the world working on Hybrid Teas, as well as numerous smaller and amateur breeders.

The evolution of the Hybrid Teas—and later the Floribundas—is unique among garden flowers, in that breeders have rejected the open flower of the Old Roses in favour of what I have called the 'bud flower'; that is to say where the beauty of the flower is concentrated entirely in the bud. The bud flower can be a thing of considerable beauty as it unfolds its petals, but once this is complete—and the process is not long—we are left with what I can only call a 'jumble' of petals that lacks

*Facing page, FELLOWSHIP, one of the best Floribunda Roses, creates a most impressive show in massed plantings*

both form and beauty. We have to catch it just at the right time if it is to have anything to offer. On the other hand, the Old Rose flower can be, and often is, also very beautiful in the bud, which is often beautifully cupped with glistening petals within—and this goes on until it achieves its full glory in the fully open flower.

The bud flower was given a huge boost by the great popularity of exhibiting roses on the show bench in the late 19th and early 20th centuries. These shows were very influential at the time. The judges insisted on the bud flower at its most perfect best and, such was their power, that breeders began to breed exclusively for this type of rose. Gradually this influence extended to the garden proper, until the time came when all roses were of this type.

The popularity of this type of flower faded a little with the arrival of the Floribundas, which often had single, semi-double or open, double flowers. It was not long, however, before these too fell before the influence of the bud flower—and it was not until the arrival of the English Roses that it began to decline.

Having said all this, I would not like to be without the Hybrid Teas and Floribundas. They add one more dimension to the incredible diversity of our flower. If they did disappear from the garden, I can well imagine a band of dedicated collectors scouring the country for surviving varieties.

# Hybrid Tea Roses

THE
HYBRID TEA &
FLORIBUNDA
ROSES

Hybrid Tea
Roses

The beginnings of the Hybrid Tea Rose can be seen in their ancestors, the Tea Roses. The Tea Roses had large petals which they had gained from one of their ancestors, *Rosa gigantea*. These tended to give them long buds which unfolded in the most attractive manner. This characteristic is not so highly developed as it is in the present day Hybrid Tea Roses. The Tea Rose reached its highest perfection in a beautiful white variety known as 'Mrs Herbert Stevens'. In general, the bud of the Hybrid Tea tended to be less heavy than that of a Tea Rose.

It was when the Tea Rose was crossed with the old Hybrid Perpetual Rose that we began to have the Hybrid Tea that we know so well today. This was in many ways a happy combination of talents: the Hybrid Perpetual provided the vigour, which was somewhat lacking in the Tea Roses, while the Tea Roses provided form of flower and a greater ability to repeat flower. Each of them brought their own fragrance—the Hybrid Perpetual, the lovely Old Rose fragrance and the Tea Rose, the Tea fragrance.

For a long time it was supposed that 'La France' was the first Hybrid Tea and that with its arrival a new class was born, but this was not, in fact, true. The first reliably documented rose that could be classified as a Hybrid Tea was 'Victor Verdier'. Bred by Lacharme of Lyons and introduced in 1859, it was a cross between the Hybrid Perpetual 'Jules Margottin'

and the Tea Rose 'Safrano'. It is by no means impossible that there were other unrecorded crosses before this, but it was only when Guillot crossed a Hybrid Perpetual named 'Madame Victor Verdier' (not to be confused with 'Victor Verdier') with the Tea Rose 'Madame Bravy', to produce 'La France' in 1867, that people began to realise a new class of roses had arrived. Even then it was a long time before the Hybrid Teas were officially recognised in countries other than France.

In Britain it was Henry Bennett who first bred Hybrid Teas. He was a farmer and cattle breeder of Stapleford, Wiltshire, and later of Shepperton, Middlesex, who turned his attention to the rose, and I must admit to a certain fellow feeling for this man, as I myself started life as a farmer. Bennett quickly saw the possibilities of the Hybrid Teas and in a very short time bred a number of important varieties—no doubt he used his experience with livestock to good effect. He was the first to use the term Hybrid Tea or, as he put it, Pedigree Hybrids of the Tea Rose. It was Bennett and a French breeder called Jean Sisley who first applied systematic cross breeding to roses. Before this, rose breeding had been a much more haphazard affair, but Bennett and Sisley made deliberate crosses with certain objectives in view and may thus be said to be the first modern rose breeders. Unfortunately Bennett's career in this field only lasted from 1879 until his death in 1890. Even so, he is usually regarded as the father of the Hybrid Tea Rose.

Since that time, many breeders have taken a hand in the development of the Hybrid Teas. These are too numerous to mention, but the names of Kordes of Germany, Meilland of France, Dickson of Northern Ireland, McGredy of Northern Ireland and, later, New Zealand, Harkness and Fryer in England and Cocker in Scotland—and in the USA, Jackson & Perkins and Weeks—have long been very much in evidence.

It is impossible to say how many millions of seedlings have been grown for selection. As a result, there are today thousands of Hybrid Teas on the market in various parts of the world—so much so, that it is difficult to make a selection. Here, I provide what is inevitably a short list of those that seem to me to be the very best. They are all varieties that I have grown myself.

*WARM WISHES, with its high pointed centre and strong colour, is a classic Hybrid Tea*

### SOME OLDER HYBRID TEA ROSES

As with the Old Roses, there are some Hybrid Teas of earlier introduction which are still worth growing, at least by the enthusiast. Unfortunately, unlike the Old Roses, they tend to be a little weak in growth. Nonetheless, the flowers have their own particular beauty and I think that many of them have greater refinement than the present day varieties. Here are a few of the older Hybrid Tea Roses that I think are worthy of consideration.

THE
HYBRID TEA &
FLORIBUNDA
ROSES

Hybrid Tea
Roses

**Dainty Bess** A single rose and one of the finest of its class. It has large rose-pink flowers with a deeper pink on the outside and contrasting red-brown stamens. The petals are slightly fringed or cut at the edges. Light refreshing fragrance. Height 90cm/3ft. 'Ophelia' × 'K. of K.' W. E. B. Archer (UK) 1925.

**Ellen Willmott** A single-flowered rose rather similar to 'Dainty Bess' from which it was a seedling, the result of a cross with 'Lady Hillingdon'. It has creamy flowers which are tinged with pink at the edges, with golden anthers and red filaments. The petals are attractively waved. Dark purple-tinted foliage. It does not perform quite so well as 'Dainty Bess'. Height 90cm/3ft. Bred by Archer (UK) 1936.

**Emma Wright** A charming little button-hole rose. It has small, perfectly formed nearly single orange-salmon buds on a dwarf plant. Glossy green foliage. Height 60cm/2ft. McGredy (UK) 1918.

**George Dickson** Very large though not very full flowers of deep scarlet-crimson. The stems are rather weak, so that it tends to hang its head. Growth, strong and tall. Fragrant. Height 1.2m/4ft. A. Dickson (UK) 1912.

**Gustav Grünerwald** An early Hybrid Tea with large, cupped, deep pink flowers. The growth is vigorous and reliable, with glossy, deep green foliage. It is a cross between the Tea Rose 'Safrano' and 'Madame Caroline Testout'. Height 90cm/3ft. Bred by Lambert (Germany) 1903.

**Kathryn McGredy** (Macauklad) Large, medium pink flowers with a strong fragrance are produced in flushes throughout the season. The large, dark-green foliage is red when young. Needs winter protection in temperatures below −7°C/20°F. Height 90–110cm/3–3½ft. Breeding 'City of Auckland' × 'Lady Rose'. McGredy (New Zealand), 1998.

**Lady Sylvia** A sport from 'Madame Butterfly'. Discovered by Stevens (UK) 1926. See 'Ophelia' below.

**La France** This famous rose is one of the earliest Hybrid Teas. Its origins are not known for certain but Guillot, who bred it in 1867, was of the opinion that it was probably a hybrid of the Tea Rose 'Madame Falcot'. It is still a worthwhile rose, although it is said to have lost some of its vigour and is rather prone to disease. The blooms are full-petalled and of globular Old Rose formation, remaining so until the petals fall. The colour is a silvery pink with a rose-pink reverse. The flowers are richly fragrant. Height 90cm/3ft. A climbing sport is also available.

**Madame Abel Chatenay** Another historic Hybrid Tea and, to me, still one of the most beautiful, retaining much of the charm of

*Mrs Oakley Fisher is a single Hybrid Tea of rich deep orange-yellow with golden-brown stamens*

a Tea Rose at its best. Raised by Pernet-Ducher and introduced in 1895, it is the result of a cross between the Tea Rose 'Dr. Grill' and the Hybrid Tea 'Victor Verdier'.

The flowers are of a charming scrolled bud formation, pale pink in colour, deepening towards the centre, the reverse side of the petals being a deeper pink. An exquisite rose that seems to retain its vigour. Delicious fragrance. Height 90cm/3ft. There is a climbing sport which is also good.

**Madame Butterfly** Discovered by Hill (USA) 1918. See 'Ophelia' p. 80.

**Mrs Oakley Fisher** One of the most beautiful of the single-flowered Hybrid Tea Roses, with neatly outlined deep orange-yellow flowers displaying golden-brown stamens. The blooms are delicately poised in small clusters on a branching bush of reasonable vigour. The foliage is bronzy green and there is a light, pleasing fragrance. Height 1.5m/5ft. B.R. Cant (UK) 1921.

79

THE
HYBRID TEA &
FLORIBUNDA
ROSES

Hybrid Tea
Roses

*BLESSINGS, reliable, prolific and continuous flowering, is an ideal bedding rose*

rather slender, growing to about 80cm/2½ft in height—all are reliable growers although rather prone to blackspot. The foliage is neat and of a greyish-green colour. All three have a delicious fragrance and were once widely grown as cut flowers. Each has excellent climbing sports and, as is so often the case with old Hybrid Teas, this may be the best way to grow them. See Chapter 7.

The origin of 'Ophelia' is a mystery. It was introduced by Arthur Paul of Waltham Cross in 1912. Paul was unable to say where it came from, although he thought it arrived with a consignment of 'Antoine Rivoire' he had bought from Pernet-Ducher in 1909. It was probably a seedling that had been included by mistake. The French firm should, therefore, share the credit, even though it must have failed to realise the true worth of the variety. It attracted little attention at the time but, eventually, both it and its sports became some of the most popular roses ever introduced and they are still in demand. It is interesting to note that 'Ophelia' was responsible for no less than thirty-six sports in all; this must be some kind of record.

**Picture** A dainty and much loved buttonhole rose, with small perfectly formed buds of a clear velvety rose-pink with reflexing petals. These are produced on a short, free flowering bush. Height 80cm/2½ft. Slight fragrance. McGredy (UK) 1932.

**White Wings** One of the most beautiful of the single Hybrid Teas. Long buds opening to large pure white flowers with conspicuous chocolate-coloured anthers. Dark green foliage. A healthy bush, but rather sparse and it may require a little time to establish. Height 1.2m/4ft. A cross between 'Dainty Bess' and an unnamed seedling. Bred by Krebs (USA), introduced 1947.

**Mrs Sam McGredy** A popular rose of the 1930s and 1940s. Its colouring is coppery-orange flushed with scarlet that is not to everyone's taste but does tone well with the glossy, coppery-red foliage. The flowers are large and have shapely, high centred, clean-cut buds that last well. The growth is branching and of moderate vigour. There is a climbing form available. Fragrant. Height 90cm/3ft. ('Donald Macdonald' × 'Golden Emblem') × (seedling × 'The Queen Alexandra Rose'). McGredy (UK) 1929.

**Ophelia** (including **'Madame Butterfly'**, **'Lady Sylvia'**) It is convenient to discuss these three varieties together, as the last two are colour sports of the first. More than any others, these roses set the ideal for the perfect Hybrid Tea buds. These are not large but are of exquisitely scrolled formation; indeed, for perfection of Hybrid Tea form, they have few rivals even today. These three roses differ only in the colour of their flowers: 'Ophelia' is blush pink, 'Madame Butterfly' is a slightly deeper shade and 'Lady Sylvia' is blush suffused with apricot. In all three the colour deepens a little towards the centre to give the most delicate effect. They do not form large bushes and are

## MODERN HYBRID TEA ROSES

**Alec's Red** Not such a popular variety today but, for many years after its introduction, this rose was widely grown. The flowers are very large and strongly scented and, although not quite classically Hybrid Tea shaped, are very resistant to rain. Their colour is cherry-red with a rather purplish tinge, making them perhaps a little dull. It is vigorous but not very upright and rather susceptible to disease. Height 90cm/3ft. 'Fragrant Cloud' × 'Dame de Coeur'. Cocker (UK) 1970.

**Alexander** ('Alexandra') Similar to its parent 'Super Star', but of an even brighter shade of vermilion, and taller and stronger, being about 1.2m/4ft in height. It must have one of the most brilliant and luminous colours to be found in roses. It is particularly thorny. Slight fragrance. 'Super Star' × ('Anne Elizabeth' × 'Allgold'). Harkness (UK) 1972.

**Blessings** A reliable, prolific and continuous flowering variety of soft pink colouring. The blooms are not large, rather loosely formed, with only a slight scent. It is an ideal bedding rose, with strong, upright, branching growth. Healthy, medium green foliage. Height 90cm/3ft. The result of a cross between 'Queen Elizabeth' and an unnamed seedling. Bred and introduced by Gregory (UK) 1967.

**Cheshire Life** Large, well-formed flowers of vermilion-orange. Strong, bushy growth of medium height, with ample, dark, leathery foliage. A particularly bright colour but with little fragrance. A good bedding rose but needs some protection against disease. Height 80cm/2½ft. 'Prima Ballerina' × 'Princess Michiko'. Fryer (UK) 1972.

**Congratulations** (*Korlift*) ('Sylvia') This is a prolific variety that produces many beautiful blooms over a long season. They are a lovely silvery-pink at the classic bud stage, paling as the flower opens and eventually shows off its stamens. It has vigorous, upright but quite busy growth and is relatively healthy. A good fragrance.

Height 1.4m/4½ft. Bred from a seedling of 'Carina'. Kordes (Germany) 1979. (Illustrated p.83)

**Doris Tysterman** Shapely, medium-sized flowers of coppery orange freely produced on a vigorous, bushy, upright plant with glossy bronze-tinted foliage. A good bedding rose. Little fragrance. Height 90cm/3ft. 'Peer Gynt' × unnamed seedling. Wisbech Plant Co. (UK) 1975.

**Dutch Gold** Large, unfading golden-yellow flowers with a strong fragrance. The growth is vigorous and upright, with good healthy medium green foliage. Height about 90cm/3ft. 'Peer Gynt' × 'Whisky Mac'. Wisbech Plant Co. (UK) 1978.

**Elina** (*Dicjana*) A beautiful and refined rose in the best Hybrid Tea tradition, with perfect bud formation, the colour being ivory-white intensifying to lemon at the centre. An extremely healthy variety with bushy growth about 90cm/3ft in height although it can be very vigorous in hot climates. An excellent variety for bedding and very

THE
HYBRID TEA &
FLORIBUNDA
ROSES

Hybrid Tea
Roses

*Far left, top, JULIA'S ROSE bears nicely shaped buds that open to rounded flowers of unique colouring*

*Far left, bottom, ELINA is one of the healthiest of the Hybrid Teas and among the best for flower form too*

*Left, DORIS TYSTERMAN bears shapely flowers on a vigorous, bushy, upright plant with glossy bronze-tinted foliage*

popular with the exhibition grower. Breeding 'Nana Mouskouri' × 'Lolita'. Dicksons (Northern Ireland), introduced 1985.

**Elizabeth Harkness** This has large flowers of shapely spiral formation, and its colour is ivory-white delicately touched with pink and amber. It can be affected by damp weather but, at its best, produces buds of pristine perfection. The growth is upright, bushy, of medium height and strength, with medium green foliage. Light fragrance. It is particularly fine when grown under glass. Height 80cm/2½ft. The breeding rather surprisingly is 'Red Dandy' × 'Piccadilly'. Raised by Harkness (UK), introduced 1969.

**Fragrant Cloud** ('Duftwolke') Large flowers, coral-scarlet at first, taking on smoky overtones as they develop, and becoming a purplish-red as they fade, particularly in hot weather. The growth is strong and bushy, about 1.1 m/3½ft in height, with plenty of large leaves. Free flowering and continuous. It lives up to its name with its strong fragrance. Occasional mildew. Unnamed seedling × 'Prima Ballerina'. Tantau (Germany) 1963.

**Freedom** (*Dicjem*) The flowers are of an unusually rich and pure yellow that fades only slightly with age. It has good, bushy growth and is an excellent bedding plant especially as it repeat flowers so well and is healthy. The flowers stand up well to the weather. Light scent. Height 80cm/2½ft. ('Eurorose' × 'Taifun') × 'Bright Smile'. Dickson (UK) 1984.

**Grandpa Dickson** ('Irish Gold') Large and perfectly formed pale yellow flowers. Although the growth is rather short and the foliage too sparse for the size of the flowers, this is a good bedding rose and repeats very well. It requires good soil and cultivation to give of its best. Slight fragrance. Height 90cm/3ft. ('Perfecta' × 'Governador Braga da Cruz') × 'Piccadilly'. Dickson (UK) 1966. (Illustrated, p. 84)

**Glorious** (*Interictera*) In recent years significantly fewer Hybrid Teas have been introduced. It is therefore particularly welcome to see this variety with large, amber-yellow blooms that are produced singly on a stem and have the classic high centre. There is a medium fragrance. Height 90cm/3ft. Bred by Ilsink (Netherlands) 2001.

**Harry Wheatcroft** This rose was named after one of the great characters of the rose world who, up to the time of his death in 1977, was as well known to the public as a pop star. He also brought some of the best foreign Hybrid Teas and Floribundas to the British Isles. A sport from 'Piccadilly', see p. 86, it has most of the qualities of that rose. The difference is that the outside of the petals is yellow, while the inside is red striped with yellow. Slight fragrance. Height 80cm/2½ft. Introduced by Harry Wheatcroft & Sons (UK) 1972.

**Ice Cream** (*Korzuri*) ('Memoire') With its huge blooms and neatly arranged petals, this is a variety well loved by exhibitors. It is, however, also easy to grow and can be grown by all. The flowers are white, sometimes with a creamy tinge to them, and have a strong sweet fragrance. Vigorous, bushy growth. Height 90cm/3ft. Kordes (Germany) 1992.

*Above,* CONGRATULA-TIONS, *produces many beautiful blooms over a long season*

*Facing page,* FREEDOM *is an excellent bedding plant because it repeat flowers well and is of a good, rich colour*

*Left,* FRAGRANT CLOUD *lives up to its name with its strong fragrance and the smoky overtones of its colour as the flowers develop*

THE
HYBRID TEA &
FLORIBUNDA
ROSES

Hybrid Tea
Roses

*Top right,*
GRANDPA
DICKSON, *being
shorter than most,
is a good choice
for a small bed*

*Right,* JUST JOEY
*is one of the most
popular of all
Hybrid Teas and
rightly so*

*Far right,*
PASCALI *may
well still be the
best white rose
in its class*

**Ingrid Bergman** (*Poulman*) This is generally regarded as one of the best red Hybrid Teas and has won many awards around the world. The pure, dark red blooms start with the classic spiral shape then open up to a fully double flower. They are usually borne singly and are excellent for cutting although unfortunately there is no fragrance. It has vigorous, upright growth and is very healthy. Height 1.4m / 4½ft. 'Precious Platinum' × seedling. Poulsen (Denmark) 1984.

**Julia's Rose** A rose of unique colouring, usually described as a mixture of copper and parchment, but hard to pin down and perhaps more parchment than copper. Its nicely shaped buds open to rounded flowers. The growth is not very strong. Slight scent. Height 80–90cm / 2½–3ft. Named for Miss Julia Clements. 'Blue Moon' × 'Dr. A.J. Verhage'. Raised by Wisbech Plant Co. (UK) 1976. (Illustrated, p. 81)

**Just Joey** Elegant pointed, coppery-fawn buds, with attractively waved petals paling a little towards the edges, the flowers remaining pleasing to the end. Growth is spreading and of medium strength, with dark green matt foliage. Quite healthy. Height 80cm / 2½ft. Fragrant. 'Fragrant Cloud' × 'Dr. A.J. Verhage'. Cants (UK) 1972.

**King's Macc** (*Frydisco*) Gareth Fryer is very proud of this rose and has very high hopes for it. The flowers are produced freely, are classically shaped and of a lovely blend of gold, apricot and cream. There is a strong fragrance. It is very healthy. Height 90cm / 3ft. Bred by Fryer (UK) 2002.

**Kronenbourg** ('Flaming Peace') A sport from 'Peace' which occurred at McGredy's Nurseries, then in Northern Ireland. 'Peace' is yellow, but in this variety the colour has become a rich crimson on the inside of the petals, the outside remaining the same yellow as its parent. The overall effect is predominantly a rich crimson which quickly turns to purple, varying considerably according to weather conditions: in cool weather it can be magnificently rich; in hot weather it becomes a not unpleasing dusky purple. Height 1.2m / 4ft. 1965.

**Lovely Lady** (*Dicjubell*) The classic, Hybrid Tea-shaped blooms start apricot-pink and then fade to pure rose pink. They have a good fragrance and make a good cut flower. In the early part of the season they are produced singly or in small clusters but in larger clusters later in the season. It is extremely healthy and perfect for bedding.

Height 90cm/3ft. 'Silver Jubilee' × ('Eurorose' × 'Anabel'). Bred by Dickson (UK) 1986.

**Memorial Day** (*Wekblunez*) Not many American bred varieties successfully cross the Atlantic but this variety is an exception. It has very large blooms that are clear pink with a lilac wash. The growth is upright but quite bushy and very healthy. The fragrance is particularly good, just like an Old Rose. It won the AARS award in 2004. Height 1.2m/4ft. 'Blueberry Hill' × 'New Zealand'. Bred by Carruth (USA) 2004.

**Nostalgie** (*Taneiglat*) A particularly striking variety with large, cream flowers that are edged with bright cherry-red. It is a very useful bedding variety: the blooms are produced on long, straight stems singly or in small clusters, it repeats well and is very healthy. It is also good if cut for the house as the flowers last well and keep their colour. There is a strong, sweet fragrance. Height 1.1m/3½ft. Tantau (Germany) 1998.

**Paddy Stephens** (*Macclack*) Keith Jones, who is the licensee for Sam McGredy's roses in the UK, is extremely enthusiastic about this variety, saying that this is one of the finest roses he has ever seen. It is extremely healthy with dark, leathery leaves and strong upright growth. The fluorescent salmon orange flowers are large and held singly on the stems. Height 1.2m/4ft. McGredy (New Zealand) 1998.

**Papa Meilland** Here we have one of the most perfect crimson Hybrid Tea Roses: the colour is rich and of remarkable purity, the flowers well formed, and there is a delicious perfume. Up to this point it is everything a red rose should be. Unfortunately there is a snag—it has very poor growth. We have to make the choice between a perfect flower and reliable constitution. If you decide to grow this variety, it is essential you treat it generously. Very fragrant. Height 80cm/2½ft. 'Chrysler Imperial' × 'Charles Mallerin'. A. Meilland (France) 1963.

**Pascali** For many years Pascali was regarded as the best white Hybrid Tea; there are now one or two competitors available but there is no doubt it is still an excellent variety. It is a cross between 'Queen Elizabeth' and 'White Butterfly', the former having passed on some of her strong growth as well as disease resistance, and in this respect 'Pascali' is unusual among white roses of this class. The flowers are not very large and have a delicate refinement. Although they give the impression of being pure white, there is a barely noticeable tinge of pink in their makeup. It is free flowering, but has only a moderate fragrance. Height 80cm/2½ft. Bred by Lens (Belgium) 1963.

**Paul Shirville** (*Harquarterwife*) A beautiful rose of elegant bud formation, with delicate apricot and peach-pink colouring. It has good, bushy growth with plenty of foliage, making it suitable for the mixed border. It

has a strong fragrance, for which it was awarded the Henry Edland Medal. Very free flowering and generally healthy. A good variety for cutting. Height 90cm/3ft. A cross between the Climbing Rose 'Compassion', which probably gives it its excellent habit of growth, and 'Mischief'. Bred by Harkness (UK) 1983.

**Peace** ('Gloria Dei', 'Madame A. Meilland') This is probably the most popular and widely grown rose ever bred. It is, in fact, the only rose to have had a book written about it—*For the Love of a Rose* by Antonia Ridge. Its influence on the development of the Hybrid Tea Rose has been enormous, not only as a parent, but also as a standard set for roses that came after it. To my way of thinking this influence has not always been for the best, and has led to a much coarser bloom. One thing is certain: it is a rose of exceptional vigour, being both tall and branching. In fact, it will form an excellent specimen shrub growing to about 1.2m/4ft in height, taller with light pruning. The foliage is large, glossy, deep green colouring. It used to be regarded as extremely healthy but does now succumb to some blackspot. The flowers are very large and full, yellow flushed with

THE
HYBRID TEA &
FLORIBUNDA
ROSES

Hybrid Tea
Roses

*PAUL SHIRVILLE has delicate colouring and a strong fragrance, for which it was awarded the Henry Edland Medal*

THE
HYBRID TEA &
FLORIBUNDA
ROSES

Hybrid Tea
Roses

*PEACE, probably the best known of all roses, has had a huge influence on the development of the Hybrid Tea*

**Pristine** The large shapely blooms of ivory-white are delicately flushed with pink and held upon a tall bush against large dark green leaves which set them off beautifully. It has good, robust leafy growth of 90cm/3ft in height. Strongly fragrant. A cross between 'White Masterpiece' and 'First Prize'. Bred by Warren (USA) 1978.

**Remember Me** (*Cocdestin*) A variety remarkable not only for the richness of its colour but also the variety of shades it goes through. The most characteristic colour is a deep copper but then it can change to orange, salmon, cinnamon and yellow. It flowers extremely freely and does well in most climates, although it is happier in cooler areas. The growth is compact and bushy with dark, glossy leaves. Fragrant. Height 90cm/3ft. 'Ann Letts' × ('Dainty Maid' × 'Pink Favourite'). Cocker (UK) 1984.

**Royal William** (*Korzaun*) ('Duftzauber 84', 'Fragrant Charm') The excellent qualities of 'Royal William' certainly justify its position as one of the most popular Hybrid Teas. The dark, unfading, turkey-red flowers are classically shaped with long pointed buds. They are very fragrant and held, usually singly, on long straight stems and so are excellent for cutting. The growth is strong and vigorous and it is very healthy and reliable. It repeat flowers quickly. Excellent as a bedding rose. Height 90cm/3ft. Bred from a seedling of 'Feuerzauber'. Kordes (Germany) 1984.

**Ruby Wedding** The flowers are a bright dark pink or pale crimson and have a light, sweet fragrance. They have many short petals and open out loosely. The growth is relatively short and bushy, benefiting from an occasional spray to help keep disease at bay. An obvious choice for an anniversary present! Height 90cm/3ft. Gregory (UK) 1979.

**Savoy Hotel** (*Harvintage*) With its high centre and beautifully swirled petals, this rose has some of the most perfectly formed blooms. The colour is a pure silky-pink with a more intense shade deep between the petals. The flowers are usually produced singly and are fragrant, making them very good for cutting and for exhibiting. A prolific, healthy and vigorous bush. Height 90cm/3ft. 'Silver Jubilee' × 'Amber Queen'. Harkness (UK) 1987. (Illustrated as a standard, p. 88)

**Silver Anniversary** ('Karen Blixen') *(Poulari)* The blooms of this variety can be superb and of exhibition quality; the long, classically shaped buds are pure white although the petals can bruise in the rain, showing up as pink spotting. It is healthy and fairly compact, growing to about 90cm/3ft tall. There is a medium, sweet fragrance. Bred by Poulsen (Denmark) 1992. (Illustrated, p.89)

**Silver Jubilee** Perhaps this is the finest rose bred by Alec Cocker in his short but highly successful career as a rose hybridist and it is good to know that his work is carried on by his wife and son. 'Silver Jubilee' is one of the most robust and reliable Hybrid Teas and has

pink, paling with age. They are produced freely both in early summer and autumn, with frequent flowers in between, and are not without beauty, being heavy and rather globular. 'Peace' was bred by Meilland in France and first budded in 1936. By the time it was ready for distribution the Second World War had started, though buds had already been sent to the United States. After the War it was distributed in the States under the very appropriate name by which we now know it and was an instant success. In France it is known as 'Madame A. Meilland'. Its rather complicated parentage is as follows: ('George Dickson' × 'Souvenir de Claudius Pernet') × ('Joanna Hill' × 'Charles P. Kilhan') × 'Margaret McGredy'. Meilland (France) 1945.

**Piccadilly** A scarlet and yellow bicolour, scarlet on the inside of the petals and yellow on the reverse, becoming suffused with orange as the flower ages. The blooms are medium sized and fairly full, with a slight scent. The growth is strong and branching with glossy bronze-tinted foliage. height 0.8m/2½ ft. McGredy's Yellow × 'Karl Herbst'. McGredy (UK) 1959

exceptionally large and plentiful foliage. The flowers are not very large, but they are well formed and of a lovely salmon-pink colour, shaded with peach and coppery-pink. They have only a slight fragrance, but are produced with exceptional freedom. Very healthy. Height 90cm/3ft. Named to commemorate the Queen's Silver Jubilee, the breeding was ('Highlight' × 'Colour Wonder') × ('Parkdirector Riggers' × 'Piccadilly') × 'Mischief'. 1978. (Illustrated, p. 89)

**Simply the Best** (*Macamster*) An excellent variety from Sam McGredy and winner of the 'Rose of the Year' trials in 2002. The beautifully shaped burnt orange flowers stand out well from the glossy, bright green foliage. With a lovely perfume and a good vase life, the blooms are excellent for cutting. Good, sturdy, vigorous growth. Height 1.1 m/3½ft. Bred by McGredy (New Zealand) 2002.

**Super Star** ('Tropicana') This is one of the most widely planted of all roses, largely because its colour—a bright vermilion—was new among Hybrid Tea Roses when first introduced in 1960. Although to some extent superseded by certain of its numerous progeny, it is still a good rose, with medium-sized, well-shaped flowers and vigorous, branching, free-flowering, if somewhat top-heavy, growth. Roses of such brilliance should be planted only sparingly if they are not to dominate all else in the garden. Only a faint fragrance. Height 90cm/3ft. Unfortunately, 'Super Star' seems to have developed a susceptibility to mildew in recent years. (Seedling × 'Peace') × (seedling × 'Alpine Glow'). Tantau (Germany) 1960.

**Thinking of You** (*Frydandy*) A classic, red Hybrid Tea with long, elegant buds that gradually unfold showing off the velvety petals of blood red and deep crimson. It starts to flower early and continues with great regularity through the summer and autumn. The bush is medium sized and particularly healthy. There is a lovely fruity fragrance. Height 90cm/3ft. Fryers (UK) 2000.

**Troika** ('Royal Dane') Medium-sized coppery-orange flowers, occasionally veined scarlet. One of the strongest, most reliable and healthy

*Left,* Savoy Hotel, with its high centre and swirling petals, has some of the most perfectly formed blooms

*Far left, top,* Pristine bears beautifully formed flowers and is an apt name to describe the delicate colouring

*Far left, bottom,* Royal William holds a justified position as one of the most popular Hybrid Teas

THE
HYBRID TEA &
FLORIBUNDA
ROSES

Hybrid Tea
Roses

roses of its colour. Glossy, medium green foliage. Little fragrance. Height 90cm/3ft. Breeding unknown. Poulsen (Denmark) 1971.

**Velvet Fragrance** (*Fryperdee*) Probably the best of the red Hybrid teas, it is renowned for the combination of beautiful blooms, fragrance and health. The flowers are large and elegantly formed and of a velvety, dark crimson. The growth is powerful, almost too strong, at times sending up very long straight stems. However it does flower very freely, the blooms being produced singly or on the end of long laterals. It is very healthy. Strong, sweet fragrance. Height 1.2m/4ft. 'Mildred Scheel' × 'Duftwolke'. Bred by Fryer (UK) 1988.

**Warm Wishes** (*Fryxotic*) ('Sweet Celebration') An excellent, absolutely traditional and very popular Hybrid Tea that does well in very different climates around the world. The flowers start with the characteristic high pointed centre, the outer petals then gradually opening out and curling back. The colour varies considerably according to the weather and climate: generally it is a mix of apricot and pink, being darker in cooler weather and fading to pink and cream in the heat. Good healthy, upright growth. Fragrant. Height 90cm/3ft. 'Pot o' Gold' seedling × 'Cheshire Life'. Fryer (UK) 1994.

*Above left,
SILVER
ANNIVERSARY
has blooms
that can be of
exhibition quality*

*Above middle,
SIMPLY THE
BEST is an
excellent variety
for the garden
and for cutting*

*Above right,
SILVER JUBILEE
is robust and
reliable, with
exceptionally
large and
plentiful foliage*

*Left, VELVET
FRAGRANCE
is probably the
best of the red
Hybrid Teas*

*Facing page,
SAVOY HOTEL,
a prolific, healthy
and vigorous
bush, it forms a
good standard,
here in a bed of
'Charles Rennie
Mackintosh'*

# Floribunda Roses

THE
HYBRID TEA &
FLORIBUNDA
ROSES

Floribunda
Roses

WHEREAS THE HYBRID TEAS are notable for the size and quality of the individual flower, the purpose of the Floribundas is to create a massed effect by the production of many flowers in large clusters. They were originally produced by crossing Hybrid Teas with Polyantha Roses. I discuss the Polyanthas in the next chapter; it is sufficient here to say that they are a small class of very hardy and extremely free-flowering bedding roses, with numerous small rambler-like pompon blooms held in very large clusters. By combining the two groups it was possible to produce a class of hardy, free-flowering and colourful roses—the Floribundas.

It was the Danish breeder D. T. Poulsen who had the idea of crossing the Polyantha 'Madame Norbert Levavasseur' with the Hybrid Tea Rose 'Richmond', with the purpose of producing a rose that would be hardy in the Scandinavian climate. The result of this rose was the rose 'Rodhatte' (Red Riding Hood). It had semi-double, cherry red flowers in large clusters. Distributed in 1912, this rose seemed to get lost in the turmoil of the First World War and little more was heard of it. After the war Poulsen's son, Svend, crossed the Polyantha 'Orleans Rose' with the Hybrid Tea 'Red Star'. And the result was 'Kirsten Poulsen', a bright red rose, and 'Else Poulsen', which was pink. These were distributed in 1924. Both proved to be great successes.

These roses were followed by others, and it was not long before breeders were producing numerous varieties. At first the class was known as Hybrid Polyanthas but, in about 1950, this was changed to 'Floribundas'. Since then there has been a continual admixture of Hybrid Tea genes, with the result that the two classes draw closer together and at times it is difficult to know where to place some varieties. The flowers of the earlier Floribundas were often single or semi-double, opening flat, but more recently they have taken on the Hybrid Tea form, and indeed at one stage it seemed as though they might overtake the Hybrid Tea in popularity.

In most climates, the value of these roses was not so much that they were hardier, but that they were very much more free flowering than the Hybrid Tea Rose and made a very colourful display when planted in the mass. They quickly became popular and soon, new varieties were appearing in quick succession.

In recent years there has been further hybridisation with Hybrid Tea Roses and as a result there is a tendency for breeders to produce Floribundas with bud flowers. Gradually, they have become more like those of the Hybrid Teas. As a result, the question now arises whether the Floribundas or the Hybrid Teas should not all be put together under the heading of Hybrid Teas. I would like to think that they are still a separate class. I think such a class is needed. Indeed, I would say that it might be worthwhile for breeders to go back to the early Floribundas for their parents and breed more and better roses of the true Floribunda type. I would like to see them in single or semi-double form, producing flowers in great profusion, but with a natural, almost wild rose appearance. Their purpose should be to produce colour, but without crudeness.

However this may be, I list here what I believe to be some of the best of the Floribunda Roses.

---

*APRICOT NECTAR is a superb variety that is perhaps more of a shrub than a Floribunda*

*Facing page, ANNE HARKNESS is very tall and robust, the flowers being produced in large sprays*

**Amber Queen** (*Harroony*) Full-petalled, shapely buds of a lovely shade of amber-yellow. The colour is similar to that of 'Whisky Mac', and blends nicely with its dark green foliage. It has a low, spreading, bushy habit of growth. The fragrance is quite strong. Height 60–80cm/2–2½ft. Parentage 'Southampton' × 'Typhoon'. Harkness (UK) 1984. (Illustrated, p. 92)

**Anne Harkness** (*Harkaramel*) Large sprays of deep apricot-coloured flowers on long stems. The growth is unusually tall and robust, and it might be used as a shrub. Starts flowering very late but then continues well. A good cut flower. Height 90–110cm/3–3½ft. 'Bobby Dazzler' × ('Manx Queen' × 'Prima Ballerina') × ('Chanelle' × 'Piccadilly'). Harkness (UK) 1980.

**Apricot Nectar** Apricot-pink flowers of almost Tea Rose form and delicacy with a good fragrance. The growth is tall and angular, forming a very shrub-like plant. It is tough, reliable and healthy and repeats well. Height 1.2m/4ft or more if pruned lightly. Seedling × 'Spartan'. Bred by Boerner (USA) 1965.

THE
HYBRID TEA &
FLORIBUNDA
ROSES

Floribunda
Roses

*Above left,
AMBER QUEEN
is a lovely shade
of amber-yellow
that blends well
with its dark
green foliage*

*Above right,
BLUE FOR YOU
bears semi-
double flowers
that open wide
to reveal the
stamens*

*Right,
CHAMPAGNE
MOMENT is
a classic Kordes
variety with
excellent health*

**Arthur Bell** A strong and reliable pale yellow Floribunda whose colour fades to a rather unattractive cream. The growth is tall, vigorous and upright, with leathery, medium green, healthy foliage. Good fragrance. Height 90cm/3ft. 'Cläre Grammerstorf' × 'Piccadilly'. Bred by McGredy (UK) 1965.

**Blue for You** (*Pejamblu*) This is something very different among the Floribundas. The flowers are semi-double, starting as long buds and opening to wide open flowers with the stamens exposed in the middle. Initially the upper side of the petals is a rich purple-mauve which then fades to a startling slate blue, while the underside is a very pale creamy-violet. It grows into an attractive rounded bush, about 90cm/3ft tall by a little less across, suitable for bedding, borders or pots. It is very free flowering and the health is well above average. The fragrance is sweet and penetrating and reminiscent of violets. Natural Beauty × seedling (dark purple Floribunda). Bred by James (UK) 2007.

**Braveheart** (*Cocjabby*) ('Gordon's College') A Floribunda that is also quite Hybrid Tea in character; the flowers are shapely and the growth is upright, although not excessively. The flowers are a good, strong coral-salmon and set off well by the particularly dark green, glossy leaves. A powerful grower that can be pruned hard if necessary. Excellent repeating and very healthy. Strong fragrance. Height 90cm/3ft. 'Abbeyfield Rose' × 'Roddy McMillan'. Bred by Cocker (UK) 1992.

**Champagne Moment** (*Korvanaber*) This was the winner of the Rose of the Year in 2006. It is an extremely healthy variety that looks well associated with perennials or planted in a bed of its own. The growth is vigorous, easily reaching 1.2m/4ft in height and so could also be classified and used as a shrub. The blooms, which are produced in large trusses, start deep apricot in the centre, paling with age to creamy white. Light fragrance. Kordes (Germany) 2006.

**Chinatown** ('Ville de Chine') An exceptionally tall, strong Floribunda, often classified as a shrub. It has large, double rosette-shaped yellow flowers that are sometimes edged with pink. Although it has its uses where a large display is required and will grow in poorer soils, all in all it is a rather stiff and coarse rose. Good fragrance. Height 1.5m/5ft. Breeding 'Columbine' × 'Cläre Grammerstorf'. Poulsen (Denmark) 1963.

**Dainty Maid** A beautiful single Floribunda with large flowers that are clear pink on the inside, carmine on the reverse. They are held in small and medium-sized clusters on a plant of vigorous, bushy growth with healthy, dark green, leathery foliage. This excellent rose is one of the parents of 'Constance Spry' and thus played an important part in the foundation of our English Roses. Slight scent. Height 90cm/3ft. 'D.T. Poulsen' × seedling. Le Grice (UK) 1938.

**Dame Wendy** (*Canson*) An attractive variety with well shaped, medium size flowers of apricot-pink. They are produced freely on a plant of average vigour and slightly spreading growth. The leaves are glossy, dark green and quite healthy. Height 8cm/2½ft. 'English Miss' × 'Momento'. Cant (UK) 1991.

**Dusky Maiden** An early Floribunda with large almost single flowers of dark red with deeper shadings and contrasting golden stamens. To me this is still one of the most pleasing of the crimson Floribundas, and all the better for being single. It has some fragrance. One of the parents of the very early English Rose, 'Chianti'. Height 60–80cm/2–2½ft. Breeding ('Daily Mail Scented Rose' × 'Etoile de Hollande') × 'Else Poulsen'. Bred by E. B. Le Grice, introduced 1947. (Illustrated, p. 94)

**English Miss** A charming variety producing large sprays of light pink, medium-sized flowers which start as pretty pointed buds and open to a camellia-like shape. Thus we have a good example of an ideal bloom— one that is beautiful at all stages. The growth is upright, rather short, and the foliage dark green with a purplish tinge. It has a good fragrance. Height 80cm/2½ft. Breeding 'Dearest' × 'Sweet Repose'. Bred by Cant (UK) 1977.

**Escapade** The almost single flowers of this variety have a simple wild rose charm far removed from that of the typical Floribunda. The rose-pink flowers have a hint of violet and are held in dainty profusion above the bush. The result of a cross between 'Pink Parfait' and the little purple Polyantha 'Baby Faurax', it is from the latter that it gains its originality, providing us with a hint as to what the breeder might do with Floribundas as a whole. It is vigorous, hardy, disease resistant and reliable. Light fragrance. Height may vary from 80–120cm/2½–4ft. Harkness (UK) 1967.

**Evelyn Fison** ('Irish Wonder') Unfading scarlet flowers of exceptional brilliance. The growth is strong and healthy with dark green, glossy foliage. This is a very reliable Floribunda providing a mass of colour, but perhaps a little ordinary in its overall

*DAINTY MAID is an excellent rose which played an important part in the foundation of English Roses*

*Left,* ENGLISH MISS *exemplifies the ideal bloom— one that is beautiful at all stages*

*Far left,* ESCAPADE *has a simple wild rose charm far removed from that of the typical Floribunda*

93

THE
HYBRID TEA &
FLORIBUNDA
ROSES

Floribunda
Roses

*DUSKY MAIDEN is one of the most pleasing of the crimson Floribundas, and all the better for being single*

*EVELYN FISON bears unfading scarlet flowers of exceptional brilliance*

appearance. Even so, it is a particularly good bedding rose. It produces numerous small to medium-sized flowers on a vigorous, bushy plant. Height 80cm/2½ft. 'Moulin Rouge' × 'Korona'. McGredy (UK) 1962.

**Eye Paint** A rose of exceptional vigour, with branching, bushy growth that would perhaps be better regarded as a shrub. Its parentage is an unnamed seedling × 'Picasso'. It thus relates back, rather distantly, to *Rosa spinosissima*, and something of this species is still evident in its growth. It bears small scarlet flowers with a white eye and reverse in large clusters. The growth is tall, dense and bushy. Unfortunately it is rather subject to blackspot. Height 1.2m/4ft. McGredy (New Zealand) 1976.

**Fellowship** (Livin' Easy) (*Harwelcome*) This is an extremely versatile variety, growing well in a wide range of climates throughout the world. It is also very reliable and healthy, doing well in massed plantings where it will create a most impressive show. The flowers are a bright orange or dark apricot and loosely double, eventually showing off their stamens. It has a good fruity fragrance. It will grow to about 90cm/3ft in height. Altogether one of the best Floribundas. 'Southampton' × 'Remember Me'. Bred by Harkness (UK) 1992. (Illustrated, p. 77)

**Fragrant Delight** With so many new varieties being introduced each year it is easy for good varieties to be lost. This was introduced in 1978 and is still a very worthwhile variety with attractive flowers that are a rich mix of coppery-orange and salmon. They have a wonderful fragrance. A neat and well balanced bush that flowers freely and stands up well to wind, rain and disease. Height 1.1m/3½ft. 'Chanelle' × 'Whiskey Mac'. Wisbech Plant Company (UK) 1978.

**Glenfiddich** Pointed buds opening to medium-sized flowers with a slight fragrance. The growth is bushy and of medium height, with healthy, glossy, dark green foliage. It is said to perform better in Scotland—the name may have something to do with this. Further south it is at its best in the autumn. Height 80cm/2½ft. Breeding 'Arthur Bell' × ('Sabine' × 'Circus'). Cocker (UK) 1976.

**Golden Wedding** (*Arokise*) Not many US bred varieties do well in the UK, but this is certainly an exception that proves the rule. It has large, golden yellow flowers that hold their form well. They are borne on a vigorous, compact plant with plentiful, shiny foliage. Light fragrance. Height 90cm/3ft. Introduced by Bear Creek Gardens (USA) 1990. (Illustrated, p. 96)

**Great News** Large blooms of rich plum-purple, the petals being silver on the reverse side—a pleasing colour effect, and one that is entirely new to the Hybrid Tea. The growth is of medium strength, but it flowers freely and has a strong perfume. Height 80cm/2½ft. Breeding 'Rose Gaujard' × 'City of Hereford'. Le Grice (UK) 1973.

**Gruss an Aachen** For a time we included this rose with the English Roses because of the very attractive, full petalled flowers. However, it is a cross between 'Frau Karl Druschki' and the Polyantha 'Franz Deegen' and has more in common with the Floribundas, although it predates them by many years having been bred in 1909. The flowers are a lovely soft pearly-pink that gradually fades to creamy-white. It is a tough variety but is rather susceptible to blackspot and benefits from good soil and generous feeding. There is a light fragrance. Height 90cm/3ft. Bred by Geduldig (Germany) 1909.

**Iceberg** ('Fée des Neiges', 'Schneewittchen') This is probably the best rose ever to come out of the Floribunda class. The flowers are small and white, lightly double, opening wide, and held in large clusters. If we study both growth and flower, we soon notice it is no ordinary Floribunda. The growth is tall, very bushy and branching; the leaves

glossy, light green and rather narrow; the stems smooth and slender. The fact is, it is not of typical Floribunda breeding, being a cross between a Hybrid Musk Rose, 'Robin Hood', and a Hybrid Tea Rose, 'Virgo'. Although 'Robin Hood' was a Polyantha on the one side, it is probable that its other parent was one of Pemberton's Hybrid Musks. This shows up in 'Iceberg' which, although it makes a first-class bedding rose, is really more of a Shrub Rose. The whole plant ~has a Hybrid Musk appearance. Lightly pruned it will form an excellent shrub of 1.2m/4ft or more in height. It flowers early and late and is seldom without bloom in between; in the cool of the autumn the flowers have a distinct blush tinge, and are then particularly attractive. In hot climates it will flower for twelve months of the year. Undoubtedly, no Floribunda makes a better standard and grown thus it seems to flower even more abundantly, forming a large, well-shaped head of growth. It will also make a fine low hedge. Its only weakness is a tendency to blackspot as the season advances, but it seems to have the ability to outgrow this. All the same, spraying is advisable for the best results. It has a pleasing, light fragrance. Bred by Kordes (Germany) 1958.

**Jenny Wren** A hybrid of 'Cécile Brünner', this variety's pollen parent is the Floribunda Rose 'Fashion'. The flowers are a creamy-apricot colour with the reverse of the petals a pale salmon-pink.

They are rather too large to be compared with those of either 'Cécile Brünner' or 'Perle d'Or', and open more loosely, but are still small and prettily shaped in the bud. They are held in open sprays and have a strong fragrance. This is an attractive little rose and it is surprising more breeders have not attempted such hybrids. Height 90cm/3ft. Ratcliffe (UK) 1957.

**Korresia** ('Fresia', 'Friesia', 'Sunsprite') This rose stands alone as the best yellow Floribunda. It is of a particularly pleasing shade, not quite so deep as that of 'Allgold', but equally unfading, making a good splash of colour across the garden. Its flowers are held in small clusters and are of average size, opening wide, with quite a good fragrance. The foliage is a glossy light green and has good disease resistance. It flowers well and repeatedly. Height 80cm/2½ft. 'Friedrich Wörlein' × 'Spanish Sun'. Kordes (Germany) 1974. (Illustrated, p. 96)

**L'Aimant** (*Harzola*) A free-flowering Floribunda that has quickly become very popular with gardeners. The individual flowers are most attractive with many short, wavy petals that are a good shade of warm salmon-pink. They are freely borne in large clusters on a well shaped plant. Medium to strong fragrance. Height 90cm/3ft. 'Southampton' × ('Radox Bouquet' × 'Margaret Merril'). Bred by Harkness (UK) 1994. (Illustrated, p. 97)

*ICEBERG, probably the best rose ever to come out of the Floribunda class, bears small, lightly double flowers, held in large clusters*

95

THE
HYBRID TEA &
FLORIBUNDA
ROSES

Floribunda
Roses

*Above left,*
GOLDEN
WEDDING
*is a vigorous,
compact plant
with well formed
flowers and
plentiful, shiny
foliage*

*Above right,*
KORRESIA,
*the best yellow
Floribunda,
flowers well
and repeatedly*

*Right,*
MOUNTBATTEN,
*is very vigorous
and much better
suited to a large
border than for
bedding*

**Margaret Merril** (*Harkully*) An excellent white rose of great beauty that has become one of the most popular Floribundas. The flowers have exquisite high pointed buds, with just a tinge of blush, and eventually open wide. They have what is probably the strongest fragrance of any in this class. The growth is of medium height, about 90cm/3ft, and it has dark green foliage, with good disease resistance although blackspot can be a problem later in the year. 'Rudolph Timm' × 'Dedication' × 'Pascali'. Harkness (UK) 1978.

**Mountbatten** This is very nearly a Shrub Rose and suitable only for the largest rose bed. The colour is usually described as mimosa yellow. It has many virtues: strong, very bushy growth, excellent disease-free foliage, and it flowers abundantly and continually. The individual blooms are large, fragrant and fully double, starting as nice buds and retaining their beauty when fully open. Height 1.5m/5ft. Parentage 'Peer Gynt' × ('Anne Cocker' × 'Arthur Bell') × 'Southampton'. Harkness (UK) 1982.

**News** A cross between an Old Rose, 'Tuscany Superb', and the Floribunda 'Lilac Charm'. It thus has a similar origin to my English Roses, but whereas these lean towards the old type of flower, this rose is of typical modern character. However, it takes from its Old Rose parent a rich purple colouring which was not previously found in Floribundas or Hybrid Teas. A more exact description of the colouring is beetroot-purple. The flowers are large, semi-double, with contrasting creamy yellow stamens. It has excellent strong, bushy growth and flowers freely over a long period. Medium green matt foliage. Slight fragrance. It is perhaps a little surprising that the parents mentioned above should have produced a repeat-flowering variety, and that this should be of typical Floribunda growth. It may well have been a second cross-back to a Floribunda. Height 80cm/2½ft. Le Grice (UK) 1968. (Illustrated, p. 98)

**Oranges and Lemons** (*Macoranlem*) A very striking rose with quite large flowers that have brilliant vermilion orange stripes set on a bright lemon yellow background. The flowers stand up well to the rain and have the best colour in a cool climate. A healthy, strong bush with dark green leaves. Height 1.1m/3½ft. 'New Year' × 'Freude' seedling. McGredy (New Zealand) 1992.

**Pretty Lady** (*Scrivo*) An excellent variety that combines beautiful flowers with exceptional health. The Hybrid Tea type blooms are a soft apricot which gradually fades with

Floribunda
Roses

*Left,
L'AIMANT bears
flowers with
many short, wavy
petals on a well
shaped plant*

*Far left,
MARGARET
MERRIL has
beautiful flowers
that open right
up and are very
strongly fragrant
in all stages*

*Near left,
PRETTY LADY
combines
beautiful flowers
with excellent
health*

THE
HYBRID TEA &
FLORIBUNDA
ROSES

Floribunda
Roses

*Above,* NEWS
*takes from its
Old Rose parent
a rich purple
colouring not
previously found
in Floribundas
or Hybrid Teas*

*Right,* THE TIMES
*creates a blaze of
colour, its double
flowers set off by
attractive foliage*

age and have a light fragrance. It has attractive, bushy growth, is very free flowering and is easy to grow. The provenance is interesting, Len Scrivens using *R. davidii elongata* in the development of this rose. Height 90cm/3ft. Scrivens (UK) 1996.

**Queen Elizabeth** ('The Queen Elizabeth Rose') Every now and again a rose appears that will sooner or later be found in almost every garden. 'Queen Elizabeth' and 'Peace' are two varieties that spring to mind when we consider the period since the Second World War. Both have the quality of extremely strong growth and near indestructibility, particularly this variety. 'Queen Elizabeth' has more in common with the Old Roses than other Floribundas. The flowers are large, clear pink and deeply cupped in shape. Although the plant is on the whole a little coarse and of rather ugly, upright habit, the individual flowers are not without their beauty, particularly when cut. The bush or shrub grows to a great height, at least 1.4m/4½ft, but often when lightly pruned it may be seen growing to 1.8m/6ft or more. It is ideal for the back of a large mixed border. When allowed to develop without restraint, the flowers tend to perch on top of the growth where they cannot be seen properly. There is no other Hybrid Tea or Floribunda quite so accommodating, for it will grow anywhere that a rose can reasonably be expected to grow. It has few, if any, practical weaknesses. The foliage is large,

THE
HYBRID TEA &
FLORIBUNDA
ROSES

Floribunda
Roses

*QUEEN ELIZABETH is an almost indestructible rose and, therefore, found in very many gardens*

dark green and very disease resistant. It flowers freely and continually. Faint fragrance. Breeding 'Charlotte Armstrong' × 'Floradora'. Raised by Dr W.E. Lammerts (USA) 1954.

**Scentimental** (*Wekplapep*) Many of the new Floribundas are quite like Hybrid Teas in appearance and could be classed as either. 'Scentimental' is such a variety, the blooms being well formed and held in small clusters. It is very distinctive with flowers that are a creamy-white striped and splashed with burgundy-red, each petal different from the next and so each bloom different too. It has a wonderful, sweet scent. The growth is bushy and healthy and it flowers freely. Height 1.2m/4ft. 'Playboy' × 'Peppermint Twist'. Carruth (USA) 1996.

**Sexy Rexy** (*Macrexy*) A very distinctive rose and not just because of its name. The medium-sized flowers are very double and open to flat rosettes; they are borne in very large clusters on long straight stems. Unfortunately they are sometimes too heavy for their own good and arch over, rather stiffly, to the ground. The colour is a pure rose pink. It flowers later than many other varieties and can be slow to repeat. Very healthy and a good choice for a large bed. Height 90cm/3ft. 'Seaspray' × 'Träumerei'. Bred by McGredy (New Zealand) 1984.

**Southampton** ('Susan Ann'). A very robust Floribunda of up to 1.2m/4ft in height, with plenty of glossy, disease-resistant foliage. The flowers are large and apricot-orange flushed with scarlet. It

99

THE
HYBRID TEA &
FLORIBUNDA
ROSES

Floribunda
Roses

*Right,*
*Trumpeter,*
*with short,*
*compact growth,*
*can appear com-*
*pletely covered*
*in flowers*

*Facing page,*
*Valentine*
*Heart is one of*
*the prettiest of*
*the Floribundas,*
*and very well*
*mannered too*

**Tatton** (*Fryentice*) A very brightly coloured variety with large, full flowers in a shade of burnt orange. The growth is strong and vigorous and it repeat flowers very well. The young growth is a very bright red, adding to the overall effect. Good fruity fragrance. Very healthy. Height 80cm/2½ft. Fryer (UK) 2000.

**The Times Rose** (*Korpeahn*) ('Mariandel', 'Carl Philip Kristian IV') In many ways this is one of the best red Floribundas; it is widely grown and very popular. The flowers are borne in large clusters; they are double and a deep and very constant red. At first they are set off by young bronzy red foliage, and then by shiny, dark green leaves. It is vigorous but compact and free flowering. Not unusual for a Floribunda, it has little or no scent and I find it a rather 'cold' rose. But it certainly creates a blaze of colour. Height 90cm/3ft. 'Tornado' × 'Red Gold'. Bred by Kordes (Germany) 1985. (Illustrated, p. 98)

**Trumpeter** (*Mactrum*) An extremely brightly coloured rose with loosely double flowers of almost fluorescent vermilion-red that sometimes veers towards dark orange. It flowers very freely and continuously and, with its short, compact growth, can appear completely covered in flowers. It is an excellent choice for a bed of roses where something particularly bright is required but not such a good choice for mixing with other colours. It is relatively healthy although may well lose its leaves later in the season unless sprayed. There is no fragrance. Height 60cm/2ft. 'Satchmo' seedling. McGredy (New Zealand) 1977.

**Valentine Heart** (*Dicogle*) I find this one of the most attractive of the Floribundas. The frilly petalled flowers are well spaced in large clusters and, because they are not very double, the delightful mix of pale and rosy pink is revealed. It is a very well shaped bush

makes a fine show as a bedding rose. Slightly fragrant. ('Queen Elizabeth' × 'Allgold') × 'Yellow Cushion'. Harkness (UK) 1971.

**Sunset Boulevard** (*Harbabble*) A particularly healthy variety that creates a strong impact when a number are planted together in a bed. The colour varies considerably with age, starting as strawberry red in bud, then going through a glowing apricot-orange and finishing as apricot-pink. It repeat flowers very quickly. Height 80cm/2½ft. 'Harold Macmillan' × 'Fellowship'. Bred by Harkness (UK) 1997.

with good, spreading growth and good resistance to disease. There is a pleasant fragrance and it flowers very freely. Height 90cm/3ft. 'Shona' × 'Pot o' Gold'. Dickson (UK) 1990.

**Wishing** (*Dickerfuffle*) The flowers are a delicate peachy pink and, when young, shaped like small Hybrid Teas. It makes a compact plant that flowers very freely and is generally healthy. Light scent. Height 80cm/2½ft. 'Silver Jubilee' × 'Bright Smile'. Dickson (UK) 1984.

# 4

# SOME SMALL ROSES

Having completed our survey of the two largest groups of Modern Roses—the Hybrid Teas and Floribundas—we are left with three other modern groups. All these are small in stature and usually have small or very small flowers. They are the Dwarf Polyantha Roses, the Patio Roses and the Miniature Roses.

Many modern houses have small gardens, often no more than a patio or a terrace, and if we wish to grow roses in such gardens, these groups can be very valuable. It is a question whether it might be better to grow just a few larger roses, perhaps in pots, with one or two climbers on the walls, but it cannot be denied that growing small roses allows us to have a wider range of varieties.

There are also uses for these three groups of small roses in the largest gardens. The Miniatures, for example, can be grown in troughs and pots, the Dwarf Polyanthas and Patio Roses are ideal for the edges of borders and all three groups are useful for small, intimate spaces.

---

## Dwarf Polyantha Roses

For the origins of the Dwarf Polyantha Roses we have to go back to the year 1860 when the French breeder, Guillot, of Lyons, sowed seed of the climbing species *Rosa multiflora* which is, as we shall see, the parent of many Rambler Roses. The resulting plants turned out to have not single white flowers, as would be expected, but flowers of varying shades of pink, some double and others single or semi-double. Most of these were sterile, but some of the seedlings were not Ramblers, but short, perpetual-flowering bushes. It is almost certain that Guillot's original *R. multiflora* had, by chance, been pollinated by a China Rose—in all probability the 'Old Blush China'. He chose two of these seedlings, naming one 'Paquerette', which he introduced in 1875, and the other 'Mignonette', which he introduced in 1880; both bore large sprays of very small pompon flowers like those of a Multiflora, and both were a soft rosy-pink fading to white with age. Thus a new class was born. However, the Dwarf Polyanthas did not

achieve great popularity and few varieties were bred. Indeed, at one time they had all but been dropped from catalogues. In recent years one or two new varieties have appeared, but these are usually of taller growth, as, for example, 'Yesterday'.

Dwarf Polyanthas are very different from other bush roses and are ideal for the edges of borders where something low growing is required, particularly if the soil is not of the best. Like their *R. multiflora* parent, the Dwarf Polyanthas are extremely tough and hardy, and produce their flowers with the greatest freedom in large, tightly packed clusters. They also repeat with continuous regularity. No sooner has one branch of flowers come into bloom than another flower shoot appears just beneath it. This virtue, together with their toughness, was to have a profound influence on the development of the rose—an effect that has by no means yet run its course. Unfortunately Dwarf Polyanthas usually have little or no fragrance.

*Facing page,*
*Marlena,*
*introduced in*
*1964 and still*
*an excellent*
*variety*

102

SOME
SMALL
ROSES

Dwarf
Polyantha
Roses

Cultivation is less demanding than for most other roses. Pruning consists merely of cutting off last year's flower heads and the removal of old and dead growth. They shoot continually from the base of the plant, and this can result in a mass of ageing growth which requires some thinning.

I include with this class a few roses that are so different as hardly to warrant inclusion here, except for the fact that one of their parents, in each case, was a Polyantha. They are 'Cécile Brünner', 'Perle d'Or', 'White Cécile Brünner' and 'Madame Jules Thibaud', which are often included with the China Roses, where they probably have less right to be. We have to place these particularly charming roses here with the Dwarf Polyanthas as they are so much out on their own and they do not really fit in anywhere else. They are like exquisite little miniature-flowered Tea Roses, with perfectly formed scrolled buds.

---

**Baby Faurax** A short grower, no more than 30cm/12in high, that might well be at home amongst the Miniature Roses. It is usually regarded as being as close to blue as it is possible to get in a rose. The colour is, in fact, reddish-violet. A very useful little rose with close sprays of tiny cupped flowers on a continuously flowering bush. Lille (France) 1924.

**Cameo** Neatly shaped clusters of dainty salmon-pink, semi-double flowers, with a slight fragrance. 50cm/1½ft. De Ruiter (Holland) 1932.

**Cécile Brünner** ('Madame Cécile Brünner', the 'Sweetheart Rose', 'Mignon', 'Maltese Rose') This rose, along with 'Perle d'Or' and 'White Cécile Brünner', is very different from all other Dwarf Polyanthas in that its flowers have buds of perfectly shaped Tea Rose formation. They are so different that a case could be made for putting them in a separate class. Nonetheless, their breeding is the same.

'Cécile Brünner' is an exquisite little rose with buds no larger than a thimble. Each of these is of perfect pointed Tea Rose formation and retains its beauty even when fully open. The colour is a pale pink which deepens towards the centre of the bud. The flowers are borne singly on thin, wiry stems, and later in the season strong base shoots appear bearing open sprays of bloom. The foliage too is small, but otherwise like that of a Tea Rose. It usually grows to a height of 90cm/3ft and repeat flowers throughout the summer. There is a faint perfume, and the bush is free of disease. One of its parents was the famous old Tea Rose 'Madame de Tartas'. Bred by Pernet-Ducher (France), distributed 1881. Another rose, 'Bloomfield Abundance', is almost identical except that it is much taller with the sepals very long,

*Near right, CÉCILE BRÜNNER has tiny buds of perfectly formed Tea Rose formation that retain their beauty when fully open*

*Far right, BABY FAURAX is is very much the shortest rose with this colouring*

SOME
SMALL
ROSES

Dwarf
Polyantha
Roses

extending well beyond the petals. This variety does not have quite such perfect flowers, but it is worth referring to page 187 before deciding which variety to grow. There is also a particularly strong-growing climbing version of 'Cécile Brünner' (see page 228) although it does not repeat flower.

**Coral Cluster** A pretty little rose with pure coral-pink flowers in large clusters. Its rich, glossy-green foliage has some tendency to mildew. Height 50cm/1 ½ft. Murrell (UK) 1920.

**Gloire du Midi** A sport from 'Gloria Mundi', with small globular flowers of brilliant orange-scarlet which retain their colour well. This is a well formed bush with bright green foliage. Slight fragrance. Height 50cm/1 ½ft. De Ruiter (Holland) 1932.

**Jean Mermoz** Pretty, airy sprays of tiny, very double flowers on nice spreading growth. They are of a deep China-pink shade, and have a slight fragrance. An ideal rose for the edge of a border. Unlike the other roses in this group, this is a cross between a *R. wichurana* hybrid and a Hybrid Tea. Height 50cm/1½ft. Bred by Chenault (France) 1937.

**Katharina Zeimet** This rose and 'Marie Pavič' both have a pleasing delicacy of flower not often found in the Polyanthas, and it is interesting to note that 'Marie Pavič' was one of its parents. The flowers are small, fully double, pure white with a sheeny texture, and are held in large clusters. It has good short, bushy growth and smooth, rich green foliage. Sweet fragrance.

KATHARINA
ZEIMET has a
pleasing delicacy
of flower not
often found in
the Polyanthas

'Etoile de Mai' × 'Marie Pavič'. Height 60cm/2ft. P. Lambert (Germany) 1901.

**Madame Jules Thibaud** This is another pretty little sport from 'Cécile Brünner' (see above), having charming little peachy-pink flowers throughout the summer. Otherwise it is entirely the same and equally good in every way.

**Margo Koster** A pretty little plant with branches of very cupped, almost bell-like flowers in a pleasing shade of salmon-pink. They are a little larger than is usual for this group and have a slight fragrance. The growth is short and bushy, about 45cm/18in in height. This rose is the result of a quite extraordinary series of sports, starting with

the Rambler 'Tausendschon', which sported to give a short bush called 'Echo'. This gave us 'Greta Kluis', which in turn gave us 'Anneke Koster', which produced 'Dick Koster', which finally resulted in 'Margo Koster'. There is little point in describing them all, as I think 'Margo Koster' is probably the best. All Polyanthas seem to have the capacity to sport and, indeed, to revert back again to their parent, so that we often find two different colours on one bush. Koster (Holland) 1931.

**Marie-Jeanne** An attractive variety, bearing very large clusters of small blush-cream rosette-shaped flowers on a bush of some 60–90cm/2–3ft in height. The foliage is a glossy light green. Suitably

pruned it will form a nice little shrub. It is almost entirely without thorns. Turbat (France) 1913.

**Marie Pavič** ('Marie Pavié') A bushy, twiggy plant that grows well and bears dainty clusters of fresh blush-white flowers, borne on a well formed bush. One of the most attractive and reliable roses in this group. Height 50cm/1½ft. Alégatière (France) 1888.

**Miss Edith Cavell** This is a colour sport of 'Orléans Rose', a classic Polyantha and a very important rose in the history of both the Polyanthas and the Floribundas. 'Miss Edith Cavell' has large trusses of small, open, scarlet-crimson flowers. It is particularly free flowering and extremely healthy, suffering from just a touch of mildew. Height 60cm/2ft. Introduced by de Ruiter (Holland) 1917.

**Nathalie Nypels** ('Mevrouw Nathalie Nypels') An excellent Polyantha bearing medium-sized flowers on a dwarf, spreading bush. It flowers almost continuously, the colour starting rose pink, paling to almost white. It has rather unusual parents for a rose of this class: 'Orléans Rose', a typical Polyantha × (a seedling from the China Rose 'Comtesse du Cayla' × *Rosa foetida bicolor*). It is, consequently, not of a typical Polyantha character, the flowers being a little larger and showing signs of its China parentage. Quite a strong fragrance. Height 90cm/3ft. Leenders (Holland) 1919.

**Paul Crampel** This rose, together with 'Gloria Mundi' and 'Golden Salmon', was the first to have the brilliant orange-scarlet or vermilion colour we associate with such modern Hybrid Teas as 'Super Star'. As such, these three Polyanthas represented an entirely new colour in roses when they were first introduced around 1930. 'Paul Crampel' is a typical Polyantha, with tight bunches of small flowers each with a tiny white eye at the centre. The growth is vigorous and erect, and the foliage light green. It has the unfortunate habit of sporting

SOME
SMALL
ROSES

Dwarf
Polyantha
Roses

*Left,* Miss Edith Cavell *is a very important rose in the history of both the Polyanthas and the Floribundas*

*Near left,* Nathalie Nypels *is not of typical Polyantha character, the flowers showing signs of its China parentage*

*Far left,* Marie-Jeanne *bears very large clusters of small rosette-shaped flowers on a shrub almost entirely without thorns*

*Facing page,* Marie Pavič *is one of the most attractive and reliable roses in this group*

107

SOME
SMALL
ROSES

Dwarf
Polyantha
Roses

*Paul Crampel was one of the first roses to have this brilliant orange-scarlet colouring*

*Perle d'Or is almost a replica of 'Cécile Brünner', with similar perfect, miniature Tea Rose buds*

*Facing page, Yesterday has a natural bushy, branching habit of growth that fits easily into the garden scene*

to flowers of a rather unpleasant crimson. Height 60cm/2ft. Bred by Kersbergen (Holland) 1930.

**Perle d'Or** Almost a replica of 'Cécile Brünner' (for a full description, see p. 104), with similar perfect, miniature Tea Rose buds. The flowers are a buff-apricot shade that deepens towards the centre, becoming tinged with pink as they open, finally fading to cream. They are of rather looser formation than 'Cécile Brünner' when fully open, but are equally, if not more, beautiful. Like 'Cécile Brünner' they are held on long, wiry stems though the growth is perhaps a little stronger. There is a sweet fragrance. Height 1.2m/4ft. It is probably the result of a cross between a Polyantha and the Tea Rose 'Madame Falcot'. Rambaud (France) 1883.

**White Cécile Brünner** A sport from 'Cécile Brünner' (for a full description, see p. 104). Unfortunately it is not quite white but tinged with buff, giving it a somewhat dirty appearance. Nonetheless, it is a worthwhile rose for those who are particularly attracted to miniature flowers. Slight fragrance. Height 90cm/3ft. Discovered by Fauque (France) 1909.

**Yesterday** A much more recent rose, bred by Harkness and introduced in 1974. Its parents were ('Phyllis Bide' × 'Shepherd's Delight') × 'Ballerina'. Both 'Phyllis Bide' and 'Ballerina' have connections with *Rosa multiflora*, and 'Yesterday' therefore has a right to be included here. It forms a rather taller bush than the older varieties, being 90cm/3ft in height. The flowers are small, flat and typically Polyantha, produced in graceful sprays and of a pleasant lilac-pink colouring paling a little towards the centre. They are sweetly fragrant. It has a natural bushy, branching habit of growth that fits easily into the garden scene.

**Yvonne Rabier** Said to be a cross between *Rosa wichurana* and an unknown Polyantha, it is therefore surprising that this rose is so very perpetual flowering, as first crosses between once-flowering and repeat-flowering roses are almost always summer flowering only. It is a vigorous, bushy rose of 90cm/3ft in height. As one would expect from two such parents, it is extremely hardy and disease resistant. The flowers, which are sweetly fragrant, are white with just a tinge of yellow and produced in abundance. It has long, slender, glossy-green foliage that shows signs of both parents. Turbat (France) 1910.

Patio
Roses

*CIDER CUP
has good, neat,
bushy growth
and is very
free flowering*

# Patio Roses

THE PATIO ROSES are closely connected with the Dwarf Poly-anthas and the Miniature Roses and are frequently the result of crossing these with Floribundas. It is, however, dangerous to be too dogmatic as to their origins for they are, in reality, the result of a variety of influences.

I regard Patio Roses as being one of the more satisfactory developments in present-day roses. They often form small, bushy plants, rather like miniature Floribundas but much more compact; indeed some of them could be described as very small, bushy or spreading shrubs. They have numerous small flowers and repeat particularly well. The growth, though short, is often cushion-like or arching, and some varieties have flowers of attractive rosette shape. Others have small pom-pon flowers like those of a Polyantha. The foliage is often small and dark and there is little trouble with disease.

Cultivation is straightforward. If breeders concentrate on beauty of flower, and not necessarily on a brilliant colour or a Hybrid Tea shape, I feel sure we could be hearing a lot more about Patio Roses in the future, particularly if they can continue to develop a good bushy habit of growth. Unfortunately they tend to have little or no scent and it may be difficult to breed this into them.

---

**Bianco** (*Cocblanco*) Small creamy-white, rosette-shaped flowers, produced with great freedom in large clusters on a short, rather open and spreading bush. There is some fragrance. Height 50cm/1½ft. 'Darling Flame' × 'Jack Frost'. Cocker (UK) 1983.

**Bright Smile** (*Dicdance*) Slightly larger flowers than is usual for this group, with deep yellow pointed buds, later opening wide to show their stamens and eventually fading. The growth is strong, neat and bushy with plentiful healthy, shiny, foliage; it is close to a Floribunda in general appearance. Free and continuous flowering. Slight fragrance. Height 60cm/2ft. Dickson (UK) 1980.

**Cider Cup** (*Dicladida*) The flowers are classically Hybrid Tea shape when young, opening to semi-double flowers, the colour being a deep apricot that fades to a paler shade. It has good, neat, bushy growth and flowers very freely. Height 50cm/1½ft. Dicksons (UK) 1987.

**Flower Power** (*Frycassia*) A particularly free-flowering variety from Gareth Fryer which, he tells us, comes from the same stable as his excellent 'Sweet Dream'. The flowers are full petalled and salmon-pink in colour. It has low, compact growth to no more than about 30cm/1ft and it is also very healthy. There is a nice, spicy fragrance. Fryer (UK) 1998.

**Greenalls Glory** (*Kirmac*) Perfectly formed buds opening to silvery white blooms with a pale pink centre. It has an excellent dwarf, bushy habit and flowers very freely. Glossy, bronze foliage. Light fragrance. Height 50cm/1½ft. Kirkham (UK) 1989.

*QUEEN MOTHER is extremely popular both because of its name and its excellent qualities*

*Sweet Dream is an excellent little rose that flowers extremely freely and has bushy, upright growth*

**Hakuun** Its name meaning 'cloud' in Danish, this rose produces tightly packed trusses of small buff to creamy-white flowers in such quantities that they are, indeed, like a cloud. A tough, reliable and bushy plant of 60cm/2ft in height. Slight scent. Poulsen (Denmark) 1962.

**Marlena** Introduced in 1964, long before the name 'Patio Roses' was conceived, this is still, I believe, the best of the group, growing to about 50cm/1½ft, it is covered with clusters of small, semi-double and slightly cupped crimson-scarlet flowers, forming a mound of colour. It is seldom without bloom and is very healthy. A very useful variety for the front of the border or for a small bed. Bred by Kordes (Germany) (Illustrated, p. 103).

**Pink Champagne** (*Peadelight*) Colin Pearce from The Limes Roses in Devon has bred a new group of roses which he has named 'New Leaf Roses', his aim being maximum health, an attractive, rounded shape and a very long flowering period. He started in 1968 using two main parents that stayed very healthy in his garden—'Aloha' (a seedling of 'New Dawn') and 'Vesper' (an orange Floribunda from E.B. Le Grice). He has been most successful and the three roses included here—'Pink Champagne', 'Pink Tiara' and 'Raspberry Royale' have been awarded top prizes and Gold Medals from Pencoed, South Wales (where it is very wet), and also from The Hague. 'Pink Champagne' is a rather taller 'New Leaf Rose', resembling a Floribunda and growing to 60cm/2ft. The flowers are about 6cm/2½in across and semi double. The colour is pink with touches of yellow and cream and it produces great quantities of blooms over a long period. Bred by Pearce (UK) 2005.

**Pink Tiara** (*Peadream*) This is one of the healthiest of the 'New Leaf Roses'. The blooms are about 7cm/2¾in across, a medium pink in colour and attractively set off by the pale green foliage. It makes a small, neat, rounded plant just 30cm/1ft tall. Bred by Pearce (UK) 2003.

**Queen Mother** (*Korquemu*) This was named for the late Queen Mother's 90th birthday and has been very popular. It is an extremely free-flowering variety with attractive, soft pink, semi-double blooms. The foliage is dark and glossy and the growth spreading and nicely rounded. Slight fragrance. Height 50cm/1½ft. Kordes (Germany) 1990. (Illustrated, p. 111)

**Raspberry Royale** (*Peacloe*) A 'New Leaf Rose' (see 'Pink Champagne') with flowers of a lovely rose-carmine colour. They retain their attractive rosette form for some time, eventually opening wide, at which point they quickly drop their petals. It is a very tough and hardy plant and, like the other varieties in this group, is also very healthy. It makes a neatly rounded plant, ideal for a small bed or a container. Height 45cm/18in. Bred by Pearce (UK) 2004.

**Regensberg** (*Macyoumis*) This is one of the best of the so-called hand-painted roses. The light pink semi-double flowers are mottled and edged with white with a white centre. These are rather larger than is usual and create a good massed colour effect. The flowers are produced very freely on a neat, healthy bush, 50cm/1½ft in height. Slight fragrance. McGredy (New Zealand) 1979.

**Sugar and Spice** (*Peallure*) A very healthy variety from Colin Pearce who also bred the 'New Leaf Roses' (see 'Pink Champagne'). It won the top award at Pencoed in 2002. The pale pink, full-petalled flowers are quite small but very pretty and contrast well with the unusually pale green foliage. It can be described as a Patio or Miniature, growing only 20cm/8in tall, and so is ideal for a pot where it creates a wonderfully rounded plant that flowers extremely freely. Bred by Pearce (UK) 1999.

**Sweet Dream** (*Frymincot*) One of the best selling of all varieties in the UK, this is an excellent little rose with bushy, upright growth and dense glossy foliage. The fragrant flowers are apricot-peach and of the most attractive, neat, full-petalled, cupped formation. Charming. Height 50cm/1½ft. Seedling × (Anytime × Liverpool Echo) × (New Penny × seedling). Fryer (UK) 1988.

**Tantalizing Mary** Sean McCann is well known in the rose world as a writer and lecturer and in his garden near Dublin he has bred a number of roses, many of them Miniatures. They are not well known in the UK but have been enthusiastically taken up by rose growers in the United States. Sean describes 'Tantalizing Mary' as a Mini-flora, a new group that is roughly equivalent to the Patios in size of plant but generally with smaller, Miniature-type flowers. It has small yellow or orange-yellow blooms that are produced with great freedom and almost continuously through to the frosts. The plant is quite upright but bushy. In cooler climates it will grow to about 80cm/2½ft but in warmer areas it can become more shrubby, the final height depending also on the severity of the pruning. It is particularly healthy. Fragrant. It was named for Mary Pullen, a great rose enthusiast especially of the Miniature roses. McCann (Eire) 2004.

**Wildfire** (*Fryessex*) A very free-flowering Patio Rose from Gareth Fryer and very brightly coloured with flowers of brilliant flame-orange. The growth is dense and compact. It is a good choice for a large pot or for the front of a border. Height 60cm/2ft. Fryer (UK) 2004.

# Miniature Roses

THESE ARE TRUE Miniatures, 12cm/5in in height in the case of 'Rouletii', but more usually from 20 to 35cm/9 to 15in tall, and some are up to 60cm/2ft or more. Variations in height depend somewhat on whether they are grown from cuttings or grafted on a stock, those from cuttings being shorter. Miniature Roses are not only diminutive in height, but also in all their parts, having twiggy growth and tiny leaves and flowers. The flowers, when closely examined, can be very pretty, either in the form of little Hybrid Tea buds or as small Old Rose rosettes.

There can be little doubt that the original variety was a miniature form of a China Rose. The earliest example of this type of rose came to Britain from China at some time around 1800 and from here travelled to France. A number of varieties were raised which became popular both in Britain and France, particularly as pot plants for the house. Later, interest faded and they were almost entirely lost. In 1918 a Swiss Army Medical Officer named Roulet discovered plants of some of these varieties growing in pots in a Swiss village, where it was said they had been grown for a very long time; this rose became known as 'Rouletii'. The Dutch hybridist Van Vink and Pedro Dot of Spain used 'Rouletii' as a parent, crossing it with various roses to found the modern race. After this a number of other breeders took a hand, and the popularity of Miniature Roses began to spread.

It is an odd fact that the Miniatures have received more attention in the land of the 'bigger and better'—the United States of America—than anywhere else. Space is usually not a problem there, while in Great Britain it frequently is. Even so, Miniature Roses have never been very popular here and their popularity in the United States must be in some degree due to the work of Ralph Moore of California. It is he who has done more than any other breeder to bring them to their present state of development. I had the great pleasure of visiting his interesting nursery during the summer of 1985, where I had the opportunity of seeing the large amount of work he has done and is doing in this field. He has numerous varieties, but sadly many of the charming little roses he has bred have never been widely distributed. Moore is the only hybridist to breed Moss Roses since the time of the Old Roses.

More recently, other breeders have taken a hand—particularly Tom Carruth of Weeks Roses in the USA, as well as a number of amateur breeders. In Britain, there seems to have been a new surge of interest in Miniature Roses. More recent varieties include roses with pretty little Hybrid Tea buds rather similar to those of 'Cécile Brünner'. I think it is true to say that the Miniature buds are often more attractive than those of larger roses.

*LITTLE FLIRT, with parents of widely differing characters, is a Ralph Moore classic*

**Cricri** A dwarf, bushy plant of 30cm/12in in height. The flowers are well formed and very double; their colour salmon-pink shaded with coral. ('Alain' × 'Independence') × 'Perla de Alcanada'. Meilland (France) 1958.

**Hula Girl** A very good Miniature that flowers particularly freely. The buds start as perfect little Hybrid Teas which quickly open up to a mass of petals that fold over at the edges. They start orange, change to salmon-pink and end closer to pink with very pale edges. The growth is neat and compact, about 60cm/2ft tall with small, dark, glossy leaves. Excellent as bedding or in a container. Bred by Williams (USA) 1975.

**Irresistible** (*Tinresist*) This variety is perhaps a little out of character in that it grows rather tall—up to about 90cm/3ft—but the flowers are very much in the style of the Miniatures. They are in the form of perfect, little Hybrid Tea buds and are white with a hint of pink in the centre and greenish markings on the outer petals. It is popular with exhibitors but also makes a good garden plant, standing up well to the rain. 'Tiki' × 'Brian Lee'. Bennett (USA) 1989.

**Lavender Jewel** Quite large, full flowers in a charming combination of pink and lavender. It flowers almost continuously. The growth is bushy, lax and of medium height. A good garden plant and regarded as one of the best Miniatures. Height 50cm/1½ft. 'Little Chief' × 'Angel Face'. Moore (USA) 1978.

**Little Buckaroo** An early variety in the history of the Miniatures, which was important in encouraging gardeners to grow them. It was

*Right, STARS 'N' STRIPES has something of the appearance of a diminutive 'Rosa Mundi'*

*Facing page, MR BLUEBIRD is compact and bushy with very good repeat flowering*

bred by Ralph Moore from the interesting cross of (*R. wichurana* × 'Floradora') × ('Oakington Ruby' × 'Floradora'). The crimson blooms are small and double, opening to reveal a white centre and yellow stamens. As might be expected from the inclusion of a climber in the parentage, the growth is rather loose and slightly spreading. There is a medium, fruity fragrance. Moore (USA) 1956.

**Little Flirt** Orange-red flowers with an orange-yellow reverse. Light green foliage and bushy growth of about 30cm/12in. The breeding is (*Rosa wichurana* × 'Floradora') × ('Golden Glow' × 'Zee'). It is interesting to note that *R. wichurana* is a giant Rambler, 'Floradora' a strong Floribunda, 'Golden Glow' a Climber, and only 'Zee' a Miniature. Moore (USA) 1961. (Illustrated, p. 113)

**Marry Me** (*Dicwonder*) Quite tall for a Miniature and classed by some as a Patio. The flowers are medium pink and start as small Hybrid Tea buds, gradually opening into little camellia-like flowers. It makes a densely bushy little, rounded shrub with glossy foliage. It is particularly free flowering. Height 60cm/2ft. Dickson (UK) 1998.

**Mr Bluebird** A charming little rose with semi-double flowers of a lovely bluish-lavender colouring. The growth is compact and bushy. In every way an excellent variety of considerable garden value. Very good repeat flowering. Height 60cm/2ft. 'Oakington Ruby' × 'Old Blush China'. Moore (USA) 1960.

**Peter Pan** (*Chewpan*) As with other groups of roses, good red Miniatures are difficult to breed. This is, however, a very good variety from Chris Warner, a good friend who lives quite close to our nursery. It has dark red, Hybrid Tea flowers and tiny, glossy foliage. A delightful and very reliable variety. Height 30cm/1ft. Warner (UK) 1998.

**Pour Toi** Creamy-white, semi-double flowers tinted with yellow at the base of the petals. Very short, being only 20cm/8in in height, but with good, bushy growth. 'Eduardo Toda' × 'Pompon de Paris'. Dot (Spain) 1946.

**Stars 'n' Stripes** Another Moore innovation. This time he has used the old striped Hybrid Perpetual 'Ferdinand Pichard' to produce a charming little striped Miniature. The flowers are semi-double with white stripes on a red ground, and have something of the appearance of a diminutive 'Rosa Mundi'. The growth is bushy and lax, forming a small shrub 60cm/2ft in height, and should appeal to those who like Old Roses. 'Little Chief' × ('Little Darling' × 'Ferdinand Pichard'). Moore (USA) 1980.

**Sweet Chariot** (*Morchari*) This variety has the dark purple Rambler 'Violette' as one of its parents and has taken on its rich dark colour, which eventually fades to lilac. The flowers are in the form of a perfect little rosette and they have a strong, damask fragrance, which is most unusual among the Miniatures. It forms a neat, compact bush which repeat flowers quickly. While the blackspot resistance is not the best, it is worth growing for its colour and overall appearance. Height 60cm/2ft. Moore (USA) 1984.

**Top Marks** (*Fryminister*) An eye-catching variety with small, double flowers of the brightest vermilion. They are produced very freely on a neat, compact and healthy bush. A useful rose for growing in a pot or for the front of a border. Height 50cm/18in. Fryer (UK) 1992.

**Yellow Doll** Still one of the best yellow Miniatures, Yellow Doll has large blooms, starting as pointed buds, eventually revealing many petals of pale yellow to cream colouring. Good spreading growth to about 30cm/12in, with leathery, glossy foliage. The pollen parent, 'Golden Glow', is an extremely hardy rambler. 'Golden Glow' × 'Zee'. Moore (USA) 1962.

# 5

# THE ENGLISH
# ROSES

THE STORY OF THE ROSE does not end. It follows the course of history, evolving as it goes—taking on new forms, new colours and new habits of growth and foliage. I have described the beautiful old European roses with their wonderful fragrance, some of which themselves had parents with their origins in the Middle East—the Gallicas, the Damasks, the Centifolias, the Moss Roses and the Albas. I have also discussed the China Roses, which flower throughout the summer, and how, in time, the ability to repeat flower passed to the Portland Roses, the Bourbons and the Hybrid Perpetuals, which had much of the same beauty as the Old Roses. These eventually gave way to the Hybrid Teas with their elegant buds and often bright colours. Later, their place was shared by their close relations, the Floribundas. During this time, roses have been developed as climbers, as shrubs, small bushes and tiny Miniatures. They have taken on many forms and colours: what is there left to do?

Many fine representatives of all these roses—old and new—are thankfully still with us; they continue to be grown in our gardens. I think that there is still much that can and should be done. This largely concerns the actual beauty of the rose. There was a tendency among plant breeders to assume that however they manipulate it genetically for colour, size, floriferousness, disease-resistance and so on, the resulting rose will inevitably retain its beauty. Unfortunately, this is not always so and some of the roses of today have declined in beauty—and often in fragrance, too—when compared with those of the past.

### THE DEVELOPMENT
### OF THE ENGLISH ROSES

Back in the late 1940s it occurred to me that it would be beneficial to combine the beauty of the Old Roses with the practical virtues of Modern Roses in one range of roses. It seemed to me that the form of flower of the Old Roses was the ideal shape for a rose, rather than the long buds of the Hybrid Tea—beautiful though these may sometimes be. Most importantly, the Old Rose shape offers a much wider range of form and beauty: the single or semi-double bloom with its delicate beauty; the flat rosette; the cupped rosette and the recurved rosette. We also have deeply cupped flowers and these may be open with exposed stamens or filled with small petals. Even these categories can vary enormously between one variety and another—but also according to the stage of the bloom: first of all as a bud; later, the partly open flower; and finally the fully open flowers—each stage offering a new type of beauty. The Hybrid Tea flower, on the other hand, is only beautiful in the bud which is, of necessity, short-lived.

Similarly, the shrubby growth of the Old Roses is not only more useful in the garden—being more suitable for mingling with other plants in the border—but is also more beautiful in itself and very importantly, is capable of displaying its flowers to much greater effect and in a variety of different ways. A bloom becomes even finer when seen on a well-formed shrub.

At the same time, the Modern Roses have their advantages. Unlike the Old Roses, they flower throughout the summer and have a much wider range of colour. The colours of the Old Roses are confined to white through pink to crimson and purple shades, whereas the Modern Roses have numerous shades of yellow, flame, apricot, peach and so on.

When I took my first tentative steps to combine the virtues of the roses of the past with those of the present day, I was simply an amateur breeder, but over the last fifty years or so I have devoted my time to the development of what I have chosen to call 'English Roses'. While putting the very com-

*GOLDEN CELEBRATION is one of the best of the English Roses, it is very free flowering and has magnificent flowers, a delicious fragrance and is very free flowering and reliable*

116

plex qualities of beauty and fragrance before all others, at the same time we have tried to encourage beauty and elegance of growth and foliage. Only after these come the very important qualities of disease-resistance, freedom of flowering, hardiness and so on for, essential as these characteristics are, a rose is of little value if it is not beautiful.

The earliest English Roses were nearly always the result of crossing old Gallica Roses with Floribundas and sometimes with Modern Hybrid Teas. Some of my very first hybrids were between the Floribunda 'Dainty Maid' and a Gallica Rose called 'Belle Isis'. The most important result of this cross was the still widely-grown 'Constance Spry', which has magnificent, large, deeply cupped flowers of a lovely shade of soft pink. It was first introduced as a shrub, in which form it easily reaches 2.5m/8ft in height and as much across, often more. Only later did we find that it is even better when grown as a climber. This rose was an immediate success, even though it was only summer flowering.

The rose 'Belle Isis' was, in fact, a short shrub and 'Dainty Maid' was a strong but not very tall Floribunda of excellent constitution and health. Graham Thomas pointed out to me that 'Constance Spry' has a myrrh fragrance, which is very rare among garden roses. He thought that 'Belle Isis' must, itself, have originally been the result of a chance cross between the Ayrshire Rose 'Splendens' and a Centifolia, as 'Splendens' was the only rose he knew that also had a myrrh scent. This would suggest that 'Belle Isis' was not a pure Gallica, in spite of the fact that it had always been regarded as such, and explained the excellent climbing properties of 'Constance Spry'. In any case, 'Constance Spry' was responsible for bringing the lovely myrrh fragrance to English Roses.

'Constance Spry' was then itself back-crossed with other Floribundas and Hybrid Teas and these gradually brought repeat-flowering to the first English Roses, which included 'Canterbury', 'Dame Prudence', 'The Miller', 'The Prioress', 'The Yeoman' and 'Wife of Bath', names all taken from Chaucer's *Canterbury Tales.*

In an attempt to bring dark crimson to our roses, I used the Floribunda 'Dusky Maiden' and crossed this with the beautiful Old Gallica 'Tuscany Superb'. As with 'Constance Spry', the result was a large shrub but with lovely deep crimson, rosette-shaped flowers and a wonderful Old Rose fragrance. I called this rose 'Chianti'. However, unlike 'Constance Spry', it formed a large but neat shrub. Again, we had the problem that 'Chianti' was only early-summer flowering, but further breeding resulted in varieties that did repeat flower, including 'Glastonbury', Othello', 'The Knight', 'The Squire', 'Wenlock' and 'Wise Portia'.

All these early roses had the true Old Rose beauty and a good fragrance. They were, however, on the whole rather weak in growth and not very healthy, in spite of the fact that their original parents were so strong. I therefore looked

*Right, CHIANTI, our first red rose, is early-summer flowering only, but well worth its place in the garden*

*Far right, OTHELLO has very large, deeply cupped blooms with a deep and powerful fragrance*

*CONSTANCE
SPRY was the very
first of the English
Roses, although
not quite typical
in that it does not
repeat flower*

119

*Right,* THE
COUNTRYMAN *is
a very beautiful
and healthy rose
with a particularly
delicious Old Rose
and strawberry
fragrance*

*Far right,*
THE MAYFLOWER
*represents
an important
breakthrough in
English Roses*

around for parents that were both vigorous and healthy and might at the same time be expected to retain the essential Old Rose character. My desire was to produce truly shrubby roses of natural growth although these did not necessarily have to be large in size.

First, we continued to cross our existing English Roses with further Old Roses, but these were usually drawn from the Portland Roses, the Bourbon Roses and the Hybrid Perpetual Roses. These, on the whole, were not quite so beautiful as the original Old Roses—the Gallicas and Damasks—but they did have the advantage that they were, at least in some degree, repeat flowering and like the earlier roses, had a shrubby habit of growth.

As time went by, we moved further afield for our parents, largely with health and vigour in mind. We used a number of roses that had in their ancestry *Rosa rugosa*, which is one of the three wild species that have natural repeat flowering and are also very disease resistant and vigorous. In addition, they have a strong Old Rose fragrance. All these qualities they are able to pass on to their progeny. Not only this, but in spite of the fact that *Rosa rugosa* is somewhat coarse in character, when crossed with existing English Roses, it produces varieties that are of true Old Rose character. The resulting roses are more in the spirit we desired.

There was one further quality I desired in my roses and that was diversity. If we look at the Modern Hybrid Teas, we cannot escape the fact that they are all very much of a kind. The blooms may vary in size and colour, but otherwise they differ only in small details. Since these roses are so widely grown, this seemed unfortunate. The rose is so popular and to see the same type of flower, however beautiful it may be, in every garden can become boring. This, I think, is the problem with Modern Roses; indeed, it is this that had enabled Graham Thomas to make the Old Roses popular once again. To achieve diversity, I decided to bring into my breeding roses of widely differing nature. It is well known that *Rosa wichurana* is a highly disease-resistant rose of great vigour. It gave us many of the best of our Rambler Roses and from these, shorter, repeat-flowering roses which became known as Modern Climbers. From these climbers I chose the variety 'Aloha', which, in fact, is barely a climber at all and more of a large shrub. It does, however, have cupped, rather Old Rose flowers and an excellent fragrance, together with glossy, disease-resistant foliage.

I crossed 'Aloha' with a number of existing English Roses and produced varieties a little closer to the Modern Rose with large, rather polished, dark green foliage, although the flowers were still of Old Rose shape and character. In addition, the seedlings from 'Aloha' came in a variety of colours, including yellow shades—something I very much wished to have. As a result of these crosses, we produced much larger shrubs, with large flowers to match. These included the giant-flowered 'Golden Celebration' and such large shrubs as 'Teasing Georgia'. While these roses had flowers of Old Rose formation and were very fragrant, they were something very different from our original Old Rose Hybrids. They make a very dramatic effect in the garden.

Further extending our search for diversity, we turned our attention to roses of Musk Rose origin or, at least, those that had Musk Rose in their make-up. For this purpose we used the Old Noisette Roses which were good repeaters and had flowers of delicate beauty, often with perfectly formed, rosette-shaped flowers. Their colours included white, soft pink, apricot and peach. Other roses with the Musk Roses in their parentage have also been used. One result is that these roses are nearly always fragrant, although not always with the Musk Rose scent. The reason is that this scent is found in the stamens of the flower rather than the petals and, because these roses are nearly always fully double, there are few stamens and, thus, very little of the Musk fragrance. The foliage and growth of these hybrids is quite distinct from other English Roses. They are usually more upright though not always; the leaves, too, are usually distinctive, being rather smaller than the others with pointed, light green leaflets.

Finally, we have used the Alba Roses. The Albas are a group of roses of great antiquity. They were originally the result of chance crosses between *Rosa canina* (the Dog Rose of our hedgerows) and the Gallica Roses. As might be expected, these roses are very hardy and robust. Crosses made with these roses have brought a whole new dimension to the English Roses. They are, as might be expected, much closer to the wild than our other hybrids. The flowers tend to be rather informal, yet this gives them their own special beauty. Their growth is more natural and tends towards the wild side.

This, then, is a very short survey of the development of the English Roses

to date. It is, of necessity, no more than a sketch; many other crosses having been made with other classes of roses with varying degrees of success. Experimentation, needless to say, continues. Recently, we have used a whole variety of species in our search for disease-resistant roses that would not need to be sprayed with chemicals. The resulting hybrids have shown hope in this direction but, rather surprisingly, they have also yielded some very beautiful roses with pleasing growth and flowers, often quite different in character from our existing varieties. But, of course, all this takes time and developments we are making now may not be seen by the public for a few years yet.

*PRINCESS ALEXANDRA OF KENT has particularly large flowers with a fragrance that changes as the flower ages*

The English Roses differ from other roses in the following respects. They are shrub roses rather than the upright bushes we have become accustomed to in the Hybrid Teas and Flori-bundas which were originally developed to grow in rose beds rather than the garden generally. This does not mean that English Roses are necessarily shrubs of large growth. They may sometimes be shorter than the Hybrid Teas and Flori-bundas, but the difference is that they have full, bushy growth, or arching growth similar to that which we might find in any other garden shrub. However, most of them are rather larger than this—around 1.2m/4ft in height. Others may be still larger—even very large shrubs. So, as you can see, we get a great variety of growth, our idea being that roses should be of natural appearance and able to mix with other plants in the border to good effect. The flowers, too, are of all the different shapes that we find in the Old Roses and many gradations between. Their fragrance is particularly strong and beautiful and varies widely between one variety and another. The num-ber of different fragrances we find in English Roses is far greater than in any other group of whatever age.

*Right,*
*WINDFLOWER*
*is an English*
*Alba Rose hybrid*
*with the almost*
*wild rose growth*
*typical of this*
*group*

As a result of all this diversity, it has become obvious that English Roses need some kind of classification if gardeners are to understand them and be able to choose which variety best suits the situation in which they intend to plant them. Consequently, I have divided them into the following six groups. None of these groups has any particular botanical significance; rather, they are each of them more a collection of roses of like type. This usually means that their foundation parents were also of similar type. I should first, however, warn my reader that these groups are by no means clear-cut, one group inevitably running into the others in some degree. They are as follows: Old Rose Hybrids, The Leander Group, The English Musk Roses and The Alba Rose Hybrids. The Climbing English Roses are discussed in Chapter 7 on Climb-ing Roses (pp. 250–57). The Cut Flowers are included in Chapter 11, Roses in the House (see p. 346).

Here I describe the English Roses that I still consider worth growing in gardens today, bearing in mind that we first introduced them nearly half a century ago and, inevit-ably, many of the earlier introductions have been superseded by superior varieties. These roses were all bred by me at our Nurseries at Albrighton in Shropshire, but I have tried to be as fair in my judgement as possible. On the one hand, I may be a little biased in their favour since they are, so to speak, my 'children', and on the other hand, I probably know them bet-ter than anyone else and, as the breeder, I am or should be their severest critic.

# English Old Rose Hybrids

THE
ENGLISH
ROSES

English
Old Rose
Hybrids

THESE WERE the original English Roses. They have much of the character of the true Old Roses—the Gallicas, Damasks and so on—although they do vary widely between one variety and another. Like the Old Roses, the flowers are not flamboyant but have an unassuming charm; their colours are, in the main, beautiful soft shades of pink, crimson and purple. They usually form small bushy shrubs and repeat flower regularly. They have a strong fragrance, often of the Old Rose type. They are excellent garden roses that mingle well with other plants.

**Barbara Austin** (*Austop*) If you know the excellent 'Gertrude Jekyll', to which this rose is closely related, you will have a fair idea of this variety. It has the same, rather upright growth and Damask Rose foliage. The form of its flowers is similar, but the colour is a very soft pink and the petals have a delicate gossamer texture. It has a particularly good fragrance which can be described as a mixture of Old Rose and lilac. It has one weakness—if weakness it be—and this is that it has a tendency to send up occasional flowerless branches from the base, rather like an Old Rose, in autumn. Such branches will, of course, have flowering shoots in the following year and the shrub will be all the better for it. A very beautiful and very tough rose.

Named after my sister, Barbara Stockitt, formerly Barbara Austin, who is an authority on hardy plants. 1.1 m/3½ft. 1997.

**Brother Cadfael** (*Ausglobe*) This rose bears some of the largest pink blooms to be found among our Old Rose Hybrids. They are deeply cupped with slightly incurved petals, providing an imposing flower which, in spite of its size, is never clumsy. Later in the season, when the plant has to carry more flowers, they may be a little smaller but are no less beautiful. The colour is a soft rose pink. There is a rich Old Rose fragrance. The growth is strong, forming a fine, medium-sized shrub. One or two blooms in a bowl of mixed roses or with other flowers, will make a strong statement. Named after the detective monk in Ellis Peters' novels. 120 × 90cm/4 × 3ft. 1990.

**Charles Rennie Mackintosh** (*Ausren*) Many people dislike the purple and lilac shades in roses, and I would agree with them where some Modern Roses are concerned. They are often altogether too harsh and metallic. I do not feel the same about this rose. It is of a pleasing shade of lilac—a little to the lilac side of lilac-pink. The flower formation is cupped at first, opening to form a nice rosette of medium size. They have a somewhat frilly, feminine appearance that has a definite appeal. They have a light Old Rose fragrance with aspects of almond blossom and lilac. The growth is upright, tough and wiry, with plentiful thorns and dusky foliage. It mixes well with other colours, both in the house and in the garden. Named after the designer, architect and painter. 110 × 90cm/3½ × 3ft. 1988.

**Chianti** (*Auswine*) A tall, broad, well formed shrub that is the result of a cross between a Gallica Rose and a Floribunda Rose. Its flowers are quite large and of fully double rosette shape; their colour a dark crimson, becoming purplish-maroon with age. There is a deep, rich Old Rose fragrance. It will be remembered that this was our first red rose (see p. 118) which was early-summer flowering only. In spite of this, it is well worth its place in the garden. It illustrates well, how, if you are willing to forgo repeat flowering in a rose, it is often possible to have a superb large shrub. This is certainly true of this rose. It will grow into a fine, very large shrub of perfect formation. Although this rose has, to some extent, been overshadowed by the better known 'Constance Spry',

*BARBARA AUSTIN is a very beautiful and very tough rose with a particularly good fragrance— a mixture of Old Rose and lilac*

THE
ENGLISH
ROSES

English
Old Rose
Hybrids

*BROTHER CADFAEL bears some of the largest blooms to be found among the English Old Rose hybrids*

*CHARLES RENNIE MACKINTOSH has cupped flowers that open to form frilly rosettes*

many people think it is rather better as a garden shrub. It was the basis from which most of the red English Roses were developed. It is, itself, quite as good as any Gallica Rose. Named after the Italian wine. Bred by David Austin and introduced jointly by Sunningdale Nurseries and David Austin Roses. 1.8 × 1.5 m / 6 × 5 ft. 1967. (Illustrated, p. 118)

**Constance Spry** (*Ausfirst*) This beautiful rose is to be found in the ancestry of the majority of the English Roses. It has truly magnificent flowers; in fact, they are larger than any Old Rose that I know and yet are never coarse or clumsy and are always in proportion to the shrub. Their colour is a lovely soft pink and they are of full, deep Old Rose formation, the outer petals gradually reflexing. The growth is very strong and it will, if left to its own devices, form a giant, sprawling shrub with large leaves and many thorns. It will require a good deal of space for development, growing to 2m / 7ft in height,

THE
ENGLISH
ROSES

English
Old Rose
Hybrids

*CORVEDALE is a good, trouble-free garden shrub with open, cup-shaped flowers that display long stamens*

with an equal spread and, under good conditions, even more. It is, in fact, somewhat ungainly, and is perhaps better when grown as a Climber (see p. 251), where it will easily achieve 4.5m/15ft or more. However it is grown, it will be a magnificent sight covered with giant blooms.

The flowers have a strong fragrance, which was described by the late Graham Thomas as being similar to that of myrrh. Fragrance is hard to classify, but Graham did go to the trouble of obtaining myrrh in order to make the comparison, and he assured me his description was correct. Before the introduction of the English Roses, myrrh was a rare perfume among roses and its origin is interesting. In Graham Thomas's opinion, the myrrh fragrance originated in the Ayrshire 'Splendens' and it would appear 'Belle Isis' must have had this rose somewhere in its ancestry. It may appear to be an odd combination but, from my experience in crossing very diverse roses, I would say it is entirely possible. Be all this as it may, the particular fragrance has persisted to a remarkable degree through the generations of 'Constance Spry's' progeny. Named after Constance Spry (1886–1960) a leading pioneer of the flower arranging movement. Introduced before David Austin Roses Ltd was formed by Sunningdale Nurseries and Roses & Shrubs Limited of Albrighton. 1961. (Illustrated, p. 119)

**Corvedale** (*Ausnetting*) This is a medium-sized rose of open, cupped shape with four rings of petals. It has clear rose-pink colouring, with long, golden-yellow stamens which add greatly to its beauty. It has a strong and pleasing myrrh fragrance. The blooms are held on a rather lax shrub, which seems to suit them ideally. The whole effect is rather like that of a wild rose. A good, trouble-free garden shrub, best suited to more informal situations. Corvedale is a most beautiful valley running parallel to Wenlock Edge in the depths of the Shropshire countryside. 1.5 × 1.2m/5 × 4ft. 2001.

**Cottage Rose** (*Ausglisten*) This rose might be said to be of the same strain as 'Mary Rose'. Its flowers are similar but perhaps of a more perfect form and a pretty rose pink with just a suggestion of an eye at the centre. It has a delicate Old Rose fragrance with hints of almond and lilac—a scent that is surprisingly diffusive when cut and placed in a warm room, or when grown in a warm climate. Its growth is upright, yet rather twiggy and bushy. Its disease resistance does not quite reach the level we would expect these days, but is easily manageable. 1.1m/3½ft. 1991.

**Darcey Bussell** (*Ausdecorum*) Being rather different in growth from other English Roses, this variety is hard to describe, but I can say that it is rather angular, close, bushy and twiggy. The leaves are small and dark. It will build up into a close, low shrub. The flowers, too, are rather different, with numerous small petals in the form of a very neat rosette. In the earlier stages the outer petals form a perfect ring. Their colour is a deep rich crimson, which takes on a tinge of mauve just before the petals drop. There is a light but pleasing, fruity fragrance with just a hint of green. Though short, this is a vigorous and healthy rose. It is an ideal shrub for the front of the border and for formal rose beds. It also makes a very good pot plant. Named after Darcey Bussell, Principal Ballerina with the Royal Ballet in London, England. 90 × 90cm/3 × 3ft. 2006.

**Eglantyne** (*Ausmak*) I regard this rose as one of the most beautiful of the English Old Rose Hybrids. The flowers are a lovely soft pink and of the most perfect formation, with a button eye at the centre. It is a close relation to 'Mary Rose' which it resembles, although it is a little stronger in growth and probably has a little more refinement.

THE
ENGLISH
ROSES

English
Old Rose
Hybrids

*DARCEY BUSSELL bears blooms of neat rosette formation and is particularly free flowering*

*EGLANTYNE has flowers of perfect formation, with a button eye at the centre*

THE
ENGLISH
ROSES

English
Old Rose
Hybrids

*ENGLAND'S ROSE, a very tough variety with medium sized, strongly fragrant flowers*

With all this, it has a lovely Old Rose fragrance. It is of rather upright growth without being stiff and is of medium vigour. Altogether, a most charming rose. Named after Eglantyne Jebb from Ellesmere in Shropshire, who founded the Save the Children Fund. 90cm/3ft. 1994.

**England's Rose** (*Auslounge*). This is a particularly tough and reliable variety. The deep, glowing pink flowers are held in large clusters, the outer petals eventually reflexing back to reveal an attractive button eye. The blooms are produced almost continuously from June right through to the first frosts. A healthy, particularly rain-resistant rose, it will form an attractive, bushy shrub, ideal for a rose border or for mixing with perennials. There is a fine, strong Old Rose fragrance, with a warm, spicy character. 20 x 90cm/4 x 3ft. 2010.

**Falstaff** (*Ausverse*) This variety produces some of the most magnificent blooms of any that we have bred. The flowers are in the form of a cupped rosette, with numerous twisted petals within. The colour is a deep rich crimson at first, paling a little towards the outer petals— eventually becoming more of a magenta-crimson. There is an excel-

THE
ENGLISH
ROSES

English
Old Rose
Hybrids

*FALSTAFF, one of
the best deep
crimson roses we
have bred, has
an excellent,
fruity, Old Rose
fragrance*

lent, fruity, Old Rose fragrance. The foliage is quite large and tends more towards the Modern Rose than the Old. Altogether, a good and reliable, crimson rose. Named after the character in Shakespeare's *Henry IV*. 1.1 x 1.1 m / 3½ × 3½ft. Rather surprisingly, this rose does well as a climber when planted against a wall (see p. 251). 1999.

**Gentle Hermione** (*Ausrumba*) I think that the outstanding feature of this rose is the perfection of its flowers. Starting as neatly rounded cups filled with petals, they develop into a perfect rosette shape. Their colour is a delicate shade of blush pink, the whole flower having an air of refinement. The growth, however, is strong—rather upright at

THE
ENGLISH
ROSES

English
Old Rose
Hybrids

*GENTLE
HERMIONE
bears perfect
flowers that start
as neatly rounded
cups filled with
petals and
develop into
a rosette*

*GERTRUDE
JEKYLL is a great
favourite, with
large flowers
and one of
the strongest
fragrances of
any rose*

first, gradually fanning out into a broader shrub. It has a powerful fragrance—Old Rose with a strong hint of myrrh. It has typical Old Rose foliage which, like all our more recent roses, is highly disease-resistant. The name is taken from Shakespeare's *The Winter's Tale*. 120 × 90cm/4 × 3ft. 2005.

**Gertrude Jekyll** (*Ausbord*) One of the most popular roses in our collection. The flowers are a lovely warm pink. Starting as pretty little Hybrid Tea-like buds, they develop—almost surprisingly—into well-filled rosettes with the petals spiralling from the centre, often with perfect precision. They are quite large, with the occasional giant bloom on the end of a very strong stem. They have a powerful Old Rose fragrance, such as we would expect from a Damask Rose. In fact, I can think of no other rose with quite so strong a fragrance. Growth tends to be rather upright and not particularly graceful. Gertrude Jekyll, as most of my readers will know, was one of the great influences in English gardening, and was the author of *Roses for English Gardens*. 1.5 × 1.2m/5 × 4ft. Old Rose Hybrid. 1986. (Also illustrated, p. 322)

This rose forms quite a small shrub, but it will climb to about 2.5m/8ft if planted against a wall. (See also p. 251)

**Glamis Castle** (*Auslevel*) This has almost pure white flowers, which is rather rare among garden roses. They are of cupped shape and typical Old Rose character. The growth is short and bushy with numerous twiggy branches, on which it bears flowers with exceptional freedom and continuity—making it ideal for both border and bedding. There is a good English Rose myrrh fragrance. Unfortunately, it does not have quite the disease-resistance we would expect in an English Rose today, but good white roses are scarce and not easy to breed. Certainly, with an occasional spraying, it will perform very well and it is a beautiful rose. Named after the childhood home of the late Queen Elizabeth the Queen Mother and the setting of Shakespeare's *Macbeth*. 90cm/3ft. 1992.

**Harlow Carr** (*Aushouse*) A tough little rose that bears medium-sized flowers of the most perfect formation—shallow cups of the purest rose pink. These hold their form to the end, the occasional petal falling back to give a pleasing effect. There is a strong, pure Old Rose fragrance that has been described as reminiscent of rose-based cosmetics. The plant has an excellent bushy habit, maturing into an attractively rounded shrub with its flowers extending almost to the ground—a characteristic that we particularly favour. The young foliage is bronze at first, later becoming green, the whole plant being of truly 'Old Rose' character. It is very disease-resistant. Harlow Carr, in Yorkshire, where a number of English Roses have been planted, is the most northerly of the Royal Horticultural Society gardens. 120 × 90cm/4 × 3ft. 2004.

**Heather Austin** (*Auscook*) The flowers of this rose have something of the character of an old Bourbon

Rose. They are a strong pink colour and distinctly cupped in shape with incurving petals. If we look inside the cup, we see golden stamens. To complete the picture, there is a strong and delicious Old Rose fragrance. Its growth is of medium height, with the flowers held well above the foliage, which tends towards the Old Rose type. It was named for my sister, now Heather Coulter. 1.2m/4ft. 1996.

**Hyde Hall** (*Ausbosky*) This variety is notable for its ability to flower with exceptional continuity throughout the summer. I know of no other Shrub Rose that can do this to such a degree—it really is quite exceptional in this respect. If lightly pruned, it makes a large shrub, but it can also be pruned to form a smaller shrub. It is tough and disease-resistant. The flowers are of rosette shape and medium size. Though not very showy individually, the flowers do have their own beauty and are produced with quite exceptional freedom. They are of soft pink colouring. Their delightfully warm and fruity fragrance is relatively light. The foliage is not dissimilar to that of a Dog Rose.

'Hyde Hall' is excellent for the back of a border and as a specimen in a lawn. Being particularly tough, reliable and healthy, it also makes a most attractive boundary hedge. Named after Hyde Hall, the Royal Horticultural Society garden in Essex, which includes many English Roses. 1.8 × 1.5m/6 × 5ft. 2004.

**John Clare** (*Auscent*) Few English Roses perform so well as this variety and not many are so beautiful. It bears shallowly cupped flowers that are deep pink. These are produced with great freedom throughout the summer, to be followed with an almost equally good crop in the autumn. The growth is of the type we so much favour—low, arching and broadly spreading. A good all-round rose with one drawback—it has no more than a light fragrance. Named after the

*HARLOW CARR has an excellent bushy habit, maturing into an attractively rounded shrub with flowers extending almost to the ground*

*HEATHER AUSTIN bears cupped, chalice-shaped flowers with something of the character of an old Bourbon Rose*

THE
ENGLISH
ROSES

English
Old Rose
Hybrids

*Above,*
*HYDE HALL*
*forms a very large*
*shrub and flowers*
*with exceptional*
*continuity*
*throughout the*
*summer*

*Right and*
*opposite, top left,*
*JUDE THE*
*OBSCURE is one*
*of only two yellow*
*varieties in this*
*group and has*
*a particularly*
*strong and*
*delicious*
*fragrance*
*reminiscent of*
*guavas and sweet*
*white wine*

rural poet who started life as a farm worker and became the finest nature poet in the English language. 80cm/2½ft. 1994.

**Jude The Obscure** (*Ausjo*) I include this rose with the English Old Rose Hybrids, even though it is of rather different origin. Its flowers are yellow and, of course, we have no yellows in this group other than 'Windrush', which is one of its parents. It bears quite large, deeply cupped flowers with incurved petals, remaining this shape to the end. The colour can be described as rich yellow on the inside of the flower and pale yellow on the outside. There is a strong and unusual fragrance with a fruity note reminiscent of guava and sweet white wine, which delights all who savour her. The growth is strong and upright although bushy, with medium green leaves. Named after the character in Thomas Hardy's novel. 1.1 m/3½ft. 1995.

**Kathryn Morley** (*Ausclub*) This rose can no longer be included among the best of the English Roses, at least from a practical point of view. It does not quite meet our standards as regards resistance to disease—however, it is a most beautiful variety of soft rose-pink colouring and true Old Rose character. The shape is deeply cupped with petals of a delicate, almost gossamer appearance, which I think gives the flower its particular charm. Rather surprisingly, it has a Tea Rose fragrance that I would not expect in such a rose. Named after Mr and Mrs Eric Morley's daughter. 1.4 × 1.1 m/4½ × 3½ft. 1990.

**Lady of Megginch** (*Ausvolume*) With its large, richly coloured flowers, this is a particularly impressive variety. The blooms begin as pretty, rounded buds, gradually opening to form very large, rather informal, full, cupped rosette-shaped flowers with the outer petals recurving slightly. The colour is a very rich, deep pink that fades slightly with age. There is a lovely, fruity Old Rose fragrance with a definite hint of raspberry. This is a very vigorous and health rose which, depending on how hard it is pruned, will grow into a medium or large shrub of rather upright but bushy habit. 120 × 90cm/4 × 3ft. 2006.

THE
ENGLISH
ROSES

English
Old Rose
Hybrids

**Lady Salisbury** (*Auscezed*). This is a variety of great Old Rose charm, with some of the character of the Alba Roses. Rich rose-pink buds open to reveal pure pink flowers, which gradually become a softer shade as the flowers age. The blooms have an informal rosette shape. At first there is a button eye in the centre, but eventually a cluster of stamens is just visible in the middle. There is a light fragrance. 'Lady Salisbury' flowers with remarkable continuity from early summer onwards. The matt green leaves and bushy growth are very much in the style of the Old Roses. This, like many other English Roses, works wonderfully when planted amongst the true Old Roses, having the very great advantage of a much longer flowering season. 'Lady Salisbury' would also be excellent in a mixed border with perennials. We are naming this to celebrate the 400th anniversary of Hatfield House in Hertfordshire, the home of Lady Salisbury. The gardens at Hatfield are very well known and loved, featuring a great many roses. Lady Salisbury is a passionate gardener and will be planting the new rose in the West Garden. 120 x 30cm / 4 x 3ft. 2011.

*Above right,
LADY OF
MEGGINCH
is particularly
impressive, with
large, richly
coloured flowers*

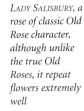

*LADY SALISBURY, a
rose of classic Old
Rose character,
although unlike
the true Old
Roses, it repeat
flowers extremely
well*

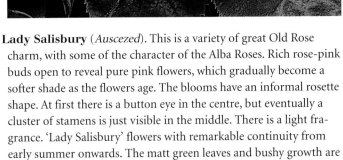

THE
ENGLISH
ROSES

English
Old Rose
Hybrids

*Right,* L. D.
BRAITHWAITE
*bears some of the
brightest crimson
flowers in
the English Roses
and is seldom
out of flower*

*Below right,* MARY
MAGDALENE *is
one of the very
best varieties for
the perfection
and charm of
its flowers*

**L. D. Braithwaite** (*Auscrim*) The English Old Rose Hybrids are
notable for their lovely dusky crimsons. 'L. D. Braithwaite' is of a
brighter shade which is slow to fade and, as such, it has long been a
valuable rose for our collection. The flowers, which are moderately
full-petalled, open wide and slightly cupped. Their scent is not
strong at first but as the flowers mature, they develop a charming
Old Rose fragrance. It forms a low, rather spreading shrub that is
seldom out of flower. Named after my late father-in-law. 120 ×
90cm/4 × 3ft. 1988.

**Mary Magdalene** (*Ausjolly*) This is one of my favourite English
Roses. It does not have quite the health and vigour I would like, but
its flowers have a charm and beauty that it is hard to equal. They are
of a soft apricot pink colour, with delicate silken petals beautifully
arranged around a button eye. These petals are small at the centre,
gradually becoming larger towards the outer edges. It has spreading
growth with matt green, Old Rose leaves. There is a possibility of
mildew in late summer and it may be necessary to spray. It has a
very beautiful Tea Rose fragrance with, rather aptly, just a hint of
myrrh. Named for our local church, St Mary Magdalene,
Albrighton. 90 × 90cm/3 × 3ft. 1998.

**Mary Rose** (*Ausmary*) This rose was introduced at the Chelsea
Flower Show in 1983 and, together, with 'Graham Thomas', received
a lot of attention from the media, which did much to make the
English Roses known to a wider public. It is not at first sight a rose of
startling beauty, but it has a modest Old Rose charm. The flowers are
of medium size, informally cupped, and loosely filled with petals,
their colour a strong rose pink that may be paler in the autumn.
They are only lightly fragrant. 'Mary Rose' forms an excellent little

*Mary Rose in a mass planting showing how the pink of the flowers blends most effectively with the green of its leaves*

shrub with a bushy, branching habit of growth. The foliage is similar to that of an Old Rose. It is quite thorny. When mass planted, the pink of the flowers blends most effectively with the green of its leaves. It is very tough and can be pruned hard or allowed to grow into a larger shrub. It has produced two good sports—'Redouté' which is a softer pink (see p. 138) and 'Winchester Cathedral' (see p. 144) which is white. Named on behalf of The Mary Rose Trust to mark the recovery of Henry VIII's famous flagship from the Solent after more than four hundred years. 1.2 × 1.2m/4 × 4ft. 1983.

**Miss Alice** (*Ausjake*) A charming rose of true Old Rose character. The growth is quite short, but bushy. The flowers are some 8cm/3½in across and a lovely soft pink at first, the outer petals turning to a pale pink which gradually spreads over the whole flower as it ages. An excellent rose for bedding or for a position towards the front of a mixed border. It has a lovely, well rounded Old Rose fragrance, with additional hints of Lily of the Valley. Named after Alice de Rothschild, who created a beautiful garden at Waddesdon Manor, Buckinghamshire. 90 × 60cm/3 × 2ft. 2000.

**Mistress Quickly** (*Ausky*) This variety has something of the character of a Multiflora. It is a tall shrub, bearing small flowers in open sprays. These are semi-double, almost double, and medium pink with the occasional tinge of lilac. They are held well above the foliage, swaying in the wind. The foliage is matt green with small leaflets. This is a very tough variety, which could be grown in groups of three plants under semi-wild conditions to give a pleasing, natural

*Miss Alice is excellent for bedding or for a position towards the front of a mixed border*

THE
ENGLISH
ROSES

English
Old Rose
Hybrids

*Mrs Doreen Pike is Rugosa in appearance although the flowers are of very beautiful Old Rose form*

*Noble Antony is a useful rose for bedding or the front of the border, especially as it has a strong Old Rose fragrance*

*Facing page, Munstead Wood bears flowers that become deep velvety crimson as the centre is revealed*

effect. Named after the good-hearted character in Shakespeare's *Henry V.* 1.2m/4ft. 1995.

**Mrs Doreen Pike** (*Ausdor*) I am never quite sure whether I should place this rose with the Rugosas or with the English Roses. It certainly has some Rugosa in its make-up but it is, in fact, some distance removed from that group. One thing that it does have is the hardiness and disease-resistance of a Rugosa. The flowers are quite small, of rosette shape, medium pink in colour and produced on arching stems. They have a strong Old Rose fragrance. It forms a beautifully shaped, mounded shrub and is pleasing even in spring, when it produces its first leaves. Its great merit is its tough reliability and it can be depended upon to grow even in poor conditions. Doreen Pike was, for a long time, our Office Manageress at David Austin Roses and was a great stalwart in the early years. 120 × 90cm/4 × 3ft. 1993.

**Munstead Wood** (*Ausingrid*) Deep crimson roses are always a welcome addition to our collection. The flowers of this variety are light crimson in the bud but become a very deep velvety crimson as the centre gradually reveals itself, while the outer petals remain lighter in colour. They are of large size and cupped at first, becoming shallowly cupped with time. As the flower ages we get glimpses of the stigma and stamens amongst the petals. The growth is quite bushy, forming a broad shrub with good disease resistance. The leaves are mid-green; the younger leaves being red-bronze to form a nice contrast. There is a strong Old Rose fragrance with a slightly fruity tinge. Our fragrance expert, Robert Calkin, assesses this as 'warm and fruity with blackberry, blueberry and damson'. 90 × 60m/3 × 2½ft. 2007.

**Noble Antony** (*Ausway*) This is a short, bushy rose that can be used for either bedding or at the front of a border. The colour is, I think, best described as a pleasing shade of magenta-crimson. The small incurved buds eventually develop into nicely formed, dome-shaped flowers. They have a lovely rich Old Rose scent, for which this variety was awarded the prize for fragrance at the Glasgow Trials. It has excellent lasting qualities and is ideal for arrangement in the house. Named after Mark Antony in Shakespeare's *Julius Caesar.* 90cm × 75/3 × 2½ft. 1995.

**Othello** (*Auslo*) Very large, deeply cupped, many-petalled dark crimson blooms that turn to shades of purple and mauve. Robust and thorny but somewhat coarse and, therefore, superseded. 1986. (Illustrated, p. 118)

**Peach Blossom** (*Ausblossom*) Here we have a rose of supreme delicacy and refinement. Although the blooms are quite large, they are produced very freely and nicely poised on airy growth. They are of sheeny pink colouring and their massed effect does, to me at least, have a blossom-like quality. A good shrubby rose of 1.2m/4ft in height. 1990.

**Portmeirion** (*Ausgard*) Perhaps the most outstanding virtue of this rose is the nature of its growth, which is in many ways ideal. It grows to about 90cm/3ft in height and is of equal width, with very full growth, so that we get a small mound which flowers almost to the ground.

THE
ENGLISH
ROSES

English
Old Rose
Hybrids

*ROSEMOOR is
a very charming
rose with rosette-
shaped flowers
and a most
delicious
fragrance*

*QUEEN ANNE is a
very versatile
variety, excellent
for both more
formal rose
gardens and
informal borders*

petals only slightly paler than the central ones. In habit 'Queen Anne' is quite upright but still bushy and has few thorns. It could be used very effectively in beds where more formal roses are required, or it would look equally at home in more informal surroundings, whether planted with other roses or mixed in with perennials. The flowers have a good fragrance with hints of pear drop at first, changing to a most attractive, rounded Old Rose scent. The 'Queen Anne' rose has been named to celebrate the tercentenary of Ascot Racecourse. The world's most famous racecourse was founded by Queen Anne in 1711. 4 x 3 ft. 2011.

**Redouté** (*Auspale*) A sport of 'Mary Rose' and similar in every way, except that it is a lovely soft pink (see p. 132 for further details). Named after Pierre Joseph Redouté (1759–1840) the most famous of all rose painters. 1.2m/4ft. 1992.

**Rosemoor** (*Austough*) A particularly charming little rose that bears small, perfectly formed, rosette-shaped flowers that remind one of the old Centifolia Rose 'De Meaux'. The colour is a lovely soft pink, deeper at the centre and lighter towards the edges. As the flower ages it pales a little and reveals a tiny green eye, which provides a most pleasing effect. There is a strong fragrance that seems to suit the character of the flower perfectly. This is basically an Old Rose fragrance, with additional hints of apple, cucumber and violet leaf. 'Rosemoor' is quite upright in growth, yet bushy and it flowers with remarkable freedom and continuity. It is also very disease-resistant. All in all, a rose of true Old Rose character in flower, leaf and growth. It is an ideal rose both for formal and informal settings where its beauty and fragrance can be appreciated to the full. Named after the beautiful Royal Horticultural Society garden in Devon, which has done so much to dispel the idea that roses cannot be grown in the south west of the British Isles. Rosemoor includes many English Roses that grow very well. 120 × 90cm/4 × 3 ft. 2004.

**St. Swithun** (*Auswith*) In common with a number of other English Roses, this variety was first introduced as a shrub but is now more often grown as a climber. Nonetheless, it is still true to say that it is very valuable in both roles. The flowers, which are soft pink in colour, are beautifully formed in an almost perfect flat rosette,

The flowers are of typical Old Rose character and of rich pink colouring; they are rosette in shape with numerous small petals enclosed within two formal rings of larger outer petals. They have a rich Old Rose fragrance. Unfortunately, it has recently shown a tendency to blackspot and may require spraying. Named for Susan Williams-Ellis, who was well known for her beautiful Portmeirion Pottery. She always took great interest in the development of English Roses. 90 × 90cm/3 × 3 ft. 1999.

**Queen Anne** (*Austruck*). This is another rose of classic Old Rose beauty, but rather more in the direction of the Centifolias or Bourbons. The medium-sized flowers are a very pure rose pink, the outer

THE
ENGLISH
ROSES

English
Old Rose
Hybrids

*St. Swithun was first introduced as a shrub but is now more often grown as a climber — valuable in both roles*

THE
ENGLISH
ROSES

English
Old Rose
Hybrids

*SHARIFA ASMA has petals with a translucent quality, and a strong fragrance reminiscent of white grapes and mulberry*

the shape being naturally rounded and unusually full of very small petals. They have a strong myrrh fragrance. The growth is tall yet bushy, with leaves of a greyish-green. It has a good health record. A rose of great charm. Named to commemorate the 900th anniversary of Winchester Cathedral. 1.2–2.5m/4–8ft. 1993.

For information on 'St. Swithun' as a Climber, see p. 255.

**Sharifa Asma** (*Ausreef*) A rose of great delicacy and beauty. The flowers are of slightly incurved rosette formation, soft pink with a touch of gold at the base of the petals, the outer petals paling with

age. These are resistant to rain but damaged by very hot sun. The strong fragrance has fruity notes reminiscent of white grapes and mulberry. All in all, they have a gentle, translucent quality which is most appealing. The growth is upright and bushy. Sharifa Asma is a Princess of the Omani Royal Family. 110 × 80cm/3½ × 2½ft. 1989.

**Sir Walter Raleigh** (*Ausspry*) This is a large and generous rose with flowers rather like those of a tree peony, some 12cm/5in across, not quite fully double, opening wide and slightly cupped, and usually showing their stamens. They are a lovely warm pink and have a strong Old Rose fragrance. The growth is tall and strong and the foliage large, with everything in proportion to the flowers although disease resistance is rather lacking. Named to mark the 400th anniversary of the founding of the first English-speaking colony in America. 1.5 × 1.2m/5 × 4ft.1985.

**Sister Elizabeth** (*Auspalette*) A unique and charming little rose of low, broad growth, which arches and branches freely to form a neat mound. Its flowers are of medium size and of similar character to an old Gallica Rose—perfectly formed rosettes, each with a button eye at the centre. Their colour is rose pink with a distinct lilac tinge. They have a sweet, spicy, Old Rose fragrance. An excellent rose for the front of the border, where it will mingle beautifully with perennials or other plants. It may also be grown as a short, neat hedge within the garden. An ideal subject for growing in containers. Sister Elizabeth is a Cistercian nun from Holy Cross Abbey in

*SISTER ELIZABETH is a little rose of low, broad growth that forms a neat mound and may also be grown as a short, neat hedge within the garden*

THE
ENGLISH
ROSES

English
Old Rose
Hybrids

*Above,* SOPHY'S
ROSE *forms
a shapely shrub
that is ideal
for the front
of a border, or
for growing in
rose beds*

Whitland, South Wales. She is a great rose enthusiast. 80 × 80cm / 2½ × 2½ft. 2006.

**Sophy's Rose** (*Auslot*) The flowers start as pretty cups, opening to form attractive, light red rosettes of medium size with a soft Tea Rose fragrance. It forms a shapely little shrub of healthy, twiggy growth. An ideal plant for the front of a border, or for growing in rose beds especially as it repeat flowers so well. Disease-resistance is good for a red rose. Named on behalf of the Dyslexia Institute after the daughter of its founder, Wendy Fisher. 90 × 80cm / 3 × 2½ ft. 1997.

**Spirit of Freedom** (*Ausbite*) The flowers of this rose start as small, rounded buds which gradually open to form a cupped flower, well filled with numerous small, spiralling petals that are slightly dished towards the centre. The colour is a lovely soft pink which gradually turns to lilac-pink as the flower ages. There is a pleasing fragrance with a hint of myrrh. A rose of charming Old Rose beauty that will form a substantial shrub. It is highly disease-resistant. We were pleased to name this rose for The Freedom Association, which does much good work campaigning for the preservation and extension of freedom. 1.5 × 1.2m / 5 × 4ft. While this rose forms an excellent shrub, it is perhaps even better as a climber, see p. 255. 2002. (Illustrated, overleaf )

**Susan Williams-Ellis** (*Ausquirk*) A delightful, unassuming little rose of typical Old Rose beauty: a pure white sport of 'The Mayflower'. The remarkable thing about these two roses is that, so far as we are aware, they are completely free from disease. Always amongst the first English Roses to flower, in late May or early June at our Shropshire nursery, continuing almost without stop until the harder frosts. It is extremely winter hardy. The fragrance is strong and perfectly Old Rose in character. It is ideal for the border, for hedging or for a container. Susan Williams Ellis founded Portmeirion Pottery, with her husband Euan Cooper-Willis. 120 x 90cm / 4 x 3ft. 2010.

SUSAN WILLIAMS-
ELLIS, *a sport of
The Mayflower
sharing the same
excellent health
and quick repeat
flowering ability*

141

THE
ENGLISH
ROSES

English
Old Rose
Hybrids

*Tess of the d'Urbervilles is very free flowering and is the brightest crimson of the English Roses*

*Facing page, Spirit of Freedom, is a rose of charming Old Rose beauty that will form a substantial shrub*

*The Herbalist was named for its similarity to Rosa gallica var. officinalis although it repeat flowers very well*

**Tess of the d'Urbervilles** (*Ausmove*) The large, fragrant flowers of bright crimson colouring are deeply cupped in the early stages and open to a looser, but still pleasing, shape, the petals turning back with age to look even more informal. The weight of the flowers bows down the branches, giving an elegant effect. The growth is robust, bushy and spreading and the foliage large and of a dark green. It will also form a good short climber. Named after the well-known character in Thomas Hardy's novel. 120 × 120cm / 4 × 4ft. 1998. (Illustrated in close up, p. 255)

**The Countryman** (*Ausman*) Like 'Gertrude Jekyll', this is a cross between an English Rose and a Portland rose and it may be helpful

to refer back to my remarks on 'Gertrude Jekyll'. The flowers are quite large, loosely double rosettes, deep pink in colour, with an exceptionally fruity Old Rose fragrance. For me, they have something of the spirit of the peonies we see in Chinese and Japanese paintings, both in character and the way in which they grow on the plant, although they are, in reality, much smaller. The leaves have something of the character of a Portland Rose, quite large with well spaced leaflets, and exceptionally healthy. It is important to remove the dead flowers to encourage quick new growth, and we can then expect two good periods of flower, although there will only be occasional blooms in between. 1987. (Illustrated, p. 120)

**The Dark Lady** (*Ausbloom*) A dark crimson rose with large, rather loosely formed, wide open flowers of rosette shape. These have a rather special character which reminds me of the flowers of a tree peony. They have a true Old Rose fragrance. They are held on a rounded, bushy shrub. Useful as a crimson rose that is particularly happy in warmer climates. In Britain it has a slight tendency to blackspot. It does very well in the southern states of the USA, where it has no disease and is remarkably resistant to red spider. The name is taken from the 'dark lady' of Shakespeare's sonnets. 1.1 m / 3½ft. 1991.

**The Herbalist** (*Aussemi*) This variety wanamed for its similarity to *Rosa gallica* var. *officinalis*, better known as the Apothecary's Rose, the great difference being that 'The Herbalist' is repeat flowering. It has the same simple beauty. It is a semi-double rose that opens wide and flat, exposing a large bunch of golden stamens. I would describe the colour of the flower as light crimson, varying to dark pink. It is a strong and reliable rose of bushy habit and typical Old Rose character. It is an ideal border plant. There is a light fragrance. 90 × 90cm / 3 × 3ft. 1991.

**The Mayflower** (*Austilly*) This rose represents an important breakthrough in English Roses: it is, we believe, virtually free of disease. Even when it gets the odd touch of blackspot, it seems to have the ability to kill this off at an early stage. Unfortunately, in warmer parts of the world it has a tendency to suffer from red spider, although this is not a problem in Britain. You never quite win them all! It is the first of the English Roses to start flowering and continues with great regularity through to the autumn. The flowers have a typical Old Rose charm and are of medium size, rosette-shaped, with a strong Old Rose fragrance. The growth is full, bushy and rather upright, with numerous twiggy branches and quite small, matt green foliage, which is also of Old Rose appearance. This is a very useful rose in the garden, where it can be placed towards the front of the border. It is very tough and hardy. I have seen 'The Mayflower' looking very pleasing in north Shropshire. We named this rose to mark the launch of our American branch at Tyler in Texas. 120 × 90cm / 4 × 3ft. 2001. (Illustrated, p. 120)

**Trevor Griffiths** (*Ausold*) Like 'The Countryman' and 'Barbara Austin', this rose has a strong streak of the old Portland Rose in its breeding. All three roses have foliage and growth that leans heavily towards the Old Roses in character. They also all have a wonderful Old Rose fragrance which, in this particular variety, has been described as reminiscent of old claret. The blooms are of beautiful formation, opening as perfect, flat, well-filled rosettes that are deep pink, paling a little towards the edges. Its disease-resistance leaves a little to be desired, but no more than we would find in an Old Rose —and it can be controlled by an occasional spraying. Named after Trevor Griffiths, the well-known New Zealand rose grower, who has done so much to introduce Old Roses to that country and is also the author of a number of beautiful books. 110 × 90cm / 3½ × 3ft. 1994.

THE
ENGLISH
ROSES

English
Old Rose
Hybrids

*Above,* WILLIAM
SHAKESPEARE
*2000, has deep
crimson flowers
and a strong
fragrance to
match*

**Wild Edric** (*Aushedge*) This is an unusually tough and reliable rose that will thrive even under difficult conditions and is not only suitable for the border but also useful for semi-wild planting or for hedges. It has quite a lot of *Rosa rugosa* in its breeding and this makes it not quite a typical English Rose. The flowers are large, semi-double and substantial. They are held in close clusters, each bloom opening in succession. Their colour is deep pink with a purple tinge at first, becoming pale pink. They have a bunch of contrasting golden stamens. The fragrance is strong and delicious, but interestingly, with a little investigation, a marked difference between the fragrance of the petals and the stamens can be detected. The scent of the stamens is pure clove, whereas that of the petals is classic Old Rose with hints of watercress and cucumber. This is a very tough and reliable rose that will grow well even under poor conditions. Wild Edric was a Saxon Lord in Shropshire, who was said to have married a fairy queen. He reproached her one day and she disappeared. Legend has it that his ghost is still to be seen

searching for her in the hills. 1.2 × 1.2m/4 × 4ft. 2005.

**William Shakespeare 2000** (*Ausromeo*) This English Rose bears superb blooms of a deep, rich velvety crimson that gradually turns into an equally rich purple. The flowers are cupped at first, eventually opening to a shallow cup with nicely quartered petals. They are of strongly Old Rose character and are set against typical Old Rose foliage. To complement these characteristics, they have the strong, warm Old Rose fragrance that we expect—but do not always find—in roses of this colour. The growth is strong, bushy and attractively spreading in habit. It has good disease-resistance, particularly for a red rose. There is a large bed of 'William Shakespeare' roses and a mixed border of English and other roses at Shakespeare's birthplace in Stratford-upon-Avon, Warwickshire. 110 × 80cm/3½ × 2½ft. 2000.

**Winchester Cathedral** (*Auscat*) A sport of 'Mary Rose' and similar in every way, except that it has flowers of pure white; a fact that makes it most valuable since there are at present very few white-flowered varieties among the English Roses. Named in aid of The Winchester Cathedral Trust. 1.2 × 1.2m/4 × 4ft. 1998.

**Windrush** (*Ausrush*) Not quite a typical English Old Rose Hybrid in character, but this variety represents a first attempt to bring yellow to these roses. The flowers are large, semi-double and of soft yellow colouring, with plentiful dark yellow stamens. There is a light, spicy Musk fragrance. The growth is strong and bushy and the foliage has something of the Old Rose character. There is a tendency to produce fine large hips which, though beautiful, tend to curb future flowering. These can be removed if you require a better crop of later flowers. Named after the river in southern England. 1.2 × 1.2m/4 × 4ft. 1984.

**Young Lycidas** (*Ausvibrant*).The flowers of 'Young Lycidas' are quite large and deeply cupped even when fully open. Their colour is new to English Roses: a blend of very deep magenta, pink and red – the outer petals tending towards light purple, in contrast to the outside of the petals, which are quite silvery in appearance. It makes an attractive, bushy shrub There is a delicious fragrance that starts as a pure Tea scent, changing to a blend of Tea and Old Rose, with intriguing hints of cedar wood. Awarded first prize for fragrance at the Barcelona Trials in 2009. 1.2 x 0.9m/4 x 3ft. 2008.

WILD EDRIC *is
an unusually
tough and reliable
rose, suitable for
the border, semi-
wild planting
and hedges*

*Far right,* YOUNG
LYCIDAS, *a rose of
quite different
character. The
blooms have a
very distinctive
colour and are
strongly fragrant*

# The Leander Group

The Leander group of English Roses is the result of once again crossing varieties of our Old Rose Hybrids with more modern varieties, often with *Rosa wichurana* in their make-up. The result is that we have a group of English Roses that lean a little more towards the Modern Rose, while their flowers are still of typical Old Rose formation. They usually form large, robust shrubs with elegantly arching growth. The flowers are often large and gracefully poised on the branch, providing a most pleasing effect. The colours are wide-ranging, including many rich yellows, apricots and some flame shades. Their fragrance is strong and varied—sometimes of the Old Rose type, sometimes Tea Rose or myrrh. These scents are frequently mixed with fruity undertones such as raspberry, lemon or apple.

---

**A Shropshire Lad** (*Ausled*) This rose is most often grown as a climber (see p. 251) but it is also very good when grown as a large shrub placed well back in the border. Its flowers are soft peachy pink and slightly cupped at first; becoming rosette-shaped—the petals turning back at the edges. They have a delicious Tea Rose fragrance. The foliage is large, of typical modern Leander character and very healthy. 1.8 × 1.5 m / 6 × 5 ft. This rose is equally good when grown as a climber, when it will cover a large area and reach a height of 2.5 m / 8 ft or more. We have a particularly fine example of it growing on an arch (see p. 250). The name comes from A. E. Housman's 'A Shropshire Lad'. 1996.

**Abraham Darby** (*Auscot*) This variety is unusual among English Roses in that it is the result of a cross between two roses that bear flowers similar to those of an Old Rose but are nevertheless Modern: the Floribunda 'Yellow Cushion' and 'Aloha', a Modern Climber. 'Abraham Darby' is very much a Shrub Rose, forming a large bush with long, arching growth and large, glossy leaves. The flowers, in spite of the parentage, are of truly Old Rose formation: large, deeply cupped and loosely filled with petals. The colour is soft peachy pink on the inside of the petals and a pale yellow on the outside. The centre petals fold and turn inwards to give a mixture of yellow and pink. All these colours fade towards the edge of the flower as it ages, providing a soft and pleasing effect. There is a delicious, strong and fruity fragrance with a raspberry sharpness. It is hardy, disease resistant and recurrent flowering. 1.5 × 1.5 m / 5 × 5 ft. 1985.

**Alan Titchmarsh** (*Ausjive*) We are always looking for better varieties with flowers of a deeply cupped shape. In 'Alan Titchmarsh' we have a prime example of such a rose. The blooms are indeed of deeply

*Far left,*
*ABRAHAM*
*DARBY has large,*
*deeply cupped*
*flowers and forms*
*a large bush with*
*long, arching*
*growth*

*Left,*
*A SHROPSHIRE*
*LAD bears rosette-*
*shaped blooms,*
*the petals turning*
*back at the edges*

*ALAN*
*TITCHMARSH,*
*bears deeply*
*cupped flowers*
*that, despite their*
*size and opulence,*
*look completely*
*'right' on the bush*

*AMBRIDGE*
*ROSE is a good*
*all-round garden*
*rose that flowers*
*very freely and*
*continuously*

cupped form, tending to incurve a little even when fully open, with numerous small, similarly incurved petals in the centre—their colour a deep pink, slightly paler on the outer petals—and they are displayed slightly nodding on a well rounded yet nicely arching shrub. They have a strong Old Rose fragrance with a hint of myrrh. Despite their size and opulence, they look completely 'right' on the bush. I know of no other rose about which I could say this with such conviction. It has dark green, typically Leander foliage. Named after the well-known television horticulturist, who has been an inspiration to gardeners over many years. 120 × 90cm/4 × 3ft. 2005.

**Ambridge Rose** (*Auswonder*) This is a good all-round garden rose. It flowers very freely and continuously, has bushy, rather upright growth and can equally well be used for a border as for a rose bed. The flowers are of medium size, nicely cupped at first, opening to a loose rosette formation; their colour is deep apricot at the centre, paling to the outer edges of the flower. The fragrance is pure myrrh and very strong. A particularly useful variety in warmer climates. Named at the request of the BBC for their long-running *The Archers* serial. 110 × 60cm/3½ × 2ft. 1990.

**Benjamin Britten** (*Ausencart*) The unusual feature of this rose is its colour, which I find almost impossible to describe. The best I can say is that it is as though you had mixed scarlet paint with a little orange. However you describe it, it is, I think, a beautiful and very lively colour that is never loud and is ideal for mixing with other English Rose colours, both in the garden and in a bowl of cut roses. The flower starts as a cup, soon opening to form a cupped rosette. The fragrance is intensely fruity, with aspects of wine and pear drops. The growth is strong and rather upright, bearing its flowers mainly at the top. Named to commemorate the life and work of the famous English composer, conductor and performer. 120 × 90cm/4 × 3ft. 2001.

**Charles Austin** (*Ausfather*) A strong, upright shrub with large, shiny modern foliage and bearing exceptionally large, full-petalled flowers of an apricot-yellow colouring paling with age and becoming very slightly tinged with pink. Strong, fruity fragrance. Although it does not repeat continuously, it can be relied on to provide a second crop in the autumn. It is perhaps a little coarse when put alongside our more recent productions, but can be impressive towards the back of a border, where it will grow much taller if lightly pruned. For other positions it is better cut down to half its height if it is not to become ungainly. Named after my father. Height 1.2–1.8m/4–6ft. 1973. 'Yellow Charles Austin' is a sport of this variety which is similar in every way except for colour, see p. 159.

**Charles Darwin** (*Auspeet*) The flowers of this variety are some of the largest among English Roses. While we would not want all roses to be of such a size, it is good to have some to use where a really bold effect is required. The blooms are full and deeply cupped at first, but open to a rather shallower flower, usually revealing a button eye. There is a strong and delicious fragrance which varies, according to weather conditions, between a soft floral Tea Rose and almost pure lemon. The colour could be described as yellow, tending towards mustard. All in all, this is an impressive and eye-catching shrub with broad, spreading growth, the flowers facing upwards on the ends of long stems. Vigorous and disease-resistant. Named after the scientist whose revolutionary work on evolution changed the course of history. He was born in Shrewsbury, Shropshire, not far from our Nursery. 1.2 × 1.1m/4 × 3½ft. 2003.

**Christopher Marlowe** (*Ausjump*) A new shade among English Roses—intense orange-red, paling a little as the flower ages—that is

not usually associated with English Roses, but we need all colours to fulfil the various requirements of the garden colour scheme. 'Christopher Marlowe' is useful where a bright splash of red is required. The flowers are rosette-shaped; the outer petals reflexing a little and paling slightly with age. They have a pleasing Tea Rose fragrance with a hint of lemon. The growth is short but very vigorous, with numerous stems arising from the base and later branching to give a continuous flow of flowers. The overall effect is that of a nicely rounded shrub. It is a very healthy rose. Christopher Marlowe, the well known playwright and contemporary of William Shakespeare, is said to have pressed a rose bud in a book, as a mark of friendship to someone with whom he had had an argument. 90 × 90cm / 3 × 3 ft. 2002.

**Crown Princess Margareta** (*Auswinter*)
The colour of this variety may be described as bright apricot-orange, which is a lovely shade that shows up across the garden, and this rose is certainly one of the finest in this range of colours. The flowers are quite large and of rosette shape. The plant is tall, vigorous and slightly arching—typical of the group—with ample dark green foliage. It will thrive even under more difficult conditions. There is a strong, fruity fragrance of the Tea Rose type. Crown Princess Margareta of Sweden was a granddaughter of Queen Victoria and an accomplished landscape gardener. 1.5 × 1.4m / 5 × 4½ft. This variety is even more beautiful when grown as a climber on a wall (see p. 251). 1999.

*Top left, BENJAMIN BRITTEN is a very lively colour that is never loud and is ideal for mixing with other English Rose colours*

*Top centre, CHRISTOPHER MARLOWE makes a bright splash of orange-red, the blooms borne with excellent continuity*

*Top right, CROWN PRINCESS MARGARETA has tall, vigorous, slightly arching growth and thrives even under difficult conditions*

*Left, CHARLES DARWIN bears flowers that face upwards and are some of the largest among English Roses*

147

*FIGHTING TEMERAIRE, with its large single blooms, is very different to most other English Roses, excellent for adding some variety to a border*

*GRACE has numerous unusually narrow petals that give the flower a very different appearance*

**Cymbeline** Large flowers of 10cm/4in or more across, opening flat and loosely filled with petals. The colouring is most unusual, a greyish almost ashen pink with tinges of brown. Although this may not please everyone, I find it beautiful and think it could be useful in garden colour schemes. The growth arches to the ground in an elegant manner showing the flowers to maximum effect, although black spot can be a problem. It is truly recurrent flowering and has a strong fragrance of myrrh. Height 1.2m/4ft. 1982.

**Fighting Temeraire** (*Austrava*). This variety is of very different character to most English Roses, making a beautiful and very useful addition to the collection. The fully open flowers are very large (10–12cm/4–5ins across), have only ten petals, and are produced with exceptional freedom. They are a rich apricot colour, with an area of yellow behind the stamens. By the time the petals are ready to drop, the colour has faded to a soft yellow-apricot. The tips of the pointed buds are red, as is the young foliage, further enhancing the effect. 'Fighting Temeraire' is particularly healthy and vigorous and will develop into a most attractive rounded shrub, the many stems producing a mass of flowers held in large heads. The fragrance is medium to strong, very fruity with a strong element of lemon zest. This is a very good choice for a mixed border, where the rich colour will create a focal point. We anticipate that it may also be suitable for growing as a climber. 'Fighting Temeraire' is a painting from 1839 by the famous landscape painter, watercolourist and printmaker, JMW Turner. This rose has been named for the Turner Contemporary Gallery on the seafront at Margate in Kent. 1.5 x 1.5m / 5 x 5ft or up to 2.5m/8ft as a climber. 2011.

**Geoff Hamilton** (*Ausham*) This variety has lovely soft pink flowers that pale towards the outer petals. Starting as a very full, cupped shape, they gradually evolve into a full-petalled rosette formation. They have an Old Rose scent with just a hint of apple. 'Geoff Hamilton' will grow into a medium sized shrub suitable for the front of the border or in more formal settings. The foliage is typically 'Leander', glossy and disease-resistant. A beautiful and very practical rose that combines delicacy and refinement with exceptional vigour and health. Named after the well-known and much-loved television gardener. 1.5 × 1.2m/5 × 4ft. 1997.

*GEOFF
HAMILTON forms
a vigorous and
healthy shrub
bearing plentiful
blooms and with
glossy and
disease-
resistant foliage,
seen here with
false mallow
(Sidalcea)*

149

Above,
JAMES GALWAY,
a superb, large
shrub with long,
slightly arching,
almost thornless
growth and neat,
domed flowers

Right, JANET
has long, elegant,
typical Hybrid
Tea buds which
open gradually to
become shapely
rosettes

**Golden Celebration** (*Ausgold*) I have always taken the view that sheer size of bloom is no great virtue in a rose, yet this is one of the largest-flowered of the English Roses. They are in the form of magnificent golden cups which hold their shape to the end. In spite of their size, they are never ungainly. I think this is because they are so gracefully held, slightly nodding, on long, arching branches. They have a strong Tea scent at first, later developing hints of Sauternes wine and strawberry. The shrub itself is quite big and is of a suitable size for the flower. Later in the season, we can expect a larger crop of flowers but these will be rather smaller and not quite so deeply cupped. The foliage is large, glossy, light green and resistant to disease. 1.2 × 1.2m/4 × 4ft. 1992. It will also make a superb climber to 2-2.5m / 6-8ft. (Illustrated in close up, p. 117)

**Grace** (*Auskeppy*) A rose with a strong individuality due, I think, to its unusually narrow petals that give the flower a very different appearance. These petals are numerous and gradually turn back to form a large, domed rosette with the hint of a button eye. Their colour is a lovely shade of apricot—deeper in the centre—and fading almost to white at the edges. All this provides us with flowers that are both charming and elegant. There is a delicious warm and sensuous fragrance. The blooms are held on an excellent shrub of rather broad, arching growth. It is vigorous, healthy and repeat flowers well. In every way, an excellent garden plant. 1.2 × 1.2m/4 × 4ft. 2001.

**James Galway** (*Auscrystal*) A superb, large shrub with long, slightly arching, almost thornless growth—typical of our Leander group. This is a tough, disease-free rose that is excellent for the back of a mixed border. The flowers are quite large and very full, with many petals arranged in a neat formation, the petals eventually turning back so that the rose becomes almost ball-like. The colour is a lovely warm pink at the centre, shading to pale pink at the edges. There is a delicious Old Rose fragrance. If not dead headed it will produce a magnificent crop of large red hips that last well into the winter. Named in celebration of the 60th birthday of James Galway, the world-famous flautist. 1.4 × 1.1m/4½ × 3½ft. 2000. An excellent shrub rose and equally good as a climber (see p. 251).

**Janet** (*Auspishus*) For many years we have been breeding roses with open flowers of the Old Rose type. Some people may be a little surprised to find that in 'Janet' we return to a flower of the Hybrid Tea type. The difference is that whereas the Hybrid Teas are beautiful in the bud, they tend to lack form in the later stages. 'Janet' has long, elegant, typical Hybrid Tea buds which open gradually to become shapely rosettes, so that we get the benefit of both types of flower in one rose.

*GOLDEN
CELEBRATION
is an excellent
all-round variety,
ideal with other
shrubs in a border,
here with* Achillea
millefolium
*'Fanal'*

*LADY OF SHALOTT*
*is an outstanding*
*variety especially*
*in terms of its*
*ability to flower*
*freely and its*
*general toughness*
*and reliability*

*Facing page,*
*JUBILEE*
*CELEBRATION*
*bears large,*
*impressive, dome-*
*shaped flowers. It*
*is healthy and*
*reliable. Shown*
*here with an*
*Astilbe*

The colour in the bud is a delightful mixture of pale and deep pinks flushed with copper, the underside of the petals being soft yellow. As it opens into a rosette shape, the flower becomes a deep glowing pink, paling a little towards the outside of the petals. Another equally important difference is that 'Janet' is not a short bush as we would expect with a Hybrid Tea, but a shrub with long, arching growth that holds its flowers beautifully—each bud hanging elegantly towards us on a long stem. There is a lovely, strong pure Tea Rose fragrance. Named for Janet, in her memory, who had a life-long love of roses. 1.2 × 1.1 m/4 × 3½ft. It forms a good climber of some 2.5m/8ft. 2003.

**Jubilee Celebration** (*Aushunter*) We were very pleased to name this rose in commemoration of the Queen's Golden Jubilee in 2002. It is a large, impressive flower, of domed shape and of a lovely rich salmon pink tinted with gold on the underside of the petals, the blooms being held well above its lush foliage. Despite the size of the flowers, they are produced with exceptional freedom and continuity. The growth is vigorous, building up into a fine large shrub. There is a deliciously fruity rose scent with hints of fresh lemon and raspberry. It is very healthy. Altogether, a most impressive rose. 1.2 × 1.2m/4 × 4ft. 2002.

**Lady of Shalott** (*Ausnyson*). This is one of the toughest and most reliable roses in our collection. It is highly resistant to disease and will bloom with unusual continuity throughout the season. The young, rich orange-red buds open to form chalice-shaped blooms,

filled with loosely-arranged petals. Each petal has a salmon pink upper side which contrasts beautifully with the golden-yellow reverse. There is a pleasant, warm, tea fragrance, with hints of spiced apple and cloves. It quickly forms a large, bushy shrub with slightly arching stems, ideal for rose beds and mixed borders. The mid-green leaves have attractive, slightly bronzed tones when young. It was named to celebrate the 200th anniversary of the birth of Alfred, Lord Tennyson. 1.2 x 1.0m / 4 x 3½ft. 2009.

**Leander** (*Auslea*) The variety that gave its name to this group of roses is no longer one of the most beautiful but it is certainly one of the toughest and most reliable, and will thrive even under difficult conditions. Its deep apricot flowers are small to medium in size, rosette-shaped and tightly packed with petals. They are held in small sprays. The foliage is shiny, disease-resistant and of modern appearance. There is a delightful raspberry scent in the Tea Rose tradition. 7 × 5ft/2.1 × 1.5m. Named after the legendary Greek lover. It also forms a good climber. (see p. 251).

**Lilian Austin** (*Ausmound*) A first-class small garden shrub of an excellent, spreading, bushy habit and one which looks very much in place with other plants in the border. The flowers are semi-double, at times almost double, opening wide to show their stamens, while their petals are slightly waved. The colour is a strong salmon-pink, shading to yellow at the centre. 'Lilian Austin' is hardy, disease-resistant and reliably repeat flowering and it has a good fragrance. Named after my mother. 120 × 90cm/4 × 3ft. 1973.

**Morning Mist** (*Ausfire*) Being a large and vigorous, single-flowered shrub, this variety is ideal for a place at the back of the border where its flowers can be clearly seen well above other subjects to pleasing effect. The colour is deep pink at first, opening to a bright salmon pink with yellow at the centre. There is a large boss of red stamens with golden anthers. The fragrance is light and a mixture of musk and cloves. If not dead headed it produces a superb crop of very large hips that last well through the winter. The growth is very strong and extremely healthy, with foliage of a rather modern appearance. 1.4m/4½ft. 1996.

**Pat Austin** (*Ausmum*) If you are one of those rose lovers who prefer pinks, blushes and reds in English and Old Roses, then it is worthwhile thinking again as regards this rose. Although the colour can only be described as a brilliant shade of copper, it is in no way gaudy. Perhaps this is because the inside of the petals is copper, while the outside is a coppery-yellow. Light shining through the petals creates a soft glow that is quite entrancing. The flower is large, well-rounded and loosely-petalled, providing an effect that is different from that of any other English Rose. This illustrates very well the great and seemingly endless form of which the rose is capable. The scent has been described as a strong Tea Rose fragrance with a warm, sensuous background. The shrub is tall and slightly arching, with the flowers held elegantly on the branch. The foliage is dark and of the kind we expect from a Leander rose. This beautiful rose is named after my wife. 1.2m/4ft. 1995.

**Princess Alexandra of Kent** (*Ausmerchant*) We are very honoured to name this rose for Princess Alexandra, who is a cousin to Queen Elizabeth II and also a keen gardener and great lover of roses. The rose that bears her name has unusually large flowers of a warm, glowing pink. They are full-petalled and deeply cupped in shape, all enclosed in a ring of outer petals of a softer pink, creating a most pleasing effect. In spite of their size, they are never clumsy; being held nicely poised on a well-rounded shrub. Because of their size, there is a lot to be said for planting in groups of three, keeping both flowers and growth nicely balanced. They have a delicious fresh Tea fragrance which, interestingly, changes completely to lemon as the flower ages—eventually taking on additional hints of blackcurrants. 110 × 80cm/3½ × 2½ft. 2007. (Illustrated, p. 121 )

**St. Alban** (*Auschestnut*) The flowers start as globular buds which gradually open up to an attractive shallow cup filled with numerous petals. The colour starts as a rich yellow, gradually tending towards a softer yellow. It has a pleasing fresh scent that is hard to define but has been described as similar to the fragrance we experience when we walk into a florist's shop. This is not a very formal flower—just a pretty arrangement of petals. The growth is of the kind we so much favour in the Leander group—a strong shrub, holding its numerous flowers nicely on arching branches. We named this rose in honour of the Royal National Rose Society, founded in 1876 and the first Society of its kind. Over the years, it has been at the centre of all matters to do with roses and has done much good work. 1.2 × 1.1 m/4 × 3½ft. 2003.

*Above,*
*Morning Mist*
*is ideal for a place*
*at the back of the*
*border where its*
*single flowers*
*can be clearly*
*seen above other*
*subjects*

*Left, St. Alban*
*is a beautiful rose*
*at all stages, from*
*globular bud to*
*shallow cup filled*
*with numerous*
*petals*

*Facing page,*
*Pat Austin,*
*a brilliant shade*
*of copper, but in*
*no way gaudy,*
*illustrates the*
*seemingly endless*
*variety of form*
*of which the rose*
*is capable. The*
*catmint, Nepeta*
*'Six Hills Giant',*
*provides good*
*contrast*

**St. Cecilia** (*Ausmit*) This variety bears medium-sized flowers of distinctly cupped, incurved formation and pale buff-apricot colouring, which can vary a little according to the season. These are held well apart in open sprays, nodding nicely on the stem. They have a strong and unusual fragrance of English Rose myrrh character, with hints of lemon and almond blossom. The growth is quite short and rather upright, making this an excellent rose for a small garden. St. Cecilia is the patron saint of music and musicians. 90 × 80cm/3 × 2½ft. 1987.

**Strawberry Hill** (*Ausrimini*) This rose bears medium to large size, pure rose pink, cupped rosettes of superb quality, the colour gradually paling to a lighter pink at the edges, eventually exposing a few yellow stamens at the centre—beautiful at all stages. It has a particularly fine myrrh fragrance with a hint of lemon. Its growth is tall, vigorous and rather informal. It is slightly arching, with very healthy and glossy, dark green leaves. This is a very good choice for a mixed border or for a border of shrub roses. It will thrive in less than ideal conditions. We expect it to be a good climber. Strawberry Hill is a beautiful house at Twickenham, built for Horace Walpole. 1.2 × 1.2m/4 × 4ft. 2006.

**Summer Song** (*Austango*) A rose of a lovely shade of burnt orange; such colours are not easy to come by and 'Summer Song' is therefore a valuable addition to our collection. The flowers start as rounded buds, opening to full cups with small glowing petals, arranged rather informally within a perfect ring of outer petals. They have a strong mixed scent, which our fragrance expert tells us 'like walking into a florist's shop: hints of chrysanthemum leaves, ripe banana and tea'. It forms a bushy, upright shrub. 120 × 90cm/4 × 3ft. 2005.

*St. Cecilia, being quite short and rather upright, makes an excellent rose for a small garden*

*Strawberry Hill is tall and vigorous—a very good choice for a mixed border or for a border of shrub roses*

*SUMMER SONG*
*is a lovely shade*
*of burnt orange*
*with a strong*
*mixed scent and*
*forms a bushy,*
*upright shrub*

Above and right,
TEASING GEORGIA
bears flowers of
a crisp, cupped
rosette formation;
growth is tall and
strong, without
being stiff, making
this rose ideal for a
mixed border or for
combining with
other shrub roses

**Teasing Georgia** (*Ausbaker*) One of the best and most beautiful members of the Leander group, the growth of 'Teasing Georgia' is tall and strong, without being stiff. Its plentiful foliage is dark, glossy and disease-resistant. The flowers are of a particularly attractive formation: a crisp, cupped rosette. The colour is a rich, glowing yellow. They are held elegantly upon the branch and have a particularly fine Tea Rose fragrance. A refined and beautiful rose. Named for Ulrich Meyer, after his wife Georgia, both of whom are well-known media personalities in Germany. 90 × 110cm/3 × 3½ft. It also makes an excellent climber of some 1.8–2.5m/6–8ft in height (see p. 255). 1998.

**The Alnwick Rose** (*Ausgrab*) This is an upright shrub that is quite broad in growth and exceptionally vigorous, with plentiful, glossy, disease-free foliage. The flowers are a glowing medium pink, the colour deepening towards the centre and attractively cupped with numerous small petals within; the pistils provide a small yellow eye at the centre. There is a lovely Old Rose fragrance with just a hint of raspberry. If you want a good, reliable shrub of the Leander Group, it would be hard to beat this rose. We named it for the Duke and Duchess of Northumberland, who have made a magnificent 5 hectare/12 acre garden at Alnwick Castle in Northumberland with a very large rose garden that includes many of our English Roses. 120 × 80cm/4 × 2½ft. 2001.

**The Ingenious Mr Fairchild** (*Austijus*) We are always keen to develop large, peony-like roses with good shrubby growth. 'Golden Celebration' and 'Brother Cadfael' are good examples of such roses —and this is another. The flowers of 'The Ingenious Mr Fairchild' are in the form of deep cups filled with crisp, upstanding petals. The

*THE ALNWICK ROSE bears deeply cupped blooms that open to reveal crinkled petals, born on an upright shrub that is vigorous and quite broad in growth*

colour on the inside of the petals is a deep pink touched with lilac; the outside is of a paler shade. Looking at the bloom in more detail, one can see that the edges are an even deeper pink, giving a most delightful fringed effect—particularly in the earlier stages. It has a strong and deliciously fruity rose fragrance, with aspects of raspberry, peach and a hint of mint. The growth is spreading, with arching branches that build up into a well-rounded, mounding shrub, with its flowers nicely poised. It is very healthy. Named after Thomas Fairchild, a nurseryman of London and Fellow of the Royal Society, who made the first recorded flower hybrid in Europe in 1720. This was a cross between a Sweet William and a carnation, which became known as 'Fairchild's Mule'. We have to thank Michael Leapman for the name, which was the title of his biography of Thomas Fairchild. 1.2 × 1.1m/4 × 3½ft. 2003.

**William Morris** (*Austir*) A tall shrub with attractive, rather arching growth and glossy foliage. The flowers are a lovely glowing apricot pink and of formal rosette shape. It is of the group which includes 'Geoff Hamilton', 'Leander' and 'A Shropshire Lad' and like them is extremely hardy and reliable, making it an ideal rose for further back in the border, where it will withstand competition better than most. It has a strong fragrance, which is difficult to describe but is nonetheless pleasing. Excellent repeat-flowering, especially for a shrub of its size. Good disease-resistance. Named to commemorate the centenary of the founding of the University of East London. 120 × 90cm/4 × 3ft. It also makes a good climber of some 2.4m/8ft (see p. 256). 1998.

**Yellow Charles Austin** (*Ausling*) A yellow sport of 'Charles Austin', which shares all its qualities and, other than colour, is exactly the same. See p. 146. 1981.

*WILLIAM MORRIS, a tall shrub bearing formal, rosette-shaped flowers, is an ideal rose for further back in the border, where it will withstand competition better than most*

# English Musk Roses

The English Musk Roses were bred by crossing our original Old Rose Hybrids with Noisette Roses. Like the Noisettes, they are lighter both in flower and growth than the previous two groups; the whole effect being one of daintiness and charm. Their colours, too, have a softness that is most appealing in a rose, with fresh pinks, blushes, soft yellows and shades of apricot and peach. The Musk Rose fragrance is unfortunately missing except in a few varieties; nonetheless, nearly all the other fragrances are to be found in these roses, sometimes mingled with the Musk scent.

*BUTTERCUP is a little-known variety that should be grown more widely. It is a wonderful colour, flowers very freely and has a most delicious fragrance*

*CARIAD is a perfect choice for a mixed border, with its more informal blooms and habit of growth*

*Facing page, ANNE BOLEYN is exceptionally free flowering, quite short but widely spreading and almost completely free of disease*

**Anne Boleyn** (*Ausecret*) An exceptionally free-flowering variety that is quite short but widely spreading, with attractively arching growth which is almost completely free of disease. The flowers are of neat rosette shape, soft pink in colour and borne in quite large sprays—the individual blooms being produced in succession with remarkable continuity. There is only a light scent. The whole impression of this rose is one of pleasing freshness. A useful and healthy, reliable shrub. Named after the second of Henry VIII's six wives. 1 × 1.2m/3 × 4ft. 1999.

**Blythe Spirit** (*Auschool*) This rose produces its flowers in sprays. The individual flowers are quite small, of cupped shape and a nice soft yellow, fading to pale lemon. They have a light Musk fragrance with a hint of myrrh. The growth is medium in height and it develops into a bushy shrub which mingles well with other plants. Its foliage is small and is, we believe, completely resistant to disease. An ideal border plant. Named after Noel Coward's play. 1.2 × 1.2m/4 × 4ft. 1999.

**Buttercup** (*Ausband*) Numerous, small cupped flowers of pure golden-yellow, held in open sprays. The effect is that of a mass of rather large buttercups—a superb display that is repeated throughout the summer. It has smooth, light green foliage and very few thorns. It will form a fine garden shrub that is very reliable and almost completely resistant to disease. An ideal rose for the mixed border where, with its light airy growth, it associates well with other plants. There is often a particularly good display in late summer. A strong, delicious scent that is difficult to describe. 1.2 × 1m/4 × 3ft. 1998.

**Cariad** (*Auspanier*). A large, airy shrub with dainty, grey-green foliage. The rose-pink flowers are held on thin, wiry stems and are semi-double in form, almost like a camellia. The fragrance is myrrh with a touch of tea at first, later becoming a spicy musk with elements of orange peel and almonds. An ideal garden shrub that will mingle naturally with other plants in the mixed border. It has excellent resistance to disease. The beautiful word 'Cariad' is Welsh for 'Love'. 1.4 x 1.1m/4½x 3½ft. 2010.

*COMTE DE CHAMPAGNE, the flowers vary greatly in colour and are perfectly complemented by a delicious honey and Musk fragrance*

*CHARLOTTE, bushy and vigorous, builds up to a small, well-filled shrub bearing cup-shaped flowers filled with twisted petals*

**Charlotte** (*Auspoly*) This variety is often compared to 'Graham Thomas', although it is not yet so well known. Its colour is somewhat less intense—a lovely soft yellow. The flower is cup shaped and filled with beautifully arranged, twisted petals. They have a strong Tea Rose fragrance. Its growth is bushy and vigorous and builds up to a small, well-filled shrub. All in all, one of our best yellow roses. Although this rose was introduced before my granddaughter Charlottwas born, I have since dedicated it to her. 90 × 80cm/3 × 2½ft. 1993.

**Claire Austin** (*Ausprior*) There is something special about white roses—they are all purity and light—and yet really good white roses are rare among English Roses and Hybrid Tea Roses alike. This is because white roses are very difficult to breed. 'Claire Austin' bears pleasingly cupped buds of a pale lemon shade at first. Gradually these open to form large, creamy white flowers of typical English Musk delicacy, their petals perfectly arranged in concentric circles, with a few more loosely arranged in the centre.

*CLAIRE AUSTIN,
with large,
rosette-shaped
flowers,
is robust and
free flowering
and forms a fine,
rounded shrub
of dense growth*

They have a strong fragrance based on myrrh with dashes of meadowsweet, vanilla and heliotrope. It forms an elegant, arching shrub with plentiful, medium green foliage. Strong and healthy. Undoubtedly our finest white rose to date. Claire Austin, my daughter, has a Nursery which specialises in Hardy Plants, including Britain's finest collection of irises, peonies and day lilies. 140 × 90cm/4½ × 3ft. It will also make an excellent climber to 2.5m / 8ft. 2007.

**Comte de Champagne** (*Ausfo*) This is an interesting rose and is, in many ways, different from other roses. The flowers are soft yellow at first—becoming pale yellow and even paler on the outside of the petals—gradually opening to form a perfect open cup of medium to large size. There is a 'mop' of deep yellow stamens; the whole providing a pleasing range of colour on the bush at one time. A delicious honey and Musk fragrance complements the flower to perfection. It is a rose of rather lax, spreading growth yet bushy, producing its flowers on slender stems. It is healthy and free-flowering. This variety was named after Taittinger's finest champagne. The president of Taittinger, M. Claude Taittinger, lives in a château built by Thibaut IV, Count of Champagne and Brie, who is said to have brought *R. gallica* var. *officinalis* (the Apothecary's Rose) from Damascus on his return to France from the 7th Crusade in 1250. The Count was a great lover of roses and wrote about them in his poetry. 90 × 110cm/3 × 3½ft. 2001.

163

**Crocus Rose** (*Ausquest*) A robust and free-flowering rose, bearing large, rosette-shaped flowers that are cupped at first; the petals later reflexing. The colour is soft apricot, paling to cream on the outer petals. The flowers are produced very freely, in large clusters elegantly poised on the end of slightly arching stems. They have a light Tea Rose fragrance. Like 'Anne Boleyn', which is of similar breeding, it forms a fine, rounded shrub of dense growth and it, too, is very free from disease. Named for the Crocus Trust, which was set up to help sufferers affected by colorectal cancer. 120 × 90cm/4 × 3ft. 2000.

**Evelyn** (*Aussaucer*) Particularly large, apricot and pink flowers of shallow, saucer-like formation with numerous petals which gradually recurve to form a rosette shape. They have a wonderful fragrance,

*CROCUS ROSE, with large, rosette-shaped flowers, is robust and free-flowering and forms a fine, rounded shrub of dense growth*

*GRAHAM THOMAS, one of the best-known of the English Roses, has much of the beauty and character of the Noisette Roses at their best and is equally good in the mixed border and as a climber*

similar in style to an Old Rose but with a sumptuous fruity note reminiscent of fresh peaches and apricot. This is a beautiful and quite startling rose, though not quite so reliable as we would like it to be, being somewhat subject to disease—although it does remarkably well in countries with a warm climate where it is an excellent climber. The growth is quite short and upright, making it useful for smaller gardens. It has typical, light green Musk Rose foliage. It was named on behalf of the perfumers, Crabtree & Evelyn. 90 × 80cm/3 × 2½ft. 1991.

**Francine Austin** (*Ausram*) A medium-sized shrub of spreading growth, bearing sprays of small, pure white, pompon flowers. As such, it is not truly an English Rose. It could reasonably have been included with the Ground Cover roses—I would, however, prefer to keep it here, as it has much of the appearance and refinement of the first Noisette Roses. The flowers are held well apart from each other on thin, wiry stems in dainty sprays. It blooms freely and continuously, its long branches wreathed with white, providing a lovely picture. Its leaves are pale green with numerous small leaflets. It is named after my daughter-in-law. 90–120cm/3–4ft and as much across. 1988.

**Graham Thomas** (*Ausmas*) One of the best-known and most widely grown of the English Roses; indeed, it has much of the beauty and character of the Noisette Roses at their best. It is probably one of the most widely grown of all roses over the last twenty years or so. It has flowers of the richest and purest deep yellow, a shade which would be difficult to match in any other rose and is hard to equal even among Modern Roses. The flowers are of medium size and deeply cupped at first, opening to form a beautiful cupped rosette, the petals mingling attractively within. They have a lovely, strong Tea Rose fragrance. The growth is very strong, breaking freely at almost every joint as well as at the base to produce further flowers. The leaves are smooth and of light green colouring. If we look for faults, we might say that the growth is a little too upright and narrow at the base but, as its namesake remarked: 'Too upright for what?' The late Graham Stuart Thomas, who chose this variety to bear his name, was the prime mover in the reintroduction of the Old Roses, was a frequent visitor to our Nursery and may be said to have paved the way for the development of the English Roses. James Mason Award and voted the world's favourite rose in 2000. 120 × 90cm/4 × 3ft. 1983.

'Graham Thomas' is equally suitable for growing as a climber, particularly on a wall where it can reach 3m/10ft (see p. 251).

**Heritage** (*Ausblush*) With 'Graham Thomas', this was one of the first English Roses of the Noisette group and it has all the delicate beauty we would expect of such a rose. Its flowers are of medium size and of a most perfect cupped formation. Their colour is a soft blush pink and the petals within the cup are each placed with exquisite perfection, giving it a shell-like beauty. The flowers are produced in small—and occasionally large—sprays. There is a lovely fragrance which has been described as having overtones of fruit, honey and carnation on a myrrh background. The stems are smooth with few thorns and typical, pointed Hybrid Musk Rose foliage. In growth and leaf 'Heritage' has much in common with the rose 'Graham Thomas', which shares the same parentage. It forms a nice, shapely rounded shrub, breaking freely along the stem to produce further flowers. If it has a fault, it is that it has a tendency to disease and needs to be sprayed. 1.2 × 1.2m/4 × 4ft. 1984.

**Jayne Austin** (*Ausbreak*) This is truly a beautiful rose. The flowers are shallowly cupped at first, later becoming rosette shaped. They are yellow, tending a little towards apricot—the outer petals being paler—and their petals have the lovely silky sheen that we find in

*Far left, top,*
LADY EMMA
HAMILTON,
*a wonderful and
rather different
English Rose with
strongly coloured
and strongly
fragrant flowers
that are set off by
the dark, bronze-
coloured leaves*

*Far left, bottom,*
HERITAGE
*produces flowers
in sprays on
smooth stems
with few thorns*

*Left,* LICHFIELD
ANGEL *shows the
pristine perfection
of the English
Musks at their best*

*Following pages,*
MOLINEUX
*flowers with
exceptional
freedom and
continuity and,
of all the English
Roses, is the best
for bedding and
for the front of
a border*

the Noisette Roses and their descendants. The growth of this rose is slender and upright—perhaps a little too much so—a tendency it owes to its parent, 'Graham Thomas'. The leaves are plentiful and pale green. It has a wonderful Tea Rose fragrance. Named after my daughter-in-law. 1.1 m/3 ½ft. 1990.

**Lady Emma Hamilton** (*Ausbrother*) The buds of this variety are dark red with dashes of orange. They open to form an incurving, cup-shaped flower of apricot-orange. The fully open flowers are a lovely mixture of rich tangerine-orange on the inside of the petals, while the outer petals are an orange-yellow; the whole is set off by dark, bronzy-green foliage which becomes dark green with age. The unusual range of colour for an English Rose is useful for creating a little excitement in the border. There is a strong and delicious fruity fragrance, with hints of pear, grape and citrus fruits. A fairly upright, rather bushy shrub of medium height, producing its flowers freely. Very healthy. Named to commemorate the 200th Anniversary of the Battle of Trafalgar. 120 × 90cm/4 × 3ft. 2005.

**Lichfield Angel** (*Ausrelate*) The flowers start as charming little peachy pink cups, gradually opening to form neatly cupped rosettes, each with a perfect ring of crisp and waxy petals enclosing numerous smaller petals. At this stage they are a creamy-apricot. Eventually the petals turn back to form domed, creamy-white flowers. They are beautiful at all stages. It is wonderfully free flowering and the overall effect in the mass is almost pure white. The fragrance is generally light, but is strongly clove at one stage. 'Lichfield Angel' will form a vigorous, rounded shrub which, with its blooms nodding attractively on the branch, is a fine sight. The fact that good white and cream roses are difficult to come by makes this rose a very welcome addition to our collection. It is useful in a border, since it goes well with all other colours and acts as an intermediary between pinks and yellows. This rose shows the pristine perfection of the English Musks at their best. We named this rose for Lichfield Cathedral. The Lichfield Angel is a carved limestone panel, from the corner of a shrine chest, possibly that of St Chad, dating from around 800AD. It was recently discovered under the nave of Lichfield Cathedral. Our Nursery is in the Lichfield Diocese. 120 × 90cm/4 × 3ft. 2006.

*MAID MARION is a rose of great Old Rose charm; the blooms are beautifully shaped, pure rose pink and have a delicious fragrance*

*PORT SUNLIGHT bears flowers of rosette formation, with a strong Tea Rose fragrance, and is particularly good as a cut flower*

**Lucetta** (*Ausemi*) Very large, wide open and flat, semi-double, saucer-like flowers of a soft blush-pink, becoming paler with age, with a large boss of stamens. This is a particularly good shrub, healthy and strong growing, to about 1.5m/5ft in height and as much across, with long, arching branches. The blooms are nicely poised and contrast well with its ample, dark green foliage. It is seldom without flowers and is in every way tough and reliable. Fragrant. 1983.

**Maid Marion** (*Austobias*). The tight buds open to rounded cups with the larger outer petals enclosing numerous smaller petals within. These become saucer-shaped rosettes in a shade of clear rose-pink, the outer petals forming a perfectly rounded rim. The growth is relatively upright, but quite bushy and compact. The soft myrrh fragrance becomes more fruity as the flower ages, with a distinct clove character. Named for the companion of Robin Hood of Sherwood Forest. 90 x 90cm / 3 x 3ft. 2010.

**Marinette** (*Auscam*) The flowers of this rose start as very long, pencil-thin buds that unfold to become wide, flat, semi-double flowers of palest pink, with a fine bunch of golden stamens. They are held on slender stems, which completes the effect of lightness and grace. They have a soft and pleasing fragrance. The growth is rounded. and well balanced; the flowers and shrub as a whole mixing easily with other plants. This rose is named for Marina Berry, known to her friends as Marinette. Not a typical English Rose, but beautiful nonetheless. 1.2m/4ft. 1995.

**Molineux** (*Ausmol*) Of all the English Roses this is, perhaps, the best for bedding, although it is also useful at the front of a border. It flowers with exceptional freedom and continuity, has short, even, upright growth and is exceptionally free from disease. Its flowers are a rich, pure yellow and in the form of a neat rosette. They have a good Tea Rose fragrance with a musky background. Not quite the 'typical' English Rose, in that it lacks that indefinable Old Rose character, but it is nonetheless an exceptionally good rose. Named for the Wolverhampton Wanderers Football Club, 'Molineux' being the name of their ground. 90cm/3ft. 1994. (Illustrated, pp. 166–67)

**Mortimer Sackler** (*Ausorts*) This rose is something a little different. The flowers are dainty, about 7cm/3in across, and borne on slender, upright stems with very few thorns. They open to shallow, dainty cups of soft pink, paling a little on the outer petals. As

they mature, they take on a rather star-like formation, gradually exposing golden stamens. There is a lovely fragrance: Old Rose with a delicious hint of fruit. The growth is tall and upright and perhaps a little bare at the base of its branches, making it really only suitable for the back of the border. The stems and leaves are red at first, gradually becoming dark green. This rose was auctioned by the National Trust to raise funds for their gardens. It was bought by Mrs Sackler for her husband Mortimer's birthday. 1.4 × 1.1 m/4½ × 3½ft. 2002.

This rose is also excellent as a climber (see p. 255).

**Pegasus** (*Ausmoon*) This rose stands a little apart from other English Roses in that it has flowers that have petals of a rather more than usually substantial and waxy quality. They are of a pleasing formality, in the form of a full rosette shape and a rich apricot-yellow. They have a strong Tea Rose fragrance. The growth is particularly arching in character, which gives it an added attraction, and the foliage is of a rather Hybrid Tea appearance. It is a particularly good rose as a cut flower, which will last well in water. It was named after the winged horse of Greek mythology, rather appropriately, for Riding for the Disabled, a charity that gives much pleasure to many disabled children. 90 × 110cm/3 × 3½ft. 1995. (Illustrated, p. 321)

**Perdita** (*Ausperd*) A good small shrub with bushy, slightly arching growth to about 1.1 m/3½ft, constantly shooting from the base and providing continuity of bloom. The flowers are fully double, of medium size, delicate apricot-blush in colour and of shallowly-dished, rather cupped formation. It has ample, dark green, foliage and red-brown stems. The fragrance is strongly of myrrh with a hint of Tea Rose, and it was awarded the Royal National Rose Society's Henry Edland Medal for fragrance in 1984. Named after the character in Shakespeare's *The Winter's Tale*. 1983.

**Port Sunlight** (*Auslofty*) This rose bears medium-sized flowers of rich apricot colouring. They are flat rosettes and slightly quartered at the centre, the outer petals falling back a little and becoming paler. They have a rich Tea fragrance. The foliage and young stems are bronzy red at first, becoming a fairly dark green. The growth is vigorous and rather upright, making it ideal for the back of a mixed border where it will compete well with other plants. It is very resistant to disease. All in all, a good, reliable variety. It is named after Model Village in the Wirral built by William Hesketh Lever, where they have a beautiful garden of English Roses. 1.5 × 1.1 m/5 × 3½ft. 2007.

*Above, MORTIMER SACKLER bears dainty, cup-shaped flowers on slender stems with very few thorns*

*Right,* QUEEN OF
SWEDEN *is a
small-flowered
rose whose
growth is tough
and reliable*

*SKYLARK is one of
the very best of
the semi double
English Roses,
flowering very
freely and also
being very tough
and reliable*

**Queen of Sweden** (*Austiger*) The flowers of a rose do not have to be large to be beautiful; there is, in fact, something appealing about small-flowered roses and often their growth is tough and reliable. 'Queen of Sweden' is such a rose. It has small to medium-sized flowers which are prettily cupped and incurved at first, gradually opening out to a neat rosette. They start a glowing apricot-pink, later becoming a lovely soft Alba Rose pink which gradually pales on the outer petals. They have a light to medium myrrh fragrance. The growth is rather rigid, a fact that only seems to add to its beauty. The foliage is typically Musk Rose and very disease-resistant. A charming little rose that grows in popularity each year. Named in celebration of the 350th anniversary of the Treaty of Friendship and Commerce between Queen Christina of Sweden and Oliver Cromwell of Great Britain in 1654. 110 × 80cm/3½ × 2½ft. 2004.

**Rose of Picardy** (*Ausfudge*) Until we introduced 'Rose of Picardy' we had no single red roses. It has single, bright scarlet-crimson flowers of exceptional daintiness. They are about 7cm/3in across with contrasting golden stamens and they have a light, fruity fragrance. It blooms with exceptional freedom, giving a display that can be seen across the garden. We felt that, for obvious reasons, this poppy-like rose was suitable to bear this very important name and so, with our French friends very much in mind, it was named to celebrate the Entente Cordiale between Britain and France. 1.2m/4ft. 2004.

**Scepter'd Isle** (*Ausland*) This charming little rose is similar to 'Heritage' but, being shorter, more upright and particularly free flowering, is suitable for bedding or for a place at the front of the border. Its flowers are medium sized and deeply cupped. Their colour is a lovely soft pink that pales on the outside of the petals. There is a very strong myrrh fragrance. The stems and leaves are light green—similar to those of 'Heritage'—showing signs of Musk Rose ancestry. The name is taken from John of Gaunt's speech, expressing his love for England in Shakespeare's *Richard II*. 90cm/3ft. 1996.

**Skylark** (*Ausimple*) It is always our desire to bring as much variety of form, fragrance and growth as possible to our English Roses and this rose is a good example. The flowers are semi-double and of open, cupped shape with prominent stamens. The colour is deep pink at first, later paling slightly to lilac-pink. At the centre of the flower there is a small white area. The fragrance is light but pleasing—Musk and Tea with clove and a hint of apple pie! The

*SCEPTER'D ISLE is suitable for bedding or for a place at the front of the border, its deeply cupped flowers having a very strong myrrh fragrance. It is accompanied here by a penstemon*

growth is light and airy, building up into a natural, well-rounded shrub. An ideal choice for planting amongst other shrubs or hardy plants towards the front of a mixed border. The name was suggested by a friend who remembers seeing and hearing a skylark when she first visited our Nursery. 90 × 60cm / 3 × 2ft. 2007.

**Sweet Juliet** (*Ausleap*) This variety is very similar to 'Jayne Austin', with flowers of the same superb quality. They are medium sized, of shallowly cupped shape and apricot-yellow in colour, paling towards the edges. There is a strong Tea scent which develops into an equally strong lemon fragrance as the flower matures. It requires harder pruning than most English Roses, otherwise the plant will become ungainly and the flowers small. Named for the heroine of Shakespeare's *Romeo and Juliet*. 110 × 90cm / 3 ½ × 3 ft. 1989.

**Tea Clipper** (*Ausrover*) This rose bears medium to large, rosette-shaped flowers. These have quite large outer petals of a pale apricot colour, enclosing numerous small, narrowly quilled petals of soft apricot—all gathering together to provide a suggestion of a button eye. Suitably for a rose of this name, it has a Tea scent. This is combined with hints of fruit and

*SWEET JULIET has shallowly cupped flowers of superb quality*

myrrh—a pleasant mixture. The growth is tall and upright, while the first crop of flowers is excellent they are not produced quiet as freely late in the season. 'Tea Clipper' was named to commemorate the centenary of the death of Frederick Horniman, who made a fortune as a tea trader and wasa great collector of artefacts. 120 × 90cm/4 × 3ft. 2006.

**The Generous Gardener** (*Ausdrawn*) A rose of delicate charm, its flowers being beautifully formed; their colour is a soft glowing pink at the centre, shading to palest pink on the outer petals. When the petals open they expose numerous stamens, providing an almost water lily-like effect. It has strong, elegantly arching growth with polished dark green foliage. This rose is most effective when placed at the back of a border, looking over other plants. Like all our recent varieties, this rose is highly disease-resistant. It has a delicious fragrance with aspects of Old Rose, Musk and myrrh. 'The Generous Gardener' was named to commemorate the seventy-fifth anniversary of the National Gardens Scheme which has, over the years, made it possible for us all to see many beautiful gardens. 1.5 × 1.2m / 5 × 4ft. It is particularly lovely as a climber (see p. 256). 2002.

**The Pilgrim** (*Auswalker*) The flowers of this variety are particularly beautiful, having a softness of character that is rare among yellow roses. Perhaps this is due to its Musk Rose background. Its blooms are pale yellow, quite large and beautifully formed in the shape of a shallowly cupped rosette. Their fragrance is a perfect balance between that of a Tea Rose and English myrrh. It will form a nice shrub of medium to large size, with soft green foliage that is very healthy and blends perfectly with the flowers. It is also a very good climber (see p. 256). Named after the pilgrims of Chaucer's *The Canterbury Tales*. 1.2m/4ft. 1991.

*Above,*
*Tea Clipper,*
*suitably for a*
*rose of this name,*
*has a Tea scent,*
*with hints of fruit*
*and myrrh*

*Right, The*
*Generous*
*Gardener*
*has beautifully*
*formed flowers*
*and arching*
*growth with*
*polished dark*
*green foliage*

THE PILGRIM
has flowers with
a softness of
character rare
among yellow
roses. The
fragrance is
between that of
a Tea Rose and
English myrrh

WILLIAM AND
CATHERINE,
altogether a rose
of outstanding
beauty, it was
named to
celebrate the
Royal Wedding in
2011

**The Shepherdess** (*Austwist*) This rose has cupped flowers of a pleasing apricot-pink. They have a slightly waxy appearance that we often find in roses of the English Musk Group. Within the cup we see attractively folded petals. The blooms are of medium size and have a lovely fruity fragrance with hints of lemon. The growth is not tall but vigorous and upright. The foliage is large for an English Musk. Named after a character in Sir Philip Sidney's 16th-century prose romance, *The Arcadia*. 90 × 60cm/3 × 2ft. 2005.

**The Wedgwood Rose** (*Ausjosiah*) This has particularly beautiful blooms of medium to large size, the petals having a delicate, gossamer-like quality and the colour being a soft rose-pink – all this adding up to a charming Old Rose effect. They have a lovely fruity fragrance on the outer petals, with a clove-like scent which comes from the stamens. Its ample foliage is dark green, glossy and very healthy, and the growth is exceptionally vigorous, sending up many shoots from the base. It forms a large shrub, although it is perhaps better trained as a short climbing rose. We named it for the famous pottery company which was founded in 1759. 1.5 x 1.5m / 5 x 5ft or 3m/10ft as a climber. 2009.

**William and Catherine** (*Ausrapper*). The flowers of this rose are particularly beautiful, having the classic shallow cup shape and the very full petalled form of many of the Old Roses. At the centre of each bloom is a button eye of small inward folding petals. As the flowers first start to open the colour is a soft creamy apricot, which quickly fades to cream and then to pure white – the overall impression being very much of white. The petals drop very cleanly, which is an important attribute in a white rose. It forms a most attractive, bushy, but relatively upright, shrub. The fragrance is pure myrrh and of medium strength. 'William and Catherine' will be excellent for mixed borders, informal rose borders and more formal beds. We have named this rose to celebrate the Royal Wedding which was held in April 2011 at Westminster Abbey. 120 x 90cm / 4 x 3ft. 2011.

**Wildeve** (*Ausbonny*) A robust and healthy rose, bearing a mass of flowers all the way along its arching branches, to form a wide, mounding shrub. The buds are blush-pink at first, opening to fully double, rosette-shaped flowers that are pink with a touch of apricot at the centre, fading to white at the edges. They are of medium size, and slightly quartered at the centre. It has a pleasing, fresh fragrance

*THE WEDGWOOD ROSE, a vigorous variety which can be grown as short climber or as a large rounded shrub*

175

*WOLLERTON OLD
HALL, named
after one of the
best private
gardens in the
UK, is very close
to our nursery in
Shropshire. It is
an excellent
variety in all
ways – beautiful,
fragrant and
extremely healthy*

*WISLEY 2008 is a
wonderfully free
flowering variety
with perfectly
formed flowers of
purest pink*

*Right,* WILDEVE *bears a mass of flowers all along its arching branches*

of medium strength. The foliage is small, clean, plentiful and free from disease. We would expect it to do well in a less than perfect position, although it is worth something better. All in all, a fine example of an English Musk Rose. 110 × 80cm /3½ × 2½ ft. 2003.

**Wisley 2008** (*Ausbreeze*). This is a rose of exceptional delicacy and charm. The flowers are shallowly cupped and about 7.5cm / 3ins across, the petals arranged in a most perfect rosette formation. Their colour is a very pure soft pink, the outer petals paling a little towards the edge. The growth is tall and slightly arching, producing flowers along the stems and building up into a fine and very healthy shrub. There is a delightful, fresh, fruity fragrance with hints of raspberries and tea. It would be an especially good choice for mixed borders and also superb as a hedge. It was awarded first prize for landscaping at the Barcelona Trials in 2009. 1.5 x 1.0m / 5 x 3½ft. 2008.

**Wollerton Old Hall** (*Ausblanket*). This is one of the most fragrant of all English Roses. It has the distinctive myrrh scent which is rarely found in roses, appearing first in 'Constance Spry', and later in 'Scepter'd Isle'. The plump buds have attractive flashes of red. These open to form round, rich buttery-yellow coloured blooms which eventually pale to a softer creamy colour. Even when the flowers are fully open, they retain their beautifully rounded chalice shape. It forms a particularly healthy and bushy shrub with many stems shooting from the base. It is relatively upright and has few thorns. With its soft shades, 'Wollerton Old Hall' will very easily blend with a wide range of colour schemes, planted with roses or other shrubs and perennials. Its more upright habit makes it suitable for both formal and informal situations. Position this rose where its strong scent can be easily appreciated. Wollerton Old Hall in Shropshire has one of the most beautiful private gardens in the country. The gardens are set around a sixteenth-century hall and feature roses in creative plant combinations, including many of our own English Roses. Wollerton Old Hall is open to the public on selected days throughout the summer. 1.5 x 0.9m / 5 x 3ft. 2011.

# English Alba Rose Hybrids

THE
ENGLISH
ROSES
English
Alba Rose
Hybrids

These are the most recent roses of the English Rose family and a little way removed from the other groups. The difference lies in their almost wild rose growth, which means they associate easily with other plants and makes them suitable not only for more formal planting, but also for the wilder areas of the garden. Their breeding originates in crosses between Alba Roses and other English Roses. They usually have light and airy growth with foliage of a similar nature. Their colours at present are confined to shades of pink. The flowers are light and dainty and some gardeners regard this group as being among the most beautiful of roses. They are not yet quite so resistant to disease as we would like them to be—the lower leaves sometimes falling off to leave a bare stem—although this does not seem to be unsightly.

---

**Ann** (*Ausfete*) This is a single-flowered rose with just the occasional extra petal. Its colour is deep pink tinged with yellow at the centre, with a nice bunch of red stamens with yellow anthers. The flowers are beautifully poised, slightly drooping on the branch. The fragrance is delicate but pleasing. The growth is quite short but broad and the plant as a whole is a picture of simple daintiness. Named after Ann Saxby, one of our longest-serving employees, who has grown our roses for Chelsea Flower Show for many years. I think this is my favourite single English Rose. 90 × 80cm/3 × 2½ft. 1997.

**Cordelia** (*Ausbottle*) Pretty, slender buds open into loosely petalled, semi-double flowers of a delightful shade of the purest rose pink. These are borne in large sprays, each bloom paling individually to provide a pleasing, mixed effect. The growth is dense and spreading, with the individual flowers held daintily above the foliage. Named after King Lear's youngest daughter in Shakespeare's play. 110 × 90cm/3½ × 3ft. 2000.

**Scarborough Fair** (*Ausoran*) It is easy to be overwhelmed by the sheer size and weight of a flower. This rose is something quite different—its flowers are modest but charming. It is not unlike the beautiful 'Windflower' except that it is low and broad in growth, making it more suitable for a position where space is limited, or indeed for a place at the front of a border. The petals in the bud curl around to form a ball, which opens to a perfect little cupped flower of pure soft pink, eventually opening wide to reveal a blush pink flower of the utmost delicacy and a bunch of golden stamens. Charming at all stages. It flowers with remarkable freedom and continuity from June until the autumn. There is a delightful light to medium, fresh 'green' Old Rose fragrance, sometimes tending towards Musk. Very healthy, tough and reliable—as we might expect from its Alba antecedents. It produces an excellent crop of hips if not dead headed. We have taken the name from the well-known medieval English folk song. 80 × 60cm/2½ × 2ft. 2003.

**Shropshire Lass** Just as 'Constance Spry' was the founding parent of the English Old Rose Hybrids, so 'Shropshire Lass' was the foundation rose of the English Alba Hybrids. It was the result of a cross between an old Hybrid Tea, 'Madame Butterfly', and the beautiful

*Facing page, SCARBOROUGH FAIR bears cupped flowers that open to reveal golden stamens, and does so with remarkable freedom and continuity*

*Right, ANN is a picture of daintiness, the single flowers beautifully poised on the branch*

*Far right, CORDELIA has loosely petalled, semi-double flowers held daintily above the foliage*

English
Alba Rose
Hybrids

*SHROPSHIRE
LASS was the
foundation rose
of the English
Alba Hybrids*

*SIR JOHN
BETJEMAN has
some of the
brightest pink
flowers of all the
English Roses. It
flowers very freely
and stays compact*

THE
ENGLISH
ROSES

English
Alba Rose
Hybrids

*THE ALEXANDRA ROSE, the flowers have a soft Musk fragrance and are produced in great abundance*

Alba, 'Madame Legras de Saint Germain'. It forms a large, strong shrub of some 2.5m/8ft in height and—like its parent—is extremely tough and disease-resistant. The flowers are blush white and almost single, 9 or 12cm/4 or 5in across, with a large boss of stamens. The fragrance is strong and delicious, with hints of myrrh. Unfortunately, being a first cross between a repeat-flowering and a non-repeat-flowering rose it is, itself, non-repeating; however, in compensation, it has enormous strength and freedom of flowering. This rose is even better when grown as a climber (see p. 255), when it will reach considerable heights of 4–5m/12–15ft. 1968.

**Sir John Betjeman** (*Ausvivid*). A rose of more modern character than most English Roses. The small buds open to neat, wide-open, full-petalled rosettes of bright, deep pink, their colour intensifying with age. The flowers are produced very freely and held in small clusters and have a light, rather 'green' fragrance. It is a healthy and very bushy shrub of medium size with a slightly arching habit. With its bright colouration, this is an ideal choice for those wishing to create some contrast and excitement in a border. Sir John Betjeman was a writer, journalist and broadcaster. 100 x 75cm / 3½ x 2½ft. 2008.

**The Alexandra Rose** (*Ausday*) A dainty, single-flowered variety with flowers of rather less than medium size. These are a soft coppery pink that quickly fades to a blush pink, giving us a delightful mixed effect in the spray. They are produced in great abundance and repeat very well. There is a soft Musk fragrance. A shrub of elegant growth with the flowers held on twiggy stems. An excellent choice for the border or for a wild area, where it will have the advantage over other shrubs of producing flowers over a long season. Named for the Alexandra Rose Day, which raises money for a variety of charities. 1.2m/4ft. 1992.

181

THE
ENGLISH
ROSES

English
Alba Rose
Hybrids

THE
ENGLISH
ROSES

English
Alba Rose
Hybrids

*SIR JOHN BETJEMAN, along with most English Roses, has the wonderful ability of flowering from the top of the plant almost to ground level*

183

THE
ENGLISH
ROSES

English
Alba Rose
Hybrids

*THE LADY'S
BLUSH, with its
almost single
flowers, is very
different to the
very full petalled
blooms of most
English Roses. It
is, however, a
most charming
variety well
worth planting in
a border*

THE
ENGLISH
ROSES

English
Alba Rose
Hybrids

*WINDFLOWER,
not unlike an
herbaceous
anemone or
windflower, this
is a rose for the
border or for
wilder areas of
the garden*

**The Lady's Blush** (*Ausoscar*) A charming, semi-double rose with delicate natural beauty. The elegant, pointed buds develop into rounded cups, their colour being a pure soft pink with a creamy-white eye at the centre and often a white stripe. The central group of golden stamens is particularly fine. The overall impression is of freshness and grace. A healthy variety that will grow into an attractive rounded bushy plant. Named for the 125th anniversary of *The Lady* magazine. 120 x 90cm / 4 x 3ft. 2010.

**Windflower** (*Auscross*) A dainty rose, holding its medium-sized blooms high up on wiry stems, giving it an appearance not unlike that of an herbaceous anemone or windflower. Pretty little buds open to loosely petalled, slightly cupped, soft pink flowers that are nicely poised on thin stems, providing a most beautiful, airy effect. They have an Old Rose fragrance with just a hint of apple and cinnamon. The foliage is of the true English Alba type, tending towards that of *Rosa canina*. This is very much a rose for the border or for the wilder areas of the garden, where it will associate well with other plants. For overall effect and almost wild flower beauty, both of flower and growth, this is one of the most beautiful English Roses. 120 × 90cm/4 × 3ft. 1994. (Also illustrated, p. 122-23)

# Some Other English Roses

*KEW GARDENS is very rare in the rose world – it is completely thornless. The flowers are held in very large clusters and it is extremely free flowering*

**Kew Gardens** (*Ausfence*). More of a Species Hybrid than a typical English Rose, 'Kew Gardens' has small single flowers, held in very large heads, rather like a hydrangea. They are produced almost continuously from early summer through to the end of the season. The soft apricot buds open to pure white, with a hint of soft lemon behind the stamens. The flowers are followed by small red hips which should be removed to encourage repeat flowering. An extremely healthy and completely thornless shrub with bushy, upright growth. It creates the beautiful effect of a mass of white blooms, as though covered with snow. An ideal choice for hedges and mixed borders. Winner of the prestigious gold standard award at the NIAB trials. 1.5 x 0.9m / 5 x 3ft. 2009.

**Princess Anne** (*Auskitchen*). An exciting new development, with its own very special beauty. The pure deep pink flowers are produced over a long period and held in large clusters. It will form a compact, bushy, upright shrub, with highly-polished foliage that is remarkably resistant to disease. It will be ideal for borders or hedging. There is a medium strong Tea Rose fragrance. Named 'Best New Plant Variety' at the Grower of the Year Awards 2011. We were honoured to name this after Her Royal Highness, the Princess Royal. 90 x 60cm / 3 x 2ft. 2010.

**Tam o'Shanter** (*Auscerise*). This has loosely formed, rosette-shaped flowers of deep cerise held on long, gracefully arching branches; the flowers opening all along their length rather as we might find on a species rose. Unfortunately the fragrance is only light. This is a rose that would look very well in an informal garden or as part of a mixed border and would need very little maintenance, especially as it is very healthy and would not need much pruning. A rose that is rather out of the ordinary but very worthwhile. It was named to commemorate the 250th anniversary of the birth of Robbie Burns – Tam o'Shanter is the hero of one of his best known poems. 1.8 x 1.5m / 6 x 5ft. 2009.

*TAM O' SHANTER is a rose of rather modest charm, although in the right position an excellent choice; it will flower very freely and create a strong focal point in a border*

*PRINCESS ANNE is
a rose of subtly
different character
to the other
English Roses. It
is extremely free
flowering and
healthy*

# 6

# SHRUB ROSES

THE ROSES THAT WE USUALLY gather together under the heading 'Shrub Roses' are the Rugosa Roses, the Hybrid Musks, the so-called 'Modern Shrub Roses' and a more recent group known as 'Ground Cover Roses'. The main characteristics they have in common are that they are nearly all large shrubs and are usually repeat-flowering. They have rampant, natural growth and are thus useful for planting with other plants and shrubs and often for growing in the wilder areas of the garden.

Shrub Roses vary widely in quality: a few of them are excellent, the remainder are either somewhat coarse or lacking in health. The reason for this is, I believe, that most of these groups have never been subject to intensive breeding and selection. They are largely chance seedlings that have been produced in the process of breeding with other objectives in mind and they often still have something of the natural beauty of their wild parents. This has been in some ways an advantage, since many breeders have a tendency to reduce the beauty of the rose they are trying to improve.

The downside of this process is that many of these roses are subject to disease. Most of them are bred from distant parents and whenever you hybridise with such parents, you tend to get this problem in the progeny. Species often have different ways of protecting themselves against disease and when we hybridise them, we are liable to—as it were—fall between two stools. The new mixture of genes often gives very little protection. This only comes by controlled selection over the years. Much the same can be said of the beauty of a rose.

With these problems in mind I have, as far as possible, selected only the most beautiful roses in this group and those with the most resistance to disease. These are, indeed, very attractive roses that are ideal for growing in the border with other roses and other shrubs and hardy plants.

## Rugosa Roses

Facing page, CORNELIA is a Hybrid Musk that forms a fine, shapely shrub bearing sprays of rosette-shaped flowers

ROSA RUGOSA is a native of northern China, Japan and Korea. It was grown as a garden shrub in China, where it was said to have been used for pot-pourri, and Bunyard in his book *Old Garden Roses* (1936) speaks of a drawing by Chao Ch'ang who lived about AD 1000. It was also grown in Japan, and this explains why its descendants are sometimes known as Japanese Roses. The exact date of its arrival in Britain seems to be in some doubt, but it is thought to have been first introduced by the nurserymen Lee and Kennedy of Hammersmith in 1796. It forms a vigorous and sturdy shrub of up to 2.5m/8ft in height and as much across. It has very numerous strong thorns and rough-textured apple-green leaves. The flowers are large, 9–10cm/3½–4in across, of a variable purple-rose colouring, and have a strong Old Rose fragrance. These are followed by giant red tomato-shaped hips of 25mm/1in or more in diameter. The stamens are creamy

rather than the usual yellow, and this assorts with the flower colour. It has two other important qualities: first, it is extremely hardy and disease resistant and secondly it is almost alone among wild roses in its ability to repeat its flowering throughout the summer, so much so that later in the season the ripe hips can be seen on the branch at the same time as the last blooms. Although the colouring of the flowers may not be to everyone's taste, it is, in fact, a very fine shrub that can be relied upon to thrive in the poorest sandy soils.

colours of the garden roses of the time. These hybrids are also large shrubs, and many of them have inherited the recurrent-flowering character of the species. Often they have lost some of the grace and bushiness of this parent, and some do not have its fine hips, but they form an often beautiful and very useful class. In spite of this, one cannot help feeling this group has never reached its full potential; since the first flush of interest little work has been done on them. This is perhaps largely due to the fact that the wrong parents have been used.

*R. rugosa* is a diploid, while most garden roses are tetraploid, and this has resulted in sterile offspring, thus blocking further progress. However, such problems can be overcome, and a rich field of endeavour is open to future breeders.

Rugosa Hybrids are not difficult to grow. Pruning can be restricted to the thinning and removal of old and weak wood, also—and more importantly—to the encouragement of a shapely shrub, particularly with those varieties that tend towards gaunt and rather upright growth.

Rugosas form excellent and impenetrable hedges or barriers, they are ideal

ROSA RUGOSA
*bears flowers
which open
from long,
slender buds,
followed by
large, tomato-
like hips*

With all these virtues, it is not surprising that a large number of hybrids have been raised and that these have become recognised as a class in their own right. Most of them were bred in the period immediately before and after the turn of the 20th century when some excellent shrubs were produced combining the shrubby virtues of *R. rugosa* with the varying

for poor soil where other roses might find it difficult to thrive, and they are useful for seaside planting, withstanding the buffeting of the wind better than most roses. I have seen them growing quite happily on sand dunes—an ability they share only with the Scots Roses, at least in so far as garden roses are concerned.

---

**Agnes** This is a cross between *Rosa rugosa* and *R. foetida* 'Persiana', and the latter parent has placed a strong stamp upon it. The result is a rose that is still very much a Rugosa but with typically Old Rose flowers and many small petals of yellow tinted with amber, later fading to cream. It is, in effect, a yellow Old Rose, and this gives it a particular value to those in favour of this form. A mixture of the not altogether pleasing scent of *R. foetida* 'Persiana', and the scent of the Rugosa, has resulted in a delicate and unusual fragrance in this rose. The growth is upright, bushy and strong, perhaps 2m/7ft in height and 1.5m/5ft across, with rather small, pale green leaves. It is subject to rust in some gardens. Bred by B. & W. Saunders (Canada), introduced 1922.

**Blanc Double de Coubert** A rose with all the appearance of a double form of *Rosa rugosa* 'Alba'. The flowers are large, pure white, sometimes tinged with blush in the bud, the petals having an almost papery appearance and opening semi-double with a strong fragrance.

The growth is very similar to *R. rugosa* 'Alba', but a little less strong. The breeder, Cochet-Cochet of France, claimed that it was the result of a cross between *R. rugosa* and the beautiful Tea Rose 'Sombreuil'. It would be easy to come to the conclusion that there has been some mistake here, not an uncommon occurrence among older roses. However, *R. rugosa* is so dominant a seed parent that it frequently leaves little trace of the pollen parent, and it is quite possible the parentage is as the breeder stated. This is one of the best of the Rugosas, growing well and flowering with remarkable continuity. There are only a few hips. Height 1.5m/5ft. Introduced 1892.

**Conrad Ferdinand Meyer** (more conveniently known as 'Conrad F. Meyer'). The parentage of this rose is ('Gloire de Dijon' × 'Duc de Rohan') × a form of *Rosa rugosa*. Its growth is very tall and upright, with unusually long strong stems shooting freely from the base, so that it can, if desired, be grown as a Climber. There are numerous strong thorns, and the foliage is about half-way between that of a

Hybrid Tea and *R. rugosa*. This rose has always been available in nursery catalogues, even at the time when Shrub Roses were almost entirely neglected. The reason lies, perhaps, in its large Hybrid Tea-like blooms. These are of a soft silvery-pink with the petals nicely rolled at the edges. Later they open into large, cupped, informal flowers. The fragrance is, to me, one of the most delicious of any to be found among roses, and very strong. *R. rugosa* is best pruned to half its height in order to form a reasonably shapely shrub, and if it is not to exhibit its flowers to the sky only. It flowers freely and produces a good second crop later in the summer. It can suffer badly from rust. The height will depend on pruning, but left to its own devices it will easily reach 3m/10ft. Bred by Müller (Germany), introduced 1899.

**Fimbriata** ('Phoebe's Frilled Pink', 'Dianthiflora') This pretty rose has, as its various names indicate, flowers fringed at the edges in the manner of a pink. This is probably the result of some breakdown in the genetic make up of the plant, due to the difficult step between its two widely separated parents, *Rosa rugosa* and the vigorous Noisette Rose 'Madame Alfred Carrière'. Such peculiarities do occur in many garden plants in the course of hybridization—in this case the result is a happy one. In spite of the robust nature of both parents, 'Fimbriata' is not a particularly vigorous shrub, although adequately so. The growth is rather slim with quite small, light green foliage. The flowers are small, soft pink, fragrant and held in clusters. It has a delicacy that is more beautiful than we find in its more robust competitors the Grootendorst Roses (see below). Height 1.2m/4ft. Bred by Morlet (France), 1891.

**F. J. Grootendorst** Like 'Fimbriata' this variety has small flowers

with fringed petals, but in this case the results are less pleasing. It is a cross between *Rosa rugosa* 'Rubra' and the Polyantha Pompon Rose 'Madame Norbert Levavasseur'. The flowers, which are of a rather dull crimson, lack the delicacy of 'Fimbriata' and are carried rather too tightly in their sprays. The growth is very strong, upright and bushy, and the leaves show signs of its Polyantha parentage. It has no scent. On the plus side it is strong and entirely reliable and flowers more repeatedly than any other of the Rugosas, except its own sport and the species itself. It has in fact three sports: 'Pink Grootendorst', 'Grootendorst Supreme' and 'White Grootendorst',

*Above, FIMBRIATA has delightful flowers with fringed edges rather like those of a pink*

*Far left, AGNES, has lovely Old Rose type flowers and is one of the very few yellow Rugosas*

*Left, F.J. GROOTENDORST is particularly bushy, reliable and free flowering with fringed petals*

*Right,*
*FRU DAGMAR*
*HASTRUP repeat*
*flowers well,*
*bears large dark*
*red hips and*
*is completely*
*disease free*

flowers are fully double and of deep crimson-purple, producing a good crop of hips in the autumn. It is strong, hardy and healthy, and from a nurseryman's point of view has the advantage that it propagates much more easily than 'Roseraie de l'Haÿ'. Typical Rugosa type. Very strongly fragrant. Height 1.2m/4ft. Introduced by Schaum & Van Tol (Holland), 1905.

**Lady Curzon** The parentage of this rose is *Rosa* 'Macrantha' × *R. rugosa* 'Rubra'—a very promising cross, and the result does not disappoint us. It forms a tangled shrub of some 2.5m/8ft in height and the same in width. The leaves are rough textured, like those of its Rugosa parent, and there are many strong thorns. The flowers are large, single and about 10cm/4in across, of a light iridescent pink, paling almost to white at the centre, with petals like crumpled silk and a fine boss of golden stamens. They are fragrant but not recurrent. This variety is excellent in the border or in the wilder areas of the garden, where it will scramble quite happily for 6m/20ft in all directions in shrubs and trees if required, providing charming natural effects. Raised by Turner (UK), introduced 1901.

**micrugosa** See Chapter 9.

**micrugosa Alba** See Chapter 9.

**Mrs Anthony Waterer** Of all the Rugosas that are of obvious hybrid appearance, this is in many ways the most satisfactory. It has excellent leafy growth of 1.5m/5ft in height, spreading broadly to form a dense and shapely, domed shrub. Both flower and foliage are close to that of an Old Rose. The blooms open wide, full and slightly cupped and are of crimson colouring, with a strong fragrance. It produces an unfailingly good crop of flowers in early summer, followed by only occasional blooms later. If it were also repeat flowering this rose would be hard to beat. It is susceptible to rust. The parents were the Hybrid Perpetual 'Général Jaqueminot' × unnamed Rugosa hybrid. Introduced by Waterer (UK), 1898.

**Mrs Doreen Pike** I list this as an English Rose, although it has a lot of Rugosa in its make-up. See Chapter 5.

**Nova Zembla** A colour sport of 'Conrad Ferdinand Meyer', see p. 190, the flowers being white with the very slightest tinge of pink. It is equally good and similar in every way to its parent, although perhaps a little less vigorous. Discovered by Mees (UK), 1907.

**Nyveldt's White** A beautiful single white rose, which might at first sight be mistaken for the excellent *Rosa rugosa* 'Alba'; closer observation reveals a rose of more refined appearance and rather more graceful growth. The leaves are smoother and their leaflets narrower and of a paler green than those of 'Alba'. The flowers are more elongated in the petal and about 10cm/4in across. They are fragrant, repeat well, and are followed by plentiful large, orange-red hips. A very good shrub and completely healthy. The parentage is stated as being (*R. rugosa* 'Rubra' × *R. cinnamomea*) × *R. nitida*. This is a little surprising, as there are no white roses in this cross, and it may be that *R. rugosa* 'Alba' was used rather than *R. rugosa* 'Rubra'. Raised by Nyveldt (Holland), introduced 1955.

**Paulii** See Chapter 9.

**Paulii Rosea** See Chapter 9.

all of which are of very similar character and detailed below. Height 1.5m/5ft. Raised by de Goey (Holland), introduced 1918.

**Fru Dagmar Hastrup** ('Frau Dagmar Hartopp') A widely planted rose and a favourite with municipal authorities, no doubt because it lends itself to mass planting, being of short, bushy growth which can be pruned fairly hard without losing bloom. It might best be described as a shorter, light pink form of *Rosa rugosa*. The flowers are beautiful and delicate in appearance, the buds long and pointed and of a rich pink, opening to a clear light pink with creamy-white stamens. They are produced repeatedly and are followed by large deep red hips. Fragrant. It is thought to be a seedling from *R. rugosa*. Height 1.2m/4ft. Hastrup (Denmark), 1914.

**Grootendorst Supreme** A sport from 'F. J. Grootendorst', see above, with darker, garnet-red flowers. It is said to be rather less vigorous than its parent, to which, except for colour, it is similar. Yellowish-green leaves. Slight fragrance. Height 1.2m/4ft. Grootendorst (Holland), 1936.

**Hansa** At first sight this variety seems to be very similar to 'Roseraie de l'Haÿ', but on closer observation it is a less beautiful rose. The

**Pink Grootendorst** A pink sport of 'F.J. Grootendorst', see p. 191. Like its parent it is vigorous, though perhaps a little less so than the original, forming a strong, bushy, reliably repeat-flowering shrub. Discovered by Grootendorst (Holland), 1923.

*Rosa rugosa* **'Alba'** An almost faultless if little sung shrub of good vigorous growth, 1.8m/6ft high by as much across, with ample foliage. It bears large 10cm/4in pure white flowers which open from long, slender buds throughout the summer. These are followed by very large tomato-like orange-red hips that ripen together with the last of its blooms. Strong fragrance. This rose was originally a sport from *Rosa rugosa typica*, and as such would not come from true seed. However, strains have been developed that are almost pure, although the occasional purple-flowered plant will still occur. Seedling bushes of both *R. rugosa* 'Alba' and *R. rugosa typica* are ideal for massed landscape planting, particularly in public places, as both flower continuously throughout the summer, spreading and suckering freely to form a continuous thicket and, most importantly in such planting, they do not have the problem of suckering from a stock. (Anyone involved in landscape designing and maintenance will be well aware of the problems presented by suckers in the middle of a hundred closely planted 1.8m/6ft tall thorny shrub roses!)

**Roseraie de l'Haÿ** A vigorous shrub, perhaps 2.5m/8ft in height, with fine, dense spreading growth and luxurious typically Rugosa foliage. The flowers are very large and double, opening wide from attractively pointed buds; their colour a rich crimson-purple with a few creamy stamens to be seen among the petals. They are studded evenly among its leafy growth, showing themselves to perfection.

It is one of the most beautiful and completely reliable shrub roses, repeating well, but with very few hips. Similar to 'Hansa' (see above), with the same very strong fragrance, but finer and of richer colouring. Said to be a double sport from *Rosa rugosa*, but this is doubtful. Bred by Gravereaux (France), 1901, and named after the magnificent rose garden near Paris.

*Above, ROSERAIE DE L'HAÿ is one of the most beautiful and completely reliable shrub roses, repeating well*

*Left, HANSA is an excellent rose by any standard, not least because of its superb fragrance*

**Sarah van Fleet** A strong, bushy, upright shrub, 2m/7ft in height and 1.5m/5ft across. It is one of the most useful and reliable of the Rugosa hybrids, both for garden and municipal planting, especially at the backs of borders. The flowers are large, semi-double, opening wide and slightly cupped, china pink in colour, with yellow stamens. They are usually held in small clusters and appear both in summer and autumn. The growth and foliage is typically Rugosa, with rough-textured leaves and many thorns. Bred by Dr Van Fleet of the USA, reputedly from a cross between *Rosa rugosa* and 'My Maryland', but a chromosome count seems to place some doubt upon this. Introduced 1926.

**Scabrosa** Whether or not this is a selection from *Rosa rugosa* or a hybrid is hard to say. Certainly it has everything in common with the species, except that it is of more substance in every way. The flowers are very large, single and about 14cm/5½in across. Their colour is a rich violet-crimson with pale contrasting stamens. The growth is strong, spreading and bushy, with large, thick, very rugose leaves and many thorns. It has a slight fragrance and bears massive hips. Height 1.2–1.5m/4–5ft. It was first introduced by Harkness & Co. of Hitchin, but Jack Harkness of that firm, in his book *Roses*, takes no credit for its breeding, saying it was discovered amongst a batch of a rose called 'Rose Apples', but otherwise being unable to say anything of its origin.

**Schneezwerg** ('Snowdwarf') Reputedly a hybrid of *Rosa bracteata*, and from this species it may have inherited its dark, shiny foliage which bears little resemblance to a Rugosa. Its outstanding virtues are compact, twiggy growth and shapely habit, together with the ability to flower continuously throughout the summer. The flowers are quite small, semi-double and purest white, with pale yellow stamens and strongly fragrant. They repeat well and are followed by pretty, small, orange-red hips. Height about 1.5m/5ft. A good and reliable shrub, if a little unexciting. Raised by P. Lambert (Germany), introduced 1912.

**Snowdon** This is a very substantial and impressive rose that is particularly useful for the back of a large border or for a corner that needs cheering up but where perhaps the soil is not particularly good. It grows to about 2m/7ft tall and about 1.5m/5ft across and so also makes an impenetrable barrier. In the first flush it will be very generously covered in pure white, double, rosette-shaped flowers; thereafter there is a steady stream of flowers until late in the year. It grows well in the UK as well as more Mediterranean-type climates. There is a delicious, true Old Rose fragrance. Altogether a very worthwhile shrub. Bred by Austin (UK), 1989.

**White Grootendorst** A white sport of 'Pink Grootendorst', the second in a line of sports from 'F. J. Grootendorst' (see p. 191), although the growth does not seem to be so strong as that of its forebears. In fact, there is often a decline in vigour when a sport occurs. Discovered by Eddy (USA), introduced 1962.

**Wild Edric** Like 'Mrs Doreen Pike', this rose is listed under the English Roses, although it has many of the characteristics of a Rugosa rose. See Chapter 5.

*SNOWDON is a substantial and impressive rose that bears a generous crop of beautiful, rosette-shaped flowers*

# Hybrid Musk Roses

THE HYBRID MUSKS are usually shrubs of 1.5–1.8m/5–6ft in height, although there are a few smaller varieties which are often of less value. The flowers are generally of small to medium size and held in sprays. Given adequate growing conditions they repeat flower well, sending up strong stems from the base to provide a second crop in late summer. Both growth and foliage are close to that of the Modern Rose, with its smooth, shiny texture.

The history of the Hybrid Musks begins in Germany in 1902, when Peter Lambert sowed what he believed to have been self-fertilized seed of a Rambler called 'Aglaia' and raised a variety that he named 'Trier', which he introduced in 1904. 'Aglaia' was itself a cross between *Rosa multiflora* and the buff-coloured Noisette 'Rêve d'Or'. 'Trier', a 1.8m/6ft shrub or short Climber bearing sprays of small, nearly single white flowers tinged with cream and pink, had the great advantage that it was both repeat flowering and shrubby in growth. Lambert saw the possibilities of this variety and used it in the development of a number of roses he called 'Lambertiana'. Most of these were, in fact, of little merit,

being not much more than rather large Polyantha Roses.

It was not long before the Reverend Joseph Pemberton took a hand. He lived in a village in Essex with the picturesque and appropriate name of Havering-atte-Bower, and here he raised a series of varieties we now call Hybrid Musks. These were the result of crosses between 'Trier' in particular, but also between certain Polyanthas and Noisettes, with a variety of different Hybrid Teas, Tea Roses and Noisettes. They were introduced by a nurseryman called J. A. Bentall, who also bred a few varieties himself, notably 'Buff Beauty' and 'Ballerina'.

The Hybrid Musks require good cultivation and adequate manuring if they are to reach their full potential. Well treated they will form graceful shrubs, bearing an abundance of bloom in summer and again in autumn. Being repeat flowering, pruning is important. Take out the old and weak wood as the shrub matures, and prune back the strong main shoots by one third to encourage new growth. Be careful to leave sufficient strong growth to enable the shrub to build up its structure, otherwise it may remain short.

---

*FELICIA makes an attractive, branching shrub that flowers very freely and makes a good hedge*

**Buff Beauty** One of the finest of the Hybrid Musks, bearing flowers of a lovely rich apricot-yellow and having a strong Tea Rose fragrance. They are semi-double to double, of medium size and held in small or large clusters on a well-balanced arching shrub which may be 1.5–1.8m/5–6ft in height. In warm climates it is generally known as a climber and even in the UK it can be grown very successfully as such. It has large, thick, dark green leaves, and its smooth stems are tinted with brown. When well grown, the whole plant has an appearance of almost tropical lushness. It is reliably recurrent flowering. One of the finest of the rather small number of yellow shrub roses available to us. 'William Allen Richardson' × unknown. Bred by Bentall (UK), 1939.

**Callisto** This is a small shrub, 1.2m/4ft in height, but quite broad and bushy. The flowers are small, rambler-like and held in tight sprays, and of a pleasing yellow shade, fading with age almost to white. Strong fragrance. A seedling from 'William Allen Richardson', it is thus probably a pure descendant from a Noisette Rose. Raised by Pemberton (UK), introduced 1920.

**Cornelia** A vigorous shrub bearing sprays of small, formal rosette-shaped flowers with three or four rows of petals. Their colour is apricot-pink at first, becoming creamy-pink with a distinct boss of yellow stamens at the centre. 'Cornelia' forms a fine, shapely shrub with quite small foliage. In the autumn large sprays of bloom are produced on the strong new stems from the base of the plant. There is a strong fragrance that carries far. 'Cornelia' will grow to about 1.5m/5ft in height and spread to 1.8m/6ft. The parents are not recorded but it appears to be closely related to 'Trier'. Bred by Pemberton (UK), introduced 1925. (Illustrated, p. 189)

*BUFF BEAUTY is one of the finest of the few yellow shrub roses available*

**Felicia** A strong and reliable shrub, flowering very freely both in summer and autumn. Its parents were 'Trier' by the Hybrid Tea 'Ophelia', and the flowers, though small and held in large sprays, have something of the character of the latter rose about them. They begin as somewhat pointed apricot-pink buds, and open to rather informal blush-pink flowers with a strong aromatic fragrance. The foliage too, leans towards the Hybrid Tea, both leaf and flower having rather more substance than is usual among the Hybrid Musks. It will form a broad, shapely, branching plant of 1.5m/5ft in height. A first class, practical shrub that will also make a good hedge. Bred by Pemberton (UK), introduced 1928.

**Francesca** A large, graceful shrub of 1.8m/6ft in height, with broad, arching growth. It is well clothed with foliage, the individual leaves being long and pointed. The long pointed buds of slim, Tea Rose elegance open to quite large, semi-double flowers which are nicely poised in well spaced sprays and coloured apricot-yellow fading to pale yellow. Strong Tea Rose scent. From 'Danaë' × 'Sunburst'. Raised by Pemberton (UK), introduced 1922.

**Moonlight** This is the result of a cross between 'Trier' and the early Tea Rose 'Sulphurea', although it leans heavily towards the former. The flowers are small, semi-double and white with yellow stamens,

and are held in medium-sized sprays, followed by very large sprays late in the summer. 'Moonlight' is useful where a tall shrub is required as it will reach 2.5m/8ft or more in height, although it is more upright than broad and has been known to ascend up to 4.5m/15ft in trees. The stems are tinted mahogany, and the foliage dark green. Strong Musk Rose fragrance. Bred by Pemberton (UK), introduced 1913.

**Nur Mahal** One of the few red Hybrid Musks. The result of crossing the old dark crimson Hybrid Tea 'Château de Clos-Vougeot' with an unspecified Hybrid Musk seedling. It is not so widely grown as many of the Hybrid Musks, which I think is unfortunate, for it is a rose of some character. The flowers are medium sized, crimson at first, opening wide and turning to mauve-crimson with contrasting yellow stamens. They have an evenness of outline that gives them a pleasing formality. The growth is wide and branching, about 1.2m/4ft in height and rather more across. Fragrant. Bred by Pemberton (UK), introduced 1923. (Illustrated overleaf)

**Pax** A cross between 'Trier' and 'Sunburst' resulting in a shrub rather similar to 'Francesca' which, in fact, shares 'Sunburst' as one of its parents. The growth is tall, broad and elegantly arching, with brown stems and dark green leaves. The flowers start as long pointed buds

*NUR MAHAL is an attractive and rather unusual variety that should be more widely grown*

and open to large, loosely formed and semi-double white flowers with golden stamens and a pleasing fragrance. They are held in sprays of medium size which have a delicacy and natural charm the equal of any of this group. Further, often massive sprays follow late in the season. Height 1.8–2.5m/6–8ft. Bred by Pemberton (UK), introduced 1918.

**Penelope** This is usually regarded as one of the most reliable of Hybrid Musk Roses, indeed of all Modern Shrub Roses, and has for many years been widely used both in private gardens and for amenity planting. It forms an excellent full branching shrub about 1.5m/5ft in height and a little more across. The flowers, which are of medium size and borne in large clusters, show some affinity to its mother parent, the Hybrid Tea 'Ophelia'. Coppery-salmon tinted buds open blush-pink and semi-double, soon becoming almost white, the overall effect being pale pink. The fragrance is strong:

*PENELOPE bears flowers in large clusters with a strong fragrance — a combination of Musk from the stamens and fruit from the petals*

a wonderful combination of Musk from the stamens and fruit from the petals. The flowers are followed by pleasing coral-pink hips — a rare bonus in a repeat-flowering rose, although it may be preferable to remove the earliest of these when the petals fall to encourage further bloom. Bred by Pemberton (UK), introduced 1924.

**Prosperity** A cross between the creamy-blush Polyantha Rose 'Marie-Jeanne' and the Tea Rose 'Perle des Jardins', 'Prosperity' is of rather different origin from most Hybrid Musks, and the influence of its Polyantha is clearly visible in its growth. However, the Tea Rose parent brings a softness and shrubbiness that renders this variety quite in keeping with the class. The growth is strong, bushy and rather upright, about 1.5m/5ft in height and slightly less across, with shiny, dark green foliage. The flowers are creamy-white, flushed with pink at first, later becoming ivory-white tinged with lemon at the centre. They are quite small and held in many flowered trusses. Good fragrance. Bred by Pemberton (UK), introduced 1919.

**Thisbe** A small shrub of moderate vigour, carrying clusters of small, semi-double buff-yellow flowers soon paling to creamy-buff. It has a strong and pleasing fragrance. The breeding is the same as for 'Prosperity' (see above) but this time we have a rose that is much closer in character to its Polyantha parent. Height 1.2m/4ft. Bred by Pemberton (UK), introduced 1918.

**Trier** The foundation rose of the class described in the introduction to this section. It is not a particularly outstanding variety, forming a rather upright shrub of 1.8–2.5m/6–8ft in height, with sprays of small, single white flowers tinted with blush and with a hint of yellow at the base. Very strong Musk fragrance. Thought to be a self-seedling from 'Aglaia'. Bred by Lambert (Germany), introduced 1904.

**Vanity** A tall shrub of 2.5m/8ft in height, bearing large, almost single, light crimson flowers which are held widely spaced in open sprays. In late summer, long, strong shoots appear, often bearing huge many-flowered heads of bloom. The whole effect is one of light and airy grace. Due perhaps to its size, the branches are not plentiful and this often results in lop-sided and very open growth. For this reason it is a good idea to plant closely in groups of two or three bushes, so that they grow together to give the appearance of one fine shrub. 'Vanity' is ideal for the back of a large border, where its dainty flowers look very beautiful when seen above other plants. The foliage is dark green and rather sparse, a feature that seems only to add to its attraction by exposing its glaucous green stalks. There is a strong and pleasing fragrance. A cross between 'Château de Clos-Vougeot' and unnamed seedling. Bred by Pemberton (UK), introduced 1920.

**Wilhelm** ('Skyrocket') In 1927 Pemberton introduced a crimson Hybrid Musk called 'Robin Hood', the result of a cross with the crimson Polyantha 'Edith Cavell'. 'Robin Hood' is a rather dull variety showing a strong Polyantha influence, and in 1934 Kordes crossed it with the red Hybrid Tea 'J. C. Thornton' to produce 'Wilhelm'. The result of all this work is a rose that is rather far removed from what I would consider to be a true Hybrid Musk. It is modern in character, with rather upright growth similar to that of a large Floribunda. For all this, 'Wilhelm' provides a fine splash of colour, with a mass of small, semi-double, dark crimson flowers in large clusters. It repeats reliably and there are long lasting orange-red hips in the autumn. There is only a slight fragrance. Height 1.5–1.8m/5–6ft.

**Will Scarlet** A scarlet sport of 'Wilhelm', similar in every way except colour and providing a brilliant display. Light fragrance. Introduced by Hilling (UK), 1947.

*TRIER, perhaps a rose of greater historical interest than of beauty, is outstandingly fragrant*

*VANITY, with its strongly coloured flowers and strong growth, is a good choice for the back of the border*

# Modern Shrub Roses

WE GROUP under this heading a large number of Shrub Roses of widely varying origins, nearly all of them bred during the last hundred years. Perhaps the most important thing they have in common is that all but a few have some Hybrid Tea in their make up, a fact that often shows up in their appearance, both in flower and growth. They might well be said to be hybrids of the Hybrid Teas or Floribundas. The other side of their parentage may come from any one of a variety of species and classes, resulting in many widely differing shrubs—although the newest varieties may be the result of much more complex breeding. The emphasis is now often on health and freedom of flowering which can, unfortunately, be to the detriment of the beauty of flower and fragrance.

Nearly all these roses are easily grown and very robust. More often than not they are recurrent flowering. They are, therefore, highly suitable for the average garden, and as this group includes some of the best known of all Shrub Roses, many are available at local garden centres. Most are very showy, producing masses of bloom. Local authorities buy them in quantity, and no wonder, for there are few shrubs of any kind that produce so much colour over so long a period.

The name of Kordes occurs again and again among these roses, and it should be said that this firm has contributed more than any other to their development. Kordes was interested in breeding hardy Shrub Roses for the North European climate. Some of these may appear a little coarse, no doubt due to the pursuit of hardiness to the exclusion of other qualities, but we have only to mention such varieties as 'Frühlingsmorgen', 'Fritz Nobis' and 'Cerise Bouquet', to realise how beautiful many of them are.

Cultivation is no problem. Good feeding and adequate pruning will yield a better performance and greater continuity of flowering, but due to the great diversity of habit of this class, it is not possible to be specific as regards pruning. Usually it best to thin out weak wood and cut back the remaining growth by about a third, but a little imagination is called for here—where the growth is closer to the wild species, greater freedom should be allowed and less pruning done, especially if they do not repeat flower.

Many of these shrubs are equally good as Climbers, perhaps for a wall, fence or pillar, and the majority of the taller kinds are suitable for growing in this manner.

---

*Right,*
*BLOOMFIELD*
*ABUNDANCE*
*is a miniature-*
*flowered rose*
*with tiny Tea*
*Rose buds of*
*perfect scrolled*
*formation*

*Far right,*
*BONICA grows*
*well in nearly all*
*climates and is*
*one of the most*
*popular and*
*widely planted of*
*all modern roses*

**Aloha** It can be grown as a free standing shrub about 1.5–1.8m/5–6ft tall and makes an excellent climber to 2m/7ft, more in warmer-climates (see p. 245). When the once-flowering Rambler Rose 'Doctor W. Van Fleet' sported to produce the repeat-flowering rose 'New Dawn', the way was open to breed new and more reliably repeat-flowering Climbers. 'Aloha' is one of the results of such endeavours. The flowers are very double, deeply cupped in form and much like those of an old Bourbon Rose, while the colour is rose-pink, deeper on the outside of the flower. There is a strong fragrance. The foliage is glossy, leathery and disease resistant. If you have a low retaining wall, this rose can be planted on top and allowed to trail downwards with the most pleasing effect. 'Mercedes Gallart' × 'New Dawn'. Bred by Boerner (USA), introduced 1949.

**Ballerina** A beautiful and very useful rose. Its small single Polyantha blooms are held in many-flowered clusters and are of a soft pink with a white centre. 'Ballerina' flowers with remarkable continuity, and combines this with quite exceptional toughness and reliability. It forms a tight, rounded shrub of 1.2m/4ft in height by almost as much across, while the flowers are held in close trusses, slightly reminiscent of a hydrangea. A mass planting of this rose can provide a pleasing effect, the flowers mingling attractively with its light green foliage. It is also excellent when grown as a standard. Slight fragrance. The parents are not recorded. Bred by Bentall (UK), introduced 1937.

**Bloomfield Abundance** A miniature-flowered rose with tiny, pale pink Tea Rose buds of perfect scrolled formation. These are so like those of the rose 'Cécile Brünner' (see p. 104), as to be almost indistinguishable at first sight. This is no doubt partly because the flowers are so small, but nevertheless the similarity is quite remarkable. The real difference is that 'Bloomfield Abundance' forms a shrub of some 1.8–2.5m/6–8ft in height, whereas 'Cécile Brünner' seldom grows to more than 1.2m/4ft. The individual blooms can easily be recognised by one characteristic: on 'Bloomfield Abundance' the sepals are unusually long and leafy for the size of the flower, trailing down as it opens; on 'Cécile Brünner' these are short. 'Bloomfield Abundance' is a tall, airy shrub, producing its blooms singly and in small clusters on long, wiry stems. Later in the year long shoots appear from the base of the plant in the manner of a Hybrid Musk Rose, and these produce dozens of widely separated flowers. It is a very reliable shrub, the result of a cross between a *Rosa wichurana* hybrid called 'Sylvia', and the Hybrid Tea Rose 'Dorothy Page-Roberts'. Bred by George C. Thomas (USA), 1920.

**Bonica** (*Meidomonac*) This must be one of the most popular and widely planted of all modern roses, chosen for the freedom with which it produces its flowers and its almost complete reliability. The small to medium sized, bright, rose-pink flowers are produced, initially, over a very long period although there is then a long gap before the late summer/early autumn flush. If not dead headed,

*BALLERINA flowers with remarkable continuity and combines this with exceptional toughness and reliability*

201

a wonderful crop of bright red hips will be
produced instead that last long into the
winter. It makes a very thick, sturdy shrub
about 1.2m/4ft tall by about the same
across, although the final dimensions very
much depend on how it is pruned. Generally very healthy but can get some blackspot
later in the year but is of little consequence.
Only a very light fragrance. Bred by
Meilland (France), 1981.

**Cerise Bouquet** A unique rose that is difficult to compare with any other. It is the
result of a cross between *Rosa multibracteata*
and the Hybrid Tea Rose 'Crimson Glory'.
The growth is tall and gracefully arching,
1.8–2.5m/6–8ft in height by as much across,
though examples of up to 3.5m/12ft are not
uncommon and, when allowed to trail
through other shrubs, up to 4.5m/15ft. The
flowers are quite small and surrounded by
attractive, leafy grey-green bracts. Starting
as prettily scrolled buds, they open semi-
double and flat to expose their stamens and
are of a pleasing cerise-crimson colour. The
particular charm of this rose lies in the fact
that the individual blooms are held on long,
leafy, hanging stems fanning out in the most
graceful manner from an already bending
branch. The foliage is small, greyish-green
and attractive. The blooms have a light,
fruit-like fragrance. There is only one period
of flowering, but then it is one of the most
beautiful shrubs in the garden. I understand
this rose will make a good Climber, and can
well imagine that it would be very fine when
so grown although it is viciously thorny.
Bred by Kordes (Germany), introduced
1958.

**Clair Matin** A rose of modern appearance,
bearing dainty, pale pink, semi-double
flowers of medium size with a slight
fragrance. It has branching, slightly arching
growth of 2m/7ft in height and about 1.8m/
6ft across. The foliage is deep green and
leathery. Perhaps its greatest virtue is that it
repeat flowers with remarkable reliability.
'Clair Matin' may equally well be grown as a
Climbing Rose, when it will achieve a height
of 3.5m/12ft. 'Fashion' × ('Independence'
× 'Orange Triumph') × 'Phyllis Bide'.
Bred by Meilland (France), 1960.

**Complicata** See Chapter 9.

**Dapple Dawn** This is a sport from 'Red
Coat' (see p. 209). The flowers are large, 10–
12cm/4–5in across, and held well apart in
open sprays. They are delicate pink, veined
all over with a stronger pink and have long
yellow stamens. The petals are quite thin,
giving them at times a gossamer-like quality,

Modern
Shrub
Roses

*CERISE*
*BOUQUET is*
*a very large rose*
*that is guaranteed*
*to make a striking*
*show in a border*
*or as a free-*
*standing shrub*

but it is the overall effect that is so pleasing. Planted in a group, with its flowers held so daintily above the foliage, this variety is an enchanting sight. Like 'Red Coat' it is an excellent shrub that is hardly ever without flowers. Light fragrance. Austin (UK), 1983.

**Dentelle de Malines** This is really a Rambler Rose but it will, if desired, make a very large shrub which will grow even under the most difficult conditions. See Chapter 8.

**Erfurt** A well-formed shrub of branching, slightly arching growth with good foliage. The flowers, which are borne in small clusters, are of medium size, semi-double, and slightly cupped, their colour being rosy-pink with a prominent contrasting white centre and a boss of golden stamens. 'Erfurt' is not a glamorous rose, but it is reliable and repeats well. It has a light fragrance. Height 1.5m/5ft. 'Eva' × 'Réveil Dijonnais'. Bred by Kordes (Germany), 1939.

**Fountain** An upright shrub, 1.5m/5ft in height, bearing large, blood-red, typically Hybrid Tea flowers with shapely buds. They are of particularly pure colouring and have a strong fragrance. There is ample deep green disease-resistant foliage. It is nice to see a Hybrid Tea flower on a good shrub. Parentage unknown. Bred by Tantau (Germany), introduced 1970.

**Fritz Nobis** A cross between the strong growing Hybrid Tea Rose 'Joanna Hill' and 'Magnifica', the latter being a direct descendant of the Penzance Sweet Brier 'Lucy Ashton'. It is remarkable how 'Fritz Nobis' has caught the strong, bushy growth of the Sweet Brier, and managed to combine this with the most charming Hybrid Tea-like flowers. The whole shrub remains in balance, growing to about 1.8m/6ft in height and the same across. The flowers start as perfect pointed buds and open to shapely semi-double flowers of a clear pink. Add to this a delicious clove scent, and we have one of the best Modern Shrub Roses. There are few roses capable of such a fine display. It is unfortunate this occurs only in early summer, but to ask for more would, perhaps, be too much, and we do have the compensation of its dark red hips that last long into the winter. The foliage is large and dark green. Bred by Kordes (Germany), introduced 1940.

**Frühlingsgold** (Spring Gold) This is one of the most widely planted of all Shrub Roses, both in gardens and public places. The reason for this is not hard to explain, for no garden rose is more hardy, so reliable, or so easily grown, even under difficult conditions.

It can get blackspot although it doesn't seem to trouble it unduly. The flowers are creamy-yellow in colour, fairly large, semi-double, with rich yellow stamens, and although they are rather untidy in form this does not matter in the mass. They have a strong fragrance that carries across the garden. There is only one period of bloom, early in the season, but what a magnificent flowering it is—the whole shrub is covered with flowers! It usually grows to about 2m/7ft high by as much across, although sometimes, if permitted, it will grow much larger. A hybrid of 'Joanna Hill' and *Rosa pimpinellifolia hispida* (now *R. spinosissima* var. *hispida*). Bred by Kordes (Germany), introduced 1937.

**Frühlingsmorgen** (Spring Morning) The second member of this series is one of the most delicately beautiful of all single roses. The flowers are large, slightly cupped and perfectly formed. According to the strength of the sun, they can vary in colour from cherry-pink to clear rose-pink, paling a little towards the centre, and they have the most attractive, long and elegant maroon-coloured stamens. The growth is not quite so unfailingly robust as in the case of 'Frülingsgold', but it will grow to about 1.5–1.8m/5–6ft in height and the same across. Like 'Frülingsgold' it can suffer from blackspot. It cannot be said to be recurrent flowering, though there are frequently a few further blooms later in the year. The foliage is of a dark and leaden green. There is a slight fragrance. Breeding ('E.G. Hill' × 'Kathrine Kordes') × *Rosa pimpinellifolia* 'Grandiflora' (now *R. spinosissima* 'Grandiflora'). Bred by Kordes (Germany), introduced 1942.

**Golden Wings** It is rather surprising that good, repeat-flowering single roses are rare among Shrub Roses of garden origin, in spite of the fact that the rose is, of course, single-flowered by nature. This variety has single flowers which are large, perhaps 10–12cm/4–5in across, sulphur-yellow, fading slightly with age, with attractive brown stamens. They open from long, pointed buds and have a sweet fragrance. With these attractions goes a genuine ability to flower throughout the summer and a good crop of large, round, orange hips. 'Golden Wings' is a beautiful rose, with something of the charm of a wild species. If it has a fault, it is the fact that its growth is rather open, stiff and stick-like, though this can be improved by careful pruning to encourage more branching growth. Blackspot can be a problem. Its breeding is both complex and interesting: Hybrid Tea

*Facing page, FRÜHLINGSGOLD has a relatively short flowering time but is then magnificent*

*Far left, FRITZ NOBIS bears shapely semi-double flowers with a delicious clove scent*

*Middle left, FRÜHLINGS-MORGEN is one of the most delicately beautiful of all single roses*

*Left, GOLDEN WINGS is a strongly coloured variety that repeat flowers very well*

JACQUELINE
DU PRÉ has semi-
double flowers of
great charm and
blooms well into
the autumn

LAVENDER
LASSIE has
something of
the character of
an Old Rose with
numerous small
petals in rosette
formation

'Soeur Thérèse' × (*Rosa spinosissima* 'Grandiflora' × *R. spinosissima* 'Ormiston Roy'). 'Ormiston Roy' was *R. spinosissima* × *R. xanthina*. 'Golden Wings' is thus closely connected with two *spinosissima* roses.

**Jacqueline du Pré** (Harwanna) A most attractive Shrub Rose that is related through 'Maigold' to the Scots Roses. The semi-double flowers are blush white and, at first, cupped but then soon open up to reveal the stamens. They start early in the season, continuing well through the year. Generally a well shaped and tough plant although it can suffer from blackspot. Lightly fragrant. It was named after the highly talented cellist who died at the age of 43 from multiple sclerosis. Height 1.2m/4ft by 90cm/3ft across. 'Radox Bouquet' × 'Maigold'. Bred by Harkness (UK), 1988.

**Lavender Lassie** Often described as a Hybrid Musk, this rose really has little in common with that group. It is more like a tall Floribunda, growing to about 1.2m/4ft in height and rather narrow. The flowers are 7cm/3in across and have something of the character of an Old Rose, with numerous small petals in rosette formation. The colour is a pale lavender, which is useful as there are few truly repeat-flowering Shrub Roses of this shade; it is, however, variable in this respect, sometimes being nearer to a lilac-pink shade. It is fragrant, repeats well and is free from disease. Bred by Kordes (Germany), introduced 1960.

**Little White Pet** This must be one of the best small Shrub Roses for sheer garden value. It is, in fact, a dwarf sport from the excellent old Sempervirens Rambler, 'Félicité Perpétue'. The flowers are exactly like those of its parent, being pure white, very small, of near pom-pon shape, with many petals, and held in large clusters. The plant grows into a perfectly symmetrical mound about 60cm/2ft in height and at least 80cm/2½ft across, and is very free flowering. Perhaps the most remarkable thing about this rose is that, in spite of the fact that its parent does not repeat flower, it does, and does so more continuously than most others. This seems to happen on the rare occasions that we have a dwarf sport of a Rambler. In fact, this rose is not repeat flowering in the manner of, say, a China Rose—it is more that each spray of flowers continues over an extended period by the production of further branches just beneath it. It is hardy, disease resistant and has a light but pleasing fragrance—indeed it has all the virtues! What a pity, then, that it has defied all attempts of the hybridizer to use it for breeding. It might have been discussed together with the Polyanthas, for which it can easily be mistaken, but it has a softness that we do not usually associate with those roses, and is much more of a shrub. Discovered by Henderson (USA), 1879.

**Magenta** Like 'Lavender Lassie' (see above), this rose has flowers in the Old Rose formation. They are not exactly magenta in colour, being perhaps better described as a mixture of lilac-pink and mauve. They are of medium size, full petalled, opening flat and rosette shaped, with the strong myrrh fragrance we usually associate with the English Roses. It forms a shrub of about 1.2m/4ft in height with rather straggly growth. A reliable rose, but perhaps a little coarse in appearance, it is the result of a cross between a yellow Floribunda seedling and 'Lavender Pinocchio'. Kordes (Germany), 1954.

**Marguerite Hilling** ('Pink Nevada') A sport from 'Nevada' (see p. 208) to which it is entirely similar except for the colour of the flowers which is a deep pink paling a little towards the centre. It sometimes seems that this rose has been overshadowed by its famous parent, and if this were so it would be unfortunate, as I think it is better in pink than in cream, although cream is a less common colour in roses. The sport occurred in Mrs Nancy Steen's garden in

*LITTLE WHITE
PET is one of the
best small Shrub
Roses, bearing
clusters of pure
white, very small
flowers*

*RED COAT is hardly ever without bloom throughout the summer*

New Zealand. It will frequently sport back and produce a branch bearing the flowers of 'Nevada', and such branches should be cut away. Height 2.5m/8ft. First marketed by Hilling's Nurseries (UK), 1959.

**Marjorie Fair** A hybrid between 'Ballerina' and 'Baby Faurax', this rose is similar to 'Ballerina', with closely packed Polyantha-like sprays, but its single flowers are a deep carmine with a white eye at the centre. It forms a small bushy shrub of 90cm/3ft by as much across, and is reliably repeat flowering, hardy and disease resistant, but not, I think, so beautiful as 'Ballerina'. Bred by Harkness (UK), introduced 1978.

**Martin Frobisher** We have here a rose that bears little resemblance to a Rugosa. The flowers are charming: small, double, rosette shaped, of Old Rose appearance and soft pink in colour, the general effect being a little like that of an Alba Rose, while the foliage bears some resemblance to that of *Rosa spinosissima*, although there are almost no thorns. The leaves are small and of a dull metallic green. It is regularly recurrent flowering. Fragrant. Height 1.2–1.5m/4–5ft. Bred by the Agricultural Research Station, Ottawa, who have done much good work in the development of hardy, disease-resistant roses. Introduced 1968.

**München** The result of the same cross as 'Erfurt': 'Eva' × 'Réveil Dijonnais', and from the same raiser, Kordes, in 1940. The growth is very similar to 'Erfurt'. About 1.5 by 1.5m/5 × 5 ft, strong and healthy with shiny dark green foliage. The flowers are semi-double, medium sized and garnet red with occasional streaks of white. They are held in clusters and repeat well. Almost no fragrance.

**Nevada** The result of a cross between 'La Giralda', an extremely strong and large-flowered Hybrid Tea Rose, and a form of *Rosa moyesii*, probably *R. moyesii* var. *fargesii*. It exhibits many of the characteristics of its *R. moyesii* parent, forming a broad, arching shrub of dense growth with long, arching, almost thornless branches. The branches bear large, creamy-white, semi-double flowers all along their branches, opening flat with yellow stamens. They are sometimes tinged with pink, particularly in warm, dry weather. Although a little untidy when taken individually, the overall effect is very pleasing. There is a second crop late in the summer and occasional flowers at other times. Somewhat affected by blackspot. 'Nevada' and its sport 'Marguerite Hilling' (see p. 206) are remarkable for their ability to repeat flower while retaining their graceful, near species-like growth. Height about 2.5m/8ft by as much across. Bred by Pedro Dot (Spain), introduced 1927.

**Pearl Drift** An interesting rose from the breeders' point of view. For many years they have tried to obtain crosses with the beautiful Climber 'Mermaid', but these have nearly always proved sterile. The aim has been to produce more Climbers with the very good qualities found in 'Mermaid'—its refined beauty, its ability to climb and repeat flower well, and an almost complete resistance to disease. After so many years, this is the first such rose to appear on the market, although I have heard of other seedlings. 'Pearl Drift' is a cross with the Modern Climber 'New Dawn'. No doubt the breeder was looking for a Climber, but in this case it has turned out to be a shrub with nice low sprawling growth of 90cm/3ft in height and about 1.2m/4ft across. The flowers are large, semi-double, tinted with pink in the bud, opening white shaded with peachy-pink. These are held in clusters and are produced very freely and continuously over a long period. The foliage is a glossy light green and has good disease resistance. Bred by Le Grice (UK), introduced 1983.

**Pleine de Grâce** Like 'Dentelle de Malines', this rose is perhaps better classified as a Rambler (see p. 286) but will also, if desired, form a fine, very large shrub.

**Red Coat** The parent of 'Dapple Dawn' described on p. 202; its red flowers seem to be of slightly greater substance, otherwise it is similar. The colour appears rather harsh when the flowers are viewed individually; this is a nice fresh scarlet-crimson at first, but later it hardens to a duller shade. When seen in the mass, however, 'Red Coat' is most impressive—the whole effect is as though a multitude of butterflies had descended upon the bushes, and this is particularly noticeable in the nursery fields. In studying 'Red Coat' and 'Dapple Dawn' at regular intervals throughout the summer, we have found them to be hardly ever without bloom, and with the exception of 'Ballerina' I know of no other roses so consistent in this respect. 'Red Coat' may be pruned as a bush when it will grow to about 1.2m/4ft in height, or as a shrub, which will achieve 1.5–1.8m/5–6ft. There is little scent. 'Parade' × an English Rose. Austin (UK), 1973.

**Rhapsody in Blue** (*Frantasia*) This rose created a great deal of excitement around the world when it was first introduced in 2003 and certainly when we first saw a row of it in our field it was very striking. It is, of course, not a true blue although, in the rose world, it is one of the closest we have to it. A difficult colour to describe, especially as it changes considerably with age of flower and climate, it is perhaps an iridescent purple that fades to slate blue. The flowers are semi-double and not particularly shapely but are produced freely over a long period. It makes a tall, bushy, healthy shrub 1.5m/4.5ft tall by 90cm/3ft across that will grow much taller in warmer weather. Many people say it has a strong fragrance but I must admit I have never found it to be so. Bred by the English amateur breeder Frank Cowlishaw, it was Rose of the Year in 2003. (Illustrated overleaf)

**Rosy Cushion** (*Interall*) From the same breeder as 'Smarty', to which it is similar except that it is rather less vigorous and the flowers are a slightly deeper pink with white at the centre. Good foliage, excellent habit of growth, continuous flowering. The breeding was 'Yesterday' × unnamed seedling. Introduced 1979. (Illustrated overleaf)

*Near left, NEVADA is a substantial variety with large semi-double flowers*

*Far left, PEARL DRIFT has an interesting parentage and is a very worthwhile garden rose*

209

*Above,*
*RHAPSODY IN*
*BLUE is not a*
*true blue, but*
*one of the closest*
*we have to it*

*Right,*
*ROSY CUSHION*
*flowers*
*continuously and*
*has both excellent*
*foliage and habit*
*of growth*

**Sally Holmes** A bushy, recurrent-flowering shrub, 1.5 m / 5 ft in height, bearing large, creamy-white semi-double flowers with a light fragrance. These can be very beautiful, but those produced on the strong main stems tend to be packed together much too closely, forming a clumsy head of bloom. When they appear on side branches it is quite a different matter, for here we have fewer flowers which can show off their delicate refinement to perfection. In warmer climates it is commonly grown as a climber. The parents were 'Ivory Fashion' × 'Ballerina'. Bred by Holmes (UK), a successful amateur breeder, introduced 1976.

**Scarlet Fire** ('Scharlachglut') A tall, vigorous shrub of graceful, slightly arching growth, with plentiful foliage. The flowers are single and a brilliant scarlet-crimson with contrasting yellow stamens. Although these appear only in the summer, they are followed by fine, large pear-shaped, orange-scarlet hips in the autumn, lasting well into the winter. Little or no fragrance. An excellent shrub, providing a brilliant splash of colour without being in any way crude. It has Old Rose connections, the result of a cross between 'Poinsettia' and a Gallica called 'Grandiflora'. Bred by Kordes (Germany), introduced 1952.

**Scintillation** A cross between *Rosa* 'Macrantha' and the Hybrid Musk 'Vanity', this rose forms an excellent low, sprawling shrub of open growth, about 1.2 m / 4 ft in height and perhaps 1.8–2.5 m / 6–8 ft across. The flowers are medium to large, semi-double and of the palest lilac-pink, opening wide to show their stamens. They are held in large sprays and produced extremely freely, indeed almost covering the whole plant. 'Scintillation' blooms only once in the summer, but then for a long period, the overall effect being one of daintiness and grace. The flowers are followed by an excellent crop of large orange hips. Very fragrant. The foliage, like that of its parent 'Vanity', is rather sparse. Bred by Austin (UK), 1968.

**Silver Ghost** (*Kormifari*) For a number of years Kordes has been concentrating on breeding varieties that are as healthy as possible, which is very beneficial to gardeners who do not want to spray at all. 'Silver Ghost' combines many good characters including extremely good disease resistance, very good repeat flowering and simple but beautiful blooms of pure white. The plant is very compact growing only about 75 cm / 2½ft tall by about 60 cm / 2 ft wide. Unusually for a single rose it also has a light to medium

*SCINTILLATION
blooms once but
then very freely
and over a long
period, the overall
effect being one
of daintiness and
grace*

fragrance. A useful rose for the front of a border or for a container. Kordes (Germany) 2001.

**Smarty** A third variety from the breeder of 'Red Blanket' and 'Rosy Cushion', and to my mind the best and most beautiful. It is a shrub of 1.2–1.8m/4–6ft high, its spreading growth bearing sprays of single, soft pink flowers of Dog Rose appearance and providing a most charming effect. It is reliably repeat flowering, almost completely disease resistant, and has a light fruit-like fragrance. Bred by Ilsink (UK), introduced 1979.

**The Fairy** This rose might properly have been included with the Polyanthas, as its flowers are of exactly their type. It is, however, a shrub rather than a bush with low arching growth spreading out in an almost fan-like manner, 60cm/2ft in height by 90cm/3ft across. The flowers are small, soft-pink in colour and borne in great quantities in broad, flat sprays. Flowering starts very late, but continues throughout the summer almost without a break, providing colour when many other roses have passed their peak. The foliage is tiny, almost like that of box. This rose has always been regarded as a sport from the Rambler 'Lady Godiva', but Peter Beales suggests it was, in fact, the result of a cross between the Polyantha 'Paul Crampel' and 'Lady Godiva'. Looking at the plant, this would seem possible, although as far as I know its breeder, Bentall, did not record his crosses. Introduced 1932.

**Thérèse Bugnet** An extremely hardy rose that was bred to survive the cold winters of Alberta and boasts two forms of *R. rugosa* and *R. acicularis*—the northernmost of all roses—in its parentage. It is fairly upright and quite tall, easily reaching 1.8m/6ft in height, and has attractive red stems with grey-green foliage that is totally disease resistant. The flowers are attractive being loosely double and a pure rose pink. They have a good, rich fragrance. After the initial flush of flowers there are some later ones although unfortunately not a great showing. A very useful rose for a tough position. Bred by Bugnet (Canada), 1950.

*Facing page, THE FAIRY starts flowering late but then continues throughout the summer almost without a break*

*Near left, ZIGEUNERKNABE has rough, dark green foliage and is one of the toughest of roses, ideal for a difficult position in the garden*

*Far left, THÉRÈSE BUGNET was bred in Canada and is remarkable for its great winter hardiness*

**Zigeunerknabe** (Gipsy Boy) A variety that would look entirely at home among the Old Roses, and indeed is sometimes classified with the Bourbons, a position to which it has little claim. It is, in fact, a seedling from a rose called 'Russelliana', which was itself probably a seedling from *Rosa setigera*. Its other parent is not known, but might have been a Rugosa. The growth is exceptionally strong and bushy, at least 2m/7ft in height and almost as much across, with many strong thorns. It has rough, dark green, Rugosa-like foliage. The flowers are a little more than medium sized, cupped in shape at first, opening flat and almost double, while the colour is a dark crimson-purple with a little white at the centre. The blooms appear only in early summer and are followed by small orange-red hips. This rose is not unlike 'Chianti' in appearance, though the flowers held in small, tight sprays, are not of the same quality and lack fragrance. It is, however, one of the toughest of roses and ideal for a difficult position in the garden. Bred by Geschwind (Hungary), introduced 1909.

213

# Ground-Cover Roses

MOST GROUND-COVER ROSES are of relatively recent introduction, although we do include here 'Raubritter' and 'Max Graf' which belong to the first half of the 20th century. Many new varieties have been introduced since the 1980s, notably the County series which are generally very healthy and free flowering. Mention should also be made of the Flower Carpet series of roses from Noack that have sold in vast quantities around the world.

The Ground-cover Roses were largely bred for public planting where dense growth and plenty of colour, together with hardiness and reliability, is required. The idea behind the use of ground-cover plants is that they save labour, which is considered particularly important for public planting. Ground-cover Roses form a thicket of growth which will smother all weeds. They have a rather tidy appearance in contrast to the often rather unruly growth of other Shrub Roses.

It is important to get rid of weeds before planting the rose, for if they get a hold before the rose has grown it may be the weeds controlling the rose, rather than the rose controlling the weeds! Moreover, it is very difficult to remove weeds or suckers from among prickly growth. For this reason, these roses are frequently grown on their own roots from cuttings, and this can be a distinct advantage.

Whether or not we favour ground-cover planting, we have here an interesting group that brings another dimension to growing roses. Furthermore, Ground-cover Roses do not necessarily have to be used only for ground cover, for their growth is pleasing in itself and they can be used in the same way as any other Shrub Rose.

All are very hardy and easily grown, and bring with them a Rambler-like charm. Most are recurrent flowering, but even those that are not bloom over an extended period.

---

**Cambridgeshire** (Carpet of Gold) (*Korhaugen*) A very bright and multi-coloured variety. The flowers start as bright orange with a yellow centre then fade to pink and end up as dark pink and cream. A single cluster can have the whole range of colours creating a quite startling effect. It repeats well and has a light fragrance. Height 45cm/18in by 1.2m/3ft across. Bred by Kordes (Germany), 1994.

**Centre Stage** (*Chewcreepy*) A truly ground-creeping rose that grows no more than about 20cm/8in tall. The thin stems are smothered in mid to pale pink, single flowers that are produced continuously from June to November. The leaves are tiny and outstandingly healthy. Pruning is very easy: simply thin out some of the stems every third year or so. Eyeopener × (*R. luciae* var. *onoei* × Laura Ashley). Bred by Chris Warner (UK), 2001.

**Flower Carpet** (Heidetraum) (Pink Flower Carpet) (*Noatraum*) The Flower Carpet series with their excellent health and continuous flowering ability created a great stir in the rose world and sell in very large numbers. This is the first of the series with bright pink, semi-double flowers. It has low spreading growth about 90cm/3ft wide and 60cm/2ft tall. Bred by Noack (Germany), 1989.

**Grouse** The parents of this rose were 'The Fairy' × a *Rosa wichurana* seedling, and it has retained something of the Wichurana's prostrate growth. It will spread over an area some 3m/10ft wide, flowering freely in July and August, followed by hips. The flowers are pale pink and single, with a dainty wild rose charm. Very disease resistant. Fragrant. Bred by Kordes (Germany), 1984.

**Hampshire** (*Korhamp*) Bright scarlet single flowers show off the golden yellow stamens in the centre. It repeat flowers very well into the autumn when there is also a good crop of orange hips. It is quite a small plant, only 30cm/12in tall by 60cm/2ft across. Bred by Kordes (Germany), 1989.

**Hertfordshire** (Tommelise) (*Kortenay*) A particularly healthy Ground-cover Rose with single carmine pink flowers. They are

*Facing page,*
*RAUBRITTER is a very distinctive variety with rounded, deeply cupped flowers of the clearest pink*

*Right,*
*CAMBRIDGESHIRE creates a quite startling effect*

*Far right,*
*FLOWER CARPET, the first in the series, created a great stir in the rose world*

*MAX GRAF forms a thicket of growth and is very useful where dense ground cover is required*

produced almost continuously in large clusters and stand up well to the rain. It is very hardy, growing well in Scandinavia. It grows about 75cm/2.5ft across by 45cm/18in tall. Bred by Kordes (Germany), 1991.

**Lancashire** (*Korstgli*) A particularly healthy rose that has won many awards around Europe including the Allgemeine Deutsche Rosen-neuheitsprufung (ADR) trials where the emphasis is on health. The small, bright red flowers are held in large trusses and produced very freely. The stems arch over to produce a rounded plant 60cm/2ft tall by 90cm/3ft across. Bred by Kordes (Germany), 1998.

**Laura Ashley** (*Chewharla*) The single, lilac-mauve flowers are produced in very large sprays of up to 30 blooms and have a light fruity fragrance. At the peak of its flowering the plant can be almost literally covered in colour. The growth habit is low and spreading, about 90cm/3ft across and 60cm/2ft tall. Marjorie Fair × 'Nozomi'. Bred by Warner (UK), 1989.

**Magic Carpet** (*Tapis Magique*) (*Jaclover*) A very pretty and rather unusual ground cover from the United States of America with 5cm/2in wide semi-double flowers. The colour varies from cherry-crimson at opening through mauve, lilac and lavender. It has a good spreading habit (about 1.8m/6ft) although it does grow rather taller than the average ground cover (about 90cm/3ft). It is also very good for the front of the border, especially as it repeat flowers very well. It has glossy, healthy leaves. Light, spicy fragrance. Bred by Zary and Warriner (USA), 1992.

**Max Graf** A trailing Rugosa that is a very useful Ground-cover Rose; the result of a cross between *Rosa rugosa* and *R. wichurana*, gaining its prostrate habit from the latter. It forms a thicket of growth about 60cm/2ft deep and spread over a wide area, its long shoots sometimes rooting themselves into the ground as they go. The flowers are of small to medium size, single, pale pink to almost white at the centre, with yellow stamens, and have the fresh, fruit-like fragrance of their Wichurana parent. It has plentiful, dark, glossy foliage, and flowers only in the early summer. A useful rose, not only in the border, but also for covering banks and other problem areas where dense ground cover is required. Bred by Bowditch (USA), 1919. There is also a white sport, known as 'White Max Graf'. It is an equally good rose.

**Nozomi** A climbing Miniature Rose which, perhaps more importantly, also has the useful ability to creep and make good ground cover. It was bred in Japan by Onodera, and introduced in 1968. Indeed, it has an oddly Japanese appearance and it is easy to picture it growing in a Japanese garden. It has small glossy leaves and sprays of tiny pearly-pink flowers in midsummer, and will spread to perhaps 1.5 m/5 ft while remaining little more than 30 cm/1 ft high. Although sometimes mixed with larger Ground-cover Roses, this is not advisable, as it will look out of place and will almost certainly be swamped. When grown as a short Weeping Standard it can be effective, and is frequently exhibited in this form at the Chelsea Flower Show. Such Standards have to be forced under glass, and this gives the flowers an attractive delicacy they do not possess when grown outdoors. A useful, not entirely satisfying rose, but one of the few that looks at home in the rock garden, and I have seen it grown over rocks by water, providing a charming effect. The breeding was Floribunda 'Fairy Princess' × Miniature 'Sweet Fairy'.

**Partridge** A rose from the same cross as 'Grouse' to which it is similar except that the flowers are pure white. It has the same wide-spreading prostrate growth and single flowers. It blooms in late July and early August, followed by hips. Kordes (Germany), 1984.

**Pheasant** The third rose in the Game Bird series, this time with double flowers of deep rose-pink borne in large clusters. It has the same vigorous prostrate growth of about 80cm/2½ft in height, spreading to perhaps 1.8–2m/6–7ft. Some repeat flowering. Bred by Kordes (Germany), introduced 1986.

**Raubritter** A cross between 'Daisy Hill' and the Rambler 'Solarium', this rose forms a sprawling shrub of 90cm/3ft in height and some 2m/7ft across, the growth developing into a low, spreading mound. The flowers are most charming: clear pink in colour, small, of a very definite cupped shape and held in clusters. It has the atmosphere of an Old Rose, although it is, in fact, quite different from any variety

*Left, PARTRIDGE and below, PHEASANT along with 'Grouse' are three excellent varieties from Kordes that have true ground-covering ability*

*Above, RUSHING STREAM bears large heads of small, single white flowers and does well in less than ideal conditions*

*Right, WORCESTERSHIRE, produces semi-double blooms through to autumn*

I know. The foliage is dark green like that of *Rosa* 'Macrantha'. Although it has some tendency towards mildew, it should still be grown, for it is a most beautiful rose. Bred by Kordes (Germany), introduced 1936. (Illustrated, p. 215)

**Running Maid** (*Lenramp*) A low shrub of excellent dome shape and close twiggy growth bearing large, nicely spaced sprays of pretty little deep pink Rambler-like flowers. It blooms only in the summer, but is good in every way, whether used for ground cover or in the border. There are tiny orange-red hips in the autumn. Bred by Louis Lens (Belgium), introduced in the UK 1985.

**Rushing Stream** (*Austream*) A most attractive variety with very large heads of small, single, white flowers. It makes a delightful, low mounding plant about 50–75cm/18in–2ft tall by about 1.2m/4ft across. The flowers are produced with exceptional continuity over a very long period and, in the autumn, there is the added bonus of a wonderful crop of bright red hips. It is a very tough rose that does well in less than ideal conditions. Bred by David Austin (UK), 1996.

**Snow Carpet** An excellent little rose of a unique habit of growth. It trails along the ground, slowly building into a small mound. It has tiny short-petalled, star-like and very double flowers of pure white held in sprays against small glossy leaves. It may be grown in rock gardens, although the purist might not think it correct in such a position. It will also form an attractive Miniature Standard Rose. Repeat flowering. 'New Penny' × 'Temple Bells'. McGredy (New Zealand), 1980.

**Suffolk** (Bassino) (*Kormixal*) One of the County series, all introduced for their good health and the freedom with which they flower. The flowers of 'Suffolk' are single and of the brightest crimson with prominent golden stamens. Later in the year they are followed by small orange-red hips. It is a low growing variety, only 45cm/18in tall, but spreading to 90cm/3ft or more. Very healthy. Useful for ground cover as well as pots. Bred by Kordes (Germany) 1988.

**Surrey** (Sommerwind) (*Korlanum*)
A particularly prolific variety. The flowers start dark pink and fade with age; they are produced continually from early summer through to the frosts. It makes an attractive spreading plant about 60cm/2ft tall by 1.2m/4ft wide. Bred by Kordes (Germany), 1985.

**White Flower Carpet** (Schneeflocke) (*Noaschnee*) This is a pure white version of the original pink 'Flower Carpet' and to our eyes a more pleasing rose. It has the same characteristics of excellent disease resistance and continuity of flowering. In growth it makes more of a rounded mound, about 60cm/2ft across and tall. Useful as both ground cover and for the front of a border. Bred by Noack (Germany), 1991.

**Worcestershire** (*Korlalon*). Very few of the ground covers are yellow and so this variety comes as a very welcome addition. The semi-double blooms are bright yellow and produced very freely through to the autumn. It has good ground-hugging growth and glossy, disease-resistant leaves. Height 60cm/2ft by 90cm/3ft across. Bred by Kordes (Germany) 1999.

*SUFFOLK*
*is low growing*
*and useful for*
*pots as well as*
*ground cover*

# 7

# CLIMBING ROSES

IT IS A REMARKABLE FACT that a genus that has been responsible for the production of so many garden shrubs—shrubs which, if considered alone, would be sufficient to make it the most important of garden flowers—should also provide us with what is, without doubt, the most important of all climbing plants. It is difficult to overestimate the value of Climbing Roses in the garden. They provide a feeling of abundance, particularly in more formal and architectural areas, which may be in need of softening and a sense of life. They bring height where it might otherwise be lacking and many of them flower intermittently throughout the summer. No plant can fulfil these functions better than the Climbing Rose.

All roses delight us, but perhaps a Climbing Rose, well grown and in full flower, does so more than any other, especially in the mass, although the individual flower is often particularly beautiful when seen looking down at us from the branch of a Climbing Rose. Perhaps it is the association of plant and architecture that gives Climbing Roses a certain advantage.

Before going further, it is necessary to explain that the Climbing Roses are divided into two main groups: the Climbers and the Ramblers. The division is an artificial one, for both are in reality climbing plants, but this division does help us deal with them more easily. A Climbing Rose usually has larger flowers such as we might find in the Old Roses or the Hybrid Teas. The Rambler Roses usually have smaller flowers in larger clusters, and are often of more lax growth. They are also inclined to send up long, sometimes very long, stems from the base of the plant. In fact, they do just what their name suggests, ramble. The Climbers may be stiffer in growth, and although they, too, produce strong base shoots, they tend to build up gradually on past growth. Most Climbing Roses are repeat flowering; the Ramblers almost never are. This is a very arbitrary division, one type frequently overlapping with the other, but in spite of this, when we see these roses there is generally little doubt as to which group they belong.

In this chapter we are concerned with the Climbers: the Noisettes with their delicate refinement, the Climbing Tea Roses, the Climbing Hybrid Teas with their flowers of many colours, the Modern Climbers with their continuous abundance, the Climbing English Roses with their delicate charm and fragrance, as well as other sorts of other classifications or of none, which are often of great beauty.

The best and most frequent use for Climbers is on walls, including house walls where, with the additional warmth that these provide, they are often the earliest garden roses to flower, thus making them particularly precious, and giving them plenty of time to make further growth and so flower again. In addition, no climbing plant is more suitable for growing over arches, on pillars, on trellises, pergolas and so on.

Annual tying and pruning is, of course, necessary with Climbers, and this can be a little more arduous than is the case with shrubs, but really need not be too great a task. All we have to do is to take away some of the long main growth where this is too plentiful, or is becoming old and worn out. This may not be required for a few years. Having done this, cut back the side shoots which have flowered in the previous year to 5 or 7cm/2 or 3in, at the same time pruning away weak or dead shoots.

When attaching the young branches to a wall or length of trellis it is best, whenever possible, to train them, if not horizontally, at least on a slant. This encourages them to form new flowering shoots all along the branch, and so provide far

*Facing page,* CLIMBING LADY HILLINGDON *has lush growth and long, elegant buds of deep apricot-yellow*

220

more flowers. Otherwise the rose will always be pushing upwards, producing its blooms only at the top, where they cannot be seen and leaving the lower parts bare. There is a special problem with pillars, for with these we have less latitude. This can be overcome by winding the growth around the pillar in spiral form.

Climbers sometimes take time to get going and a little persuasion may be necessary. A liberal quantity of some form of natural manure, mixed with the soil where they are to grow, will work wonders. If such material is readily available, it may be used very freely, and you will be amply rewarded in the years to come. Roses planted against walls may well require the most attention for such areas are usually very dry, due to the fact that the soil here is protected and may receive little or no rain. The rose will not begin to move until its roots have themselves moved out into more moist ground. A hosepipe can be useful in the first year or two. Give Climbers in such positions an occasional very heavy watering, one that will soak down deep into the soil. It is vital to avoid drying out early in the life of the rose.

# Noisette Roses

EVEN BEFORE the China Rose was hybridized with various Old Roses to produce the first European recurrent-flowering roses I describe in Chapter 1, it was cross fertilized with the Musk Rose to give us the first repeat-flowering Climbing Roses. This is rather surprising, for it has never been easy to breed such Climbers. Credit for this innovation goes to John Champney, a rice planter of Charleston in South Carolina in the early 1800s. Champney produced a rose which was first named *Rosa moschata hybrida*, but later became known as 'Champney's Pink Cluster'. It is sometimes said he obtained

*GLOIRE DE DIJON, for many years a great favourite of many gardeners, bears large flowers that are richly coloured and highly fragrant*

this rose by crossing the then new 'Parsons' Pink China' (now *Rosa × odorata* 'Pallida') with pollen from the Musk Rose, but it is more likely it was an accidental hybrid, as the deliberate cross fertilization of roses was not practised at that time.

Philippe Noisette, a nurseryman, also of Charleston, sowed seed from 'Champney's Pink Cluster' to produce a variety known as 'Blush Noisette' (now *Rosa* 'Noisette Carnée') which, although not so tall in growth as its parents, was repeat flowering. Thus it was that the Noisettes were born. 'Blush Noisette' was later crossed with 'Parks' Yellow China' (now *Rosa × odorata* 'Ochroleuca'), to give us yellow Noisettes. Noisettes were also freely crossed with the Tea Rose, further widening their range and improving their quality—and the Noisette Roses are, even today, some of the most beautiful of all Climbing Roses. These qualities they frequently combine with tall, lax, rampant growth—something breeders still find very hard to achieve. In addition, the colour yellow was added to the repertoire of garden roses—and we are short enough of yellows among Climbing Roses, even today.

The period of development of Noisettes was brief, and one cannot help feeling that there is a job not yet completed and with very considerable possibilities for further progress. Once again, as with the Rugosas and the Hybrid Musks, the problem is that Noisettes are diploids and this tends to make further development difficult, most roses being tetraploid.

The Noisettes as a class have a refinement and delicacy that is hard to equal elsewhere. The flowers are in the true Old Rose tradition. They are of a rosette formation with petals of a lovely silky texture, and nearly all have a good fragrance. The winter hardiness of some of the Noisettes is, unfortunately, a little questionable, but this should not prevent us from growing them in anything but the coldest positions. Given the protection of a warm wall, they will be perfectly safe. The majority are, in fact, quite hardy.

**Aimée Vibert** ('Bouquet de la Mariée', 'Nivea') This rose, which was raised by Vibert of France in 1828, is not a typical Noisette, but a cross between a Noisette, probably 'Blush Noisette', and *Rosa sempervirens*, the 'Evergreen Rose'. It has the plentiful, long, graceful, rich green foliage of *R. sempervirens*, and bears open sprays of small, pure white, double flowers with yellow stamens. These have a simple charm that is hard to compare with any other Climber. There is a slight musky fragrance. From the Noisette it gains the ability to flower again, starting early in warm climates and often continuing well into the autumn. It is somewhat tender, although it will survive most winters it is likely to encounter in the UK. Early flower shoots are sometimes cut back by frost and this will delay flowering until July or even later. It will climb to a height of 4.5m/15ft in a warm position and may also be grown as a giant, sprawling shrub. Either way it is a most beautiful rose. We have here a variety that is, in fact, a perpetual-flowering Rambler of strong growth, and it is thus something rather unusual. It might have been more accurately included with the Ramblers, but it is by ancestry a Noisette.

**Alister Stella Gray** ('Golden Rambler') Bred by A. H. Gray, a Tea Rose enthusiast, this rose was introduced by George Paul in 1894. It bears small yolk-yellow buds of tightly scrolled formation which open into prettily quartered flowers, later fading to a creamy-white and remaining beautiful at all stages. The flowers have a silky texture and are held in small sprays on the ends of long, thin stems. Later in the year large heads of bloom appear. They have a delicious tea scent. This rose may be grown either as a Climber and will achieve 4.5m/15ft on a warm wall, or as a large arching shrub. A most charming rose.

**Blush Noisette** ('Noisette Carnée') Said by some to be the first Noisette, although arguably 'Champney's Pink Cluster' has more right to that claim to fame. It is hardy, very tough and a great survivor, and still to be seen in old gardens where it may have been planted long ago. The flowers are almost double, small, Rambler like and cupped, and are held in tight clusters. They are of a lilac-blush colour with exposed yellow stamens and have a strong clove fragrance. Although of modest appearance, the flowers are pretty and produced in profusion, repeating well and creating a pleasing massed effect. This variety has a tendency to remain short and bushy, in fact it will form a good shrub. It needs the encouragement of a wall to achieve height, where it can grow to 3.5m/12ft. Noisette (France), before 1817. (Illustrated, p. 224)

**Bouquet d'Or** A seedling from 'Gloire de Dijon', and thus one of the roses that were known as the Dijon Teas. The flowers are quite large and full petalled with a slight scent, their colour a coppery-salmon with yellow at the centre. It is hardy and fairly vigorous, growing to a height of 3m/10ft. Bred by Ducher (France), introduced 1872.

*ALISTER STELLA GRAY bears small yolk-yellow buds of tightly scrolled formation which open into prettily quartered flowers*

223

**Céline Forestier** Although not a strong rose, this is one of the most beautiful, and given a warm wall and careful treatment it will do well. The flowers are fully double, neatly rounded, opening quartered with a button eye. Their colour is a pale yellow, the petals having a silky texture. There is a rich Tea Rose fragrance. Given time it will grow to about 2.5–3m/8–10ft, perhaps more in a warm climate. A charming rose of delicate refinement. Bred by Trouillard (France), introduced 1842.

**Champney's Pink Cluster** Small, blush pink, double flowers in large, loosely formed clusters. Light green foliage. Repeat flowering. Disease-free. Arguably the first Noisette. 4.5 × 2.5m/15 × 8ft. (Champney 1802).

**Claire Jacquier** ('Mademoiselle Claire Jacquier') Here we have a truly vigorous Noisette that will grow to as much as 9m/30ft but, as is often the case with Climbing Roses, what it gains in vigour it loses in its ability to repeat flower. A very good early flush of bloom is followed by only occasional flowers later. The individual flowers are rather loosely formed, rich yellow at first, paling with age to pale yellow. They have a delicious fragrance. They are held against plentiful light green foliage. Hardy. Bred by Bernaix (France), introduced 1888.

**Cloth of Gold** ('Chromatella') A self-sown seedling from 'Lamarque' and, like its parent, rather tender. If planted against a warm wall it can do well. The flowers are double and of a soft sulphur-yellow which deepens towards the centre. Fragrant. Height 3.5m/12ft. Introduced by Coquereau (France) 1843.

**Crépuscule** The Flemington race course in Melbourne is famed for its roses, which are planted in large beds, in borders, mixed in with perennials and covering large arches and obelisks. Perhaps the most impressive sight is a 100m/330ft or so stretch of fencing covered with 'Crépuscule'. The flowers overall give the impression of a beautiful, rich apricot-yellow but closer inspection shows a whole range of colours from deep, rich apricot to butterscotch and buff and paling with age to soft yellow. The flowers, which are produced almost continuously, are perfectly set off by the bronze coloured young leaves. They have a strong sweet and musky fragrance which is further enhanced by the great abundance with which the blooms are produced. While the colours are more intense in cooler weather it does grow better in a warmer, Mediterranean type climate. It is not particularly vigorous. Height 2.5m/8ft. Bred by Dubreuil (France), 1904.

*CHAMPNEY'S PINK CLUSTER bears small double flowers in large clusters*

*Left, CRÉPUSCULE, with many different colours in the flowers, gives an overall effect of a very pleasing rich apricot-yellow*

*Facing page, BLUSH NOISETTE is still to be seen in old gardens where it may have been planted long ago. It is hardy and a great survivor*

**Desprez à Fleurs Jaunes** ('Jaune Desprez') An excellent Climber blooming freely and with remarkable continuity. The flowers are medium sized, opening flat, with many silky petals and a button eye, their colour a warm yellow shaded with peach, becoming paler with age. They have a strong and pleasing fragrance. Growth is vigorous, reaching 6m/20ft on a warm wall. The result of a cross between 'Blush Noisette' and 'Parks' Yellow China'. Bred by Desprez (France) 1835.

**Gloire de Dijon** A famous old Climbing Rose, that was once found in many a cottage garden, where it was often known as 'Old Glory'. There can be few roses that have given more pleasure to more people since its introduction in 1853. It is said to have been a cross between

*Right, DESPREZ À FLEURS JAUNES is an excellent Climber which, on a warm wall, flowers freely and with remarkable continuity*

*Far right, RÊVE D'OR has pretty, rather informal flowers, although it really needs a warm climate to look its best*

a Tea Rose, the name of which is not known, and the old Bourbon 'Souvenir de la Malmaison' (see pages 65 and 233), and indeed its general appearance would seem to support this. It has large, globular, buff-yellow flowers that flatten and become quartered later, taking on pink tints, particularly in hot weather. They have a strong, rich fragrance. There is no doubt this is a much hardier rose than the typical Noisette, probably due to the fact that it is in part Bourbon. It is truly recurrent flowering. The foliage is thick and heavy, more like that of a Hybrid Tea. A charming Old Rose but one that, today, is outclassed by more recent introductions. Bred by Jacotot (France) 1853.

**Lamarque** Not an easy rose to grow, but well worth a little extra attention. The flowers are in the form of quite large rosettes of palest lemon-yellow (almost white), quartered and flat and of exquisite delicacy. It will grow to about 3m/10ft, but I would expect much more in warmer climates. 'Blush Noisette' × 'Parks' Yellow China'. Bred by Maréchal (France), 1830.

**Ley's Perpetual** This rose was given to me by Mr Wyatt, who for some time edited an excellent magazine called *The Rose*, which unfortunately ceased publication. A seedling from 'Gloire de Dijon', it has a great deal in common with that rose. The flowers are cupped, medium sized, and of a pleasing pale yellow colour, with a Tea Rose fragrance. It will grow to about 4.5m/15ft in height. A beautiful and worthwhile rose deserving more attention. Bred by Ley (UK) 1936.

**Madame Alfred Carrière** If a very strong, reliable and repeat-flowering, white Climber is required, you need look no further than this variety. Even today, there are few white Climbing Roses to rival it in performance. The flowers are large, cupped and creamy-white with just a tint of pink, and have a Tea Rose fragrance. They cannot be said to be particularly shapely, and the growth is rather stiff and upright, though this stiffness can be overcome by careful training. It gives a magnificent display in June and July with good continuity till late in the season. The foliage is large and plentiful. Reliably hardy. Bred by Schwartz (France), introduced 1879.

**Maréchal Niel** Until Pernet-Ducher introduced the blood of *Rosa foetida* into the Hybrid Teas at about the turn of the 20th century, there was no rose of such a truly deep yellow, other than a few less developed varieties such as *R. hemisphaerica* and 'Persian Yellow' (now *R. foetida* 'Persiana'). 'Maréchal Niel' was highly prized for this reason, as well as for the perfection of its large, pointed buds. In fact it was treated with near reverence. Its long, hanging, strongly fragrant flowers of pure yellow and perfect Tea Rose shape were unique at the time. The trouble was that it would not withstand our cold winters and damp summers, and for this reason the Victorians nearly always grew it under glass; indeed lean-to greenhouses were built with the main object of growing this rose. Whether it is worth going to such lengths today is rather doubtful, although there is still nothing finer than a perfect example of its waxy blooms. Unfortunately it does not always grow very well, and requires careful treatment if it is to thrive. The late Graham Thomas suggested that it should be grown like a vine, with the roots in the open soil and the growth trained into the house on a framework, under the slope of the glass. Given such conditions it may be expected to grow to up to 4.5m/15ft. Believed to be a seedling from 'Cloth of Gold'. Bred by Pradel (France), 1864.

**Princesse de Nassau** At one time known as *R. moschata* 'Autumnalis', this has semi-double flowers of creamy-buff with a strong musky fragrance. They are held in dainty sprays, appearing unusually late in the season (in August) and continuing until autumn. This rose needs and deserves a sheltered position in full sun to hasten the blooms. We know nothing of its origin, but it has many similarities to a Noisette, which in fact it may be. Height 2.5m/8ft.

**Rêve d'Or** ('Golden Chain') A seedling from 'Madame Schultz', itself a seedling from 'Lamarque', this too is only for a warm wall. The flowers are semi-double, buff-yellow with pink shadings, paling with age, and of a rather informal shape. They are produced freely, and repeat particularly well. The foliage is plentiful and glossy. Little fragrance. A first class Climber. Bred by Ducher (France) 1869.

**William Allen Richardson** This once famous rose was a sport of 'Rêve d'Or', to which it is similar except for the distinct yolk-yellow colouring at the centre of its flowers. Unfortunately the growth is rather weak, and it is probably not worth growing except by the collector. It requires a warm wall. Height 3m/10ft. Bred by Ducher (France), introduced 1878.

*MADAME ALFRED CARRIÈRE is a very strong and reliable Climber that gives a magnificent display in summer with good continuity to late in the season*

227

# Various Old Climbers

THERE ARE A NUMBER of old Climbing Roses that do not fit comfortably into the categories I use here. These are usually by-products of the repeat-flowering Old Roses, or sometimes crosses that have been made with Species Roses. They include some very beautiful and—as one might expect—highly individual varieties.

**Belle Portugaise** ('Belle of Portugal') (Tea) A cross between *Rosa gigantea* and the early Climbing Hybrid Tea 'Reine Marie Henriette'. *R. gigantea* is the largest-flowered of all Climbing Species and, as we have seen, is one of the main ancestors of our modern roses. It was, therefore, obviously a good idea to back-cross some of our modern roses to this species. Unfortunately such hybrids are not hardy in the UK, though this variety, and one or two others, will survive most winters in warmer areas if given a protected position, when 'Belle Portugaise' may be expected to grow to 6m/20ft. It has long, silky, pointed buds that hang their heads in the most elegant and pleasing manner. Their colour is a pale salmon-pink and their petals beautifully scrolled, eventually opening to rather loose flowers which appear in mid-June only, but in some abundance. It has fine, long, pointed, grey-green, drooping foliage. Strong Tea Rose fragrance. Raised at the Botanic Gardens, Lisbon, 1903.

**Blairi Number Two** ('Blairi No. 2') Were it not for the fact that this Bourbon Rose does not repeat flower and has a tendency to mildew, I would be inclined to regard it as one of my favourite Climbers. The flowers are the very personification of an Old Rose at its best. They are cupped in shape, full of petals, pale pink at the edges, and deepening towards the centre. The growth is rather lax, perhaps 3.5–4.5m/12–15ft in height, with the blooms borne elegantly on the branch. The young shoots are mahogany coloured, and the mature leaves rough textured and matt green. The whole plant makes a most charming picture. Raised by a Mr Blair of Stamford Hill in 1845, it is said that the parents are *Rosa chinensis* (now *R. × odorata*) × 'Tuscany'. There is also a 'Blairii No. 1', which is very similar, but the flowers are less fine, and I think there is little point in growing them both, although the colour of the latter is a more even pink. I have only seen 'Blairii No. 1' growing at Hidcote Manor in Gloucestershire.

**Cécile Brünner, Climbing** A description of the bush form of this variety is to be found in Chapter 4. This rose has miniature, blush-pink, Hybrid Tea Rose blooms, with scrolled buds of the utmost perfection. It may, therefore, come as something of a surprise to find that its climbing form is of exceptional vigour, with fine luxuriant foliage. It can, in fact, achieve 8m/25ft of rampant growth. The flowers are exactly similar to those of the bush, except that they can be a shade larger, as are the leaves. It is certainly one of the most free-flowering of climbers although unfortunately, unlike the bush form, it does not repeat flower. It is a most charming and reliable Climbing Rose, and free of disease. A good variety for growing into trees. Discovered by Hosp (USA) 1894.

**Cramoisi Superieur, Climbing** This is a climbing form of the bush China Rose described in Chapter 1. I find it grows to a height of 2m/7ft, although I understand it will reach very much further with the protection of a sunny wall. It produces small, cupped, crimson flowers in clusters. The growth is twiggy and bushy with

*CLIMBING CÉCILE BRÜNNER is incredibly free flowering with fine luxuriant foliage*

small, dark green leaves. It repeat flowers quite well, but hardly so well as we would expect from a China Rose. Climbing sport discovered by Couturier (France) 1885.

**Dream Girl** A cross between the Wichurana Rambler 'Doctor W. Van Fleet' and a Hybrid Tea called 'Senora Gari', though it does not really fit in with the Wichurana Hybrids. The flowers are of a lovely soft coral-pink and of typical Old Rose rosette formation with numerous small petals. The growth and foliage is rather similar to 'Doctor W. Van Fleet', but it will achieve no more than 3 m/10ft in height. There is a strong spicy fragrance. 'Dream Girl' flowers very late, continuing for a long time, but cannot be said to be repeat flowering. A charming rose, ideal for a pillar. Bred by Bobbink (USA) 1944.

**Fellemberg** ('La Belle Marseillaise') A rose of doubtful origin, sometimes regarded as a Noisette, but perhaps better classified as a China Rose. It bears small, semi-double cupped flowers in rather close clusters, their colour being cerise-crimson with yellow stamens. This rose flowers freely and repeats well, while the growth tends to be bushy, to 2.5–3 m/8–10ft, indeed it will form a good broad shrub or may even be pruned for bedding. Good, dark green, disease-free foliage. A useful and reliable if somewhat dull rose. Bred by Fellemberg (Germany), introduced 1857.

**Gruss an Teplitz** ('Virginia R. Coxe') A rose of no particular persuasion, but rather a mixture of Bourbon, China and Tea Rose, the breeding being ('Sir Joseph Paxton' × 'Fellemberg') × ('Papa Gontier' × 'Gloire des Rosomanes'). The flowers are dark crimson and

have retained the quality of a China Rose, in that the colour intensifies rather than fades in hot sunshine. They are medium sized, loosely and informally double, and have a rich, spicy fragrance. The foliage is purplish at first, becoming green later. This rose is frequently grown as a rather straggly shrub of some 1.8 m/6ft in height, but is perhaps more satisfactory as a Climbing Rose when it will grow to a height of 3.5 m/12ft. Bred by Geschwind (Hungary), introduced by P. Lambert (Germany) 1897. (Illustrated overleaf)

*Above,* BLAIRI NUMBER TWO *bears flowers that personify an Old Rose at its best*

*Left,* FELLEMBERG *flowers freely and repeats well; it can be used in a number of different ways according to the way it is pruned*

*Above,* GRUSS AN
TEPLITZ *is a great
favourite in warm
climates where its
colour intensifies
in hot sunshine*

*Right,* MAIGOLD
*is a very tough
rose that thrives
under the most
difficult con-
ditions and starts
flowering very
early in the year*

**Hume's Blush China** (*R.× odorata* 'Odorata', 'Odorata', 'Spice')
(Tea) An ancestor of many of the Tea roses and so important too in
the history of many of our modern-day varieties. It was originally
brought over from Canton in 1809 to the garden of Sir Abraham
Hume and named after his wife. In the early part of the 20th century
it was thought to be extinct and was only known from illustrations,
notably that of Redouté (identified as *Rosa Indica Fragransin*).
However the rose 'Spice' found growing in Bermuda is thought to
be the same and more recently Roger Phillips and Martyn Rix found
(probably) the same rose growing in a village garden in Pingwu,
Sichuan. Although perhaps not the ideal rose for the British climate
it is relatively hardy and, in a sheltered position, is well worth
grow ing for both its garden value and its historical background.
The flowers are a cupped, pale pink with few long petals, have a tea
fragrance and are produced over a long season. It has low arching
growth with stems up to 2m/6ft long that would undoubtedly
scramble up into trees given the chance and the climate. *Rosa
chinensis × Rosa gigantea.*

**Kathleen Harrop** A soft pink sport from 'Zéphirine Drouhin' (see
p. 233) with a deeper pink on the reverse of the petals, but otherwise
entirely similar, except that it may be a little less vigorous. It has
perhaps the more pleasing colour of the two. Discovered by Dickson
(UK) 1919.

**Lawrence Johnston** (originally known as 'Hidcote Yellow') A
hybrid between the Hybrid Perpetual Rose 'Madame Eugène Verdier'
and *Rosa foetida* 'Persiana', it is strange this cross should produce
such a vigorous Climber which can be relied upon to reach 6m/20ft,
and often as much as 9m/30ft. As is usually the case with *R. foetida*
crosses, it is this species that dominates. The flowers are large, of
loosely-cupped shape, and of a bright clear yellow that shows up well
against the excellent, glossy, dark green foliage. They have a strong
fragrance and are produced in one magnificent crop early in the season, with the chance of an occasional bloom later. If it has a weakness, it is a susceptibility to blackspot, a not surprising fact in a *R.
foetida* hybrid, but please do not let this deter you from growing it, as
it is one of our finest Climbers. Raised by Pernet-Ducher of France,

230

*Above,*
*LAWRENCE*
*JOHNSTON*
*flowers in one*
*magnificent*
*crop early in*
*the season, with*
*the chance of*
*an occasional*
*bloom later*

*Right, MERMAID,*
*one of the most*
*beautiful of all*
*Climbing Roses,*
*bears large,*
*delicately scented*
*flowers*

in 1923, who rather surprisingly rejected it. Lawrence Johnston, of Hidcote Manor fame, rescued it when visiting the French nursery, and it was eventually made available to the public by Graham Thomas.

**Le Rêve** A sister seedling to 'Lawrence Johnston', from 'Madame Eugène Verdier' and *Rosa foetida* 'Persiana', it was selected by Pernet-Ducher in preference to 'Lawrence Johnston', although it has, in fact, turned out to be inferior. We should not be too surprised at

this, for it is difficult even to be sure of a new Shrub Rose until it has been grown in gardens for some years. With Climbers, which may take many years to reach their full potential, the task becomes even more difficult. Nonetheless, the virtues of this variety should not be totally obscured by its more illustrious sister, for 'Le Rêve' does have a certain grace that is its own. It is similar to 'Lawrence Johnston', but a little less robust, with almost single flowers of a paler yellow which are deliciously fragrant. Fine, glossy-green foliage. Growth 8 m / 20 ft. Introduced in 1923.

**Maigold** A cross between 'Poulsen's Pink' and 'Frühlingstag', which makes it three generations removed from *Rosa spinosissima* var. *hispida*, and it still carries many of the qualities of that rose, particularly in that it is extremely tough and hardy and will thrive under the most difficult conditions. Indeed, it would be hard to think of any Climbing Rose of moderate height that is more suitable for such conditions. It has short, reddish buds which open to quite large, strongly-fragrant, semi-double flowers of bronzy-yellow with golden stamens. There is one very free-flowering period, early in the season, with occasional flowers later. The growth is extremely vigorous, producing strong, very thorny stems to a height of 3.5 m / 12 ft, with plentiful, glossy-green foliage. Although often recommended as a shrub, I find the growth rather too untidy for this. Little or no disease. Raised by Kordes (Germany), 1953. (Illustrated, pp. 230–231)

**Mermaid** A true classic—one of the most beautiful of all Climbing Roses, bearing large, single, soft canary-yellow flowers of 12cm/5in and more across, with a boss of long, sulphur-yellow stamens that remain attractive for some time after the petals have fallen. Its flowers are delicately scented and of a soft sheeny texture, the slightly waved petals giving an elegantly sculptured effect. 'Mermaid' blooms with remarkable regularity throughout the summer; in fact few Climbers can rival it in this respect. The result of a cross between *Rosa bracteata* and an unspecified yellow Tea Rose, one cannot but wonder what this Tea Rose might have been to provide such a lovely shade of yellow. The foliage is similar to that of *R. bracteata*, but larger, and almost evergreen, with a smooth, shiny surface. It is no doubt due to *R. bracteata* that 'Mermaid' is almost completely resistant to disease. Inevitably there is one snag: it is not completely hardy, but it is certainly worth growing in all but the coldest areas, and deserves the best wall you have—if this is out of the morning sun to avoid too quick a thaw after a night of frost so much the better. 'Mermaid' has, rather surprisingly, proved successful on a north-facing wall where it is protected from cold winds. It is frequently slow in the early stages, making little progress in the first two or three years, but once it starts it can grow quickly, easily achieving 8m/25ft. Little pruning is necessary or desirable—no more than to keep it within bounds. It may also be grown as a sprawling shrub, but needs a warm corner if it is not to stay short and appear impoverished. The credit for this fine rose goes to William Paul (UK), who introduced it in 1918, and it must be regarded as the crowning glory of that famous rose breeder.

**Pompon de Paris, Climbing** ('Climbing Rouletii') A sport of the Miniature Rose, it makes dense, twiggy growth up to 2m/7ft in height, providing a good display of small rose-pink, pompon flowers in June, although the first flowers can appear as early as April, but rather surprisingly has very little bloom later. The foliage is small, to match the flowers, and of a greyish-green. It enjoys considerable popularity, perhaps more than it deserves, although no doubt it is useful for very small gardens and certain positions in larger gardens.

**Souvenir de la Malmaison, Climbing** The climbing form of this famous old Bourbon Rose has strong growth and will achieve a spread of 3.5m/12ft. It is possible that its beautiful, delicate, flesh-pink flowers will not be quite so fine as the bush variety and they are easily spoilt or, indeed, never open in the rain. Nonetheless, they take on an added charm when seen on a Climber rather than on the somewhat squat growth of the bush. Unfortunately the Climber does not repeat quite so well. Climbing sport discovered by Bennett (UK) 1893.

**Zéphirine Drouhin** A Bourbon Rose. This variety was introduced in France as early as 1868 and is still popular but, by today's standards, perhaps undeservedly so. It flowers freely and continuously. The blooms are a very bright cerise-carmine, semi-double, although of no very definite form, and have a wonderful fragrance. It is completely thornless. However, it is susceptible to disease—blackspot, rust and mildew—and needs to be sprayed regularly. It can actually do better on a north-facing wall as the ground tends to be moister. It will achieve anything up to 4.5m/15ft, maybe more on a north wall. Although sometimes recommended as a shrub, I have never found it to be very satisfactory when so grown, the growth often appearing too open and straggly, but perhaps if closely planted in a large group the appearance would be quite different. It is said that it will form a good hedge. Parentage unknown. Bred by Bizot (France) 1868.

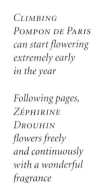

*CLIMBING POMPON DE PARIS can start flowering extremely early in the year*

*Following pages, ZÉPHIRINE DROUHIN flowers freely and continuously with a wonderful fragrance*

# The Climbing Tea & Hybrid Tea Roses

I include the Climbing Tea Roses and the Climbing Hybrid Teas in one group, as most of the Tea Roses have at least a little Hybrid Tea in their make-up and their appearance is, for the most part, very much the same.

Very few of these roses were purposely bred, perhaps because it is not an easy thing to do, or because it was thought to be much less profitable than the breeding of bush roses. In spite of this there are innumerable varieties of these roses to choose from. The explanation for this apparent anomaly lies in the fact that both bush Hybrid Tea and Tea Roses have proved very prolific in the production of climbing sports, and this is what most of them are. They form an important contribution to our stock of Climbing Roses, not least because they extend the colour range considerably.

Anyone whose preferences lie with the Old Rose, or perhaps has some prejudice against Modern Roses, should think again in the case of the Climbing Tea Roses and Climbing Hybrid Teas, for even those bearing flowers which may look rather ordinary on a short bush often have greater appeal when seen from the branches of their climbing form. This illustrates better than anything else the advantage a shrub rose has over a bush rose, or, likewise, a Climbing Rose over a bush; that is to say, the advantage of scale—the balance between the size of the flower, and the growth of the plant.

There can be little doubt that, in general, the older Climbing Tea Roses and Climbing Hybrid Teas make better climbing sports than those of more recent introduction. The early varieties were rather weak in growth, but it is an odd fact that such roses often produce strong climbing forms. They also have the advantage that they often inherit the more lax and elegant growth of their parent so that the flowers, instead of looking up towards the sky, look down on us for our appreciation. They have a further advantage in that they tend to be more gentle in colour, substance and general appearance. Fortunately it is the Tea Roses and the earlier Hybrid Tea Roses that have produced the most Climbers. This may be because they were the result of rather distant crosses and had not settled down genetically. The contemporary Hybrid Tea bushes are of much stronger growth, with the result that their climbing sports have a tendency to make growth and foliage at the expense of bloom and, more often than not, their flowers stand up like ramrods.

The climbing forms of the early Tea Roses and Hybrid Teas Roses may then be said to be good Climbers, growing strongly and often repeating well. In fact, if the early varieties are to be preserved, it is perhaps as Climbers that this is best done.

---

**Allen Chandler** (Hybrid Tea) A vigorous Climbing Rose bearing very large, semi-double flowers of brilliant crimson, opening to show contrasting yellow stamens. It blooms very freely early in the season and regularly thereafter. Good red Climbing Roses are rather scarce and this is one of the best of them. It will grow to about 4.5 m/15 ft, sometimes much more, is fragrant and has ample large foliage. A cross between 'Hugh Dickson' and an unnamed seedling. Bred by Chandler (USA), 1923. (Illustrated, p. 238)

**Château de Clos-Vougeot** (Hybrid Tea) One of the darkest of dark red roses: rich, velvety crimson overlaid with garnet, unfading and pure. It is not a typical Hybrid Tea flower, having numerous rather short petals and opening wide, with a particularly strong and rich fragrance. The growth is suitably lax, holding its flowers well. I have not found it to be very strong, although the growth is quite adequate with good cultivation. It should reach 4.5 m/15 ft on a wall. Sport found by Morse (UK), 1920, from the original Hybrid Tea bred by Pernet-Ducher (France).

**Crimson Glory, Climbing** (Hybrid Tea) A particularly fine rose in its climbing form. The flowers start as typical Hybrid Tea buds of deepest velvety crimson, becoming an attractive informal cup of a pleasing purplish shade. They are richly fragrant and evenly placed along the branch, holding themselves admirably. In summer the whole plant is studded with flowers, followed by occasional blooms later. Height 3–3.5 m/10–12 ft. We have found it to be very successful

on a tall pillar. Bush bred by Kordes (Germany), 1935; sport discovered by Jackson & Perkins (USA), 1946. (Illustrated, p. 238)

**Cupid** (Hybrid Tea) Very large, single, delicate flesh-pink flowers shaded with apricot; these may be 12 cm/5 in across with attractively waved and crinkled petals and ample stamens. Although summer flowering only, this variety has large orange-red hips in the autumn. It will grow to 4.5 m/15 ft or more. Graham Thomas suggested it might be allowed to trail over shrubs, and I can imagine it being very effective when so grown. Fragrant. Bred by Cant (UK), 1915.

**Devoniensis, Climbing** ('Magnolia Rose') A sport from the bush variety discovered by Pavitt and introduced in 1858, the original bush having been bred by a Mr Foster of Devonport, and introduced in 1838. 'Devoniensis' was the first Tea Rose to be bred in England, although due to the climate it is not surprising that very few were raised in the UK. This variety is, in fact, quite hardy on a warm wall. Its flowers are creamy-white, attractively flushed with pink and apricot at the centre. At their best, they are beautiful with a silky sheen and a strong Tea Rose fragrance. The parentage is not known.

**Easlea's Golden Rambler** Although this rose bears the name Rambler, it is, in effect, a Climber. The buds are tipped with red and open to large loosely-filled deep yellow flowers, with a strong fragrance. They are held either singly or in small clusters. The growth is heavy and robust with thick, olive-green, shiny leaves. A reliable rose that will reach 4.5 m/15 ft. Bred by Easlea (UK), 1932.

*Facing page,
MADAME
GRÉGOIRE
STAECHELIN
has a delicious
fragrance and is
one of the most
spectacular of all
Climbing Roses*

**Elegance** In spite of the strong mixture of *Rosa wichurana* in this Climber, it has much of the appearance of a Climbing Hybrid Tea. It does, as the name suggests, have truly elegant blooms, which start as long shapely buds of clear yellow, opening to very large, very full blooms of pale lemon. The foliage is a dark glossy green. There is one profuse blooming, with only occasional flowers later. A beautiful rose that will grow to a considerable height: 4.5–5.5m/15–18ft. Its parentage is 'Glenn Dale' × ('Mary Wallace' × 'Miss Lolita Armour').

**Ena Harkness, Climbing** (Hybrid Tea) This is a good climbing sport of the Bush Hybrid Tea, with pointed buds of bright crimson-scarlet. The bush form, popular in the 1940s and 1950s, had a weakness in that it tended to hang its head. In the climbing form this becomes a virtue, enabling us to view the blooms from below. Vigorous growth of at least 5.5m/18ft. Introduced by Gurteen and Ritson (UK), 1954.

**Étoile de Hollande, Climbing** (Hybrid Tea) A climbing sport of the once popular bush Hybrid Tea, and still one of the best and most reliable crimson Climbers. It has long buds of deepest crimson and the rich heavy fragrance we expect of such a rose. The buds open to a rather shapeless flower, but this is made up for in quantity, both early and late in the season. It has been said 'Climbing Étoile de Hollande' does not like cold, but this has not been my experience. It will grow to 5.5m/18ft. Discovered by Leenders (Holland), 1931, on the bush by Verschuren, also of Holland.

**Fortune's Yellow** ('Beauty of Glazenwood', 'Gold of Ophir', 'San Rafael Rose') This famous old rose was brought to England from China by the well-known plant collector Robert Fortune in 1845, having been discovered in the garden of a rich Mandarin at Ningpo. Its flowers are held either singly or in small clusters and are semi-double, bright coppery-yellow in colour, shaded with white. It will grow to about 1.2–1.5m/4–5ft in height, and much taller in a favourable climate. It is not recurrent flowering, and is only suitable for the collector.

**Général Schablikine** (Tea) A rose which is only barely a Climber, and which might well have been included among the bush varieties. On a wall it may be expected to achieve perhaps 1.8m/6ft. When well grown it can produce rather small, perfectly scrolled flowers of a deep coppery-pink which hang elegantly from their stems. Under poor conditions it does not have such beautiful buds, as the petals remain short and open quickly into

*Top right, ALLEN CHANDLER, with its large semi-double flowers, creates a striking display*

*Near right, CLIMBING ENA HARKNESS bears classic Hybrid Tea type flowers and has a wonderful fragrance*

*Far right, CLIMBING CRIMSON GLORY is studded with flowers in summer and very successful on a tall pillar*

informal rosettes. It can be particularly fine when grown under glass. Bred by Nabonnand (France), introduced 1878.

**Guinée** (Hybrid Tea) The result of a cross between 'Souvenir de Claudius Denoyel' × 'Ami Quinard', the first of which has 'Château de Clos-Vougeot' as one of its parents, and the exceptionally deep colouring of that rose has been passed down with equal intensity. 'Guinée' has pointed buds opening to attractive, flat, neatly formed blooms. They are so dark that in the shade they can appear almost black; indeed, they become barely visible against its dark green foliage. For this reason it is best grown against a light background. A few contrasting stamens are visible, and there is a very rich fragrance. Although perhaps just a little lacking in strength, with generous treatment it will grow well to about 4.5 m/15 ft. The problem may be that it is not altogether hardy and would be better grown on a warm wall. Bred by Mallerin (France), introduced 1938.

**Josephine Bruce, Climbing** As a bush, this variety produces shapely flowers of a particularly rich and pure crimson. They are very fragrant. It is perhaps even better as a Climber, growing to 4.5 m/15 ft and flowering well, with another crop of flowers in late summer. Discovered by Bees (UK), 1954, on the bush form bred by the same firm.

**Lady Hillingdon, Climbing** (Tea) One of the best Tea Roses still in existence. Indeed, I would place it high in any list of Climbing Roses. It is remarkably hardy for this class, so much so that it is hard to believe it is the result of a cross between the Tea Roses 'Papa Gontier' and 'Madame Hoste'. It would be easy to believe a Hybrid Tea comes into its breeding somewhere, but the records say otherwise. Nonetheless, I would still give it the protection of a wall. The flowers are made up of large petals which result in long, elegant buds of deep apricot-yellow. These hang gracefully from the branch and emit a strong and delicious tea fragrance. Although not shapely when they open, this does not matter so much with a Climbing Rose whose flowers are usually seen from a distance. 'Climbing Lady Hillingdon' has lush growth, with large dark green leaves tinted with red when young, and it continues to flower with admirable regularity. It may be expected to grow to 4.5 m/15 ft. The bush variety was bred by the English firm of Lowe & Shawyer in 1910, making it one of the latest of the Tea Roses to be introduced. The Climbing sport was discovered by Hicks (UK), 1917.

*Climbing Etoile de Hollande is certainly one of the best and most reliable crimson Climbers with the rich heavy fragrance we expect of such a rose*

*Guinée has blooms so dark that in the shade they can appear almost black and are barely visible against its dark green foliage— hence it is best grown against a light background*

*CLIMBING
MADAME
CAROLINE
TESTOUT is
a very distinctive
rose with large,
globular flowers
of rich silvery-
pink, the petals
rolling back at
the edges; it is
extremely tough
and repeat
flowers well*

**Lady Sylvia, Climbing** (Hybrid Tea) I discussed 'Ophelia' and its two sports, 'Lady Sylvia' and 'Madame Butterfly', under the early Hybrid Teas in Chapter 3. 'Climbing Lady Sylvia' has all the qualities of the bush form with exquisitely shaped buds of flesh-pink tinged yellow at the base. As a Climber it is first rate, growing to about 6m/20ft and repeating well. This rose, 'Ophelia' and 'Madame Butterfly' are all particularly fine in the greenhouse, where they will produce flowers of the utmost perfection. Outside, they are among the best of the Climbing Hybrid Teas, although they are a little upright in habit. Discovered by Stevens (UK), 1933.

**Lady Waterlow** (Hybrid Tea) Large blooms opening to loosely formed, almost semi-double flowers of salmon-pink edged with carmine and with attractive veining. It produces strong growth to about 3.5m/12ft, and is often recommended as a pillar rose, although it is equally suitable for a wall. Delicious tea scent. 'La France de '89' × 'Madame Marie Lavalley'. Bred by Nabonnand (France) 1903.

**Madame Abel Chatenay, Climbing** (Hybrid Tea) I have already said that the bush form of this rose is one of the most exquisitely beautiful of all Hybrid Tea Roses. The Climbing form is no less desirable, although with me it has not proved too reliable. When well grown it will achieve 4.5m/15ft, with attractive, not too stiff growth, and slightly nodding flowers. These are pale pink, deepening towards the centre with a darker reverse and lovely fragrance. Discovered by Page (UK), introduced 1917; bush form bred by Pernet-Ducher (France) 1895.

**Madame Butterfly, Climbing** (Hybrid Tea) The Climbing form of the beautiful bush rose described among the early Hybrid Teas, having the same perfect buds and blush-pink colouring. An excellent rose of up to 6m/20ft, with good repeat-flowering qualities, the later blooms being finer than those in early summer. Very fragrant. Discovered by E.P. Smith (UK) 1926. See also 'Lady Sylvia' above.

**Madame Caroline Testout, Climbing** (Hybrid Tea) The bush form of 'Madame Caroline Testout' was, in its day, almost as popular as 'Just Joey' is in our time. Like 'Just Joey' it is extremely tough, and the climbing form is no less so; it also repeat flowers well. We have on our house an interesting example: photographs taken in 1919 show it as a mature Climber even then, and it is still there today, growing strongly and flowering well. This is in spite of the fact that it was cut to the ground in the winter of 1981/2 when, in Shropshire, we suffered the lowest temperatures ever recorded in England. It is interesting to note that this plant was budded on a Rugosa stock, which is usually regarded as short lived. The flowers are large and globular, of an even silvery-pink colour, not particularly full, with the petals rolled back at the edges. The growth is strong and rather stiff with the flowers held upright, though this does not seem to matter with a bloom of this form. It will achieve at least 6m/20ft. Only a slight scent. Discovered by Chauvry (France), 1901, on the rose bred by Pernet-Ducher (France) 1890.

**Madame Edouard Herriot, Climbing** ('Daily Mail') (Hybrid Tea) A rose of unique and mixed colouring, so much so that the descriptions we read are as various as they are numerous. *Modern Roses* says: 'Coral-red, shaded yellow and light rosy-scarlet, passing to prawn-red', but in fact the overall effect is an almost terracotta shade. However we put it, it is beautiful and ever-changing in appearance. The individual flowers are not outstanding, being loosely double, but they provide a sheet of bloom in early summer, and are followed by occasional blooms later on. The foliage is glossy green and there are very few thorns. It will grow to about 4.5m/15ft.

Fragrant. Breeding 'Madame Caroline Testout' × unnamed Hybrid Tea. Bush bred by Pernet-Ducher (France); climbing sport discovered by Ketten (Luxembourg), 1921.

**Madame Grégoire Staechelin** (Hybrid Tea) A fine Climbing Rose bred by Pedro Dot of Spain, who also gave us the Shrub Rose 'Nevada'. Known in some countries as 'Spanish Beauty', this is perhaps a more suitable name, for indeed it is one of the most spectacular of all the Climbing Roses. The flowers start as slender buds of deep pink, but soon open wide and flat to form very large semi-double blooms of fresh, glowing pink, with a deeper shade on the reverse. The stamens are visible, and there is a delicious fragrance. This Climber produces one magnificent flush of flowers in early summer, but nothing thereafter. Perhaps this would be too much to expect, although it is followed by a good crop of large hips. It has strong growth, usually to about 4.5m/15ft, but often more on a wall. The foliage is dark, glossy and luxuriant. If it has a fault, it is that the lower part of the plant becomes bare as it ages, the flowers appearing mainly on its upper branches. To avoid this it is necessary to train it horizontally so far as possible. A good rose for growing on a north wall, it is generally tough although it can suffer badly from rust. The result of a cross between 'Frau Karl Druschki' with 'Château de Clos-Vougeot', an almost pure white and one of the darkest of dark red roses, it was introduced in 1927. (Illustrated, p.237)

**Madame Jules Gravereaux** (Tea) Large, very full flowers of soft flesh-pink, shaded with peach and yellow. I am not fully acquainted with this rose, but understand it will reach 3.5m/12ft on a wall. The foliage is dark and glossy, the scent only slight. It is not a pure Tea Rose, being a cross between 'Rêve d'Or' and the Hybrid Tea 'Viscountess Folkestone'. It would appear to be well worthy of preservation. Bred by Soupert & Notting (Luxembourg) 1901.

**Meg** This Climbing Rose is thought to be the result of a cross between 'Paul's Lemon Pillar' and 'Madame Butterfly', and its general appearance would suggest that this is, in fact, true. It bears very large, single or semi-double flowers of pale apricot-pink, with a large boss of quite dark stamens. The flowers are fragrant and held in small clusters. This is a beautiful rose that may be grown on a pillar or wall, but is perhaps best of all when encouraged to clamber over bushes or hedges. Here its large and elegantly waved blooms display themselves with the most pleasing effect. There is only occasional repeat flowering after the first flush. Height 2.7m/9ft. Bred by Dr A.C.V. Gosset (UK) 1954.

**Mevrouw G.A. van Rossem, Climbing** ('Climbing Mrs G.A. van Rossem') A Climbing Hybrid Tea of unusual and beautiful colouring, its large flowers a mixture of dark golden-yellow and orange attractively veined with bronze. These are held on long, rather too rigid stems and have a strong fragrance. Vigorous growth to about 3.5m/12ft, and deep bronzy-green foliage. Bush bred by Van Rossem (Holland); the climbing sport discovered by Gaujard (France) 1937.

**Mrs Herbert Stevens, Climbing** (Tea) The result of a cross between 'Frau Karl Druschki' (which I have described in Chapter 2 in the section on Hybrid Perpetuals as being very close to a Hybrid Tea) and the old Tea Rose 'Niphetos'. It could, therefore, more accurately be described as a Hybrid Tea, but it is close to a Tea Rose in appearance. The flowers are white with long pointed buds tinged with green towards the centre, and have a strong, typically Tea Rose fragrance. They are produced freely and repeat well. The foliage is light green. This rose will grow strongly on a wall, often reaching

*Top, CLIMBING
MRS HERBERT
STEVENS bears
superb flowers
with the lovely
Tea Rose form*

*Middle, PAUL'S
LEMON PILLAR
will grow to a
considerable
height—at least
6m/20ft on a
warm wall—
bearing majestic
flowers with a
wonderful
fragrance*

*Bottom,
PAUL LÉDÉ
has blooms of
great beauty
with a strong
and delicious
tea fragrance*

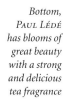

5.5m/18ft. Unfortunately, the flowers are easily damaged by rain, more particularly if planted away from a wall, where it is otherwise usually quite hardy. The original rose was bred by McGredy (UK), and the Climbing sport was discovered by Pernet-Ducher (France) in 1922.

**Mrs Sam McGredy, Climbing** (Hybrid Tea) A good example of an early Hybrid Tea that is much better in its climbing form. The bush is not strong, but the Climber has no such trouble and will easily achieve 4.5m/15ft. Its flowers are coppery-orange flushed with scarlet, with crisp buds, and associate well with the glossy, dark, bronzy foliage. The growth is not too rigid and the flower stems suitably lax. It repeats well. Bush bred by McGredy (UK); climbing sports have been discovered by various people, the first being Buisman (Holland), 1937.

**Niphetos, Climbing** (Tea) Not a rose for the outdoors in Great Britain, for if it survives the frost, the flowers are likely to be spoiled by rain. These are large and hang their heads slightly, with perfect creamy buds opening to pure white. They have a light Tea Rose fragrance. It would be worth growing this rose under glass—in fact its bush parent was once widely used for this purpose. Discovered by Keynes, Williams & Co (UK) 1889.

**Ophelia, Climbing** (Hybrid Tea) A good Climber that will achieve anything up to 6m/20ft, with beautifully formed blush-pink flowers repeating well and a rich fragrance. Discovered by A. Dickson (UK), 1920. See Chapter 4 and also 'Climbing Lady Sylvia' and 'Climbing Madame Butterfly'.

**Parks' Yellow China** (*R. × odorata* 'Ochroleuca') (Tea) Along with 'Old Blush China', 'Hume's Blush China' and 'Slater's Crimson China' this is one of four main (so-called stud) varieties that were introduced from China and were so influential in the future development of the repeat-flowering roses. It was introduced from Canton to England in 1824 by John Parks. The rose being grown today was discovered by Peter Beales and is thought by many to be the true variety, although there is a certain amount of doubt. It has fragrant, pale sulphur-yellow flowers, the colour deepening slightly with age. They are produced freely in the first flush but then there is only the occasional flower. Like 'Hume's Blush China' it benefits from a warm position but it will grow satisfactorily in the warmer parts of the UK as a short climber and can achieve 3m/10ft.

**Paul Lédé** (Tea) A sport discovered by Lowe in 1913 on the Bush Rose bred by Pernet-Ducher in 1902. Its hardiness perhaps belies its Tea Rose ancestry, but however this may be it is a rose of great beauty and has a delicious tea fragrance. The flowers are large, semi-double, with exposed stamens, and of a rather loose formation. They have a lovely buff-yellow colouring and are flushed with carmine at the centre. The growth is strong, to about 3.5m/12ft, and it flowers well later in the year. All in all, a most pleasing and reliable Climbing Rose.

**Paul's Lemon Pillar** (Hybrid Tea) A cross between 'Frau Karl Druschki' and 'Maréchal Niel', two roses of classic bud formation and, as we might expect, this rose has flowers of similar perfection. Their colour is a creamy-yellow with a tint of green at the base of the petals. They are very large, hanging slightly with their weight, the petals being neatly scrolled at the edges as the buds unfold. It will grow to a considerable height, at least 6m/20ft on a warm wall. However, it is surprising it should bear the name 'Pillar', for which it is not particularly well suited. There is no repeat flowering. A majestic flower with a wonderful fragrance. Bred by William Paul (UK), introduced 1915.

**Paul's Scarlet Climber** A once-popular Climbing Rose bearing small clusters of semi-double, scarlet-crimson flowers in late June. It is, perhaps, not so worthwhile today, as it does not repeat and the flowers are not of outstanding quality—equally good Climbers can be found amongst the Moderns which do repeat. Nonetheless, it flowers freely and is hardy and reliable. Slightly fragrant. A good pillar rose; height about 3m/10ft. The parents were probably 'Paul's Carmine Pillar' × 'Rêve d'Or'. Bred by William Paul, introduced 1916.

**Reveil Dijonnais** (Hybrid Tea) The result of a cross between the Hybrid Perpetual 'Eugène Fürst' and the Hybrid Tea 'Constance', this rose is, therefore, not too distantly related to *Rosa foetida*, and this fact is evident in its appearance. It is a short-growing Climber with glossy, deep green leaves. The buds are of Hybrid Tea type, opening to large, semi-double flowers of bright scarlet-crimson with a yellow centre, and yellow tints on the reverse of the petals, giving a distinct bicolour effect. It flowers in late June and, to a limited extent, later. Slightly fragrant. Growth 3m/10ft. Somewhat subject to blackspot. Bred by Buatois (France) 1931.

**Sombreuil** (Climbing Tea) A rose bred by Robert of France in 1850, little is known of its parentage other than that it was a seedling from a Hybrid Perpetual called 'Gigantesque'. However, the refinement of its flowers would make it almost certain the other parent was either a Tea Rose or a Noisette. It is, therefore, really a Hybrid Tea, but to place it in that section would be most misleading. In fact, it is really a variety that stands on its own. The flowers have numerous petals, and open to form flat rosettes that can only be described as the most perfect Old Roses. They are creamy-white with the slightest flush tint at the centre, have a delicious tea scent and in quality and refinement compare with the very best of the Old Roses. 'Sombreuil' is completely hardy and may be grown on a pillar or other support, though is perhaps best on a wall where it will reach 3.5m/12ft. I know of no other old variety that produces better flowers in autumn.

**Souvenir de Claudius Denoyel** (Hybrid Tea) The breeding of this rose is 'Château de Clos-Vougeot' × 'Commander Jules Gravereaux', and it has the rare unfading crimson of the first parent, though in a brighter shade. The flowers are large, opening to a rather informal, semi-double cup shape, with a strong, rich fragrance. It is laden with bloom hanging nicely from the branches in early summer, and has a rather smaller crop later on. It is not a vigorous rose and responds well to generous feeding and watering when it will achieve 3–3.5m/10–12ft. Bred by Chambard (France), introduced 1920.

**Souvenir de Madame Léonie Viennot** (Tea) Not one of the finest Tea Roses, but worth a place in our list. The flowers are of loose Tea Rose shape, pale yellow shaded with coppery-pink. Although not very free flowering it is recurrent and hardy. The growth is strong and quite hardy, to about 3.5m/12ft in height. Fragrant. Bred by Bernaix (France) 1898.

**Sutter's Gold, Climbing** The climbing form of one of the most beautiful Hybrid Teas. It has the same shapely buds of orange-yellow colouring, flushed with pink and veined with red, and a delicious fragrance. Growth about 3.5m/12ft. Discovered by Armstrong Nurseries (USA) 1950.

**Vicomtesse Pierre du Fou** It is difficult to know where to place this variety as it is the result of crossing the Noisette 'L'Idéal' with the Hybrid Tea 'Joseph Hill'. However, I think it leans towards the latter parent. The flowers are of a coppery-pink colour, deeper at first, paling a little later on. They open to a quartered formation hanging nicely from the branch. The growth is vigorous, spreading to 6m/20ft, the foliage large and bronzy-green. Tea Rose fragrance. Bred by Sauvageot (France), introduced 1923.

*SOMBREUIL, with its very many petals and perfect rosette form, is comparable to the best of the Old Roses*

# Modern Climbers

IF WE LOOK BACK over this chapter, it will be seen that there has been very little in the way of the deliberate breeding of Climbing Roses. With the exception of the Noisettes, most Climbing Roses have been either sports or chance offspring from the breeding of bush roses. It was only after the summer-flowering Rambler Rose 'Doctor W. Van Fleet' sported to produce 'New Dawn' in 1930 that any definite move was made towards breeding Climbing Roses, and even then nothing happened until the 1950s. 'New Dawn' has many of the characteristics of a repeat-flowering Climber, having pearly, blush-pink flowers of almost Hybrid Tea size and form, like its parent. It was eventually crossed with various Hybrid Teas to produce a number of useful repeat-flowering Climbing Roses. Along with these, other crosses were made between bush roses and Ramblers, and sometimes between strong-growing Hybrid Teas to produce further Climbers. It is a combination of all these roses that we gather together under the heading 'Modern Climbers'.

To obtain recurrent flowering in a Climbing Rose is no easy matter, and many of these roses do not grow to a great height. However, taller varieties are now appearing. On a pillar or more open structure they will often remain rather short, but given the benefit of a wall, this will draw them up to a considerable height. Here they can achieve 3 m/10ft or more. There are, of course, times when a short Climber is required, as on a low wall, or fence, and here Modern Climbers come into their own. Most of them are in the modern mould, often with strong colours and with very much of the appearance of a Hybrid Tea. One thing is certain—they can be relied on to give continuity of colour over a long period.

**Alchemist** A vigorous climber of 3.5m/12ft with plentiful, glossy foliage. The flowers, a mixture of yellow and yolk-yellow, are unusual among Modern Shrub Roses in that they are of typical Old Rose rosette shape, opening flat—in fact rather similar to those of the English Rose 'Charles Austin', though less cupped in shape. They have a strong fragrance, but there is no second crop. 'Alchemist' can equally well be grown as a shrub, when it might grow to 1.8m/6ft. This variety is the result of a cross between the Hybrid Tea 'Golden Glow' and a *Rosa eglanteria* hybrid. Bred by Kordes (Germany), introduced 1956.

**Aloha** It makes an excellent climber to 2m/7ft, more in warmer climates and can also be grown as a free standing shrub about 1.5–1.8m/5–6ft tall (see p.201). When the once–flowering Rambler Rose 'Doctor W. Van Fleet' sported to produce the repeat-flowering rose 'New Dawn', the way was open to breed new and more reliably repeat-flowering Climbers. 'Aloha' is one of the results of such endeavours. The flowers are very double, deeply cupped in form and much like those of an old Bourbon Rose, while the colour is rose-pink, deeper on the outside of the flower. There is a strong fragrance. The foliage is glossy, leathery and disease resistant. If you have a low retaining wall, this rose can be planted on top and allowed to trail downwards with the most pleasing effect. 'Mercedes Gallart' × 'New Dawn'. Bred by Boerner (USA), introduced 1949.

**Altissimo** Large, single flowers of unfading blood-red, each some 12cm/5in across, opening flat and neatly rounded, with a large boss of deep gold stamens. They have no scent but are produced freely, both in early summer and quite regularly later. The growth is strong, to at least 3m/10ft, with large, deep matt-green leaves. A very good Climber, but perhaps a little artificial in appearance. Such a colour is best kept away from red brick and is better against a light green background or perhaps clambering over shrubs. It can also be grown as a large shrub if kept in check by pruning. Bred by Delbard–Chabert (France), introduced 1966.

**Anne Dakin** A rose that always creates a very striking show in our garden. The medium-sized flowers are a very bright coral-pink on the upper sides with a much yellower shade on the reverse. They start as a very full flower, the petals arranged in a most attractive rosette. With age, they gradually open up and the colour changes to bright, medium pink. It is reasonably vigorous, growing to about 3m/10ft and, with its relatively flexible stems, it is easy to train. Unfortunately it doesn't repeat flower but the blooms are followed by rounded, orange hips. It is healthy apart from some blackspot later in the season. Mrs Anne Dakin is very well known to us as she lives in the neighbouring village and is closely associated with flower arranging. She was instrumental in the planting of the Shifnal Sensory Millennium Garden which features many roses. Bred by Holmes (UK) 1974.

**Breath of Life** A low–growing Climber of 2m/7ft, bearing large, full, well-formed Hybrid Tea flowers of a lovely apricot colouring which turns to apricot-pink. Fragrant. Bred by Harkness (UK), 1982.

**Casino** Clusters of large, globular, soft-yellow flowers, with dark, glossy, light green foliage. A cross between 'Coral Dawn' and the tall Hybrid Tea 'Buccaneer'. Height 3m/10ft. Bred by McGredy (UK), 1963.

**Compassion** Well-shaped Hybrid Tea flowers with a sweet fragrance, their colour being salmon-pink tinted with apricot-orange. The growth is rather stiff and bushy and there is plentiful dark green foliage. One of the best and most popular roses in this group, as well as being one of the most fragrant. Height 3m/10ft. It may also be

*Left and facing,* ALCHEMIST *is unusual among Modern Shrub Roses in that the flowers are of typical Old Rose rosette shape*

*Left,* COMPASSION *is one of the best and most popular roses in this group, as well as being one of the most fragrant*

grown as a shrub. Breeding: 'White Cockade' × 'Prima Ballerina'. Harkness (UK), 1973.

**Copenhagen** Medium-sized flowers of good Hybrid Tea shape and dark scarlet colouring. The growth tends to be upright, to about 2m/7ft. Quite fragrant. Breeding seedling × 'Ena Harkness'. Bred by Poulsen (Denmark), 1964.

**Coral Dawn** Quite large, full blooms of coral-pink colouring, against plentiful, healthy, dark green foliage. Fragrant. Growth 3–3.5m/10–12ft . ('New Dawn' × a yellow Hybrid Tea) × an orange-red Polyantha. Bred by Boerner (USA), 1952.

**Crimson Cascade** (*Fryclimbdown*) This has some of the darkest red flowers on any rose, they are also very large — about 10cm/4in across. The blooms start in the form of a classic Hybrid Tea then open up to a less attractive form. Unfortunately there is no fragrance. It has stiff, upright growth, reaching a height of about 3m/10ft and is very healthy. Bred by Fryer (UK) 1991.

**Danse du Feu** Bright orange-scarlet flowers of medium size, the colour deepening with age. The buds are quite short but well formed and the flowers open flat. They are produced very freely and continuously against plentiful foliage. Little scent. Growth 2.5m/8ft. Breeding 'Paul's Scarlet' × unnamed Multiflora seedling. Mallerin (France), 1953.

**Dortmund** In the early 1940s the rose 'Max Graf', a hybrid between *Rosa rugosa* and *R. wichurana*, produced a chance seedling which Herr Wilhelm Kordes named *R.* × *kordesii*. This turned out to be tetraploid, and may have been a chance hybrid with another rose. It was a very hardy Climber, and Kordes hybridized it with other garden roses to produce a race of hardy Climbers, most of which are repeat flowering. I include here 'Dortmund', 'Leverkusen' and 'Parkdirektor Riggers'. 'Dortmund' is a vigorous Climber, with very dark, glossy green leaves. It bears large, single, crimson flowers, with a white eye at the centre and yellow stamens, and will bloom recurrently if dead headed, otherwise there will be numerous hips. A very reliable, disease-free, hardy rose, but perhaps a little coarse. Height 2.5–3m/8–10ft. Breeding seedling × *R.* × *kordesii*. Kordes (Germany), 1955.

**Galway Bay** Large, double, Hybrid Tea flowers of salmon-pink colouring. A vigorous plant with plentiful, glossy, dark green foliage. Height 3m/10ft. 'Heidelberg' × 'Queen Elizabeth'. McGredy (UK), 1966.

**Gloriana** (*Chewpope*) Chris Warner (who lives quite close to our nursery in Shropshire) has bred a group of very good roses, naming them Patio Climbers. They are characterised by small flowers which are freely produced over a long season and over the whole height of

*DORTMUND is a reliable, disease-free and very hardy Climber of strong colouring*

the plant. The flowers of 'Gloriana' are a rich shade of purple and like miniature Hybrid Teas. It will grow about 2.5m/8ft tall and is very healthy. 'Laura Ford' × 'Big Purple'. Bred by Warner (UK), 1998.

**Golden Future** (*Horanymoll*) The late Colin Horner was arguably the most successful amateur rose breeder in the world. In later years he succeeded in developing varieties that were extremely healthy. 'Golden Future' is excellent from this point of view and has fragrant, yellow, Hybrid Tea flowers. The growth is quite upright, reaching a height of 3m/10ft or so. It repeat flowers well. The parentage is rather complex but includes *R. bella*; Colin often using this species to help confer disease resistance to his seedlings. Bred by Horner (UK), 1999.

**Golden Showers** A short growing Climber of many virtues. Large, open golden-yellow flowers, fading to light yellow. The individual blooms may be of no exceptional beauty, but they are produced very freely and continuously throughout the summer, providing a good splash of colour. The plant grows well and it is unusually happy on a north wall, perhaps more so than any other rose except 'Zéphirine Drouhin'. Also good as a shrub. 'Charlotte Armstrong' × 'Captain Thomas'. Lammerts (USA), 1956.

**Handel** Quite small semi-double flowers that are closer to a Floribunda than a Hybrid Tea in character. The colouring is unusual, being creamy-blush and edged with pink. The growth is tall, perhaps 3.5m/12ft and it repeats well. There is some tendency to blackspot. 'Columbine' × 'Heidelberg'. McGredy (UK), 1956.

**Highfield** A sport from 'Compassion' (see above), with all the virtues of that rose. Here we have light yellow flowers with occasional peachy tints. Fragrant. Harkness (UK), 1981.

**High Hopes** (*Haryup*) The medium-sized, fragrant flowers are light pink at first then fading to palest peach; they are susceptible to blotching in the rain. With 'Compassion' in its parentage, it is not surprising that the growth is stiff and upright and so probably best suited to a wall or fence. Height 3m/10ft. 'Compassion' × 'Congratulations'. Bred by Harkness (UK), 1994.

**Iceberg, Climbing** Floribundas, unlike the Hybrid Teas, have not been fruitful in the production of climbing sports and I am aware of only two worthwhile varieties, this and 'Climbing Masquerade'. 'Climbing Iceberg' lives up to the high expectations we would have of its parent, and even takes on a new elegance with its longer growth. Its only drawback is a tendency to revert to the bush form when first planted. When this occurs it is worth trying again with another plant. Growth 3m/10ft. Discovered by Cant (UK), 1968.

**Laura Ford** (*Chewarvel*) ('King Tut', 'Normandie') One of the first of Chris Warner's Patio Climbers, 'Laura Ford' has great quantities of small, loosely double, deep yellow flowers. They are borne over the height of the plant and it repeat flowers very well. The growth is upright with small dark, glossy leaves and it reaches a height of about 2.5–3m/8–10ft. Bred by Warner (UK), 1989.

*GOLDEN SHOWERS is particularly happy on a north wall where it will keep its colour for longer*

**Leaping Salmon** (*Peamight*) The flowers of this variety are very large, 13cm/5in across, and have the classic high centre of the Hybrid Teas. They are salmon-pink, have a wonderful fragrance and are good for cutting. The growth is relatively upright but bushy and the leaves are a glossy, dark green. Height 3m/10ft. Bred by Pearce (UK), 1983.

**Leverkusen** Perhaps the most attractive of the Kordesii hybrids, the result of a cross between *Rosa × kordesii* and the climbing Hybrid Tea 'Golden Glow'. It bears quite large, double rosette-shaped flowers of rather Old Rose appearance and of a creamy-yellow colouring, deepening towards the centre. There is a pleasing, fruit-like fragrance. The growth is strong and rather bushy, to a height of 3m/10ft, and the foliage is a deep glossy green, with rather small leaflets. This rose flowers freely in summer and, to a lesser extent, later on. Kordes (Germany), 1954.

**Masquerade, Climbing** The climbing sport of the Floribunda of the same name that was bred by Boerner (USA) and introduced in 1949. As a climber it will grow to 5.5m/18ft and flower freely, but only in the summer. Its unusual mixture of yellow, pink and deep red has its uses in the garden scheme. Light fragrance. Discovered by Gregory (UK), 1958.

**New Dawn** As I said in the introduction to this section, this is a recurrent-flowering sport from the summer-flowering Rambler 'Doctor W. Van Fleet', and an important influence in this group. With its conversion to repeat flowering, the growth reduced from 6m/20ft in its parent to about 3m/10ft in this rose. It has pretty, rather pointed buds, opening to medium-sized, pearly-blush coloured flowers held in large clusters and with a sweet fragrance. The growth is vigorous with plentiful foliage. It may be pruned to

247

form a shrub, or grown as a hedge. 'New Dawn' is one of the most disease-free of roses, and was the first rose ever to receive a patent. Discovered by Somerset Rose Nursery (USA), introduced 1930.

**Parade** Here we have a rose that deserves more attention. Like 'Aloha' the growth is short, with large, deep cerise-pink flowers that are fully double and of almost Old Rose persuasion. They have a strong fragrance. It is exceptionally free and continuous in flower. The growth is very vigorous and healthy, and will achieve 2–2.5 m / 7–8ft, though it can also make a good lax growing shrub. Bred from a seedling from 'New Dawn' × 'World's Fair'. Boerner (USA), 1953.

**Parkdirektor Riggers** A rose similar to 'Dortmund', but with large clusters of semi-double flowers of deep velvety crimson. It has similar glossy, dark green foliage. Recurrent flowering. Slight fragrance. Height 3.5 m/12ft. R. × kordesii × 'Crimson Glow'. Bred by Kordes (Germany), 1957.

**Penny Lane** (*Hardwell*) When 'New Dawn' first appeared in 1930 it was quickly seized upon as a useful parent for producing climbers and has been responsible for a number of varieties including 'Aloha'

and 'Pink Perpétué'. It is also responsible for this variety. While, arguably, none of its seedlings quite come up to the high standard of 'New Dawn', 'Penny Lane' has very pretty flowers, very much in the style of the Old Roses. They are honey-champagne in colour and have a pleasing fragrance, although they are not produced particularly freely. The stems are quite lax and so easy to train. It won the Rose of the Year award in 1998. Bred by Harkness (UK), 1998.

**Pink Perpétué** A variety that will grow a little taller than most of the others, perhaps to 3.5 m/12ft. In colour it is a rather harsh pink with a carmine reverse, the flowers being medium sized, double, slightly cupped and held in trusses. The growth is vigorous and reliable and it repeats well. There is some fragrance. 'Danse du Feu' × 'New Dawn'. Gregory (UK), 1965.

**Schoolgirl** This has been a popular Climber for some time but, although a beautiful rose at its best, having shapely buds in a pleasing coppery-orange shade, it is not reliable. The foliage is not good and is rather subject to blackspot, often resulting in poor growth. Fragrant. 3m/10ft. 'Coral Dawn' × 'Belle Blonde'. McGredy (UK), 1964.

**Summertime** (*Chewlarmoll*) A Patio Climber from Chris Warner, it won Rose of the Year in 2005. It is an extremely free-flowering variety with the small, full petalled, lemon-yellow flowers being produced from top to bottom. Fragrance is not such a feature with the Patio Climbers but 'Summertime' has a sweet fragrance of medium strength. It grows to a perfect height for a fence, trellis, pillar or arch, about 2.5 m/8ft. 'Laura Ford' × 'Golden Future'. Bred by Warner (UK) 2005.

**Swan Lake** One of the most beautiful Modern Climbers, with large, well-shaped, white Hybrid Tea blooms delicately flushed with pale pink at the centre. Good, dark green foliage. Slight fragrance. 2.5 m/8ft. 'Memoriam' × 'Heidelberg'. McGredy (UK) 1968.

**Sympathie** Shapely, high-centred blooms of bright blood-red. Vigorous growth, with large, glossy foliage. It will achieve 3–3.5 m/10–12ft . A good reliable variety, flowering intermittently throughout the summer. Kordes (Germany) 1964.

**Warm Welcome** (*Chewizz*) Certainly the brightest coloured of the Patio Climbers, the almost single flowers are a bright orange that is extremely eye catching. The leaves are small, dark and glossy and set the flowers off well. It is very free flowering, carrying on into the early frosts. It won the Royal National Rose Society's President's International Trophy in 1991 and the prestigious James Mason Award in 2006. Height 2m/7ft. ('Elizabeth of Glamis' × ['Galway Bay' × 'Sutter's Gold']) × 'Anna Ford'. Bred by Warner (UK) 1991.

**White Cockade** A rose which produces some of the most beautiful and shapely flowers in this group. They are pure white and most attractive against its large, dark green leaves. Unfortunately it does not grow very quickly, nor to a great height, so would perhaps be better grown as a shrub. A good cut flower. Fragrant. 'New Dawn' × 'Circus'. Cocker (UK) 1969.

*Right,
New Dawn,
an important
variety in the
history of the
rose, is one of
the most popular
with gardeners*

*Facing page,
Warm
Welcome,
with its brightly
coloured flowers
and long
flowering season,
is guaranteed
to create an eye-
catching show*

# English Roses as Climbers

ENGLISH ROSES form a diverse group. Indeed, it has always been my wish that this should be so. This has been possible because they, themselves, were bred from a great diversity of very different parents. Some of these parents were Climbing Roses. The difference between a Climbing Rose and a Shrub Rose is often somewhat nebulous. We used these Climbers largely with a view to giving our roses greater vigour and disease-resistance—and because we wanted not only small shrubs but also large shrubs, in order that we would have roses for all parts of the garden. The result is that we have a number of large shrubs that are equally suitable for growing as Climbing Roses.

The fact that the taller English Roses are—so to speak—dual purpose, does not mean that when grown as Climbers they are in any way second best. Indeed, some varieties are even better when grown in this way. The Old Rose flowers of the English Roses are, I think, if anything more beautiful when seen high up—perhaps when growing on a wall or pillar. The very nature of English Roses seems to lend itself to this purpose.

There is something of a dearth of really good Climbing Roses. Such Climbers as there are—though often beautiful—tend to be subject to disease, perhaps because many of them are climbing sports of early bush Hybrid Tea Roses which were, themselves, subject to disease. There are some very good Modern Climbers, but these seldom have the Old Rose flower which many people desire. English Climbers do have the Old Rose style of flower. They are reliably repeat flowering and more disease resistant than most other Climbing Roses—and of course, they are very fragrant.

It has to be admitted that most English Climbers do not reach a great height, though many of them will easily achieve 3.5 m/12ft on a wall and this is about as much as most people require. A Climber growing to a greater height is difficult to manage. English Climbers are ideal for trellis work, pillars, arches and the like, although these should not be too tall. They are, I think, best of all when grown on the walls of a house.

Of all the developments in English Roses in recent years, I think the use of them as Climbers is the one that gives me the most satisfaction. As such, they fulfil a very useful role and one that, up to the present time, has not been well filled. I can strongly recommend them. The following descriptions refer to English Roses when grown as Climbers. Further, more complete details, are given in Chapter 5.

*A SHROPSHIRE LAD forms an excellent all-round climber and is particularly suitable for an arch. The flowers have a delicious fruity fragrance in the Tea Rose tradition*

**A Shropshire Lad** (*Ausled*) (Leander Group) This is a versatile variety that is related to 'Leander', from which it inherits its vigorous, healthy, almost thornless growth. It forms an excellent all-round Climber and is particularly suitable for an arch. The flowers are soft peachy pink and of cupped rosette formation. They have a delicious fruity fragrance in the Tea Rose tradition. This rose can also be grown as a large, arching shrub. (See also p. 145)

**Constance Spry** (English Old Rose Hybrid) Originally introduced as a large shrub, it soon became clear that 'Constance Spry' was better when grown as a Climbing Rose. It is unfortunately only early-summer flowering and will not repeat but, while it does flower, it provides us with one of the most superb pictures in the garden. It is a most beautiful rose with clear pink blooms of true Old Rose formation. They are exceptionally large, with a luminous yet delicate quality that is hard to compare with any other variety. There is a strong myrrh fragrance. 4.5 m/15 ft or more. (See also p. 125)

**Crown Princess Margareta** (*Auswinter*) (Leander Group) This is not a tall Climber but it has plenty of vigour and can be relied upon to reach 2.5 m/8 ft on a wall. It is a variety that shows itself off particularly well when the flowers look down at us in a delightful manner. They are large, neatly formed rosettes in a lovely shade of apricot-orange and they have a strong, fruity, Tea Rose fragrance. 1.8–2.5 m/6–8 ft. (See also p. 147)

**Falstaff** (*Ausverse*) (Old Rose Hybrid) This rose and 'Tess of the d'Urbervilles' are the only crimson English Roses that qualify as Climbers. 'Falstaff' is turning out to be particularly valuable in this respect. The flowers are a rich, dark crimson that eventually turns to a most pleasing shade of rich purple—both colours are particularly satisfactory. They have a powerful Old Rose fragrance. It will have little trouble in reaching 2.5 m/8 ft or more in height. (See also p. 128)

**Gertrude Jekyll** (*Ausbord*) (Old Rose Hybrid) To those who know this beautiful rose it may seem an unlikely candidate for inclusion with the Climbing English Roses, as it seems to be so very much a shrub. Nonetheless it will, with proper encouragement, achieve a good height—which is particularly welcome in English Old Rose Hybrids, not many of which develop as Climbers. Its flowers are in the form of large, flat rosettes of true Old Rose character and rich

pink colouring. They have a particularly strong and delicious Old Rose fragrance. 2.5 m/8 ft. (See also p. 130)

**Graham Thomas** (*Ausmas*) (English Musk Rose) As a shrub, this rose—although vigorous—tends to be rather too slender in growth to be ideal and this obviously points to its possibilities as a Climbing Rose. It is, in fact, an excellent climber that will cover a considerable area and I think it is true to say that it is better as a Climber than as a shrub. The flowers are in the form of a shallowly cupped rosette in an unusually rich and pure yellow. They have a fresh Tea Rose fragrance with a cool violet character. James Mason Award 2000. 3 m/10 ft. (See p. 164)

**James Galway** (*Auscrystal*) (Leander Group) This is a vigorous climber with strong, almost thornless growth, that will reach a fair height. The flowers are large and full, with many petals arranged in the form of a neat rosette. The colour is a lovely warm pink at the centre, shading to pale pink at the edges. There is a delicious Old Rose fragrance. 3–3.5 m/10–12 ft. (See also p. 150)

**Janet** (*Auspishus*) (Leander Group) This is the first English Rose that can be said to have flowers of an almost Hybrid Tea type in the early stages. Such flowers look well on a Climber, where the beauty of the opening bud can be seen to perfection. The difference is that the buds of 'Janet' open into a classic full rosette shape, so that we get the beauty of both types of flower. The colour is a combination of soft pink and soft yellow. They have a strong, fruity fragrance. 2.5 m/8 ft. (See also p. 150)

**Leander** (*Auslea*) (Leander Group) There is a strong element of *R. wichurana* in this rose, which has given it an inclination to climb. This shows up in its appearance as a whole, with its glossy foliage and small, tightly formed flowers of rich apricot. It is a very easy rose to grow and would, I think, clamber into trees if planted in the right position. More normally, it is very much in place on walls and trelliswork. 3.5 m/12 ft. (See also p. 152)

**Malvern Hills** (*Auscanary*) (English Musk) This variety might be better described as a repeat-flowering Rambler. It sends up long, trailing branches to a considerable height and still finds the energy to flower again later in the season. Very few Ramblers will do this. Its flowers are small and of typical Rambler form, with a Musk

*Above left,*
GRAHAM
THOMAS *is an*
*excellent climber*
*with flowers*
*of an unusually*
*rich and pure*
*yellow*

*Above right,*
CROWN PRINCESS
MARGARETA,
*a particularly*
*reliable and*
*beautiful climber,*
*is excellent for a*
*wall or arch and*
*bears flowers with*
*a strong fruity Tea*
*Rose fragrance*

*Following pages,*
MALVERN HILLS
*is a wonderful*
*rose, close in*
*appearance to*
*a rambler but*
*with good repeat*
*flowering*

fragrance. The colour is buff, becoming pale yellow. It has polished leaves with small leaflets. An ideal rose for covering arches or trellis-work, it might also be encouraged to scramble over shrubs or into a small tree. It has almost complete disease-resistance. Named after the beautiful hills in Worcestershire, which were the home of the composer Sir Edward Elgar. 4m/14ft or more.

**Mortimer Sackler** (*Ausorts*) (English Musk) This rose is really better as a Climber than it is as a shrub. Its growth is rather still and upright as a shrub but will, if given the chance, gradually form a good Climber as it grows and branches. Its flowers are of small to medium size, not showy, but with an almost star-like formation that is most appealing. The colour is soft pink, paling slightly with age. The stems are thin and wiry with narrow, Noisette-like leaves that are almost red in the early stages, gradually becoming dark green. The fragrance is of the Old Rose type with a hint of fruit. 3–3.5m/10–12ft. (See also p. 168)

**Shropshire Lass** (English Alba) This tough and disease-resistant rose bears blush white, almost single flowers with a strong and delicious fragrance. These are borne freely but not repeatedly. Height 6m/20ft or more. (See also p. 178)

**Snow Goose** (*Auspom*) (English Musk) This might best be described as a repeat-flowering Rambler (see also p. 286). It bears large sprays of numerous, small, glistening white flowers with yellow stamens just visible, giving it a charming, almost daisy-like appearance. The stems are almost thornless. It is a good rose to train over an arch, wall, fence or trellis. Very healthy and reliable. There is a slight Musk Rose fragrance. 2.5–3m/8–10ft.

**Spirit of Freedom** (*Ausbite*) (English Old Rose Hybrid) Very large flowers with numerous petals of a soft glowing pink, which gradually turns to lilac pink with time. A flower of typical Old Rose beauty with a pleasing fragrance. It forms a particularly good Climber. 2.5m/8ft. (See also p. 141)

**St. Alban** (*Auschestnut*) (Leander Group) Rather similar to the giant-flowered 'Abraham Darby', but not quite so large, this has better disease resistance. Cupped blooms of rich yellow gradually open to shallow and more open cups well filled with petals. The growth is typical of the Leander group, with fine, glossy foliage. It will form a good Climber of about 2.5m/8ft on a wall. It has a pleasing fragrance. (See also p. 155)

**St. Swithun** (*Auswith*) (English Old Rose Hybrid) If not among the very best of English Climbers, this rose is certainly one of the most beautiful. It bears blush pink, perfectly formed, rosette-shaped flowers filled with small petals, reminiscent of one of the old Alba Roses. Although it is of no more than medium height when grown as a shrub, trained as a Climber it can be relied upon to grow to 2.5m/8ft or more. It has a lovely pure myrrh fragrance and pleasing grey-green leaves, which are smooth and blend ideally with the flowers. (See also p. 138)

**Teasing Georgia** (*Ausbaker*) (Leander Group) This is one of the most beautiful and reliable of the Leander roses. It forms an excellent Climber, holding its flowers perfectly on a wall and looking straight at us. These repeat well and are of a glowing strong yellow, paling a little on the outside petals and in the form of a perfect rosette. There is a lovely strong Tea Rose fragrance. Some people think this is one of the best of the English Climbers. Height 1.8–2.5m/6–8ft. (See also p. 158)

**Tess of the d'Urbervilles** (*Ausmove*) (English Old Rose Hybrid) There are not many good crimson Climbers, which makes this variety most valuable. It bears bright crimson flowers that are

*SPIRIT OF FREEDOM has very large and very full flowers of typical Old rose beauty*

*Left, TESS OF THE D'URBERVILLES has flowers of a particularly bright crimson and with a good fragrance*

*Facing page, SNOW GOOSE repeat flowers well and is a lovely rose to train over an arch, wall, fence or trellis*

deeply cupped at first, the petals gradually turning back to form a more rosette shape that is less formal. It will form a short Climber of 1.8–2.5m/6–8ft. There is a lovely Old Rose fragrance. (See also p. 142)

**The Generous Gardener** (*Ausdrawn*) (English Musk) I am often asked which is my favourite English Rose and I always decline to answer. I find it an almost impossible question. Nonetheless, at the present time I am prepared to say that 'The Generous Gardener' is my favourite English Climbing Rose. It is one of the few English Roses that is better when grown as a Climber than as a shrub. It has the most beautifully formed deeply cupped flowers of pale pink colouring. The scent is a mixture of tea and myrrh. It is of true climbing habit—tall, strong and disease resistant—and repeat flowers admirably. It also has attractive foliage with pale green leaves that are rather larger and broader than we would expect in a rose of the English Musk group. Height 3.5m/12ft or more. (See also p. 172)

**The Pilgrim** (*Auswalker*) (English Musk) This is a very good Climbing Rose with flowers of a pale to medium yellow colour. They are quite large and of cupped rosette formation. They have a softness of character that is most pleasing in a rose of this colour—yellows are often a little harsh. Although as a bush it is not always very tall, when grown as a Climber it can reach a considerable height. The scent is a pleasing mixture of Tea Rose and myrrh. Height 3m/10ft or more. (See also p. 172)

**William Morris** (*Auswill*) (Leander Group) A healthy and vigorous Climber with rosette-shaped flowers of a lovely, glowing apricot pink—gradually becoming shallowly cupped. Ample glossy, dark green foliage. Height: 1.8–2.5m/6–8ft. (See also p. 159)

*Near right, THE PILGRIM makes a first-class Climber, the flowers being produced over the whole height of the plant*

*Far right, THE GENEROUS GARDENER is an English Rose that is better when grown as a Climber than as a shrub—tall, strong and extremely healthy*

# 8

# RAMBLER
# ROSES

THE TYPICAL RAMBLING ROSE has long, lax growth and bears large sprays of often small flowers in abundance, which provide a massed bower-like effect of great beauty. Most flower only in the summer, although certain varieties frequently provide some blooms later on and a few are reliably repeat flowering. Many people associate Ramblers with the past, and indeed their popularity was at its height in Edwardian times and soon after. They do not, however, belong to the more distant past, as most of them were introduced in the first quarter of the 20th century. Prior to this time a very limited selection was available, bred mainly from *Rosa arvensis* (the Field Rose), *R. sempervirens* (the Evergreen Rose) and *R. moschata* (the Musk Rose). It was only with the introduction of certain climbing species Ramblers from the Far East— notably *R. multiflora* and *R. wichurana*—that the majority of the varieties that we now enjoy came into being. These two species were crossed with the garden roses of the day—the Tea Roses, the Hybrid Perpetual and the Hybrid Teas—thus providing a much wider variety of colour and form of flower.

In more recent times, the popularity of Ramblers in the average garden has given way to the more continuous flowering Modern Climbers, and there are only a few varieties to be found in the average nursery catalogue or garden centre. This could not be more unfortunate, for Rambling Roses have a place in the garden that no other rose can fill, and are capable of a beauty that is hard to equal. They have a natural grace, often exceeding that of the Climbing Roses, their branches and large sprays hanging gracefully from their support. They are frequently very vigorous and can grow to a great height.

The way Ramblers can be used is, perhaps, more varied than for any other class. While they are not always suitable for growing on walls, since they may be difficult to manage and some of them are inclined to suffer from mildew when so grown, they are ideal for trellises, arches, pergolas, pillars, tripods, the covering of small unsightly buildings and other objects, as well as for growing into trees and over shrubs and hedges. In fact, the possibilities are almost endless, providing great scope for ingenuity. Rather surprisingly, some varieties can be grown successfully without support as large shrubs, and where space can be spared they will grow into great arching mounds. There are also a number of very lax-growing varieties that will creep along the ground, forming excellent ground cover. These many and varied uses are discussed in greater detail in Chapter 10.

Ramblers are usually fragrant and, since they arise from many different species, many different fragrances can be found among them. Some have the fresh, sharp, fruit-like fragrance of *R. wichurana*, others have a Musk Rose fragrance, but it is possible to detect among Ramblers most of the fragrances of the rose, and indeed the scents of other flowers. The scent of the double white Banksian Rose (*R. banksiae* var. *banksiae*) is, for example, said to be similar to that of violets.

The pruning and maintenance of Ramblers need not give us much trouble. Although there are exceptions in the case of the Multifloras, Ramblers are often best left to run their own course. Pruning is better kept to a minimum so that plants can create their own natural effect, with no more than an occasional tidying and removal of old growth. Tying will, of course, be necessary, as will the careful and artful guidance of growth, but as time goes on new growth will often intertwine with the old and become, to some degree, self-supporting. Ramblers are in general the most disease free and trouble free of roses; the worst that we can say is that a few varieties suffer from mildew. This matters less than with other roses, since we view Ramblers from a greater distance.

*Facing page,*
*RAMBLING*
*RECTOR is*
*probably the most*
*free flowering of*
*all ramblers,*
*the plant being*
*literally covered*
*in flowers*

258

# Sempervirens Hybrids

*ROSA SEMPERVIRENS*, the Evergreen Rose, is a native of Southern Europe and North Africa. It is a climbing or trailing species which, as its name suggests, has the ability to hold its foliage well into the winter, and has passed something of this quality on to its hybrids. Early in the 19th century the French breeder Jacques, gardener to the Duc d'Orléans (later King Louis-Philippe) used *R. sempervirens* to create the small but very beautiful group which we call Sempervirens Hybrids. They were almost exclusively the result of his work, and since his time little has been done with them. This is unfortunate, for few Ramblers bred since have been able to rival them for their grace of growth or for the charm of their flowers. These are small, typically Rambler, and held in graceful sprays.

Although *R. sempervirens* is not completely hardy, its hybrids seem to be almost entirely so. They have long, lax growth that is excellent for almost any purpose required of a Rambler, including growing on pillars or as weeping standards. They may also be grown as low, sprawling shrubs. Their foliage is small and neat and the flowers are usually fragrant. Most Sempervirens Hybrids flower only once in summer.

---

**Adélaïde d'Orléans** One of the most beautiful of Rambling Roses, not only for its creamy-white, semi-double flowers, but also for the elegance with which they hang down, like the flowers of a Japanese cherry. Each flower is held a little apart from the next in small dainty sprays, and the whole effect is charming. All this makes it an ideal rose for an arch or pergola. The growth can be slight by comparison with others in this robust group, but under reasonable conditions can be relied on to reach 4.5 m/15 ft. It has a pleasant myrrh fragrance. Jacques (France) 1826.

**Félicité Perpétue** A very beautiful rose which must be regarded as one of the most reliable and generally useful of the Ramblers. It flowers with great abundance, the individual white blooms being small, of neat full-petalled pompon formation, and held in large, slightly hanging sprays. They have a light fragrance. The foliage is dark, small and neat, holding well into the winter. The whole plant has a look of 'rightness' and balance. It is hardy, and often to be seen in old gardens, where it may have been for a long time. This rose should not be pruned more than is necessary to keep it within

*ADÉLAÏDE D'ORLÉANS is a very beautiful and particularly healthy variety with elegant, lax growth*

*FÉLICITÉ
PERPÉTUE is
one of the most
beautiful and
reliable of
Ramblers; it is
quite vigorous
and so best for
trees or for
covering garages,
sheds and so on*

*Above,*
*Princesse*
*Louise holds its*
*clusters of flowers*
*with typical*
*Sempervirens*
*elegance and the*
*growth is long*
*and pliable*

*Right, Flora, is*
*a very distinctive*
*Rambler with*
*attractive, full-*
*petalled flowers*

bounds, as this will lead to more growth and less bloom. It flowers late in the season and is quite happy on a north wall. Growth 4.5m/ 15ft. The name refers to two Christian martyrs who died in AD 203, although I am told by Professor Fineschi of Italy that these were also the names of the breeder's daughters. Bred by Jacques (France) 1827.

**Flora** A free-flowering Rambler with attractively cupped blooms opening flat and filled with petals. The colour is lilac-pink with deep pink at the centre, and there is a delicate perfume. Strong but graceful growth to about 3.5m/12ft . Raised by Jacques (France) 1829.

**Princesse Louise** A very similar rose to 'Félicité et Perpétue', described above, and much of what I have said about that rose can equally well be applied to this one. It differs in the soft pink colour- ing of its buds which soon turns to a creamy-blush, fading almost to white. The flowers are held in large clusters with typical Semper- virens elegance and are in every way delightful, while the growth is long and pliable with small, dark green foliage. Growth 3.5m/12ft. Jacques (France) 1828.

**Spectabilis** An altogether shorter rose than the other Sempervirens Hybrids, growing to about 2m/7ft in height. The flowers open from pretty rounded cupped buds into the most perfect delicate pink rosettes with closely packed petals, and have a sweet fragrance. It flowers late with occasional blooms in the autumn and is a charm- ing little rose worthy of extra encouragement. This rose has also been known as 'Noisette Ayez', and there is little doubt that it is a Noisette Hybrid. Breeder unknown, introduced 1848.

# Ayrshire Hybrids

*ROSA ARVENSIS* is the wild trailing rose of British hedgerows that flowers a little later than the Dog Rose. The Ayrshire Hybrids are a descendant of this species, and it seems that the Sempervirens Hybrids may also have had some part in their development. Unfortunately, there are no precise records, but the Ayrshire Hybrids, as their name would suggest, appear to have originated in Scotland. They cannot be said to be in the front rank of Ramblers, but all of them are very hardy, and have the advantage that they will grow under the partial shade of trees better than any other climbing rose. They are useful if only for this reason and, like nearly all older roses, do have their own modest beauty.

Of the Ayrshire Hybrids that remain, the following four varieties are worth consideration.

**Bennett's Seedling** ('Thoresbyana') This was raised or discovered by Bennett, gardener to Lord Manners at Thoresby, Nottinghamshire, in 1840. It appears to be a double form of *Rosa arvensis* with fragrant white flowers. It is very hardy and particularly suitable for growing in partial shade. Growth to 6m/20ft.

**Dundee Rambler** Small, very double, white flowers, tinted with pink at the edges. Spread 6m/20ft. It has been suggested it is *Rosa arvensis* × a Noisette Hybrid. Raised by Martin (Scotland), about 1850.

**Splendens** ('The Myrrh-scented Rose') One of the more worthwhile of the Ayrshire Hybrids. Its flowers are blush-white, tinted with cream and cupped at first, opening to a semi-double flower. They have a pleasing myrrh scent that was at one time almost unique amongst roses, although we do find it in the Sempervirens Hybrids, and again in the English Roses. It will grow vigorously to over 6m/20ft. The breeding is not known, nor do we know who raised it.

**Venusta Pendula** A distinctive rambler with wide, semi-double flowers of white touched with pink on the outer petals. The flowers open wide to reveal the dark stamens and release a strong, musky fragrance. The growth is vigorous, to about 4m/13ft, and lax, producing wonderful festoons of flowers when growing through trees. It is a very hardy variety and particularly popular in Germany where it was re-introduced by Kordes in 1928.

*VENUSTA PENDULA has vigorous, lax growth and is very hardy*

# Multiflora Hybrids

ROSA MULTIFLORA is a native of Korea and Japan, and was introduced to Britain in 1862. It is a rather stiff-growing Climber or shrub that is both robust and hardy, and is frequently used as a root stock in continental Europe, producing large plants with few suckers. Before the introduction of the species, a garden variety known as *R. multiflora* 'Carnea' had been brought to England from Japan by Thomas Evans of The East India Company in 1804. This had clusters of small double pink flowers. In 1817 the 'Seven Sisters' Rose' arrived from Japan, and later, in 1878, another Rambler known as 'Crimson Rambler'. It was these three roses from Japan, hybridized with various other garden varieties, that gave us the basis for the Multiflora Hybrids.

It is usually not difficult to differentiate between the Multiflora Hybrids and the Wichurana Hybrids. The former have rather stiff growth like the original species, with many strong shoots arising from the base of the plant. Their leaves are usually of a duller, more opaque green. The Wichuranas, on the other hand, are inclined to be more flexible in growth, with long thin stems and frequently have more polished, darker green leaves.

Multiflora Hybrids nearly always have small flowers in large, tightly packed clusters and have the advantage in that many of them flower earlier than the Wichuranas, thus lengthening the season of bloom. *R. multiflora* has a pleasing fragrance which carries well, and this quality is often to be found in the garden varieties. Generally, the flowers of the Multiflora Hybrids have the appearance of what most people would consider to be typical Rambler Roses, whereas the flowers of the Wichuranas tend a little more towards the Climbing Roses. They flower only once in the summer.

By the nature of their growth, many varieties of this class make excellent large shrubs, as do a number of other Ramblers. Indeed, it is surprising that they are not more often seen growing in this form in the wilder areas of large gardens. They are also ideal for municipal planting, roadside sites, public places, or anywhere where a large space has to be covered. I cannot think of a less expensive or more satisfactory way to do this.

It is not possible to be too dogmatic about pruning Ramblers in general, but insofar as the Multifloras are concerned, we can say that much of the old growth should be removed at the base in order to encourage the remaining young growth. This is because the Multifloras tend to make so much growth from the base that they easily become choked. However, gardeners should use their discretion, paying due attention to the result they may wish to attain and the general state of the plant. Pruning is best done immediately after flowering.

---

*BLEU MAGENTA is valuable for its rare colouring, a violet-cerise shade fading to pale violet*

**Aglaia** A very little-known variety that should be planted more widely, its main attribute being the great freedom with which it flowers. The cupped, double flowers open a pale yellow, quickly fading to cream and white. It is also very useful and rather unusual amongst the Ramblers in not being too vigorous—3–4m/10–13 ft tall—and virtually thornless, although this does mean it has to be tied in to prevent the stems being blown about. It has a strong, musky fragrance. An important rose historically, it was the basis of Peter Lambert's breeding lines which gave us many of the best Hybrid Musk and Polyanthas. *Rosa multiflora* (or hybrid) × 'Rêve d'Or'. Bred by Schmidt (Germany) 1896.

**Bleu Magenta** The Multifloras are notable, among other things, for the fact that they have produced the only truly purple flowers among the Climbers and Ramblers. Later, through the Polyantha Pompon Roses, they were responsible for such purple shades as we find in the Polyantha 'Baby Faurax'. That they should have this capacity is somewhat surprising, but such are the mysteries of genetics. Other rather similar Multifloras of purplish colouring include 'Rose Marie Viaud', 'Veilchenblau' and 'Violette'. All are beautiful in their own way, valuable for the rarity of their colouring, and particularly desirable for mingling with roses of other colours, especially the pink shades. 'Bleu Magenta' is the last of the four to flower. It is of a violet-cerise shade fading to pale violet. The flowers are small, double and held in closely

packed clusters. Growth of about 4.5m/15ft may be expected. There is little scent. It was brought to England by Graham Thomas from Roseraie de l'Haÿ. Nothing is known of its breeding.

**Blush Rambler** Once one of the most popular Ramblers, this rose was bred by B. R. Cant, in 1903, from a cross between 'Crimson Rambler' and 'The Garland'. It is, therefore, one quarter Musk Rose, although in fact it is of very typical Multiflora appearance. The flowers are blush-pink, small and cupped, opening to show golden stamens. They are held in quite large, closely-packed, rather conical clusters. It flowers very freely and the growth is vigorous, with ample light green foliage. Deliciously fragrant. A good Rambler worthy of more attention.

**Bobbie James** The parents of this rose are not known, but its overall appearance indicates it has at least some connection with the Multifloras, so it seems reasonable to place it here. It is a Rambler of exceptional vigour, growing far taller than other Multiflora Hybrids. Indeed, it is one of the five or six varieties that we, as nurserymen, tend to recommend when asked for a rose to cover large areas such as an unsightly building, or to grow into a tree. It produces long, thick stems with glossy, pale green leaves. The flowers are small, semi-double, cupped in

shape, pearly-white in colour, with yellow stamens, and are held in enormous clusters which, with their weight, tend to hang down from the branch. In fact each large cluster provides what I can only describe as a glistening, pearly effect. This is a very heavy rose that produces a mass of bloom, and it requires a strong structure to support it. It has an exceptional fragrance. Small oval hips. Growth to at least 8m/25ft. Introduced by Sunningdale Nurseries (UK) 1961, and named in honour of the Hon. Robert James, at Richmond, Yorkshire.

*Above, BLUSH RAMBLER flowers very freely and is worthy of more attention*

*Left, BOBBIE JAMES has exceptional vigour and produces vast quantities of strongly fragrant flowers*

*GOLDFINCH, one
of the few yellow
Ramblers, has
a strong and
delicious fruity
fragrance and
almost no thorns*

**Crimson Rambler** ('Turner's Crimson Rambler', the 'Engineer's Rose'). This is one of the original Ramblers brought to England from Japan in 1878. In China it was known as 'Shi Tz-mei' or 'Ten Sisters', and in Japan as 'Soukara-Ibara'. Sent to a Mr Jenner in England from Japan, by Professor R. Smith, an engineer, Jenner named it in Smith's honour. Charles Turner, a nurseryman of Slough, purchased the entire stock of this rose and introduced it in 1893 as 'Turner's Crimson Rambler'. It soon became a popular rose, and although there are not many crimson Ramblers, we do not value it very highly today. The flowers are small, crimson, soon fading to an unattractive bluish-crimson. It is particularly subject to mildew. There is little or no scent. Height 4.5 m / 15 ft.

**Ghislaine de Feligonde** This rose has attracted considerable interest in the last few years because of its repeat-flowering capabilities, although it doesn't compare too well next to most modern repeat-flowering varieties. From orange buds the flowers open apricot with a yellow base and then fade to peach, pink and white. In the autumn the flowers tend to be pinker. They are small and have an attractive scent. It can be grown as a climber (to 4 m/13 ft) or a rounded shrub (to 2 m/6 ft). Bred by Turbat (France) 1916.

**Goldfinch** A vigorous Rambler of typical Multiflora growth and character, bearing close bunches of small button-like flowers of a buff-apricot colour, fading almost to white, with yellow stamens and a strong fruit-like fragrance. There are not many yellow Multifloras and this must be regarded as one of the most satisfactory. It makes dense growth with many stems coming from the base and so may require quite a lot of thinning. It will also form an unusually fine, arching shrub of 2 m/7 ft in height and, eventually, considerably more across. There are almost no thorns. A hybrid between 'Hélène' and an unknown variety. Bred by George Paul (UK), introduced 1907.

**Phyllis Bide** This rose is of truly Rambler-like character, with typical small flowers in clusters, while at the same time being reliably repeat

*Far left,
GHISLAINE DE
FELIGONDE has
the advantage of
repeat flowering
and very good
disease resistance*

*Left, PHYLLIS
BIDE is very
different
from most
Ramblers, being
repeat flowering
and quite short*

flowering. Its colour is pale yellow flushed with pink, and it has a pleasant fragrance. A dainty rose of modest beauty, which should be used in such a way as to display itself to full effect without being lost among more robust neighbours. Growth about 3 m/10 ft. Bred by S. Bide of Farnham, Surrey, in 1923, who gave the parentage as 'Perle d'Or' × 'Gloire de Dijon', though there is some doubt about this statement.

**Rambling Rector** Rose names are not expected to amuse, but here we have an exception, evoking all sorts of images. The rose itself bears large heads of bloom which are small, semi-double, cream at first, later fading to white, with yellow stamens and a good fragrance. These are produced in great abundance on strong, unusually dense and bushy growth of 6 m/20 ft or more. Such growth makes it ideal for growing as a shrub, but it is also well suited for scrambling over trees and bushes. A magnificent sight in full bloom with numerous small hips in autumn. Origins unknown. (Illustrated, p. 259)

*Right,
RUSSELLIANA,
valuable for
demanding
conditions, bears
clusters of semi-
double flowers
with the Old Rose
fragrance*

*Facing page,
THE GARLAND
with small semi-
double flowers,
growing on the
same support as
PAUL NOËL,
a Wichurana
described on
page 278*

**Rose Marie Viaud** This is the second of our purplish Ramblers, its colour being a rich violet at first, fading by degrees to a pale lilac, providing a pleasing mixture of shades. The flowers are small, of neat rosette shape, borne in large clusters, and appear late in the season. The growth is vigorous, to about 4.5 m /15 ft. It has little or no scent. Like 'Veilchenblau', from which it is a seedling, it has some tendency to mildew, but this need not worry us too much in a Rambler. Bred by Igoult (France), introduced 1924.

**Russelliana** This is probably a Multiflora / Rugosa cross, with predictably coarse results but with equally predictable toughness and hardiness, giving it a certain value for demanding conditions. It has small, semi-double crimson-purple flowers with the Old Rose

fragrance. They are held in small clusters. The foliage is dark green, the growth robust and thorny. It flowers freely, providing a pleasing colour effect from a distance. The shrub rose 'Zigeunerknabe' is a seedling from this variety. First introduced in 1840, and from time to time variously known as 'Russell's Old Cottage Rose', 'Scarlet Grevillea' and 'Old Spanish Rose'.

**Seven Sisters' Rose** (*Rosa multiflora* 'Platyphylla', *R. m.* 'Grevillei') This rose was brought to Britain from Japan by Sir Charles Greville in 1817. Very popular in Victorian times, it is still worthy of a place in the garden. It gained its name from the varying shades of colour to be found in its flowers as they pass on to maturity—the idea being that there were seven different colours to be seen at one time. The flowers are double, quite large for a Multiflora, and held in big clusters, while the colour ranges from cerise to pale mauve, and eventually almost to white. It is free flowering and strong growing, to a height of about 5.5 m /18 ft. Fresh, fruit-like fragrance.

**The Garland** ('Wood's Garland') An early Rambler believed to be the result of a cross between *Rosa moschata* and *R. multiflora*. The flowers are small and semi-double, with quilled petals giving the blooms an unusual daisy-like appearance, while the buds are cream tinged with blush, opening to white, with yellow stamens. The clusters are of small to medium size and are held upright on the branch. Vigorous and bushy in growth to about 4.5 m /15 ft, with quite small, dark green leaves, it will also form a good shrub. There is a strong fragrance that carries well, and small, oval hips. Bred, or perhaps discovered, by a Mr Wells, 1835.

**Veilchenblau** ('Violet Blue') The third of the purplish Multifloras, this is a vigorous Rambler of 3.5–4.5 m /12–15 ft and typical Multiflora character, with large, closely packed clusters of small, cupped, purple-violet flowers. These are white at the centre with yellow stamens, and have an occasional streak of white. The colour becomes dark violet later, and finally turns to lilac-grey, presenting an attractive range of colour. Better colours are achieved in a shady position, where there may also be less likelihood of mildew, to which it is subject. There is a fresh, fruity fragrance. The foliage is light green, the growth almost thornless. A cross between 'Crimson Rambler' and 'Erinnerung an Brod'. Bred by Schmidt (Germany) 1909.

**Violette** The fourth of our purplish-coloured varieties, bearing large sprays of small, cupped, crimson-purple flowers turning to maroon-purple, with an occasional white streak and contrasting yellow stamens. Light, fruit-like fragrance. The growth is vigorous, attaining about 4.5 m /15 ft, with few thorns and dark green foliage. Breeding unknown. Bred by Turbat (France), introduced 1921.

*Right,
VEILCHENBLAU
flowers freely
and produces
a wide range of
colours; it is the
most popular
of the purplish
Ramblers*

*Far right,
VIOLETTE has
perhaps the
darkest coloured
flowers of all
the Ramblers*

# Wichurana Hybrids

THE WICHURANAS are the largest and most important group of Rambler Roses. The species, *Rosa wichurana*, comes from Japan, East China, Korea and Taiwan. Unlike *R. multiflora*, it is a naturally prostrate, trailing or scrambling rose, which is equally capable of being grown as a Climber, and no doubt frequently does so in its natural state. It has large clusters of quite small flowers (although bigger than those of Multiflora) of about 4–5cm/1½–2in. Brought to Britain in 1891, the breeders wasted no time in making use of it in the development of new Ramblers.

While *R. multiflora* is rather stiffly upright in growth—perhaps too much of a shrub to be quite what we require for a Rambler—no such complaint can be levied against *R. wichurana*. Its long, trailing growth, great vigour and glossy disease-free foliage have made it an ideal parent.

Whereas the Multifloras usually have small, typical Rambler flowers, the flowers of the Wichurana Hybrids vary considerably between varieties, having a wider range of colour and form than the Multifloras, often with flowers that are more like those of the Climbing Roses. These frequently differ from the Old Rose colouring and come closer to those of the Modern Roses, but they are never crude or garish. They are nearly always fragrant, often with the delicious fruit-like scent of fresh apples. It is interesting to note that many Wichurana Hybrids were hybrids of the crosses with the early Hybrid Teas. In this Wichuranas were fortunate, for it enabled them to perpetuate something of the delicacy of those roses. Where we have Wichuranas crossed with Hybrid Perpetuals or with Multiflora Hybrids, we have a rose much closer in appearance to that of a Multiflora Hybrid and such varieties are often less beautiful. The Wichuranas often grow to a greater height than the Multifloras, frequently to 6 or 8m/20 or 25ft, and tend to be of a more branching and attractive habit of growth. All Wichuranas have one season of flowering, although a few of them, such as 'Alberic Barbier' and 'Paul Nöel', frequently have a small crop of flowers in the autumn.

The Wichurana Hybrids have a great many uses, such as for growing into trees, over arches and pergolas, or perhaps over a wall. They also include some of the best roses for weeping standards, while others, like 'Alberic Barbier', easily take on the trailing habit of the species, making them suitable for ground cover.

When pruning Wichuranas, we can allow a great deal of latitude, according to the position in which they are grown and the tastes of the grower. Where there is plenty of space, I like to see them run riot so that the growth builds up into a twiggy mass. We can afford to leave them for some years although, of course, the time will come when we have to start removing old growth.

*ALBÉRIC BARBIER is a particularly valuable Rambler since it is extremely healthy, almost evergreen and repeat flowers quite well*

**Albéric Barbier** A very vigorous Rambler that will easily reach 8m/25ft under suitable conditions. Its parents were *Rosa wichurana* × 'Shirley Hibberd', the latter being a yellow Tea Rose. Its pretty buds open into quite large, fully-double, quartered flowers of a creamy-white shade with a strong fruit-like fragrance. These are held in small clusters and produced with great freedom. The long, thin, flexible stems have excellent glossy, dark green foliage that will last well into the winter. I had a particularly fine specimen which grew on the wall of an old granary; gradually, without any assistance, it clambered on to the roof, covering it completely and providing a most magnificent effect. Unfortunately it was killed by the exceptionally severe winter of 1981/2. In spite of this, 'Albéric Barbier' should not be regarded as tender in the British climate, and we are unlikely to encounter such a winter again for a long time. This Rambler has some capacity to provide flowers later in the year, no doubt due to the influence of its Tea Rose parent. One of the best and most reliable in this class. Bred by Barbier (France), introduced 1900.

**Albertine** One of the most popular of Ramblers available from most garden centres and not without good reason, for it is a most reliable rose that blooms very freely. It was the result of a cross between *Rosa wichurana* and the Hybrid Tea 'Mrs Arthur Robert Waddell', and its flowers, though of loose, open formation, have something of the

*ALEXANDRE
GIRAULT
produces strong,
lax stems and
great quantities
of strongly
coloured flowers*

*Following pages,
ALBERTINE is one
of the best known
Ramblers and, at
its best, one of the
most beautiful
and most free
flowering*

stamp of a Hybrid Tea. Starting as salmon-red buds, they open into large, coppery-pink flowers with a rich fragrance. The growth tends to be branching and bushy, making it an excellent subject with which to cover a fence. The leaves are small, thick, deep green, and have something of the Hybrid Tea about them. It will grow to 8 m / 25 ft as a Climber, and will, if desired, form a dense shrub of 1.5 m / 5 ft in height, spreading broadly. Bred by Barbier (France), introduced 1921.

**Alexandre Girault** With some repeat flowering, this is a useful Rambler, providing strength of colour in a class rather lacking in strong shades. The flowers are tinted red in the bud, turning to a deep coppery-carmine on opening, and have numerous slightly quilled petals. There is a green eye and yellow stamens. Growth is vigorous, to 6 m / 20 ft, with dark, glossy foliage and few thorns. It makes a magnificent and unusual massed colour effect. Parentage *Rosa wichurana* × the Tea Rose 'Papa Gontier'. Barbier (France), introduced 1909.

**Alida Lovett** Large, double blooms of soft shell-pink, shaded yellow at the base and opening to flat flowers with a good fragrance. The growth is quite vigorous and the foliage is dark, glossy green. Height 3.5 m / 12 ft. Breeding 'Souvenir du Président Carnot' × *Rosa wichurana*. Van Fleet (USA) 1905. (Illustrated, p. 274).

271

*Right,
AMERICAN
PILLAR
has extremely
distinctive
flowers, and is
also very tough
and reliable*

*Far right,
ALIDA LOVETT is
a charming rose
worthy of being
planted more
widely*

**American Pillar** This is a striking and extremely reliable variety, although one could argue that its colouring is harsh and it is rather stiff in character—both in flower and growth. Nonetheless, we still receive some demand for it. The single flowers are produced in large clusters and are bright carmine-pink with a distinct white centre. It is tough and robust, but may have some mildew. There is no scent. Breeding (*Rosa wichurana* × *R. setigera*) × a red Hybrid Perpetual. Bred by Dr W. Van Fleet (USA) 1902.

**Auguste Gervais** For me one of the most beautiful of the Wichurana Ramblers. It does not produce flowers with the abundance that we might expect of a first class Rambler, but they have a Tea Rose delicacy and are beautifully poised on elegant growth, providing the most pleasing effect. The flowers are semi-double, with large petals arranged in nicely sculptured informality, their colouring being a delicate mixture of cream-apricot and pale yellow, with copper flame-pink on the reverse. They are deliciously fragrant, and are produced over an extended period, with an occasional bloom later. Height 5.5 m/18ft. Good on a pillar. The breeding was *Rosa wichurana* × the yellow Hybrid Tea Rose 'Le Progrès'. Barbier (France) 1918.

**Crimson Shower** A comparatively new variety with two particularly useful qualities: it is a richer crimson than any other Rambler, and it does not begin to flower until midsummer, continuing into September. The flowers are small and rosette shaped and held in large clusters. There is little scent. 'Crimson Shower' will grow to about 3.5 m/12ft in height, and has small, very glossy foliage. Its long, flexible growth makes it ideal for a weeping standard. A seedling from 'Excelsa', it was bred by the successful amateur breeder A. Norman (UK), introduced 1951.

**Débutante** This excellent and charming rose bears small, cupped flowers of a fresh rose-pink colouring, the petals gradually reflexing and paling to blush-pink. They are held in quite small, dainty sprays and have a delicate and pleasing fragrance. The growth is healthy and strong, to about 4.5 m/15ft, with dark green foliage, the whole adding up to a most delightful picture. Rather surprisingly, there are not many soft pink Ramblers, and this is one of the most beautiful. It was the result of a cross between *Rosa wichurana* and the Hybrid Perpetual 'Baroness Rothschild'. It has provided us with an equally fine though rather different seedling called 'Weetwood'. Bred by Walsh (USA), introduced 1902.

**Dorothy Perkins** In its day the most popular Rambler, but it has fallen from grace in more recent times. This is not surprising, as it is by no means one of the best and suffers badly from mildew. We should not be too hard on it, however, as it does have a certain appeal with its large sprays of small, double or semi-double flowers

274

and flexible growth. The colour is a strong, almost matt pink, and unlike that of any other Rambler. It seems to require a good moist soil, and does not like to be in a baked, sunny position—certainly not against a wall where it is sure to have mildew. Fragrant. Growth about 3.5 m / 12ft. The breeding was *Rosa wichurana* × Hybrid Perpetual 'Madame Gabriel Luizet'. Bred in 1901 by Jackson & Perkins (USA), who are still leading American rose specialists.

**Doctor W. Van Fleet** This rose has, to a large extent, been succeeded by its own sport 'New Dawn', a repeat-flowering form that has been influential in the production of many of the Modern Climbers of the present day. The two are, in fact, identical, except that 'New Dawn' is considerably shorter in growth, due, no doubt, to the fact that more energy is taken up by its long season of flowering. For this reason it is worth retaining the parent variety which will grow to at least 6m/20ft. Its flowers are double, medium sized, with pointed buds and of a soft, even, pearly blush-pink. These are produced with great freedom, making an excellent effect in the mass. Breeding (*Rosa wichurana* × Tea Rose 'Safrano') × Hybrid Tea 'Souvenir du Président Carnot'. Bred by Dr W. Van Fleet (USA), introduced 1910.

**Emily Gray** Medium-sized clusters of semi-double buff-yellow flowers are shown off to advantage by glossy, dark green foliage, which is richly tinted with brown when young. The growth, unfortunately, is somewhat variable, and not entirely hardy, probably due to the fact that this rose is three-quarters China and Tea Rose, its breeding being 'Jersey Beauty' × 'Comtesse du Cayla'. In a warm position it will grow to 6m/20ft, but in less favourable places it can languish at 2.5 or 3m/8 or 10ft. It is, at its best, an attractive rose. Bred by Williams (UK), introduced 1918.

**Evangeline** Clusters of small, single, pale pink flowers, make a dainty effect against dark green foliage. They are fragrant and appear late in the season. It is good to have a single-flowered Rambler, but it is prone to blackspot. Growth to 5.5m/18ft. Breeding *Rosa wichurana* × 'Crimson Rambler'. Bred by Walsh (USA), introduced 1906.

**Excelsa** ('Red Dorothy Perkins') Large clusters of small, double, crimson flowers of globular formation, with white at the centre. It is vigorous, growing to 5.5m/18ft, with glossy, light green leaves. Its flexible branches make it suitable for a weeping standard, or for growing in prostrate form. Somewhat inclined to mildew. Bred by Walsh (USA), introduced 1909.

**François Juranville** An excellent, tall and vigorous Rambler of 8m/25ft, with flowers of a rich coral-pink that deepens towards the centre, and with a touch of yellow at the base, eventually fading with age. They are of medium size, opening flat and double, with slightly quilled petals, and have a fresh, fruit-like fragrance. They are held in small clusters on graceful lax growth with purple-red stems. The foliage is glossy green, tinted with bronze at first. A useful rose for pergolas or growing into small trees, but not suitable for a wall, where it may develop mildew. A cross between *Rosa wichurana* and the China Rose 'Madame Laurette Messimy'. Bred by Barbier (France), introduced 1906. (Illustrated overleaf)

**Gardenia** Small sprays of prettily pointed buds, opening to creamy-white flowers that deepen to yellow at the centre and eventually fade almost to white. These are of medium size, very full, slightly quartered, and have a fresh apple scent. The growth is vigorous, with graceful, flexible stems and small, dark, glossy green leaves. Height 6m/20ft. A cross between *Rosa wichurana* and Tea Rose 'Perle des Jardins'. Bred by Manda (USA), introduced 1899.

*CRIMSON SHOWER has flowers of a richer crimson than any other Rambler; it starts later than most but then continues into September*

275

*Above,* MARY
WALLACE
*has some of the
largest flowers
of the Ramblers
and makes a
striking show*

*Right,*
FRANÇOIS
JURANVILLE *is
an excellent
Rambler with
richly coloured
flowers and
glossy, dark
green leaves*

*Facing page,*
MAY QUEEN
*is particularly
free flowering
and the flowers
are beautiful
both individually
and en masse*

**Gerbe Rose** Large, cupped, quartered flowers of a soft pink, with a lovely fragrance. The growth, though robust, is not typical of a Wichurana Hybrid, being short and rather stiff with large, glossy, dark green leaves. This is no doubt due to its Hybrid Perpetual background—it is a *Rosa wichurana* × 'Baroness Rothschild' cross, and it appears that the latter parent has been influential. It is, however, a good pillar rose, and has some ability to flower again after its main crop. Growth 3.5 m/12ft. Bred by Fauque (France), introduced 1904.

**Lady Godiva** A sport from 'Dorothy Perkins' to which it is similar, except for the colouring of its small flowers which are blush-white, turning to almost pure white, and a shade that is perhaps more distinct and pleasing. Subject to powdery mildew. Fragrant. Growth 3.5 m/12ft. Discovered by G. Paul (UK), introduced 1908.

**La Perle** A tall and vigorous Rambler with a spread of up to 9m/30ft, the result of a cross between *Rosa wichurana* and the pale yellow Tea Rose 'Madame Hoste'. It seems that the Tea Roses, with their close relationship to *R. gigantea*, often produce tall Ramblers, and frequently combine this with flowers of exquisite delicacy. In 'La Perle' they are creamy-white, deepening to yellow at the centre. They are cupped at first, opening flat with quilled petals, and have a strong, fresh fragrance. The young leaves are tinted with brown, becoming a glossy green as they develop. Bred by Fauque (France), introduced 1905.

**Léontine Gervais** I regard this as one of the most attractive of the Wichurana Ramblers. It is the result of a cross between *Rosa wichurana* and the dainty Tea Rose 'Souvenir de Catherine Guillot'. The flowers are a delicate mixture of pink, copper and orange; they have large, gracefully sculptured petals, and are held nicely poised on rather branching growth, providing a beautiful airy effect. Fragrant. It will grow to about 8m/25ft, but can successfully be confined to a pillar. Bred by Barbier (France), introduced 1903.

**Mary Wallace** A cross between *Rosa wichurana* and an unnamed Hybrid Tea, showing the influence of the latter parent, the flowers being large, loosely-formed, semi-double and of a warm rose-pink colouring. It has a good fragrance. The growth is strong and rather upright, spreading to about 8m/25ft, with rather sparse foliage. Bred by Van Fleet (USA), introduced 1924.

**May Queen** Graham Thomas tells us there were two Ramblers of this name, both from

*SANDERS'
WHITE starts
flowering late but
then produces
great quantities
of powerfully
fragrant flowers*

The colour is a clear rose-pink, and there is a fresh, fruit-like fragrance. Individually the flowers are of considerable beauty, and this is equalled by the massed effect, the plant producing numerous long shoots that intertwine to form a mat of growth. It will grow to about 4.5 m/15 ft in height and will also form an excellent large shrub.

**Minnehaha** Large clusters of small, double, pink flowers, fading almost to white, on a strong Rambler. Once a very popular rose, perhaps more so than it deserved, although it will make a good weeping standard. Height 4.5 m/15 ft. *Rosa wichurana* × 'Paul Neyron'. Bred by Walsh (USA) 1905.

**Paul Noël** An excellent Rambler with the added advantage of repeating quite well in late summer. The flowers are most attractive, being very full with the quill-shaped petals radiating out from the button eye. They start a soft salmon pink, quickly fading to a medium pink. It flowers freely and is not too vigorous, about 4m/13 ft tall, and has the attractive, lax growth typical of this group and so is ideal for training horizontally on pergolas and over garages and sheds or against a wall. Apple fragrance with a hint of Chrysanthemum. Breeding is probably *R. wichurana* × 'Monsieur Tillier'. Bred by Tanne (France), introduced by Turbat, 1913. (Illustrated, p. 269)

**Paul Transon** After many years of confusion we now realise that the rose we were selling as 'Paul Transon' should correctly be called 'Paul Noël'.

**Réné André** Gracefully hanging sprays of small, semi-double flowers of a soft apricot-yellow which later becomes flushed with pink. The growth is vigorous with long, slender, flexible stems and plentiful dark, glossy green foliage. Fresh, fruit-like scent. Occasional repeat flowering. Growth about 4.5 m/15 ft. *Rosa wichurana* × 'L'Idéal'. Bred by Barbier (France), introduced 1901.

**Sanders' White** ('Sanders' White Rambler') A very good white Rambler, bearing large clusters of small, semi-double flowers with golden stamens and a wonderful fragrance—more powerful than any other member of this class. The growth is vigorous, long and flexible, to 5.5 or 6m/18 or 20ft, with glossy foliage. An altogether beautiful rose, it flowers with great freedom, and does so when most other Ramblers have nearly finished. It will also make excellent ground cover. Bred by Sanders & Sons (UK), introduced 1912.

**Thelma** Small to medium-sized clusters of quite large semi-double flowers in a delicate mixture of coral-pink and carmine, with a hint of yellow at the centre. This variety is not always very vigorous, but it will flower freely when well grown. Height 3.5 m/12 ft. *Rosa wichurana* × 'Paul's Scarlet Climber'. Bred by Easlea (UK) 1927.

the USA, and introduced in the same year, 1898. One was bred by Manda from *Rosa wichurana* × 'Champion of the World'; the other by Dr Van Fleet from *R. wichurana* × 'Madame de Graw'; the pollen parents in each case being Bourbons. It may be that neither breeder was willing to step down and change the name; it is more likely that the distributor confused two roses and sent them out under the same name. Such a confusion is by no means unheard of. The variety we have shows distinct signs of Old Rose parentage, the blooms starting as rounded shallow cups, well filled with petals, later becoming flat and eventually reflexing. They are of medium size, and, in fact, not dissimilar to those of the Bourbon 'Louise Odier'.

# Other Rambling Roses

As with the Climbing Roses, there are inevitably a number of Ramblers, some of them particularly beautiful, that do not belong to any of the previous four groups. Some belong to very small groups like the Boursault Roses that, nevertheless, stand very much on their own. Others included here are one-off hybrids between various species.

**Baltimore Belle** A hybrid between *Rosa setigera* and a Gallica Rose bred by an American nurseryman called Feast in 1843, this rose bears hanging sprays of very double cupped flowers of pale pink fading to ivory-white. They have an attractive formality which gives some hint of the Gallica parent, and are freely produced on a strong but graceful plant, with good, medium green foliage. Flowering occurs late in the season, after most other Ramblers. It will grow to 3.5m/12ft.

**Belvedere** This variety has been known as 'Princesse Marie' and used to be placed with the Sempervirens Roses. It may well have connections with that class, but these are slender at best; indeed it is difficult to say what are its origins. Graham Thomas has suggested it should be named 'Belvedere' after the house in Ireland, whence it was procured by Lady Ross. It is a very robust Rambler of 6m/20ft and frequently much more under favourable conditions. It bears large trusses of small flowers that are distinctly cupped and remain so to the end. Their colour is a strong clear pink which fades a little with age, and they have a pleasant fragrance. This is a most charming Rambler, but unfortunately it has one bad fault —it tends to become shabby in the rain. It appears to require a rich soil and a cool climate. In drier areas the flowers are often a dirty white. In the richer soil at Nymans Garden, West Sussex, it is beautiful, growing into trees. If you can provide suitable conditions, I would certainly recommend this rose. It is also ideal as a large shrub.

**BOURSAULT ROSES** These form a small group of almost thornless Ramblers which were once thought to be the result of crossing *Rosa pendulina* with *R. chinensis*, but it has since been discovered that the chromosome count excludes this possibility. We are thus left with a mystery. They have never become a major class, but they do have an Old Rose character that still appeals.

    **Amadis** ('Crimson Boursault') Small

*BELVEDERE grows very strongly and has small, distinctly cupped flowers*

*MADAME SANCY DE PARABÈRE, the most beautiful of the Boursaults, has large flowers and is completely thornless*

279

semi-double, cup-shaped flowers of deep
crimson-purple with an occasional white
streak. These are held in both small and large
clusters and produced freely on strong, rather
bushy growth of about 4.5 m/15 ft. The foliage
is dark, and there are no thorns. An attractive
Rambler in the mass, providing a splash of
rich colouring. There is no fragrance. Bred
by Laffay (France) 1829; **Blush Boursault**
('Calypso', 'Rose de l'Isle', 'Florida') Double
flowers of pale blush-pink, opening flat and
with a rather ragged appearance. Long, arching, thornless growth, with plentiful dark
green foliage. 4.5 m/15 ft. 1848; **Madame
Sancy de Parabère** A unique rose, and the
most beautiful of the group, with large, double, soft pink blooms up to 12 cm/5 in across,
opening flat. These are unusual in that the
small inner petals are frequently, but not
always, surrounded by distinctly larger
outer petals, creating the attractive effect of
a rosette within a single flower. They have
a slight scent, and are produced early in the
season. It has good dark green foliage and
no thorns. Its large flowers and general habit
would make it more suitable for inclusion
amongst the Climbers, but as it is a Boursault Rose I place it here. 4.5 m/15 ft. Bred
by Bonnet (France), introduced 1874.
(Illustrated, p. 279)

**Dentelle de Malines** This rose was bred by
Louis Lens who used a very wide and interesting range of parents and carried on with
the development of the Hybrid Musks. He
used *Rosa filipes* in his breeding programme
and, from it, introduced a number of excellent vigorous shrubs or climbers. Lens sent
us this variety for trialling as a ground cover
rose; we planted it in our garden not far from
a trellis to which it immediately attached
itself and covered with great speed. It is
exceptionally free flowering, the small
flowers at first being a rich pink that then
fade to soft pink. Unfortunately it doesn't
repeat at all and only has a light fragrance.
It is however very healthy and reliable. As
a Rambler it will quickly achieve 4m/13 ft,
as a shrub it would probably be 2m/6ft tall
and more across. *Rosa filipes* × ('Robin
Hood' × 'Baby Faurax'). Bred by Lens
(Belgium) 1986.

**Francis E. Lester** One of the surest and
most reliable of Rambler Roses. A seedling
from the Hybrid Musk 'Kathleen', this rose
is thus of rather mixed origin. The flowers
are single, delicate blush-pink at the edges,
soon becoming almost white, and giving
something of the impression of apple blossom. They are held nicely spaced in large

280

*DENTELLE DE MALINES was originally sent to us as a ground cover rose but it makes a superb Rambler*

*FRANCIS E. LESTER is one of the very best Ramblers, very free flowering, with beautiful single flowers that are fragrant and followed by a large crop of hips in the autumn*

trusses and have a particularly strong and pleasing fragrance. This rose blooms with exceptional abundance and in autumn there are plentiful small, oval, orange-red hips. The growth is strong and bushy, to about 4.5 m/15 ft, and it will, if desired, make a first class large shrub. The foliage is elegant, a glossy dark green, with pointed, widely spaced leaflets and extremely healthy. Bred by Francis E. Lester, founder of the Californian nursery now known as 'Roses of Yesterday and Today', introduced 1946.

**Kew Rambler** A cross between *Rosa soulieana* and 'Hiawatha', this rose might have been included with the Multiflora Hybrids, but *R. soulieana* has placed a very definite stamp upon it, providing us with quite a different rose. The foliage is an attractive grey-green colour, similar to that of *R. soulieana*, the growth vigorous, bushy,

very thorny and rather stiff. The flowers have a wild rose charm, being single, of soft pink colouring, with a white centre and yellow stamens. They are held in close but not over-packed trusses. The fragrance is strong and typically Multiflora, and there are small orange-red hips in autumn. It will achieve about 5.5 m/18ft. Raised at Kew, introduced 1912. (Illustrated, p. 287)

**Little Rambler** (*Chewramb*) A Patio Rambler that is not dissimilar to 'Open Arms' (see p. 285) but has much smaller and more double flowers giving a very tight and neat effect. The very small buds are crimson but open to pure pale pink fading to almost white with age. Being fairly lax it is easy to train along a fence or over an arch where it will flower almost continuously through to the frosts. Good musky fragrance. Bred by Warner (UK) 1994.

*MOUNTAIN SNOW bears semi-double flowers in shapely sprays, making cascades of pure white*

**Long John Silver** With its very stiff, upright growth and large flowers, this could be classed as a climber and indeed is better suited to being trained against a wall rather than in a tree or on a pergola. It is a very vigorous and needs a big space to accommodate it. The blooms are about 10cm/4in across, a pure, luminous white and full petalled. There is a medium musky fragrance. Tough and reliable. *Rosa setigera* × 'Sunblest'. Bred by Horvath (USA) 1934.

**Lykkefund** A seedling from *Rosa helenae*, thought to have 'Zéphirine Drouhin' as its pollen parent. If this is true, it is a rather interesting cross, for I know of no other rose that has 'Zéphirine' in its make up. The two roses have this much in common: they are both entirely thornless. The flowers are of medium size, semi-double, pale creamy-yellow, deeper at the centre, and tinged with pink which soon fades in the sun. They are held in medium-sized clusters and produced with great freedom. The growth is strong and bushy, probably to 3–4.5m/10–15ft, the foliage a deep glossy green, with rather small leaflets. 'Lykkefund' is suitable for growing in trees, and may also be used as a large shrub. Strong fragrance. Bred by Olsen (Denmark), introduced 1930.

**Malvern Hills** See Chapter 5.

**Mountain Snow** Although this rose was bred at our nursery, I am ashamed to say I have no idea of its parentage. It was one of those little mysteries that are apt to occur from time to time in rose breeding, but I feel it is worth preserving. The growth is particularly robust, with plentiful dark green foliage. The semi-double, medium sized flowers are borne in large, shapely sprays, providing a cascade

283

of pure white. It makes a good Rambler or may be used as an elegantly arching shrub. It may be expected to reach 3.5–4.5m/12–15ft as a rambler or 1.5m/5ft by 2.5m/8ft as a shrub. Bred by David Austin (UK) 1985.

**Open Arms** (*Chewpixel*). In addition to his Patio Climbers, Chris Warner has introduced two Patio Ramblers—'Open Arms' and 'Little Rambler'—that are distinct in having a rather more lax habit; otherwise they are similar with small flowers, excellent flowering capabilities and very good disease resistance. The small, almost single flowers of 'Open Arms' open a pale salmon-pink quickly fading to pure pale pink, the bright yellow stamens becoming very prominent. It flowers very freely from top to bottom and continuously through to the frosts. The leaves are small and generally very healthy. There is a light musky fragrance. Height 2.5m/8ft. 'Mary Sumner' × 'Laura Ashley'. Bred by Warner (UK) 1995.

**Paul's Himalayan Musk** This is the attractive, if somewhat fanciful, name for a very beautiful Rambler; indeed, to me, it is one of the most beautiful of all the Ramblers. It will grow to 9m/30ft over a pergola or into trees, making long, thin, flexible branches, trailing gracefully and hanging down from their support. Its small, dainty, fully-double, soft pink, rosette-like flowers are held in large open sprays, with each bloom held separately from the next on long, thin stems, giving a delicate, airy effect; the whole plant being garlanded with beauty in season. The light greyish-green foliage is long and pointed. Small, oval hips. There is a strong and delicious Musk fragrance. First distributed by W. Paul (UK) 1916.

**Plaisanterie** A most interesting rose that has the old China Rose 'Mutabilis' as one of its parents, the other parent being 'Trier', the Multiflora Rambler that was the origin of the Hybrid Musk group of roses. It has the unmistakable look of 'Mutabilis', with flowers that change in colour from deep orange in bud, through yellow and then to pink when fully open. They are rather smaller, about 4cm/1½in across, but produced in large heads and giving a wonderful mixed display from very early in the year. It is certainly more vigorous than 'Mutabilis' in British climates and, while normally grown as an arching shrub about 1.5m/5ft tall, we have grown it in our garden as a climber to 2.5m/8ft. It is very healthy. 'Trier' × *R.* x *odorata* 'Mutabilis'. Bred by Lens (Belgium) 1996.

*Facing,* PAUL'S HIMALAYAN MUSK *creates a delicate, airy effect, the whole plant being garlanded with beauty in season*

*Left,* OPEN ARMS, *is a Patio Rambler with small, almost single flowers that bloom continuously*

*Left,* PLAISANTERIE *bears flowers that change from deep orange in bud, through yellow and then to pink when fully open*

285

*Near right,*
*PLEINE DE GRÂCE*
*has flowers that*
*are held in huge*
*clusters of up to a*
*hundred, followed*
*by equal numbers*
*of orange hips,*
*creating a*
*stunning effect*
*in both summer*
*and autumn*

*Far right,*
*TREASURE TROVE*
*has the same vig-*
*our as its parent*
*'Kiftsgate' but*
*with attractive,*
*dark bronze-green*
*foliage and loosely*
*double flowers*

**Pleine de Grâce** ('Lengra') Another extraordinarily free-flowering variety from Louis Lens using *Rosa filipes* as a parent. The flowers are pure white and small and held in huge clusters of up to a hundred, followed by equal numbers of small orange hips, creating a stunning effect in both summer and autumn. It is most commonly grown as a rambler to about 4m/13ft but, if there is space, as a free standing shrub it will achieve impressive proportions and be an unforgettable sight. Each flower has a strong musky, clove fragrance which wafts on the air. It is very healthy and reliable. 'Ballerina' × *Rosa filipes*. Bred by Lens (Belgium) 1983.

**Princesse Marie** (Now known as 'Belvedere', see p. 279).

**Rambling Rosie** (*Chewhorjasper*) A new and very good, bright red, repeat-flowering Rambler from Colin Horner. The blooms are almost single and small, only about 2.5cm/1in across, but they are produced in huge groups and so provide a wonderful overall effect. It is of medium vigour, growing 3–4m/10–13ft tall and so ideal for trellises, obelisks, arches and so on. As with most of Colin Horner's varieties, it is very healthy. Bred by Horner (UK) 2005.

**Russelliana** ('Russell's Old Cottage Rose', 'Scarlet Grevillea', 'Old

Spanish Rose') This rose is probably a Multiflora/Rugosa cross, with predictably coarse results, but with equally predictable toughness and hardiness, giving it a certain value for demanding conditions. It has small semi-double crimson-purple flowers with the Old Rose fragrance. They are held in small clusters. The foliage is dark green, the growth robust and thorny. It flowers freely, providing a pleasing colour effect from a distance. The shrub rose 'Zigeunerknabe' (Gipsy Boy) is a seedling from this variety. First introduced in 1840.

**Silver Moon** The breeding of this rose is considered to be (*Rosa wichurana* × 'Devoniensis') × *R. laevigata*. It is a particularly vigorous climber, capable of 9m/30ft, and has abundant dark, glossy foliage, inherited from *R. laevigata*. The buds are yellow, opening to form large, single or semi-double flowers of creamy-white, with a bunch of yellow stamens. These are borne in clusters, and have a strong fruit-like fragrance. It starts flowering in mid-June but does not repeat. Raised by Dr W. Van Fleet (USA), introduced 1910.

**Snow Goose** (*Auspom*) An excellent pure white, repeat-flowering Rambler that we bred and is, therefore, included and illustrated on page 254. The flowers are semi-double with quite narrow petals that give a very pretty, almost daisy-like appearance and are borne in long sprays on stems that have very few thorns. It is very healthy and equally at home in the UK as in warmer climates. There is a sweet, Musk fragrance. It is particularly useful around doorways. It will grow to about 3m/10ft. Bred by Austin (UK) 1996.

**Super Dorothy** (*Heldoro*) We list here three of the repeat-flowering Ramblers from Karl Hetzel. They are based on 'Dorothy Perkins' and have the advantage of repeat flowering and much better disease resistance, although still little or no scent. 'Super Dorothy' is, in fact, a seedling from 'Dorothy Perkins' but is slightly darker pink than the original with long sprays of up to fifty small flowers. It has a very lax habit and so makes a most effective weeping standard. Height 3m/10ft. Bred by Hetzel (Germany) 1986.

**Super Excelsa** (*Helexa*) This is a cross with the old rambler 'Excelsa' and has fully double, carmine-crimson flowers that fade to a more purple colour with age. It is very healthy, reliable and free flowering and, indeed, won the prestigious ADR award from Germany. It is moderately vigorous (2.5m/8ft) and, with its lax habit, is very good for arches and small pergolas. It can also be grown as a ground cover rose and makes a very good weeping standard. Bred by Hetzel (Germany) 1986.

**Super Fairy** (*Helsufair*) The most vigorous of this group, growing to 4m/13ft or more, it has delicate, soft pink, fully double flowers. As with the others, the blooms are produced in large groups on lax growth, making it particularly good for arches and pergolas. It is very healthy. Bred by Hetzel (Germany) 1992.

**Treasure Trove** This aptly named, self-sown seedling, was discovered in the garden of Mr John Treasure of Burford House, Tenbury Wells, Hereford, growing beneath a plant of *Rosa filipes* 'Kiftsgate', and was introduced in 1979. The other parent is believed to have been the Hybrid Musk Rose 'Buff Beauty', and indeed if we had been planning a yellow hybrid it would have been hard to have found a better pollen parent. 'Treasure Trove' has the vigour of 'Kiftsgate', and will grow to a similar size (10.5m/35ft), although it may not be quite so hardy. It flowers profusely in summer, bearing sprays of about twenty blooms which are loosely double, cupped, about 5cm/2in across, and have a delicious fragrance. Its colour, a warm apricot that fades with age, is particularly valuable in a rose of such growth.

**Wedding Day** A seedling of *Rosa sinowilsonii*, raised by Sir Frederick Stern in 1950. The other parent is not recorded. Like *R. sinowilsonii*, 'Wedding Day' has fine, glossy foliage, although the individual leaves are smaller, but unlike *R. sinowilsonii* it is completely hardy. The growth is very strong, to at least 8m/25ft. The flowers are single and held in large clusters which mingle with the dark foliage. They are yellow in the bud, opening to creamy-yellow, but almost immediately becoming white, the massed effect being white dotted with yellow. The petals are wedge shaped, narrow at the base, broadening to the outer edges. Its only fault is that the petals become spotted in wet weather and the petals hang on too long, becoming a rather unpleasant pink. An ideal rose for growing in trees or to cover some unsightly object. Exceptionally fragrant.

*KEW RAMBLER has wild rose charm; it flowers very freely, has a delicious fragrance and bears orange hips*

# 9

# SPECIES ROSES
# & THEIR NEAR
# HYBRIDS

HAVING PROGRESSED ALL THE WAY from the earliest garden roses to those of the present day, we must now return to the very first roses—the wild roses of many lands. It might quite reasonably be said that we should have begun at this point. There are, however, certain advantages in placing them at the end of the story. We are concerned here with these roses not so much from a botanical point of view, but as a garden plant. The Species and their hybrids are, generally speaking, quite different in character from those of horticultural origin, often occupying a different place in the garden. They are children of the wild, or, at least, close relatives of such roses, whereas the garden roses are very much the product of civilisation. The Species are all single flowered, double flowers being the result of selection by man.

Like the garden roses, the Species have an interesting background, not so much from a human point of view—except perhaps for the often dauntless men who first collected them—but because of the many lands and widely differing terrains which form their natural habitat. Although the cultivated rose has spread to virtually every country in the world, as a garden plant it is found wild only in the Northern Hemisphere. North America, Europe, across Russia, through China and into Japan—almost every country has its wild roses. China, in particular, is extremely rich in roses, as it is in many other plants.

The pleasure of wild roses lies not so much in their colourfulness or the showiness of their flowers, but more in their simplicity, as well as in the elegance of their growth, the daintiness of their foliage and their often richly coloured fruit. Indeed, hardly any of the wild roses are lacking in beauty, but it is a beauty that has to be looked for. Through the long process of their evolution, they have taken on many forms in order to deal with the vagaries of different climates and terrains. Between one Species and another, there are to be found infinitely varying patterns of growth and leaf.

Wild roses tend to form rather large shrubs and climbers, but not all are large in growth and some are suitable for the smaller garden. In larger gardens, particularly those in the country, there must always be a place for at least one or two wild roses. It would be wrong to think of the Species as being of purely botanical interest, or even for growing only in the wild garden. The occasional Species Rose, such as *Rosa hugonis* or *R. moyesii* or one of the smaller Species Hybrids, can be useful to bring a change of mood to a border of mixed Old Roses or English Roses, or other Shrub Roses. The Species Roses seem to bring lightness to the whole border. They are, of course, ideal for the shrubbery and for wild areas of the garden, even in fields, hedges and open woodlands. The Climbing Species, which I deal with in the second half of this chapter, may be encouraged to scramble over bushes and hedges and up trees—sometimes quite large trees. In fact, the Species include some of the best roses for these purposes.

Usually the Species will not require much in the way of attention. The occasional removal of old branches to encourage the new is generally sufficient, or perhaps a little cutting back to stop them becoming excessively large or smothering their neighbours. However, pruning should not be too heavy or it may promote growth at the expense of flowers and fruit, and perhaps destroy the natural grace of the plant. For this reason it is worth studying a rose's ultimate size with some care before making a decision on planting. Where a Species Rose has been left unpruned for many years, and perhaps been a great source of beauty during that time, there is a tendency for it to fill up with old and dead wood, thus becoming unsightly. This is nature's pruning, but not desirable from a

*Facing page*, ROSA SPINOSISSIMA 'DUNWICH ROSE' *is an extremely beautiful shrub, its flowers produced in great quantity along its elegant branches*

garden point of view. In such cases it is sometimes best to cut the shrub hard back and begin again.

The Species Hybrids are usually hybrids between Species, although sometimes they are hybrids between Species and garden varieties. All of them have the nature of wild roses, with certain exceptions, such as the Scots Roses, which I place here more for convenience than for any other reason.

The Species are not the choice of man, but a development of nature, and as such they do not come as a conveniently standardised product to fit neatly into a book. Each Species may vary considerably, according to the area from which it was originally collected. With the more varied Species, such as *Rosa moyesii*, it is important to see that your nursery or garden centre has a good form.

There are some one hundred and sixty different Species Roses; all have their beauty, as indeed do all plants, but some are more suitable for the garden than others. I describe only those that I consider to be of true garden worth.

SPECIES
ROSES &
THEIR NEAR
HYBRIDS

Species Shrub
Roses & their
Hybrids

# Species Shrub Roses & Their Hybrids

**Rosa alpina** See *R. pendulina*.

**Rosa altaica** See *R. spinosissima* 'Grandiflora'.

**Rosa californica** 'Plena' (*R. nutkana* 'Plena') Opinions differ as to the origins of this rose. Some say it is a double form of *R. californica*. The late Graham Thomas, however, suggested that it may be related to *R. nutkana*. The fact that it is double suggests to me the other parent was of garden origin, for it seems rather too much of a coincidence we should find a Species Hybrid that was also double. This is a very fine shrub and a better garden plant than its parent. Its semi-double flowers are deep pink, fragrant, and borne on long, pendulous branches in cascading abundance. The foliage is small, dark and plentiful, forming dense cover. It is hardy and grows vigorously, often suckering profusely, and would, I am sure, be very useful for municipal planting. Height, 2.5 m / 8 ft. Introduced by Geschwind (Hungary), 1894.

**Rosa canina** The Dog Rose of our hedgerows, and also to be found across Northern Europe and into Western Asia in varying forms. Although it will not require much description to people of the British Isles, for those of other countries it can be described as an open shrub of 3 m / 10 ft in height, bearing 5 cm / 2 in flowers either singly or in small clusters. Between different shrubs these may vary in colour from white to almost crimson, but are more often of a soft pink shade. It is unique among roses for its excessive variability, particularly in the colours of its flowers, but also in growth and leaf. In fact, if we study it in the wild, we seldom find any two plants that are the same. This is due to an unusual variability in its genetic make up, and not, as it may seem, to differences in soil conditions. The flowers have their own typical fragrance, and are followed by scarlet hips of long, oval shape. Those of us who have access to this rose will not perhaps consider planting it, although it is a beautiful shrub. Some people think it worth planting in hedgerows and wild places. I can well remember it on my parents' farm near Shrewsbury, in woodlands that had been cut some twenty years previously and where it was to be seen growing in great masses to a height of anything up to 6 m / 20 ft, providing an almost overwhelming profusion of bloom in season. I have come across few rose scenes to equal this since.

*R. canina* has been the parent of a number of hybrids, most of which are excellent shrubs, often with larger flowers, but usually keeping close to it in appearance. These include *R.* 'Complicata' and *R.* 'Macrantha' which are described separately.

**Rosa canina** Abbotswood (*R.* 'Abbotswood') A semi-double seedling of the Dog Rose showing little sign of hybridity. In spite of this I suspect it is a hybrid, as I have myself hybridised *R. canina* with other roses and obtained very similar results. This variety appeared in a hedgerow at Abbotswood in the garden of Mr Harry Ferguson, of tractor fame, and was discovered by his gardener, Mr Tustin, who gave it to Graham Thomas. It forms a 2.5 m / 8 ft shrub with pink flowers of a sweet Canina fragrance followed by orange-red hips. 1954.

**Rosa canina** Andersonii (*R.* 'Andersonii') Probably a Canina × Gallica Hybrid with typically Dog Rose flowers but larger and of a richer, more brilliant pink, and blooming over an extended period. The leaves are long and downy on the underside. It has the bright red Canina hips. Fragrant. 1.8 × 2.5 m / 6 × 8 ft. First recorded by Hillier (UK), 1912.

**Rosa canina hibernica** (*R.* × *hibernica*) This rose has all the signs of being a Canina / Spinosissima Hybrid. It forms a neat, bushy, twiggy, slightly arched shrub of medium size, with attractive pale pink flowers of about 2.5 cm / 1 in across appearing late in the season. It will grow to approximately 2.5 m / 8 ft in height, forming a dense bush, and has greyish-green foliage, midway between that of Canina and Spinosissima. In autumn it bears quantities of large hips. The original was discovered in 1802 by a Mr John Templeton of Belfast who received a prize of five guineas from the Botanical Society of Dublin for a new indigenous plant. This was hardly an accurate description as it is, in fact, a chance hybrid.

**Rosa Cantabrigiensis** See *Rosa hugonis* hybrids below.

**Rosa 'Complicata'** Probably a hybrid of a Gallica Rose and *R. canina*. Indeed, it is often classified as a Gallica, although it is really very much a wild rose. The flowers are large, about 12 cm / 5 in across, slightly cupped at first, opening flatter, and of the purest bright pink paling to white at the centre, with a large boss of golden stamens. In mid-June the whole shrub is completely covered with a mass of oversized Dog Rose blooms. These are followed by a good crop of not particularly colourful hips. The growth is extremely robust but quite compact, about 1.5 m / 5 ft in height, with ample large foliage. It is very tough and can be relied on to do well even under rather poor conditions. Nothing is known of the age of this rose, or of its origin. (Illustrated overleaf)

*Facing*, ROSA
CALIFORNICA
'PLENA' *is*
*a superb shrub*
*with great*
*quantities of*
*deliciously*
*fragrant flowers*

291

SPECIES
ROSES &
THEIR NEAR
HYBRIDS

Species Shrub
Roses & their
Hybrids

ROSA
COMPLICATA is
probably a hybrid
but very much
a wild rose in
appearance, with
slightly cupped
flowers that
open flatter

size of its flowers, *R. elegantula* 'Persetosa' is often known as the 'Threepenny Bit Rose', a name that may soon have little meaning to future generations of gardeners. It is a dainty little shrub, with tiny, clear salmon-pink flowers lacing its arching growth, and with small leaves and many hair-like thorns. The foliage turns to a purple shade in autumn, and there are numerous small orange-red hips which persist well into the winter. Height 1.5m/5ft. (Illustrated, p.297)

***Rosa fedtschenkoana*** A large and very strong growing bristly shrub of 2.5m/8ft or more in height which, if grown on its own roots, suckers very freely, spreading far and wide—so much so that it can become a problem. Perhaps its chief virtue is its pleasing grey-green foliage, but it also has the distinction of being one of five wild roses that have a natural ability to flower throughout the summer, the other four being *R. rugosa, R. beggeriana, R. foliolosa* and *R. bracteata*. The flowers are white and about 5cm/2in across, but although they continue over a long period I have not found them to be very plentiful. The short-lasting hips are long, pear shaped and bright red with persistent hairy sepals. The flowers are strongly and distinctly fragrant. A native of Turkestan, it was discovered by and named after a Russian in 1868/71, arriving at Kew in 1890.

***Rosa foetida*** (*R. foetida lutea*, 'Austrian Yellow') This rose is often, rather misleadingly, known as the 'Austrian Brier'. It is, in fact, a native of Iran and Kurdistan, and has been with us since the late 16th century. *R. foetida* was a very important Species in the development of garden roses, being the main source of yellow colouring in our Modern Roses through its variety *R. foetida* 'Persiana'. This has been a mixed blessing, as *R. foetida* suffers from blackspot and has passed something of this fault on to its progeny. Indeed, it frequently and rather unfairly receives the total blame for the problem. It bears 6cm/2in flowers of bright sulphur-yellow with a scent that does not appeal to everyone. The foliage is pale green and the stems brown with greyish coloured thorns. It forms a pleasing, rather sparse shrub of 1.5m/5ft in height. This Species and its varieties provide a most brilliant effect early in the season. If your garden is subject to blackspot it might be better to grow *R. × harisonii* 'Lutea Maxima' (see p. 296) which is less prone to this disease.

***Rosa foetida*** Bicolor (*R. lutea punicea*, Austrian Copper) A dramatic and intriguing sport from *R. foetida*. The upper surface of the petals has become a dazzling coppery-red, while the under-surface remains bright yellow. Otherwise it is identical to its parent. If we look at this rose, it is not hard to see how the Modern Rose arrived at its present state of often excessively bright colouring. This rose, however, is beautiful and well worth a place in the garden. It was grown in the Arab world as far back as the 12th century. Height 1.5m/5ft.

***Rosa foetida*** Persiana ('Persian Yellow') An attractive double form of *R. foetida* with flowers of similar bright sulphur-yellow colouring. It will achieve a slender 1.2m/4ft in height, although I understand that it will grow more strongly in a warmer climate.

***Rosa davidii*** A graceful, upright shrub of about 2.7m/9ft in height, bearing 5cm/2in mallow-pink flowers borne in large open clusters and elegantly poised along its branches. There is a pleasing fragrance, and the flowers are followed by slim, flagon-shaped hips of bright orange-red. The leaves are rough textured and of a greyish-green. It is one of the last of the Species to flower. This rose has shown a tendency to die back in my garden but soon renews itself. It grows wild in West China and South-east Tibet, and was first collected by E. H. Wilson in 1903.

***Rosa*** Dupontii This beautiful rose is probably a hybrid between *R. damascena* and *R. moschata*. It may have been raised at Malmaison, and appears in Redouté as *R. damascena subalba*. The flowers are about 8cm/3in across and single, with occasional extra petals. Their colour is white, sometimes tinged with blush, and they are held in nice Damask-like sprays of five or more blooms. They have a clean-cut shape and a purity which adds much to their attraction, particularly when viewed against their elegant, downy-grey foliage. It is a strong and rather loose-growing shrub of perhaps 2m/7ft in height and rather less across. There is a sweet fragrance. Late flowering. *c.* 1817.

***Rosa ecae*** A compact shrub of about 1.5m/5ft in height and almost as much across, with slender, thorny, dark brown branches and small, dark green fern-like leaves, similar to those of *R. hugonis*. The flowers are small, no more than 2.5cm/1in across, deep buttercup-yellow, and set all along its branches. A good shrub, but not always easy to establish. It is best in a warm, sunny position. A native of Afghanistan, it was first collected by Dr Aitchison in 1880. The name derives from the initials of his wife, E.C.A.

***Rosa eglanteria*** See *R. rubiginosa*.

***Rosa elegantula*** Persetosa (*R. farreri* 'Persetosa', *R. farreri* var. *persetosa*) This rose was selected by E. A. Bowles from seed of *R. elegantula*, collected by Reginald Farrer (1880–1920) from West China in 1915. It has deeper pink flowers than is usual for the typical Species which is now very rare in cultivation. Owing to the small

SPECIES
ROSES &
THEIR NEAR
HYBRIDS

Species Shrub
Roses & their
Hybrids

*Left*, ROSA FEDT-
SCHENKOANA
*is one of five
wild roses that
have a natural
ability to flower
throughout
the summer*

*Following pages*,
ROSA DAVIDII
*is a graceful,
upright shrub
whose flowers are
followed by slim,
flagon-shaped
hips of bright
orange-red*

SPECIES
ROSES &
THEIR NEAR
HYBRIDS

Species Shrub
Roses & their
Hybrids

Its  flowers are cupped in shape and have a rather Old Rose appearance. Introduced to England, probably from Iran, in 1838 by Sir Henry Wilcock.

*Rosa forrestiana* A shrub of some 1.8 or 2m/6 or 7ft in height, and 1.8m/6ft across, bearing rosy-crimson flowers of about 3cm/1in with creamy-yellow stamens. These are fragrant and borne in dense clusters, and have large, leafy bracts. The hips are flask shaped, bright orange-red and rather bristly, the green bracts persisting. A most attractive shrub. A native of West China, first cultivated in 1918.

*Rosa glauca* (*R. rubrifolia*) A native of Central Europe usually grown for the beauty of its foliage. It is a shrub of some 2m/7ft in height, and nearly as much across, with smooth, almost thornless purple-red stems and glaucous coppery-mauve leaves which provide an excellent colour contrast in the border or in an arrangement of cut flowers. Its blooms are not very conspicuous, being light pink, quite small and held in rather tight bunches, but in spite of this they  have a certain charm among the tinted colour of the leaves. The  hips, which are small and globular, provide us with a further pleasing effect.

*Rosa* × *harisonii* '**Lutea Maxima**' Almost certainly a hybrid of *R.  foetida*, from which its flowers would have obtained their strong buttercup-yellow colouring, which is the brightest yellow in this group. The foliage is less typically Spinosissima, being more plentiful and downy on the underside. The growth is less robust and it will  usually reach a height of 1.2m/4ft. Hips black and globular. The fragrance shows some similarity to *R. foetida*.

*Rosa hemisphaerica* (*R. sulphurea*, *R. glaucophylla*, the Sulphur Rose) This rose has little claim to a place among the Species, but

*Right,* ROSA FORRESTIANA *bears rosy-crimson flowers that are very attractive to bees and are followed by very shiny, bright orange-red hips*

*Facing page,* ROSA ELEGANTULA PERSETOSA *has tiny flowers lacing its arching growth and small leaves with hair-like thorns*

since it is difficult to know where to put it, I include it here. It bears large double, full-petalled, sweetly fragrant, deeply globular flowers of typical Old Rose appearance which are pale sulphur-yellow in colour. Indeed at one time it was, quite erroneously, known as the 'Yellow Provence Rose'. The growth is rather loose, up to 1.8m/6ft in height, the foliage a pale greyish-green and the blooms hang their heads from the branches: all of which sounds very attractive, and indeed it is, but unfortunately the flowers seldom open, and then only in the driest and most favourable seasons. A little rain, and they ball up and soon decay, although the plant itself is completely winter hardy. The protection of a warm sunny wall can be a help. This rose was a favourite of the old Dutch painters, and there is a particularly

fine Redouté print which shows how good it can be. Unfortunately this happens only occasionally. Gordon Rowley has suggested that it  is a double-flowered sport of the species *R. rapinii* which is found in Turkestan and Iran. It is known to have been in cultivation in Europe as early as 1625.

*Rosa hugonis* (the Golden Rose of China, Father Hugo Rose) A  shrub of 2.5m/8ft in height, with long, graceful branches, brown bark, many thorns and small, pale green fern-like foliage which turns a bronzy colour in autumn. It is worthwhile for its growth and foliage alone, but in mid-May its branches are wreathed along their length with dainty, slightly cupped flowers of soft yellow colouring, each 3–5cm/1–2in across. These are followed by small, round, maroon-coloured fruit. If it has a fault it is that the flowers do not always open completely, the petals tending to be crumpled. Although this is quite attractive, in some seasons it can be excessive. Possibly it  may be due to our climate. *R. hugonis* is, however, the parent of some fine hybrids that are very similar and may be preferable; these are described below. They are all particularly good shrubs, with similar dainty foliage, flowering long before most other roses appear. *R. hugonis* probably grows best on its own roots. It was originally collected in West China by the missionary Hugh Scanlon (known as Pater Hugo) who, in 1899, sent seed to Kew where the original plants still thrive.

• *ROSA HUGONIS HYBRIDS*: **Cantabrigiensis** (*R. pteragonis* 'Cantabrigiensis'). An excellent shrub similar to *R. hugonis* but stronger in growth, easily achieving 3m/10ft in height. The flowers are saucer-shaped, rather larger, of a paler yellow, and more symmetrical in form than *R. hugonis*. They are produced in great profusion, providing a magnificent sight in mid-May. It  has graceful growth and dainty foliage, similar to that of *R. hugonis*. There is a light fragrance. It was a self-sown seedling discovered at the University Botanic Garden, Cambridge, and was named in 1931. It may have been the result of a cross between *R.  hugonis* and *R. sericea hookeri*. **Golden Chersonese** A comparative newcomer which is a hybrid between *Rosa ecae* and *R.  xanthina* 'Canary Bird', and thus only one  quarter Hugonis. It has very numerous, small, deep buttercup-yellow, sweetly-scented flowers which are held closely along its branches. A good shrub, stronger and hardier than its parents, with flowers of a  particularly rich colour. It is of unusually upright growth, a fact that gives it a certain added value in the garden, even though we are grateful that most species do not share this habit. Fragrant. 1.8m/6ft. Bred by E.F. Allen, 1963 (Illustrated overleaf). **Headleyensis** A  seedling of *R. hugonis*, probably hybridized with *R. spinosissima* 'Grandiflora', and one of the best of this group. It is very vigorous, achieving 2.7m/9ft in height and considerably more across. It thus requires space if it is to develop properly. Its broad, graceful, open growth carries ample fern-like foliage. The creamy-yellow flowers are particularly fine and plentiful, and are fragrant. Raised by Sir Oscar Warburg (UK), 1920. **Helen Knight** This is named after the wife of the former Director of the Royal Horticultural Society's gardens at Wisley, where I understand it is a great favourite. It is of unusual upright growth; some might think a little too stiff and upright, but we do not require roses to be all the same,

SPECIES
ROSES &
THEIR NEAR
HYBRIDS

Species Shrub
Roses & their
Hybrids

*GOLDEN
CHERSONESE
is a hybrid of*
Rosa hugonis
*with unusually
upright growth
and flowers of
a  particularly
rich colour*

besides which there are positions in the garden where a rose of this habit can be a definite asset. It is a seedling of *R. ecae*, probably hybridized with *R. spinosissima* 'Grandiflora', and will grow to 1.5 or 1.8m/5 or 6ft bearing deep yellow flowers with dark stamens. F. P. Knight (UK) 1966.

***Rosa hulthemia*** (*R. persica*) Some time ago this Species was listed with the genus *Rosa*. It was then decided that it was a separate genus, *Hulthemia*. However, the botanists have changed their minds yet again. Whatever the truth may be, it is very unusual. It is an interesting shrub in that it occurs in the semi-desert conditions of Iran, Afghanistan and neighbouring Soviet republics. It forms low, twiggy, spiny growth of about 80cm/2ft in height, spreading by means of runners. The foliage is silvery-grey. The flowers are small, about 3cm/1in across, of deep golden-yellow with a red-brown blotch in the centre. No rose is of quite such a brilliant yellow. Later, there are small bristly hips. In its native territory it is extremely hardy and persistent, and I understand it has been known to push its way up through concrete. It is not easy to grow in a northerly climate, but not impossible if given a warm, dry position. Recently it has been a subject of much interest with rose breeders who are working on repeat-flowering hybrids with the same contrasting blotch of colour at the base of the petals. First introduced to Europe around 1790.

***Rosa* Macrantha** A fine, arching shrub, sending out long, thin growth, to a width of 3m/10ft and 1.5m/5ft in height. The flowers are large and borne in small clusters from mid-June to early July. Their colour is pale pink, fading almost to white, with a good boss of stamens and a pleasant fragrance. They have something of the appearance of much bigger Dog Roses. Little is known of its origin. The rather dull, rough-textured foliage and the form of its flowers seem to suggest a Gallica as one parent. *R. canina* is often suggested as the other, but cytological analysis rules this out, nor does the growth fit in with this theory. Its appearance points to the possibility of some trailing rose like *R. arvensis* in its parentage. However this may be, *R.* 'Macrantha' is a truly beautiful rose that is not only good as a shrub, but also very useful for covering banks, the stumps of old trees, or growing into other shrubs and over hedges. It has round, red hips, that persist well into autumn.

***Rosa macrophylla*** A very large shrub of 3.5m/12ft in height and as much across, possibly more under suitable conditions. This is one

Rosa *Macrantha*, a vigorous variety with long arching stems, is useful for covering banks and the stumps of old trees or growing into other shrubs and over hedges

of the most magnificent of the Species, its exuberant growth and large leaves — which may be 20cm/8in in length and have up to eleven leaflets — forming a thick canopy. It has few thorns and dark red-brown stems. The flowers are a deep rose-pink, 8cm/3in across, and are held nicely poised either singly or in small clusters. In autumn it has long, bristly, bright red, flagon-shaped hips hanging elegantly from its branches. A common and widely varying shrub, found wild in an area spreading through North India, West China and the Himalayas. Introduced *c.*1888.

• *ROSA MACROPHYLLA* HYBRIDS: **Doncasterii** This is thought to be a hybrid between *R. moyesii* and *R. macrophylla* and is

*Left & far left,* Rosa macrophylla *one of the most magnificent of the Species, bears nicely poised flowers, followed by long, bristly, flagon-shaped hips*

a worthwhile alternative to the latter as it is rather more arching and less tall. The flowers are bright pink to light red and are followed by large, pear-shaped hips. The stems are plum coloured and the leaves purplish-green. 1.8 × 1.2m/6 × 4ft. raised by E. Doncaster (UK) 1930. **Master Hugh** Collected in Nepal in 1966, this is similar to *R. macrophylla* but taller, more upright and more open in growth, and with exceptionally large hips that hang like miniature lanterns. Height 4.5m/15ft. Mason (UK) 1966.

*Rosa × micrugosa* A hybrid of *R. rugosa* and *R. roxburghii*. The latter was formerly known as *R. microphylla*—hence this variety's name. The foliage leans towards Rugosa in character, although it is a little coarse in texture. The growth is very dense and twiggy, forming a shapely shrub with plentiful foliage. The flowers are pale pink, about 10cm/4in across, opening flat. Individually they are among the most beautiful of single roses, nestling amongst the leafy growth and having a lovely silky texture. They are followed by round, bristly, orange-red hips. Flowering may not be plentiful in the early stages, but as it matures it does so more freely. It will, if required, form an impenetrable barrier. Height 1.5 or 1.8m/5 or 6ft. A self-sown seedling found at Strasburg Botanical Institute in 1905.

*Rosa moyesii* Certainly one of the finest of the Species Roses. A native of North-west China, it was brought to the British Isles by E.H. Wilson and introduced in 1903, when it caused a considerable stir in horticultural circles. This is not altogether surprising, as there was nothing quite like it among wild roses. The flowers vary from rose-pink to blood-red, 6cm/2in across, with overlapping petals and a neat ring of contrasting pale stamens. They have no fragrance, but are followed by magnificent, long flagon-shaped, orange-red fruit which hangs down from the branch, providing an attractive effect from late August to October—or perhaps later. The growth is open, with long, sweeping, widely spaced canes to a height of 3m/10ft and 2.5m/8ft across. The foliage is dark green and attractive, with up to twelve leaflets. This is a useful shrub for the mixed border, as its tall growth can be encouraged to stand above other plants without smothering them. It should be noted that in the wild *R. moyesii* is more often of deep pink colouring. The rose we grow in gardens is a selected form. As with some other Species Roses it is extremely variable. If we grow this Species from seed it will usually revert to the pink type. It is therefore important, when purchasing a plant, to be sure that you obtain a red form. I have noticed that bees prefer *R. moyesii* to any other rose in our collection; indeed, they almost ignore the rest when it is flowering. It was named after the Reverend E. J. Moyes, who was a missionary in China.

  • *Rosa moyesii* forms and hybrids: **Eos** This is a hybrid, *R. moyesii* × 'Magnifica', the latter being a self-sown seedling of the Sweet Brier 'Lucy Ashton'. It bears flat, almost single flowers of coral-red along its branches, providing a brilliant effect. The growth is rather gaunt and bare at the base. Height 3.5m/12ft. There is rarely any fruit. Bred by Ruys (USA), introduced 1950. **Geranium** This is probably the most useful form for the average garden, as it is a smaller shrub than *R. moyesii*, with more compact growth of about 2.5m/8ft in height. The flowers are bright geranium-red, the hips rather larger, with more plentiful bright green foliage. Raised by B.O. Mulligan at Wisley (UK), 1938. **Highdownensis** A seedling from *R. moyesii*, selected by Sir Frederick Stern at Highdown in Sussex. It is a good shrub, with tidier, less open and more bushy growth than the typical Species. The light cerise-crimson flowers with a paler centre are borne in larger clusters. It is tall and vigorous, to about 3.5m/12ft in height, and bears particularly fine orange-red hips. **Hillieri**

(*R. × pruhoniciana*) The outstanding feature of this rose is the dark crimson colouring of its flowers, certainly the darkest to be found in this group, and as dark as any we might find in a Hybrid Tea or Hybrid Perpetual. A mystery surrounds its breeding; some say it is a *R. moyesii* × *R. willmottiae* cross, but we would not expect this to produce such a depth of colour. The growth is more arching and graceful than *R. moyesii*, the foliage small and rather sparse, and it does not flower quite so freely, but continues over a long period. It will grow to 3m/10ft in height by 3.5m/12ft across. The hips are large and flagon-shaped, but not always plentiful. Light fragrance. Long thin thorns. Introduced by Hillier (UK), 1920.

*Rosa multibracteata* A wide and gracefully arching shrub, with prickly stems and fragrant grey-green foliage of seven to nine leaflets. The flowers are plentiful, lilac-pink, 5cm/2in across, with prominent bracts along their stems which provide an attractive effect. They are held singly or in small clusters. The fragrance is unusual, similar to that of *R. foetida*. One of the parents of the beautiful 'Cerise Bouquet'. Height 2m/7ft by 1.8m/6ft across, more in favourable conditions. Collected by E.H. Wilson from West China, introduced 1908.

*Rosa nitida* A low-growing, suckering shrub of 60cm/2ft in height which, once established on its own roots, will spread freely, forming a thicket of excellent ground cover. It sends up slender, twiggy growth, with many thin thorns and shiny green leaves of seven to ten leaflets which in autumn develop beautiful scarlet-crimson tints. The flowers are about 5cm/2in across and of an unfading deep pink, but its foliage is perhaps its chief asset. Hips, small, bright red, round, and rather bristly. A native of Canada and the north-east USA, first cultivated 1807.

*Rosa nutkana* A native of western North America, growing to about 1.8m/6ft in height by 1.2m/4ft across, with ample greyish-green foliage which turns to brown in the autumn. The flowers are

SPECIES
ROSES &
THEIR NEAR
HYBRIDS

Species Shrub
Roses & their
Hybrids

lilac-pink, 5–6cm/2–2in in width, and are followed by a good display of globular hips which persist well into the winter. Introduced to Britain in 1876.

*Rosa omeiensis* See *R. sericea omeiensis* below.

*Rosa* **Paulii** (*R. rugosa repens alba*) *R. rugosa* × *R. arvensis* hybrid, bred by George Paul (UK), and introduced at some time prior to 1903. It is an extremely vigorous, procumbent shrub of about 1.2m/4ft in height, producing long stems that can gradually spread to as much as 3.5m/12ft, although it can, of course, be restricted by pruning. The flowers are pure white, about 8cm/3in across, the petals being wedge-shaped, narrow at the base so that they do not overlap, and providing a rather star-like effect similar to that of a clematis. They have golden stamens, the petals are inclined to be crinkled and there is a clove-like fragrance. The foliage is rough textured, similar to that of *R. rugosa* in appearance, and there are many vicious thorns. It is very tough, growing well under adverse conditions, and ideal where a large expanse of ground cover is required.

*Rosa* **Paulii Rosea** This appears to be a hybrid of *R.* 'Paulii', from which it differs quite considerably in strength of growth. Although vigorous, it is much less so than its parent. It bears large clear pink flowers with a white centre and yellow stamens. The petals have a crinkled, silky appearance, and overlap in the more usual manner. A beautiful rose with a strong fragrance. Height 90cm/3ft by 2.5m/8ft across.

*Rosa pendulina* (*R. alpina*) A native of the foothills of the Alpine regions of Central and Southern Europe, usually regarded as growing to about 1.2m/4ft in height, although in my experience it will easily achieve 1.5 or 1.8m/5 or 6ft under good garden conditions. The growth is erect and slightly arching, the stems are tinted with red and purple, and are smooth with few thorns. The foliage is finely divided, with anything from five to nine leaflets. The flowers are about 5cm/2in across, of a variable purplish-pink colouring with yellow stamens and are held singly or in twos and threes. They are

ROSA ROXBURGHII *has some of the largest flowers of the Species Roses, and these are followed by large, round, bristly hips*

followed by bright red pear-shaped hips of about 2.5cm/1in in length, making a conspicuous show. This rose is sometimes difficult to establish, but seems to prefer light soil. An attractive shrub.

*Rosa primula* This rose is similar to *R. hugonis*, to which it is closely related, having the same finely divided, fern-like foliage and dainty flowers carried along its arching branches. These are of a delicate primrose-yellow, with a light scent, and it is one of the first roses to flower in mid-May. It is also known as the 'Incense Rose' for the fragrance of its foliage, a fragrance that carries far on the air. It may grow to 1.8m/6ft and as much across. However, like other yellow-flowered species, whole branches tend to die back. A native of the region spreading from Turkestan to Northern China. First discovered near Samarkand by the American collector F. H. Meyer, 1911.

*Rosa* × *richardii* (*R. sancta*, Holy Rose, Sacred Rose of Abyssinia) Probably a natural hybrid between *R. gallica* and *R. phoenicea*, this forms a sprawling but shapely bush of 90cm/3ft in height and 1.2m/4ft across, and bears large pale pink flowers in small clusters. It was introduced into Britain by Paul of Cheshunt in 1902.

Not only is this one of the most beautiful single-flowered roses, but it also has a long and intriguing history. Dr Hurst speculates on its origins, suggesting that St Frumentius, who brought Christianity to Abyssinia, may have introduced it to that country in the 4th century, and that it was planted in the precincts of Christian churches and thus preserved throughout the centuries. He goes on to relate how in 1888 the eminent archaeologist, Sir Flinders Petrie, discovered the remains of this rose twined into garlands in burial sites at Fayum in Upper Egypt. This would date them to a period between the 2nd and 5th centuries AD. He also tells of Sir Arthur Evans's excavations at Knossos in Crete. Here Evans found a representation of a rose that was part of a wall painting and which Hurst felt bore a striking resemblance to the 'Sacred Rose'.

*Rosa roxburghii* (*R. microphylla*; also popularly known as the Burr Rose, the Chestnut Rose, the Chinquapin Rose). An unusual rose from China and Japan, it forms a vigorous shrub of about 2m/7ft in height and the same across, with stiff, angular branches and attractively flaking light brown bark. It has strong hooked thorns in pairs, just below the leaves. The leaves themselves are long, with up to fifteen evenly-arranged leaflets. The flowers are usually solitary, 10cm/4in across, and of a clear pink fading to white, with plentiful golden stamens, the stalk and calyx being covered with prickles. These are followed by large, round, bristly hips (hence Chestnut Rose). The whole effect is that of an attractively gnarled shrub. In cultivation prior to 1814.

*Rosa roxburghii* f. *roxburghii* (*R. roxburghii* 'Plena') This is a double form, probably of Chinese origin, and thought to be of great antiquity. The flowers are very full, giving the appearance of a beautiful Old Rose. They have large, pale pink outer petals, while the numerous shorter centre petals give a deep pink effect. They have a light fragrance. Height 80–90cm/2–3ft. A curious and interesting rose. Introduced to Britain by Dr Roxburgh, from Canton, 1824.

*Rosa rubiginosa* (*R. eglanteria*, the Sweet Brier) A native of Britain and Northern Europe, this rose is greatly valued for the rich and spicy fragrance of its foliage which is emitted from glands on the underside of the leaves, and is particularly in evidence on a warm, moist day, when it can fill the garden around it. An even stronger fragrance can be obtained by crushing the leaves between the fingers. Graham Thomas wisely recommended that in the British Isles it should be planted on the south or west side of the garden to catch the warm, moist winds. This is a strong, easily grown shrub of 2.5m/8ft in

SPECIES
ROSES &
THEIR NEAR
HYBRIDS

Species Shrub
Roses & their
Hybrids

ROSA
× RICHARDII,
*one of the most
beautiful single-
flowered roses,
has a long and
intriguing history*

SPECIES
ROSES &
THEIR NEAR
HYBRIDS

Species Shrub
Roses & their
Hybrids

been in existence before this date. It is a rather smaller shrub than the Species, 1.8m/6ft in height, with scented flowers that are semi-double, cherry-pink and attractively veined with pale pink, the centre being almost white. The foliage is rather coarser and less fragrant than the Species. **Lady Penzance** An attractive shrub, the produce of a cross between *R. eglanteria* and *R. foetida* 'Bicolour'. It bears dainty single yellow flowers that are flushed with coppery-pink towards the outer edges. Unfortunately it has inherited some of *R. foetida*'s susceptibility to blackspot. The foliage has only a slight fragrance, while the flowers have the scent of *R. foetida*. Height about 1.8m /6ft. **Lord Penzance** *R. eglanteria* × 'Harison's Yellow'. Not so robust as the others, but with foliage that is quite strongly aromatic. The flowers are single, fragrant and of a soft rosy-yellow with pale yellow at the centre. Height 1.8m/6ft. **Lucy Ashton** Attractive single white flowers edged with pink. Foliage with above average fragrance. 1.8m/6ft. **Manning's Blush** An old variety of a date prior to 1799. It is a much smaller shrub than *R. eglanteria*, about 1.5m/5ft in height, with pretty little full-petalled flowers which are pink in the bud and pale to blush when they open. The foliage has a slight fragrance. **Meg Merrilies** Semi-double, bright crimson flowers. The foliage has a good fragrance. Scarlet hips. 2.5m/8ft.

***Rosa rugosa*** This important species is the parent of the Rugosa Hybrids, and I have dealt with it in the section on those roses in Chapter 6.

***Rosa sericea omeiensis*** (*R. omeiensis*) A vigorous, usually thorny shrub, occurring in a wide area extending over Northern India, the Himalayas, North Myanmar and Western China, and first collected in 1822. It is unique amongst roses in that its flowers have only four petals, although occasionally it is to be found with the normal five. These flowers are small, white or sometimes yellow, 3–5cm/1–2in across, cupped, with the petals only just overlapping; they are held very closely along the branch early in the season in mid-May. The foliage is small and fern-like with many leaflets. The hips, which are small, red and pear shaped, drop rather quickly. Height 3m/10ft.

*R. sericea* does not make a great show in the garden, although the growth and foliage are attractive. It has given rise to a number of forms and hybrids. The following two are worthwhile.

***Rosa sericea*** **Heather Muir** The most beautiful form with creamy-white, scented flowers which are much larger than the species—about 8cm/3in across. These are produced with great freedom over a long period throughout the month of June. It will form a very large shrub of 3 by 3m /10 by 10ft or more. The hips are small and orange-red. It was named after the creator of the famous Kiftsgate Garden. Mrs Muir obtained the original seedling from E. A. Bunyard, and it was eventually distributed by Sunningdale Nurseries in 1957.

***Rosa sericea* f. *pteracantha*** This unique rose differs from *R. sericea* in the enormous size of its red thorns. These are triangular and flat, up to 2cm /¾in wide at their base, and are the rose's chief attraction. When young, they are a translucent red-brown so that the sunlight shines through them, giving a brilliant effect. For this reason it is worth placing the rose where the sun can catch it, and cutting it hard back annually to produce new growth and, consequently, young thorns. Alternatively, it

height and across, with many thorns. It will form an impenetrable barrier where this is required, and may also be used as a hedge. The flowers are clear pink, about 5cm/2in across, and they too are fragrant. Later there is a mass of bright red, oval-shaped hips that last well into the winter. There are a number of hybrids, all with fragrant foliage, but never of quite such power as the original.

• ROSA RUBIGINOSA HYBRIDS INCLUDING PENZANCE BRIERS During the years 1894 and 1895 Lord Penzance introduced a number of Sweet Brier hybrids that he had bred himself. These were mainly crosses between *R. rubiginosa* (previously *R. eglanteria*) and various Hybrid Perpetuals and Bourbons. They have a certain garden value, combining as they do a variety of colours with the fragrant foliage of the wild Sweet Brier. They are nearly all extremely robust, usually about 2.5m/8ft in height, though most of them are inclined to grow into what are, to me, rather coarse shrubs of upright growth. They all have aromatic foliage, but not to the extent of the Sweet Briers. Where space can be found for only one such rose it might be best to plant *R. rubiginosa* itself. It is probable that the Penzance Briers are the result of a very few crosses, with little selection. Here are a few examples: **Amy Robsart** Semi-double flowers of deep clear pink. Extra strong growth. Not very fragrant foliage. Good, scarlet hips. Height 2.7m/9ft. **Janet's Pride** ('Clementine') This was distributed by W. Paul & Sons (UK) in 1892, but it may well have

*Above, AMY ROBSART bears brightly coloured flowers, followed by rounded scarlet hips*

*Right, ROSA SERICEA F. PTERACANTHA, is grown mainly for its very wide, translucent thorns which can be an effective deterrent*

SPECIES
ROSES &
THEIR NEAR
HYBRIDS

Species Shrub
Roses & their
Hybrids

ROSA SETIPODA
*is in every way an
excellent shrub—
in flower, leaf,
fruit and general
demeanour*

is sometimes useful as a barrier to halt both four-legged and two-legged intruders, for no rose has quite such a formidable armoury. The flowers are white, similar to *R. sericea*, with four petals, and not very conspicuous, although they have a certain quaint charm amongst the thorns. 2.5 by 1.8m/8 by 6ft. Western China, 1890.

**Rosa setigera** (the 'Prairie Rose'). There is some doubt as to whether this should be regarded as a Species Shrub or a Species Rambler. It is so large that I think for most garden purposes it is best treated as a Climber, when it will climb to 4.5m/15ft. In late July and early August it bears small sprays of rose-pink flowers that fade almost to white. These are followed by 5cm/2in round, red hips. The foliage is an attractive dull green colour. It is a useful rose for growing in a small tree or over bushes. Where space can be found it is also an excellent shrub, sending out long, trailing stems and form-ing a mound of sprawling growth. It is a native of the Eastern United States, and has been used in the breeding of Rambler Roses, more notably 'American Pillar' and 'Baltimore Belle'.

**Rosa setipoda** In every way a beautiful shrub: in flower, leaf, fruit and general demeanour. It will grow to about 3m/10ft in height and the same across. The foliage is very fine, the leaves being about 18cm/7in long, with nine neatly formed leaflets of a glaucous-green, and with a slight Sweet Brier fragrance. The flowers are quite large for a species, 6 to 8cm/2 to 3in across, opening flat, the petals turn-ing back slightly at the edges. They are held nicely poised upon thin, bristly purplish stalks, have a light fruit-like fragrance and appear in the latter part of June. The hips are very large, orange-red, flagon-shaped and bristly, with persistent sepals. A native of Central China, brought to Britain by E. H. Wilson in 1895.

305

SPECIES
ROSES
& THEIR
NEAR
HYBRIDS

Species Shrub
Roses & their
Hybrids

*Rosa spinosissima* (*R. pimpinellifolia*) This rose was, until very recently, *R. pimpinellifolia*, having been *R. spinosissima* before that, but the botanists have now come down on the side of *R. spinosissima* after all. It is more popularly known as the Scots or Burnet Rose. A native of the British Isles, it is to be found growing in poor sandy conditions, often on seaside banks, anywhere from Cornwall to Scotland. It also grows in Europe and West Asia, and is occasionally to be seen naturalised in North America. It is one of the hardiest, toughest and most reliable of roses. Its height will vary according to conditions. In the wild, in a windswept seaside position, it may grow to no more than 15cm/6in. In the garden it may be about 90cm/3ft in height, but in good soil it can reach up to 1.8m/6ft. It forms a thicket-like growth, sending up slender stems with many bristles and small, fern-like foliage. In May and June it produces numerous creamy-white flowers of 5–8cm/2–3in across close along its branches. They have a distinct, refreshing fragrance. Later, there are round maroon-black hips. When grown on its own roots it will sucker far and wide, producing dense ground cover. This may be an asset, but can sometimes be a problem, and will not occur if the union of the stock and the rose is kept above the surface of the soil when planting. It is a particularly useful rose for large-scale public planting, and for this purpose it is usual to use seedlings rather than budded stock. So grown it will cover big areas at minimum cost, producing a most satisfactory effect.

There are a number of good forms and hybrids, and these have been used with some success in the breeding of modern garden shrubs. There is also an old race of double-flowered garden varieties (see Old Garden Varieties of the Scots Rose below). All are similar in foliage and general appearance and are equally hardy.

• ROSA SPINOSISSIMA FORMS AND HYBRIDS: *Rosa* **'Robbie Burns'** (*Ausburn*) This variety, which was bred at our nursery in 1985, was the result of a cross between *R. spinosissima* and the English Rose 'Wife of Bath'. It is of strongly Scots Rose appearance. The flowers are medium-sized, neat and rather cupped, of a soft rose-pink at the outer edges shading to a distinctly white centre, and have a delicate beauty. They are followed by large, mahogany-coloured hips. The growth is quite tall, perhaps 1.5m/5ft, and a little heavier than one would expect from these roses, but otherwise similar. Fragrant. Like all Scots Roses, extremely hardy, even in the central Provinces of Canada. *Rosa spinosissima* **'Dunwich Rose'** (*R. pimpinellifolia* 'Dunwich Rose') I know very little about the origin of this rose. It was found in 1956 on the sandy cliffs at Dunwich in Suffolk, and, according to Richard Mabey, it can still be seen growing wild in heathland near the sea there. What I do know is that it is an extremely beautiful shrub — one of the finest of this group. It is typically Spinosissima in flowers, foliage, thorns and hips, but differs in the habit of its growth, which is its chief virtue. It spreads broadly, fanning out into a symmetrical dome of low, arching growth. My specimen reached 90cm/3ft in height and about 1.5m/5ft in width in four years. The flowers are of a creamy-yellow, about 3cm/1½in across, and produced in great quantities along its long, elegant branches, covering the whole shrub with a mass of bloom. I feel it must be a hybrid, but of what I cannot say (Illustrated, p. 289). *Rosa spinosissima* **'Grandiflora'** (*R. pimpinellifolia altaica*, *R. sibirica*, *R. spinosissima altaica*) Commonly known as *R. altaica*. A native of West Asia, this is very similar to *R. spinosissima* but grows rather taller, to about 1.8m/6ft, and has larger flowers. These are pale yellow when opening, but quickly turn to creamy-white. The

*Right*, ROSA SPINOSISSIMA, *more popularly known as the Scots or Burnet Rose, forms a thicket-like growth and produces numerous flowers with a distinct fragrance*

*Far right*, ROSA SPINOSISSIMA 'ORMISTON ROY' *is an excellent shrub, the yellow fading with age to give a wonderfully mixed effect*

SPECIES
ROSES &
THEIR NEAR
HYBRIDS

Species Shrub
Roses & their
Hybrids

*Above* ROSA
'*STANWELL*
*PERPETUAL*' *is
unique among
the Scots Roses in
that it is reliably
repeat flowering*

hips are globular and maroon-black. It has all the hardiness of
*R. spinosissima*. Fragrant. An excellent hardy shrub. ***Rosa spinosissima* var. *hispida*** A variant from North-east Asia, usually growing
to about 1.8m/6ft. It is not so inclined to sucker as the typical Species
and the stems are covered with slender brown bristles. The flowers
are of considerable beauty, being a soft creamy-yellow. Known to
have been in cultivation in 1781. ***Rosa spinosissima* 'Ormiston
Roy'** The result of a cross between 'Allard' (a *R. xanthina* Hybrid)
and *R. spinosissima* has provided an attractive, large, rounded shrub,
bearing neatly formed bright yellow single flowers with attractive
veining. These are followed by large maroon-coloured hips. Height
1.8m/6ft. Doorenbos (Holland), 1938.

• OLD GARDEN VARIETIES OF THE SCOTS ROSE These are
double-flowered garden varieties of *R. spinosissima*. I therefore have
little right to include them with the Species, but place them here to
avoid making too many divisions and thus causing unnecessary com-
plication. They appear to have been largely the result of pure selection
from the Species. We grow *R. spinosissima* seedlings in large numbers,
mainly for municipal authorities, and I have frequently noticed that
there will nearly always be a few individual bushes with at least some
sign of blush-pink in their flowers. I assume that this group is the
result of selecting individuals of this kind. They were, as the name suggests, developed in Scotland, and indeed they are ideal roses for the

more extreme climate of the North. It is difficult to say when Scottish
interest in these roses began, but in the early 1800s, Dixon & Brown of
Perth were probably the first nurserymen to grow them on any scale.
Later the firm of Austin & McAslan of Glasgow listed 208 varieties, but
there is no mention in their catalogues of those that we grow today. We
may assume that a few of them at least survive under other names.

Although the Scots Roses flower for a very limited period early
in the season, and are not particularly showy, they do have certain
virtues, not the least of which is the dense, bushy, compact nature
of their growth. These bushes are covered with pretty little flowers in
season, and the result is a charming picture. They are also extremely
tough, and will grow under poor conditions, particularly on sandy
soils. This gives them a special value which it would be difficult to
replace with any other garden rose. They nearly all have their own
pleasant perfume. **Andrewsii** Small semi-double, deep pink flowers
of rather cupped formation. Dense, bushy growth of about 1.2m/4ft
in height. **Double Blush** Blush-pink flowers, deepening towards
the centre and paler on the reverse side. Height 1.2m/4ft. A pretty
little rose. **Double White** An excellent shrub. It forms a fine, well
rounded, dense and bushy plant of about 1.5m/5ft. In May and early
June it is studded with small, double, deeply-cupped flowers with a
delicious fragrance (Illustrated, p. 310). **Falkland** Semi-double, delicate pink flowers fading almost to white against a background of

ROSA 'ROBBIE BURNS'
*bears fragrant flowers of*
*delicate beauty but is*
*extremely hardy*

SPECIES
ROSES &
THEIR NEAR
HYBRIDS

Species Shrub
Roses & their
Hybrids

greyish-green leaves give a charming effect. Height 1.2 m/4 ft. **Glory of Edzell** This attractive rose is always particularly welcome, as it is one of the first of all to flower. It has single, clear pink flowers that pale towards the centre. A sprightly little shrub of 1.5 m/5 ft. **Harisonii** ('Harison's Yellow', × *harisonii* 'Harison's Yellow') There is some doubt as to the origin of this rose, but it was probably raised by George Harison of New York in 1830. It is almost certain that it is a hybrid between a Scots Rose and *R. foetida*. It forms a rather slender, upright shrub of 1.5 m/5 ft, bearing bright sulphur-yellow double flowers which are cupped at first and open to a more flat formation, usually exposing their rather darker stamens. The foliage is of a slightly greyish-green. It provides a most satisfactory exclamation mark of bright colour in a border of Old Roses before most of them

are in flower. Fragrant. **Lochinvar** (*Aus-bilda*) This beautiful rose retains all the good characteristics of a Scots Rose and repeat flowers throughout the summer. The flowers are a lovely fresh blush pink and loosely double—about 3 cm/1 in across. Typical thorny, bushy growth. Charming fragrance of medium strength—Old Rose with a little geranium. 120 × 90 cm/4 ft × 3 ft. **Marbled Pink** Small semi-double, cupped flowers, opening wide with the outer petals turning back. In colour it is blush-pink at first, marbled darker, becoming almost white. It forms an attractive, low, dense but spreading shrub of 90 cm/3 ft in height. **Mary, Queen of Scots** This charming rose has small, double flowers in a mixture of purple and lilac-grey, paler on the outside. There is a legend that it was brought from France by Mary Queen of Scots. Height 90 cm/3 ft. **Mrs Colville** A shrub of 80 cm/2 ft in height, thought to be a hybrid with *R. pendulina*. The flowers are single, crimson-purple, white at the centre, with yellow stamens. The young wood is red-brown, and it bears elongated hips of darkest red. **Single Cherry** Small cherry-pink flowers, with a lighter reverse and prominent stamens. Height 90 cm/3 ft. **Stanwell Perpetual** The first Old Rose I grew and still a favourite of mine. It was discovered in a garden in Essex, and introduced in 1838 by a nurseryman called Lee, of Hammersmith. It is highly probable that it was the result of a chance cross between *R. pimpinellifolia* and an Autumn Damask, as it is unique among Scots Roses in that it is reliably repeat flowering. Its growth is more lax than is usual in these roses, and the foliage a rather greyish-green, but otherwise it is typical, showing little sign of the Damask parent. It is not so free-flowering as the others in this group, but this is made up for by a succession of later blooms. The flowers start as the most perfect little cupped buds of clearest blush-pink. These open to flat, semi-double, rather informal flowers of about 8 cm/3 in across, with quilled petals and a button eye. They have the most delicious fragrance. The height is about 1.5 m/5 ft. Like all these roses, it is very tough and hardy. (Illustrated, p. 307) **Williams' Double Yellow** (× *harisonii* 'Williams' Double Yellow', 'Double Yellow', 'Scotch Yellow', 'Old Double Yellow', 'Scots Rose') This is similar to 'Harisonii' and probably came from the same parents. It was said to be a seedling from *R. foetida*, raised in 1828 by John Williams who lived near Worcester, and must have been a chance cross with a Scots Rose. At first sight it is easy to confuse it with 'Harisonii', but closer examination reveals it is much nearer in growth to its Scottish parent. It has pale green carpels, not stamens, in the centre of its small bright yellow double flowers that open to an informal formation. These have a strong fragrance, similar to that of *R. foetida*. In Scotland it is known as

'Prince Charlie's Rose'. Height 1.2m/4ft. **William III** A dwarf bush of no more than 60cm/2ft in height, suckering freely when on its own roots and forming a dense thicket. The flowers are semi-double, purplish-crimson fading to lilac-pink, and are followed by small, round, maroon-coloured hips.

*Rosa stellata* (*Hesperhodos stellatus*) A native of the South-western USA, from the west of Texas to Arizona, this is a wiry, thicket-like shrub of about 60cm/2ft in height, with grey-green stems, pale sharp prickles and hairy, deeply toothed leaves of three leaflets, similar to those of a gooseberry. The flowers are solitary, 5–6cm/2–2½in across, soft rose-pink, with deeply-notched petals and yellow anthers, having something of the appearance of a cistus. Strong almond fragrance. The hips are round, brownish-red and about 1cm/½in wide. Very hardy, but likes sun and a well-drained soil.

*Rosa stellata* **var. *mirifica*** ('Sacramento Rose') Similar to *R. stellata*, but more vigorous, attaining 1.2 to 1.8m/4 to 6ft in the wild, usually with leaves of five leaflets. The flowers are slightly larger and it is more free flowering than *R. stellata*. It requires similar conditions. Both are roses of some charm.

*Rosa sweginzowii* A very vigorous shrub, similar to *R. moyesii* in many respects, but larger, growing to 3.5m/12ft in height and the same across, with very large thorns and numerous bristles. The flowers are rose-pink, 3–5cm/1–2in across, and held in small clusters. These are followed by long, bristly, flagon-shaped, orange-red hips. It is a native of North-west China. Introduced 1906. (Illustrated overleaf)

*Rosa villosa* Also known as the Apple Rose for the exceptionally large size of its round hips which make a fine display in autumn. It is a vigorous, well-formed shrub of 2.1 by 2.1m/7 by 7ft, with large, downy, grey-green foliage, against which its clear rosy-pink flowers show themselves to good effect. These are about 6cm/2in across, with slightly crinkled petals and a light fragrance. A native of Central Europe and Western Asia.

*Above,*
WILLIAM III
*suckers freely when on its own roots and forms a dense thicket*

*Left,*
ROSA STELLATA
VAR. MIRIFICA
*bears flowers of the clearest rose-pink that have a strong almond-like fragrance*

311

SPECIES
ROSES &
THEIR NEAR
HYBRIDS

Species
Shrub Roses
& their
Hybrids

**Rosa villosa** Duplex (*R*. 'Duplex', Wolley-Dod) This is a semi-double form or hybrid of *R. villosa*. Although it may be a little shorter in growth, it is otherwise similar. In spite of this, the chromosome count suggests that it is, in fact, a hybrid of a garden rose. The hips are less plentiful and perhaps a little smaller, the flowers rather larger, but we have the same attractive combination of flower and leaf. It is known to have been in existence prior to 1797.

**Rosa virginiana** A dense, suckering shrub, notable for the varying colours of its foliage. This is bronzy when young, becoming green, and finally turning to wonderful autumn tints of red and yellow. The stems are tinged with red, and have few thorns. The flowers appear later than many other Species and continue from late June to early August. They are quite small, cerise-pink, paler at the centre, with pointed buds. The hips are small and bright red, persisting throughout the winter. It will grow to 1.2 or 1.5m/4 or 5ft in height, and sucker freely on its own roots. A useful rose for municipal planting or for the more natural areas of the garden. Many seedling strains of this rose have become rather mixed and show distinct signs of hybridity. A native of North America.

**Rosa virginiana alba** A white-flowered form or hybrid of the rose described above, with green stems and pale green leaves which do not turn to autumn tints. Height 1.2 or 1.5m/4 or 5ft.

**Rosa webbiana** A pretty Species Rose closely related to *R. willmottiae*. It is of dense growth, with slender, reddish-brown, twiggy stems in long, arching sprays, along which are borne pale lilac-pink flowers, each about 5cm/2in across, with a slight scent. These are produced in early June. They are followed by narrow flask-shaped, scarlet-red hips about 2cm/¾in long, making a particularly dainty display; indeed, few other Species can match it in this respect. The foliage is made up of up to nine small, finely divided leaflets. It will grow to about 1.8m/6ft in height and 1.8m/6ft across. A native of the Himalayas, Afghanistan and Turkestan, it grows at 1,800 to 5,500m/6,000 to 18,000ft. First cultivated in 1879.

**Rosa willmottiae** (*R. gymnocarpa var. willmottiae*) Of all the Species, this is perhaps the most graceful in growth and foliage. It is a prickly shrub of 2.5m/8ft in height and rather more across, with arching growth bearing small, finely divided greyish-green foliage, giving a dainty spray-like ferny effect. The flowers are small but pretty. They do not last for very long, but while they do they provide a pleasing picture. Their colour is lilac-pink with creamy stamens. Later, there are small pear-shaped orange-red hips. A native of Western China, collected by E. H. Wilson in 1904.

**Rosa woodsii** var. **fendleri** *R. woodsii* is a variable shrub native to central and western North America. *R. woodsii* var. *fendleri* is the form usually seen in gardens, reputedly found in the southerly areas of this region — sometimes as far south as Mexico — although it is quite hardy. It forms a dense bush of 1.8 by 1.5m/6 by 5ft, and has graceful growth, greyish-green leaves and small lilac-pink flowers with creamy stamens. These are fragrant and borne singly or in small clusters. In autumn the branches are hung with round, shiny, red hips that persist well into winter. These are perhaps its greatest asset. First cultivated in 1888.

**Rosa xanthina** Canary Bird One of the most popular and best known of the Species, mainly because of the deep yellow colouring of its flowers. Although it is a good shrub, I am not quite sure it deserves such pre-eminence. It has 5cm/2in flowers, graceful growth, chocolate-brown bark and dainty fern-like, grey-green foliage. The hips are dark maroon, but not very conspicuous. An excellent rose, although not always very robust and it is inclined to suffer from die-back unless on its own roots. Height 2m/7ft.

*Right & below left,* ROSA SWEGINZOWII *has rose-pink flowers, followed by long, bristly, flagon-shaped hips*

*Below right,* ROSA XANTHINA CANARY BIRD *is popular because of the colour of its flowers and dainty foliage*

*Facing,* ROSA VIRGINIANA, *is a dense suckering shrub notable for its very brightly coloured flowers and hips and wonderful autumn colour*

# Climbing Species Roses

SPECIES
ROSES &
THEIR NEAR
HYBRIDS

Climbing
Species
Roses

Apart from the shrubby Species, there are a number of good Climbing Species. In the wild these would climb over shrubs and into trees to find the light. The majority are of the Synstylae family (see below) and of very strong growth, producing large sprays of small, white flowers with a powerful fragrance .

In addition there are a few Climbing Species of other families, including hybrids of *Rosa banksia* and *R. laevigata*. These vary considerably and include some exotic roses of great beauty (see pages 317 to 319). Unfortunately, many of them are rather tender, but where this is the case they are usually well worth trying on a warm wall.

Nearly all the Climbing Species are best left to their own devices, with little pruning, at least in so far as space allows. They will require very little other attention.

---

## CLIMBING SPECIES OF THE SYNSTYLAE FAMILY

Species of this family are so distinct as to make it helpful to include them in a section of their own. The name refers to the fact that all these roses have the styles of their flowers in one piece, and not separated and held individually as is the case with all other roses. This is how botanists identify them. It is by crossing Species from this family with garden varieties that all our Rambler Roses have been developed.

A reader who is not familiar with the Synstylae roses might be excused if he or she complained that they seem to be all very much the same. They do, however, vary greatly in height, and as we get to know them better we find that they have many subtle differences which are hard to put into a few words. They usually have a strong, sweet fragrance, and flower with exceptional freedom. They include some dramatically tall and rampant roses ideal for growing in trees and over bushes, and indeed for covering any large structure.

ROSA FILIPES
BRENDA COLVIN
*has all the strength
of 'Kiftsgate'
and a delicious
fragrance*

**Rosa arvensis** (the Field Rose) A common rose of the British hedgerows, flowering after the Dog Rose and having rather smaller white flowers. It also grows wild over much of Europe. A climbing or trailing Species it is usually found scrambling over bushes. From a horticultural point of view it is mainly important as the parent of the Ayrshire Roses. The flowers are borne in small bunches along reddish stems, and are followed by ovoid, red hips. Contrary to what we often read in books, it is fragrant and is indeed the 'Sweet Musk Rose' extolled by Shakespeare and Spenser. This rose will grow to a great width if permitted—perhaps 6 by 3m/20 by 10ft in height. It is worth growing in wild places, and is sometimes used for roadside planting.

**Rosa brunonii** (*R. moschata nepalensis*, the Himalayan Musk Rose) A variable Species and one of the most beautiful of this family. A native of the Himalayan region, extending into China, it grows extremely vigorously, to a height of 9 or 12m/30 or 40ft, making it excellent for climbing into larger trees. The foliage is particularly fine, with very large, elegantly poised leaves of seven widely-spaced, long pointed leaflets. These are grey-green and downy on the underside. The flowers are creamy-white, about 3cm/1in across, with yellow stamens, and are held in

SPECIES
ROSES &
THEIR NEAR
HYBRIDS

Climbing
Species
Roses

very large clusters in late June and early July. They have a strong fragrance. This Species is not completely hardy and can be caught by severe frosts, but it is entirely worthwhile in most areas. First cultivated in 1822.

**Rosa brunonii La Mortola** A superior form of *R. brunonii* in almost every way, and should generally be grown in preference. It has larger white flowers of about 5cm/2in across, which are held in larger clusters. The leaves also are larger, more grey and more downy. In other respects it is as described in the Species above. Height 9 or 12m/30 or 40ft. It was named after the famous garden in Italy, close to the French border, and was brought from there to England by E. A. Bunyard. It was introduced in the UK in 1954.

**Rosa filipes** A strong and rampant climber that will grow to 9m/30ft. The flowers are white and borne in large corymbs. They are of a pronounced cup-like formation, and each is held on a long, slender thread-like stem. They have a strong fragrance and are followed by very small oval hips. We do not grow this Species — it has been almost entirely superseded in the garden by *R. filipes* 'Kiftsgate'. A native of West China, first collected by E.H. Wilson in 1908.

**Rosa filipes Brenda Colvin** A seedling from 'Kiftsgate' described below. It has all the strength of that massive rose, and small semi-double flowers in large clusters. The difference lies in the colour: this is a soft blush-pink which quickly turns to white. Unfortunately, the pink is so indistinct as to be almost white in massed effect. There is a delicious fragrance. A chance seedling discovered by Miss Colvin, first distributed by Sunningdale Nurseries in 1970.

**Rosa filipes Kiftsgate** This is the form of *R. filipes* usually sold by nurseries. It has become well known among keen gardeners as a climber for large trees and there is no better rose for this purpose. It is a prodigious grower and an astonishing bloomer. It can easily achieve 12m/40ft and bears enormous corymbs of bloom, sometimes with hundreds of flowers. Individually these are small, cupped and creamy-white with yellow stamens. They have a strong fragrance. The flowers are followed by an equally wonderful crop of small pinky-red hips. It can at times be a little choosy as to the position in which it is grown, and refuse to live up to its reputation as a massive grower. Mrs Muir of Kiftsgate Court, Gloucestershire, purchased this rose from E.A. Bunyard in 1938. Where he obtained it from we do not know, but it was eventually introduced by Murrell (UK) in 1954. Mrs Muir's original plant is now some 18m/60ft in width, and almost as high.

**Rosa moschata** (the Musk Rose) Not, in fact, a wild Species, but a rose of ancient garden origin. It may have been brought to England in the time of Elizabeth I and has many romantic associations. Later, it had an important effect on the breeding of garden roses, being one of the original parents of the Noisette Roses. On a sunny shel-

*ROSA FILIPES KIFTSGATE is well known among keen gardeners as a climber for large trees and there is no better rose for this purpose*

tered wall it can be very fine, but in a less than favourable position it may not be so impressive. The flowers are single, creamy-white and held in widely branching sprays. It has lovely grey-green foliage and a general air of daintiness. It has two important merits: its delicious musk fragrance, and the fact that it does not bloom until August, and then continues until autumn. Height about 3m/10ft.

**Rosa mulliganii** For a long time this rose was available as *R. longicuspis*, but according to Bean's *Trees and Shrubs*, it should properly be known as *R. mulliganii*. *R. longicuspis* is distinct, with much darker leaves, and is perhaps even more vigorous. *R. mulliganii* vies with *R. filipes* 'Kiftsgate' for the position as the largest tree-climbing rose. It is usually not quite so strong, but will reach 9m/30ft, and has fine, glossy, almost evergreen foliage, with leaves of seven leaflets, the young shoots being tinted with brown. The flowers are creamy-white, almost 5cm/2in across, and are held in huge broad trusses of anything up to 150 individual blooms. They have a strong fragrance. In autumn there are small orange-red hips. It flowers late in the season, from the end of June to mid-July. A native of West China, it was collected by F. Kingdon Ward in about 1915.

**Rosa multiflora** (*R. polyantha*) A vigorous Climber or shrub sometimes used as a root stock in Britain, but more often on the Continent. For this reason it is frequently found surviving in gardens long after the garden rose which was budded on to it has died away. However, this is not to say it is not a useful garden plant, although it is perhaps a little stiff in growth as a Climber, and there are better Species. It has considerable value for large-scale planting in municipal landscapes, as it grows very vigorously, forming a great mass of tall growth. For this purpose it should be grown from seed. It bears tight clusters of small, 2.5cm/1in creamy-white flowers with golden stamens in late June and early July. These have a strong fruity fragrance which carries extensively. There are small, oval, red hips in autumn. Its dimensions as a shrub are 2.1m/7ft high by 3m/10ft across; as a Climber it will grow considerably taller, and may reach 6m/20ft or more in a tree. It was one of the ancestors of the Multiflora Ramblers and the Polyantha Pompon Roses, eventually influencing the Floribundas. It is thus one of the most important ancestors of our Modern Roses. A native of North China, Korea and Japan. Known to have been in Britain before 1869.

**Rosa polyantha** Grandiflora is usually known as *R. gentiliana*, but it is more likely that it is a *R. multiflora* Hybrid, as no one seems to have any knowledge of it in the wild; and more conclusively by the fact that the styles of its flowers are separated, indicating it is not a pure member of the Synstylae family. In late June to mid-July it bears masses of small, single white flowers in rather small clusters. These have orangey-red stamens, a strong fruit-like fragrance, and are followed by light red hips which last well into winter, making a fine display. It flowers freely and has plentiful, glossy foliage, which is tinted with bronze at first. Height 4.5 to 6m/15 to 20ft. It is thought to have been brought from China, and introduced in 1886.

**Rosa sempervirens** This Species is a native of Southern Europe and North Africa and is best known as the parent of the beautiful Sempervirens Hybrids. It is, in fact, an attractive Species in its own right, with larger flowers than others of this family and of pleasing individual character. These are borne in small clusters on long, graceful, trailing growth. They have a slight fragrance. The foliage consists of five to seven leaflets and is almost evergreen. Not entirely hardy in the British Isles.

**Rosa sinowilsonii** This rose has the most magnificent foliage of all the Species, and it is grown mainly for this reason. The leaves are of a dark, glossy green, very large, and may be up to 30cm/1ft in length. They are deeply corrugated, tinted with purple beneath, and have seven leaflets. The flowers are not outstanding, being white, 3cm/1in across, and borne in small sprays. Most unfortunately, it is not completely hardy in the British Isles. It was brought from China to Britain in 1904 by E.H. Wilson, who was responsible for bringing so many good Species from that country, so much so that he became known as 'Chinese Wilson'.

**Rosa soulieana** A very strong, loose-growing Climber or shrub, with long, arching stems, distinctly greyish leaves, and hooked yellow thorns. The flowers are pale yellow in the bud, opening white, about 3 cm/1 in across, and freely produced in clusters. There is a very strong clove-like fragrance. Bunches of small, ovoid orange hips make a good show in autumn. As a Climber it will grow to 3.5 or 4.5 m/12 or 15 ft. As a shrub it will create a mound of growth 3 m/10ft high and the same across. It is excellent for wild areas, where it can be grown as a shrub or into trees and over bushes. In the British Isles it may be cut back by cold frosts. Collected in West China by Père Soulié, and sent to France, arriving at Kew in 1899. (Illustrated overleaf)

*Rosa wichurana* A vigorous, trailing rose, native to Japan, East China, Korea and Taiwan. Best known as the parent of the Wichurana Ramblers, it is a useful garden plant in its own right. It will make excellent ground cover where space permits, sending out trailing growth of great length which will keep close to the ground or climb into bushes and trees with the help of its hooked thorns. It does not flower until August, when it has attractive pyramid-shaped clusters of small white flowers shading to yellow at the centre. These have a strong fruit-like fragrance. The foliage is a bright, glossy green and almost evergreen. Later we have small, ovoid, dark red hips. It is also a most attractive Climber, growing to 6 m/20ft, its long shoots hanging gracefully from their support.

## OTHER CLIMBING SPECIES

**BANKSIAN ROSES** The Banksian Roses form a small group of Ramblers that stand very much on their own. The wild species is a native of West China, growing at 1,500 m/5,000ft in Hunan, Shaanxi and Hubei, and both this and its garden forms have an individuality and character that places them among the most desirable of all climbing roses. Small flowers, with a strong fragrance, are borne in hanging sprays and appear in late May or early June, long before most other Ramblers. The branches are almost thornless, the foliage pale green with long, glossy pointed leaflets of polished appearance. As a group these roses appreciate plenty of warm summer sun to ripen their wood. They flower well in most of the British Isles, suffering only from an unusually hard frost. The flowers are produced on the second and third year's growth, and for this reason it is necessary to confine pruning to the removal of old wood and generally keeping the rose tidy and within bounds. In a favourable position Banksian Roses may be expected to reach the roof, or at least 8 m/25ft. Propagation is best done from cuttings or by grafting, for the Banksian Roses will not bud successfully on to the usual root stocks.

*Rosa banksiae* **var.** *banksiae* This variety, frequently known as *R. banksiae* 'Alba-Plena', was brought to England by William Kerr on behalf of the Royal Society in 1807. He discovered it in a Canton garden. It was named after Lady Banks, the wife of the famous Director of Kew Gardens at that time, thus giving its name to the species. The flowers are white, small (no more than 25 mm/1 in across) full petalled and form a near button-like rosette with a strong fragrance that is similar to that of violets. *Rosa banksiae* **'Lutea'** The most widely grown of the Banksian Roses, this is rather more free-flowering than the white form, and probably a little hardier, although it does not grow quite so strongly. The flowers are small, cupped and double, of a lovely deep yellow colour, but have only a light scent. Introduced from China by J. D. Park for the Horticultural Society of London, it first flowered in Britain in 1824. One of the great classic roses. *Rosa banksiae* **'Lutescens'** This form has small, single

ROSA BANKSIAE VAR. NORMALIS *is the wild species from Western China with a particularly strong fragrance*

ROSA BANKSIAE LUTEA *is one of the great classic roses and the most widely grown of the Banksian group*

canary-yellow flowers in sprays. It is believed to have been brought to England in 1870 from La Mortola, the famous garden on the Italian Riviera. It has a strong fragrance. **Rosa banksiae var. *normalis*** The wild species from Western China, bearing sprays of single white flowers with a strong fragrance that is more powerful than any other in the group. Probably introduced to England in 1877. (Illustrated, p. 317)

**Rosa bracteata** (the Macartney Rose) A most beautiful and exotic rose, but unfortunately not completely hardy in the British Isles. It will, given a warm and sheltered wall, survive most winters, certainly in the warmer parts of the country. The flowers are large, up to 10cm /4in across, pure white, with a silky texture and a large boss of orange-red stamens. They are fragrant and borne singly on short stalks, with attractive, large, leafy bracts around the buds. The fruit is globular and orange-red. It has fine, smooth, dark green leaves with up to nine leaflets, and is almost evergreen. The growth is bushy, to about 3.5m/12ft in height in a suitable position, and it will in warmer climates form a good shrub. Unusually among Species it continues to flower until autumn. It is a native of Eastern China, collected by Sir George Staunton, and brought to Britain by Lord Macartney in 1793. In the warmer regions of the Southern USA it has become naturalized and is regarded as something of a weed in certain areas. It is one of the parents of the beautiful 'Mermaid'.

**Rosa gigantea** The most splendid of the wild Species Roses. Sadly, it is too tender to be grown in the British Isles, except in the very warmest areas, but even then it seldom blooms. In its native habitat of South-west China and Upper Myanmar the flowers are very large, 12 or 15cm/5 or 6in across, and may be pale yellow, cream or white, with large, overlapping petals and a boss of golden stamens. The fragrance is similar to that of Tea Roses. It has huge, 23cm/9in glossy dark green leaves, and will make massive growth to as much as 16m/50ft, even 24m/80ft in warm climates. The hips, too, are very large, about 3cm/1in across, and globular. Indeed, it is in every way gigantic. Gault and Synge, in their *Dictionary of Roses,* tell us how the giant hips are sold for eating in the bazaars of Manipur State in north-eastern India. Discovered by Sir George Watt, 1882, introduced by Sir Henry Collet, 1889.

*R. gigantea* is of particular interest to us as one of the great influences in the development of Modern Roses, and this has been discussed at some length in earlier chapters. It was this rose, above all, which was responsible for the transition of Old Roses to what we now call Modern Roses. It is so huge and so different that it was certain to change the whole character of garden roses.

**Rosa laevigata** (R. sinica, R. cherokeensis) A vigorous Climber or shrub, with dark green leaves which are unusual in that they each have only three coarsely-toothed leaflets. It has 10cm/4in creamy-white, deliciously fragrant flowers borne singly or in pairs in late June. This is a beautiful but tender Rambling Species. It will flower well in the UK, but requires a warm wall if it is to survive. A native of China, it has adapted itself to the wild in south-eastern North America, where it has become known as the 'Cherokee Rose'. Growth 6m/20ft. Introduced 1759.

• ROSA LAEVIGATA HYBRIDS **Rosa Anemone** (*R. anemonoides, R. sinica* 'Anemone') This is a hybrid of *R. laevigata*, probably with a Tea Rose. It is more delicate in appearance than the former, with sparse growth, less foliage and finer stems. The flowers, however, are very similar to those of *R. laevigata*, and are of supreme beauty, being a clear shell-pink, lightly veined with deeper pink and paler on the reverse side. In spite of its refined appearance it is hardier than *R. laevigata*, but still requires a warm wall. It starts flowering in early June and, although not repeat flowering, continues over an extended period. It will grow to 4.5m/15ft in a suitable position. Slight fragrance. Bred by J. C. Schmidt (Germany), 1895. **Rosa Cooperi** ('Cooper's Burmese Rose') This is a Species closely allied to *R. laevigata*, and a native of Nepal, North Myanmar and South-west China. Its flowers are large, about 10cm/4in across. They are held singly and are of glistening pure white, with a large boss of yellow stamens. It has fine, very glossy foliage, with three (occasionally five) leaflets. Unfortunately it is tender and fails to flower in my garden, although at Sissinghurst Castle it flowers freely early in the season on a sunny wall. In England it will grow to about 3.5m/12ft, although in its habitat it is a giant. We have a plant under glass where it flowers freely and would no doubt grow to a great length. It was first brought to the UK in 1931 by Mr R. E. Cooper, and grown at the then National Rose Society's Trial Ground at Haywards Heath, West Sussex. Our stock was brought to us by Mr and Mrs Cooper-Willis from Nepal, where they saw valleys of it growing to the tops of tall trees, and sweeping in long, trailing stems almost to the ground. This must be the most wonderful rose spectacle in the world. **Rosa Ramona** A sport from R. 'Anemone', discovered by Dietrich and Turner of California in 1913. It is similar in every way, except for the colour of the flowers. This is cerise-crimson with a greyish tint on the reverse. A very beautiful rose.

*Left,* ROSA 'ANEMONE' *is a very distinctive rose with large flowers of clear shell-pink that are lightly veined*

*Facing page,* ROSA SOULIEANA *is excellent for wild areas, where it can be grown as a shrub or into trees and over bushes*

# 10

# ROSES IN THE GARDEN

IN SPITE OF ITS GREAT POPULARITY, the rose is not always used in the garden to its full potential. As we have seen, there is now available to us a great range of roses that vary so widely in growth, flower and overall character that there is something for every style of gardening and for almost every part of the garden. In beds and borders, on walls and fences, over trees and bushes, on arches and pillars, and in pots and containers—the rose has its place. It no longer need be confined to rectangular rose beds or, in small gardens, to narrow borders around the house. The rose tends to be admired for the beauty of the individual flower and its delicious fragrance. Wonderful though these qualities are, it is a shame to allow them to overshadow the value of the rose as a garden plant. For it is a particularly good garden plant. In fact, it would be hard to think of another that is its equal.

## Roses in a Mixed Border

It is in the mixed border that roses are most valuable and yet few gardeners use them here—and garden writers and broadcasters hardly ever mention them for this purpose. I am, of course, talking about Shrub Roses of all kinds—Old Roses, Modern Shrubs and English Roses, as well as the Species, rather than Hybrid Teas and Floribundas, which are too short and stiff in habit to combine with other plants.

To some extent I can sympathise with this attitude, for roses do require special treatment. First, there is the fact that they are shrubs but are not really suitable for a shrub border. They are successful planted in a mixed border of hardy perennials and shrubs, but do not seem to mix easily with shrubs alone.

Roses are most at home in a mixed border of hardy perennials. To be seen at their best they should take centre stage and the area immediately around them should be planted with perennials that complement the roses in form as well as colour, such as sprawling herbaceous geraniums, wafting grasses, tall penstemons and iris or low-growing diascias and

*Right, CERISE BOUQUET is a very large rose that looks superb with late-summer-flowering Clematis viticella growing through it*

*Facing page, JOHN CLARE combines well with valerian and delphiniums*

320

ROSES
IN THE
GARDEN

Roses in
a Mixed
Border

lavender—to name but a few. None should be too strong or invasive, otherwise they will get the better of the roses. While roses are confined to their root stocks, many hardy plants can spread at will—and this gives them the upper hand.

Here, I would like to make an important point: in anything but the smallest gardens, roses should nearly always be planted in groups of two, three or more bushes of one variety. These should be so close that they gradually grow together to form what is, to all intents and purposes, one shrub. Many roses, when planted singly, have—as it were—a rather straggly appearance. This is because they have been bred to flower throughout the summer and this places a considerable strain upon them. A 'shrub' made up of a number of plants has in effect a number of points of access to the soil, thus greatly enhancing its vigour. (For further details on planting roses, see the chapter on Cultivation.)

Quite apart from these practical advantages, group planting has aesthetic advantages—it makes a statement and we can see each rose in all its beauty. Most good gardeners advise group planting for the majority of plants. Of course, the group can vary in size according to the impression you wish to make, and there will be occasions when a single shrub will make the desired effect. Indeed, in small gardens there may not be enough space for group planting but here everything is on a smaller scale.

*Near right,* GERTRUDE JEKYLL *is a wonderful border plant and, even though it can reach quite a height, should be planted close to the edge so that its delicious fragrance can be easily and frequently appreciated*

*Far right, a mixed border at Wollerton Old Hall includes* ST. CECILIA *in the foreground and* LAVENDER LASSIE *immediately behind*

## A Border of Roses

If you wish to have a collection of roses of any size, it is worth considering a border made entirely of roses. Such a border can be filled with bloom throughout the summer and, with the variety of roses available to us today, it need never be boring. In a border of roses it is vital to plant in groups to avoid a jumble of bloom and to enable each variety to express itself to the full.

A border of Hybrid Teas and Floribundas would inevitably be somewhat 'flat' in appearance, but with Shrub Roses

we can, by careful choice of varieties, vary the height to give the border form, which is more important than colour in a border of roses. With form, I would include texture and weight. Consider the growth of a Gallica, a Damask or an Alba Rose, then think about the vast variation in height and kind of the English Roses, or compare the rough texture of the Rugosas and the smooth leaves of the Hybrid Musks. Add to these a few smaller roses such as 'Little White Pet' and mix with them the occasional Wild Species Rose, and it soon becomes obvious that we have a wide-ranging palette which is more than capable of providing us with a border of unending interest and beauty. All these roses seem to live happily together, one with another. Perhaps this is not surprising, as all the subjects are of the same species and have a natural affinity. Highly developed flowers mingle with lighter, more natural flowers, to their mutual benefit.

The rose is by nature a flower of soft colouring: pinks, blushes, pale yellows, apricots and peaches—the pink shades deepening into red and crimson. All these colours go well together. They are beautiful and just what we require in a rose but, used to excess, they can become a little monotonous. There are, however, a number of brighter colours—flames, oranges, coppers and so on, as well as reds—and if we use these with care they will create highlights and bring the whole border to life. They should be used sparingly. There are of course many bright colours among the Hybrid Teas and Floribundas—indeed, too many—but these are too different in habit to mix well with a border of Shrub Roses.

## A Simple Rose Garden

It is only a small step from a border of roses to a rose garden consisting of two borders facing each other and divided by a path. This is the simplest of rose gardens, but the one that I find most satisfactory. If the path leads to some sort of focal point at the end, so much the better. A garden seat, an urn or a piece of sculpture are all satisfactory, and sculpture is especially so. To give the garden the feeling of being an entity, it is best to enclose it by a hedge, a walk, trelliswork, or simply Climbing and Rambling Roses growing on posts and rails. This will have the effect of transforming two simple borders into a rose garden. It will also provide a background against which the roses can be seen to best effect. A gate at each end, with perhaps an arch of Climbing Roses, will complete the picture.

I can think of few more beautiful sights than a garden of this kind well-planted with roses in groups and the groups almost touching each other—their growth overflowing on to the path and giving a wonderful feeling of abundance. The path between the borders may be narrow so that we almost have to find our way between the roses, or it may be wide to give a sense of spaciousness, in which case it is important to make the width of the borders in proportion to the path.

## A Garden of Roses

The conventional design for a rose garden is one of formal beds. This was the fashion throughout the 20th century and, to a large extent, still is. There can be no doubt that this is the

*Left,*
SCINTILLATION *and* BLEU MAGENTA *are two of the varieties lining this path in the Long Garden which leads to a place to sit and admire the many different types of rose*

*Facing page, our rose garden in Wales includes* GEOFF HAMILTON *and* THE MAYFLOWER, *creating a colourful contrast with the fields and hills beyond*

325

*Tall Ramblers and Climbers, such as ALCHEMIST (left) and THE GARLAND (centre) grow up brick pillars and across horizontal wooden poles in the Long Garden*

best kind of garden for Hybrid Tea and Floribunda Roses. Although there are some English Roses that are of suitable size for this purpose, they are usually a little too muted in colour and informal in growth to be ideal. Formal gardens of this kind require intense colours and short, upright growth and the Hybrid Tea Roses and Floribundas were designed for this purpose. Some of the more recent varieties of these roses are rather too tall for bedding, but this can be overcome to some extent by hard pruning.

It is usual to recommend the use of one variety per bed—and I am inclined to believe that this is best. Unfortunately it does not leave much scope for the imagination or, indeed, for a wide selection of varieties. Having said this, a single isolated bed of mixed roses can be a fine sight. Of course, rose beds do not have to be rectangular—there can be variations on this theme, but not many. For example, a circular garden with curved beds is a possibility. An ornament placed at the centre of the formal garden can do much to give it a sense of purpose.

The true rose enthusiast, with no more than a small garden, may consider using the whole area at the front of a house or, alternatively, at the back of the house, as a rose garden, which would never be without interest, particularly if the varieties were to be changed as the roses age. Roses that give the greatest pleasure are a source of enduring interest.

## Larger Rose Gardens

I have mentioned two forms of rose garden but, of course, the possibilities do not end here. There is an infinite range of types and styles, and many more than I can include. The best I can do is to describe the gardens at our Nurseries and hope that you may find some inspiration from these. Unfortunately, most of them are rather larger than the average plot, unless you are willing to make the whole of your garden into a rose garden. This, I feel, would be a little too much for most gardeners—even though he or she could have something of great beauty in this way. My aim is not that our gardens should be copied, but rather that they should provide ideas and inspiration.

Our gardens cover about 0.8 hectares/2 acres, divided into four gardens, each in a different style. The whole area and all but one of the gardens within it is surrounded by a hedge. With one exception, they are all formal—in structure, that is, rather than content. It seems to me that roses require a structured setting. They are so rampant and informal in themselves that they require some kind of order if they are to be seen at their best. Most garden roses are, so to speak, man-made and they are more at home in a man-made setting.

Our main garden, which we call The Long Garden, is in the nature of a large entrance hall off which other gardens lead. It consists of three double borders, about 90m/100 yards long, running parallel with paths between. Each set of double borders is divided from its neighbour by a low yew hedge with brick pillars rising out of it; the pillars being joined by wooden poles. On these we grow Rambler Roses and a few Climbers that are strong enough to compete with the hedge, small though this is. This arrangement has the advantage that it gives us height, avoiding the rather 'flat' appearance of many rose gardens. We have more Rambler Roses in front of the hedges in The Long Garden. These are grown on wires strung between metal uprights. Viewed from the path, you do not see the structure, only the roses.

*Short and colourful patio and miniature roses, including MARLENA, surround the sculpture by Pat Austin that gives The Lion Garden its name*

The central walk of this garden leads to a sculpture of three life-size dancing figures carved from one large piece of stone by my wife, Pat Austin. This makes a perfect focal point. Walking up and down the paths, we have long views with roses on each side and, at the same time, glimpses across the border to other borders—as if through windows. The long paths are traversed by other paths leading into the other gardens, further extending the interest and variety of the scene. We are thus surrounded by abundant planting on all sides. The Long Garden is planted with a mixture of all kinds of Shrub Roses, Old Roses and Modern Shrub Roses, freely mixed with English Roses to ensure continuity of bloom throughout the summer and a wider colour range.

The first of the other gardens is known as The Lion Garden because it has a large carving of a lion at its centre. It is a traditional formal rose garden made of rectangular beds such as I have already described. Around them are herbaceous borders which include, in their planting, specimens of larger-growing Shrub Roses. This garden has not, on the whole, been a great success and we are planning to redesign it in what we hope will be a more pleasing form. Nonetheless, it is useful, in that it enables us to show the Hybrid Teas and Floribundas that we grow.

The second of the adjoining gardens, which we call The Renaissance Garden is the grandest. The centrepiece is a summerhouse that has at least a passing resemblance to a classical Greek building, open at the front with six pillars. It is slightly raised from the ground and contains seats from which visitors can view the garden. Its role is to take the place of the house at the centre of the gardens. In front of this building and flowing away from it is a canal which leads to the entrance from The Long Garden. On both sides of the canal there are grass paths, each with a border at either side. All this forms the centre of the garden which is backed by a low yew hedge.

Behind the hedges are two areas of massed English Roses, which have been long pruned to form large shrubs. Winding through them is a grass path with roses growing to head height on each side to give the feeling of walking through a sea of blooms. These two areas give an idea of what can be done with English Roses in an informal garden.

*Left, shorter English Roses, such as DARCEY BUSSELL, each variety planted in tight groups of five plants, flank the canal in the Renaissance Garden*

*Following pages, a mixture of Climbers, such as MAY QUEEN on the pergola, Old Roses, English Roses and other shrub roses in the Long Garden, with a statue by Pat Austin terminating the vista*

*Above, CHIANTI
(centre) and
A SHROPSHIRE
LAD (on the
right) in the outer
border of the
Round Garden
at our nursery in
Shropshire, at its
height in late
June/early July
and continuing to
look good through
to late summer
and into autumn*

*Right, THE
PILGRIM, one
of the best of the
shorter English
Rose Climbers,
has large, fragrant
flowers and each
of the very many
petals is perfectly
arranged in the
form of a rosette*

*Facing page,
concentric rings
of beds in the
Round Garden
contain roses
of gradually
decreasing size
towards the
centre, where the
arching growth
of FRANCINE
AUSTIN
surrounds
the statue*

The last of the formal gardens is circular and known as The Round Garden. It is surrounded by a 2.5m/8ft wall of a pleasing, pale brick, which is relatively new, although the garden has been there for some time. Within are three circular borders with a large carving in stone at the centre, the borders diminishing in width towards the centre—the largest having large shrubs, graduating to the smallest in the centre. This garden, with its abundance of flowers and their delicious fragrance, is very different from any other rose garden I know. There is a peace about it that is almost other worldly.

The wall also has a practical function, which is very important to us. English Climbing Roses look their best against a wall. It provides the ideal background. I have strung horizontal wires along the wall, each about 50cm/18in apart and about 7.5cm/3in away from the wall, so that we have only to tuck the branches under them to keep the roses in position.

## Walls

Up to this point in this Chapter, I have written mainly of Shrub Roses. There is another part of the rose kingdom which is of equal importance—the Climbing Roses. The first and most important place for these roses is on the walls of the house or, indeed, any other building. A rose that is grown in this way becomes very intimate to us and probably gives us more pleasure than any other individual rose in the garden. It is possible that we pass it several times a day. And a flower seldom looks better than when it is seen on the branch of a Climbing Rose. The individual flowers look us in the face and, against a suitable background, show themselves off to the very best effect.

Most Climbing Roses can be planted to grow against walls but the English Climbers and Modern Climbers are particularly suitable. Both groups have several advantages: they usually grow

*The Climbing English Rose* TEASING GEORGIA *is not too vigorous and so a very good choice for an arch*

to cover a larger area; indeed, some varieties grow so vigorously that they will smother a small building. They are Old Roses and there are not many varieties still with us. A few are less vigorous but they are usually hybrids of the Tea Roses.

## Arches and Pergolas

A well-clothed arch can be an appealing feature in any garden wherever a suitable position can be found. Where you place it is important. There must be a certain logic to its placement, as, for example, where one part of the garden leads to another. Alternatively, a series of arches along a path can be attractive. No doubt many other ideas will suggest themselves.

Short Rambler Roses are ideal for arches, except for the fact that they only have one brief period of flowering. English and Modern Climbers are also suitable, but only the taller varieties—otherwise they will fail to meet at the top of the arch. Whatever rose you choose, it should have suitably lax growth so that it can be trained neatly over the arch. Try, insofar as possible, to select varieties that are well clothed with bloom almost to the ground.

A pergola can be a very attractive feature. The structure itself can be made from a variety of materials. In our Rose Garden we have used brick pillars joined by wooden poles. Stone pillars would be even better. Our long pergola starts at a point where visitors have the choice either to go down it or proceed in one of two other ways. It is interesting that they nearly always choose to go down it. There is something about a pergola that draws one on.

Ramblers are the best roses for a pergola. They are certain to fill the structure completely and their lax growth and abundant sprays of flowers provide just the effect we need. Be

to heights that can be managed easily without danger to life or limb; they hold their flowers lower down, where they can more easily be appreciated; and, not least, they are reliably repeat flowering, which is something that cannot be said for many other Climbing Roses.

I do not wish to dismiss other groups of climbers. The Hybrid Teas are at their most beautiful in their climbing forms. Regular repeat flowering should not be expected from most of these roses. A good display in early summer and a lesser crop in late summer is about as much as they can manage. Almost every Climbing Rose requires some spraying against pests and disease, but the Climbing Hybrid Teas *must* have regular treatment if they are not to lose their leaves soon after flowering.

The Noisettes are among the most beautiful of Climbing Roses, although they are limited in their colour range. Most varieties are both vigorous and healthy. They are particularly useful where we need

*Ramblers, such as* PAUL'S HIMALAYAN MUSK *and* ALEXANDRE GIRAULT, *adorn the brick pillars and wooden poles of the Pergola Walk, creating a tunnel-like effect*

careful when selecting varieties—remember that they not only have to cover the arch but also join up with the next arch and this takes a lot of energy. Unfortunately, as always, there is the problem that they flower only once in the summer. You can overcome this to some extent by working in a few repeat-flowering Climbers using a Rambler on one side and a Climber on the other—but this is not always satisfactory, particularly on a wide pergola.

An idea that is often put forward is to plant clematis to grow with the Ramblers. In this way the flowering period can be extended. The only trouble is that the clematis will often overwhelm the Ramblers. Roses—however strong—do not like any form of competition. The selection of partners should be made with great care and if the clematis threatens to overwhelm the rose, it must be removed.

## Hedges and Fences

I will not say that the rose makes an ideal hedging plant, but bushy varieties can be successfully used as an internal hedge to divide one part of the garden from another, at the same time providing a continual display of bloom. Such a hedge can be short or tall, according to the effect you wish to create. For small hedges I would suggest an upright, low-growing variety like 'The Mayflower'. This rose is one of the few varieties that are completely disease-free—and it is reliably repeat-flowering. In fact, it is seldom out of flower. It is of neat, upright growth and can easily be kept within bounds. For a larger hedge there are numerous suitable roses, although it is as well to choose bushy varieties.

If you have a bare fence that you would like to make into something a little more decorative, English Climbers are probably best. They are not too rampant and produce their fragrant Old Rose flowers with admirable continuity. Their growth will tend to be quite dense compared with other Shrub Roses and if they are trained along the fence, it will be hard to distinguish it from a hedge. We have these roses on a fence in the car park at our Nursery and they never fail to attract attention.

## Pillars

Pillars are often useful features in the garden. They can be placed at intervals in a border, thus giving it height. There are a number of very good light structures for this purpose available from garden centres. Some are no more than 1.2m/4ft tall, but for a border where we don't require great height, they are ideal.

A tall pillar can be effective as an obelisk at the end of a vista or as the centre point of a rose garden. Both Modern Climbers and English Climbers can be used according to the height of the pillar. Many of these do not grow too tall and are ideal for the purpose. The pillar may be of brick, stone or metal-work, or simply a stout timber post. Oak is ideal.

*Above left, PEGASUS planted 90cm/3ft apart on a post and rail fence provides a long season of colour and scent as it repeat flowers well and has a strong Tea Rose fragrance*

*Left, MORTIMER SACKLER, with its pretty soft pink flowers, makes a charming pillar rose and has the added advantage of being almost completely thornless*

333

## Trelliswork

Trelliswork is easy to obtain through most garden centres and can be particularly useful in a small garden to divide one part from another or as a background to a border. It can be used against a building and covered with Climbers—a quite ordinary or even unsightly building can be brought to life by using roses in this way. Climbers can easily be trained up trelliswork by threading the long main growth in and out of its bars.

## Growing Roses into Trees and over Bushes

A dramatic and most satisfactory way to grow Rambler Roses is simply to let them do what they do naturally—climb up into trees and over bushes. An old apple or pear tree makes an ideal host. For a larger tree, choose a rose of rampant growth, probably of the Synstylae group. Plant the rose near to the tree and it will soon find its way up and, from there, its branches festooned with bloom will hang down, making a most magnificent sight. I am particularly fond of 'Paul's Himalayan Musk' for this job. It has the most beautiful fruit-blossom-like flowers and if your tree is a fruit tree, you will have a second crop of flowers after the first has finished. Of course, you will get very little fruit. Other varieties include 'Rambling Rector' and *Rosa filipes* 'Kiftsgate'—these two being excessively strong ramblers—or 'Alberic Barbier', 'François Juranville', 'Léontine Gervais', and 'May Queen'.

Smaller Ramblers will do if the rose is to climb over bushes.

Be sure that the rose is not too strong for its host, otherwise it will eventually smother the tree or shrub—and perhaps kill it. On the other hand, if the tree is too strong for the rambler, it will never succeed in climbing it. It is something of a balancing act to get the two partners right. If the ground is dry and poor, which it frequently is around a tree, the rose will have to be a strong one and it will need feeding and watering in the early years. It will also require a little guidance so that it finds its way up into the tree.

## Pots, Urns and Other Containers

Roses are very satisfactory plants for growing in containers of all kinds. Many of us have small gardens; indeed, often no more than a patio. With the careful use of pots and urns of varying sizes, it is possible to have a rose garden in a very small space and it is surprising how many pots you can get in a small area. The rose, with its long flowering season, is ideal. There are roses for growing in anything from the smallest pot to the largest urn—and these can be objects of beauty in themselves.

Of course, the use of roses in pots is not confined to small gardens. They can also be very attractive features in larger gardens—on paved areas, around the house, or along a long, broad path. Wherever they are placed, they will provide that

ROSA BANKSIAE *LUTEA is very vigorous and needs plenty of space; here it is starting to cover a summer house in California*

ROSES
IN THE
GARDEN

Pots, Urns
and Other
Containers

*With vigorous but
graceful growth,
Belvedere
makes a stunning
show; one of the
best places to
grow ramblers is
up into trees and
over hedges*

lived-in feeling that is often so pleasing.

For the smallest pots there are Miniature Roses which have been greatly improved in recent years. Choose bushy varieties that will not become too lanky—an occasional light trim will also help to avoid this. It is a good idea to place two or three plants in a pot if this is of any size—in this way you will get a nice, bushy specimen.

With large pots or even very large urns, a whole range of roses becomes possible. English Roses are ideal as many varieties are bushy and will grow into fine, well balanced specimens. If you grow the larger varieties, it is a good idea to treat them as small climbers. Many garden centres sell small structures on which they can be trained and these are ideal. There may also be an opportunity to grow the larger English Climbers. They can still be grown in large pots and trained up a wall, if it is not possible to grow them in the ground.

Another possibility is to grow a Standard, or half Standard, in a pot. These can be very effective, forming a good head of growth above an attractive pot. On a patio, pots can be grouped with larger or Standard Roses towards the centre and smaller pots around to give a pleasing effect, In larger gardens, a row of Standards in pots can look very trim in front of a large house, or placed along the edges of a wide path.

No doubt many other ideas and arrangements will suggest themselves, whether the garden be small or large. Also, one great advantage of this type of gardening is that pots can be arranged and rearranged according to what is in flower.

As regards cultivation, it is important to remember that a rose grown in a container is entirely dependent on you for its sustenance. Use a good, soil-based compost and give it regular watering and feeding. After three years or so, the rose may need re-potting. Knock it out of the pot, remove most of the soil and replant in a good, soil-based compost. Re-potting does not seem to have any lasting ill effects on the roses; in fact, they often seem to thrive on this treatment. Alternatively, you may prefer to plant a new bush.

## Roses for Public Places

Many towns and cities have public parks and much of what I have written in this book applies to them. Such gardens are frequently rather dreary with large beds of roses, each of one variety, lacking in interest and beauty. I cannot help thinking that Park Superintendents should allow themselves, or be allowed, to be more imaginative. Often, the problems are that they do not hold the same position for very long and it is difficult for them to act independently. Because there is neither enough time nor money to make changes, they are forced to accept what has been handed down to them. All the same, I think they should do the best they can to make their gardens as attractive as possible—for many people the park is the only garden they have.

*One of the best varieties for growing in a pot, ANNE BOLEYN has arching growth, beautiful individual flowers and repeats well*

337

*The rose garden planted with a huge collection of English Roses, Old Roses, Shrub Roses, Climbers and Ramblers is one of the most popular features of the Alnwick Garden in Northumberland*

I would like those who maintain and design these gardens to consider planting rose gardens as I have described earlier in this chapter. I frequently walk through the gardens at our Nursery and never cease to be surprised at the enormous pleasure they give and the interest people take in the various roses we grow. Visitors can walk from one area to another and make new discoveries as they go. The whole garden is not seen at once. The mixture of Old Roses, English Roses, Shrub Roses, Climbers and Ramblers, and so on means that varieties are seldom repeated and roses of many different kinds can be enjoyed. I am sure that gardens of this kind would give more pleasure than the typical formal gardens of the past and I would expect them to cost no more to maintain.

It is important that these gardens should be of Shrub Roses rather than Hybrid Teas and Floribundas, although there is no reason why these should not have an area of their own. It is even more important that each variety of a rose should be planted in a close group and that the groups should, themselves, be close enough to create an ongoing mass of flowers that will make the maximum impact. Gardens of this kind bring bloom over a long period and they may be underplanted with bulbs so long as these do not get in the way of the all-important annual mulching. Thus we can have colour for a long period of the year. This, as every Park Superintendent will agree, is so important in all public planting.

Not all public planting is in gardens or parks. A large part of it is in borders alongside roadways. Here, Shrub Roses are ideal. We generally do not get much chance to look at these in depth, although they do cheer us on our way. The Ground Cover Roses are best for such positions. They are tough and hardy and have little disease—and provide a mass of bloom throughout the season.

Roses can also play their part in open and more natural areas. Here, the Species are ideal as well as some of the larger shrubs. I can think of few better sights than a well grown group of the beautiful Shrub Rose 'Cerise Bouquet', with its crimson flowers and beautifully arching growth. The largest English Roses are also contenders.

# Roses with Other Plants

SHRUB ROSES associate happily with a great variety of plants. It is hard to go very far wrong in placing them, but it is important to avoid mixing them with flowers of too strong a hue, as this may overwhelm their usually softer colours. As well as flower colour, it is worth considering flower forms to contrast with roses—including spikes (*Aconitum*, *Delphinium*), plates (*Achillea*) and fluffs (*Thalictrum*, *Gypsophila*, *Crambe*)—as well as foliage texture, from feathery grasses to sword-like irises and deeply cut *Cynara*. Most people never really consider such matters and still achieve good results. There is, however, no doubt that a little planning can often lead to very pleasing effects, and certain plants spring immediately to mind.

Shrubs such as silver-leaved *Elaeagnus* 'Quicksilver' and purple foliaged *Cotinus*, *Sambucus* and *Berberis* can be beneficial in a mixed border, relieving an unbroken mass of rose foliage. Other useful shrubs include *Buddleja*, larger *Hebe* and *Lavatera* × *clementii* with midsummer roses, and *Caryopteris* and *Perovskia* with late roses. A proportion of evergreens will help with interest through winter and give structure towards the back of the border.

Here, then, is a small selection of plants that in my opinion associate well with roses and which will in some cases extend the season of flowering in a border. It is wise to avoid vigorous plants that may overpower the roses. The list is intended as a starting point from which to develop your own ideas.

---

*Achillea* Beautifully feathered silver foliage. Huge colour range from salmon ( 'Lachsschönheit'), cream (*A.* 'Mondpagode') and white (*A. ptarmica* 'The Pearl') to pink (*A.* 'Christine's Pink' and 'Heidi'), red (*A. millefolium* 'Kelwayi') and yellow (*A.* 'Lucky Break', *A.* 'Credo' and 'Martina'). 40–60cm/16–24in. Summer. *A. filipendulina* and its cultivars are good when a taller plant is needed and are the most architectural of the genus. 1.2–1.5m/4–5ft.

*Aconitum* **'Stainless Steel'** Deeply cut, dark green foliage and silvery blue flowers over a long season that blend in with a wide colour spectrum *A.* × *cammarum* 'Bicolor' and *A.* × *c.* 'Eleanora' have white flowers edged or tinged with violet-blue, 90cm/3ft. Mid to late summer.

*Agapanthus* Round umbels of blue or white upright flowers. A good contrast to roses when planted towards the front of the border. 80cm/2½ft. Mid to late summer. 'Torbay' is especially good —floriferous and strikingly erect.

*Alchemilla mollis* An ideal companion for Shrub Roses. Flowers lime green. 45cm/18in. Early summer. Cut back after flowering for fresh foliage and some reblooming and to prevent seeding.

*Allium* The onions are valuable plants for combining with roses, different species flowering all through the summer months and some with attractive seed heads. The leaves become untidy as the flowers reach their peak and need other companions to disguise them. *A. cernuum* has bell-shaped deep pink flowers. 30–60cm/12–24in. Among the globe-shaped alliums *A. hollandicum* 'Purple Sensation' (up to 90cm/3ft) coincides with early roses and *A. cristophii* (up to 60cm/24in) flowers from late spring to early summer.

*Alstroemeria psittacina* (Peruvian lily) Strap-shaped leaves make spring ground cover. Clusters of attractively marked flowers appear in summer. Good varieties include 'Apollo' (white with a soft gold eye), 'Friendship' (cream) and 'Golden Delight (soft gold). 90cm/3ft. *A. ligtu* hybrids are grey leaved with flowers in white, blush pinks, brighter coral tones and carmine. 60cm/2ft.

*Amsonia orientalis* A discreet plant with willowy leaves and wiry stems, producing soft blue flowers over a long period. 45cm/18in. Mid to late summer.

*Anaphalis margaritacea* Downy grey leaves and large pearly white everlasting flowers with yellow eyes. 30–45cm/12–18in. Late summer.

*Anemone* × *hybrida* Pretty flowers with a refined elegance, in

*The frothy, flowering heads of* Alchemilla mollis *make a wonderful surround to the large flowers of* WINCHESTER CATHEDRAL

339

whites and pinks. Can be over vigorous. 'Honorine Jobert' is one
of the best. *A. hupehensis* 'Hadspen Abundance' is purple-pink and
adds sparkle to white roses. 1.2m/4ft. Late summer to late autumn.

***Anthemis punctata* subsp. *cupaniana*** Single pure white daisy
flowers above dense silver foliage. For the front of a border. 30cm/
1ft. Spring to summer. Susanna Mitchell ('Blomit') is also very good
and showy.

***Artemisia*** (wormwood) *A. absinthium* 'Lambrook Silver' and
*A.* 'Powis Castle' make clumps of silver-grey finely cut foliage. 90cm/
3ft. *A. stelleriana* 'Boughton Silver' is good at the front of the border
and can be used with *Allium cristophii* (see also *Senecio viravira*).

***Astrantia major*** Numerous airy white flowers held above attractive deeply cut foliage. Deadhead to extend the flowering season.
60cm/2ft. Many crimson varieties, including 'Hadspen Blood' and
'Ruby Wedding'. Summer/autumn.

***Ballota pseudodictamnus*** Evergreen pale woolly textured leaves
for the front of a border. 30–60cm/1–2ft.

***Calamintha nepeta* subsp. *nepeta*** Flowers mauve-white, giving
a pleasing hazy effect. Aromatic foliage. Bees love this plant. 30cm/
1ft. Summer to autumn.

***Camassia leichtlinii*** Linear leaves and creamy white star-shaped
flowers. 60–130cm/24–54in. Late spring. *C.l.* 'Semiplena' has double
flowers, which gives them more substance and makes them last
longer.

***Campanula*** (bellflower) Particularly good varieties for association
with roses are *C. lactiflora*, *latiloba* and *persicifolia*, giving a soft blue
or white combination which highlights the pink blooms of roses
beautifully.

***Centaurea* 'John Coutts'** Pink flowers, leaves pale green, white
beneath. Seldom without bloom. 60cm/2ft. Early summer.

***Chamerion angustifolium* 'Album'** (white-flowered rosebay
willow-herb) Tall spires of white flowers on strong stems associate
well with roses. 1.2m/4ft. Summer.

**Clematis** The more slender cultivars can blend well with roses and
look charming scrambling into and over them.

***Coreopsis verticillata* 'Moonbeam'** Fine hair-like foliage and
loose daisy-flowers in pale yellow. Deadhead to prolong flowering.
Showy but not reliably perennial, though it can be planted each year
like a bedding plant. 45–60cm/18–24in. Late summer. *C.* Crème
Brûlée ('Crembru') is much more persistent and showy—it needs
shearing over after first flush but should last from mid summer into
mid autumn.

***Cosmos bipinnatus*** Annual with feathery foliage with white,
pink or crimson flowers with yellow centres. It is important to get
a named cultivar, and even then most don't flower before the frost.
Sonata Series are perhaps the best. Up to 1.5m/5ft. Summer.

***Crambe cordifolia*** Attractive coarse foliage. A noble sight when
the branching stems give way to gypsophila-like clouds of white
scented flowers. 1.8m/6ft. Use only where scale allows. Early summer.

***Cynara cardunculus*** Magnificent silvery, deeply-cut foliage. The
large stems usually need some support and can become untidy by
the end of the summer but removing them encourages another flush
of handsome basal foliage. 2.1m/7ft. Summer.

***Delphinium*** Charming effects can be achieved by combining the
long blue spikes of delphiniums with pink roses. 1.2–2.1m/4–7ft.
Summer.

***Dianthus*** Pinks are ideal companions for roses, with their attractive
old-fashioned flowers and grey foliage. Their only drawback is their

fragrance which is so strong it can overwhelm that of the roses, at
least at a distance. Old varieties flower once, modern varieties such
as the Devon Series flower throughout the summer.

***Dictamnus albus*** Clump-forming perennial with spikes of white,
pinkish white or crimson flowers, followed by star-shaped seedpods.
Early summer. 40–90cm/16–36in. Early summer.

***Digitalis purpurea*** A few one-sided spikes of the common foxglove
rising up between Shrub Roses can provide a pleasing picture. They
will probably seed freely, and the subsequent plants should be
thinned out so that they do not become too much of a feature.
White-flowered *D.p.* f. *albiflora* is also elegant and non-white seedlings can be rogued out by removing those with a pink flush in the

leaf midrib. 1.8m/6ft. With even more substance and flowers all round the spike are Excelsior Group (also 1.8m/6ft) and Foxy Group (5ft/1.5m), the latter's height suiting more roses. *D.p.* 'Sutton's Apricot' can also look marvellous with white, peach or soft yellow roses. *D. parviflora* has close spires of bronze bells. 90cm/3ft.

*Eryngium* There are sea hollies with blue flowers and silvery stems that range from *E. giganteum*, Miss Willmott's ghost, (1.5m/5ft) to *E. bourgatii* 'Oxford Blue' or 'Picos Blue' (45cm/18in). Other good ones for use with roses are *E. × oliverianum* and *E. × tripartitum.*

*Euphorbia characias* subsp. *wulfenii* Worth planting with roses for its dramatically contrasting form, which is especially effective in cultivars with cylindrical inflorescences such as 'Lambrook

Gold'. The flowers coincide with early roses but still look respectable as the main rose season starts. Even after they fade, the good foliage remains.

*Foeniculum vulgare* **'Purpureum'** Feathery bronze or copper fennel can be a very attractive foil to roses. Remove the tiny yellow flowers that appear in late summer if you want to prevent a rash of seedlings. 90–180cm/3–6ft.

*Gaura lindheimeri* Airy pink-tinged white flowers on willowy stems, good with white, pale pink or crimson roses. 90cm/3ft.

*Geranium* (cranesbill)  There can be few flowers more suitable as companions for roses. They give little trouble, have beautiful foliage and dainty unobtrusive flowers. Numerous species and varieties are

*The double mixed border at Wollerton Old Hall (as it used to be) is mostly roses but has the tall white rosebay willow herb (Chamerion angustifolium 'Album') as a sharp contrast, with shorter plants including pinks (Dianthus) and Artemisia along the edge of the path*

available, most of which are ideal. Here are a few: 'Kashmir Blue', with finely cut leaves forming dense cover, blue flowers. 30cm/1 ft, early summer to autumn. *G. pratense* 'Plenum Violaceum', double warm-blue flowers touched with lilac, 75cm/30in. *G. renardii*, sage-green rounded leaves, white flowers with a suspicion of violet, 30cm/1 ft, early to mid-summer. *G. sanguineum* var. *striatum* 'Splendens', dark green leaves and clean pink flowers, 23cm/9in. 'Blue Cloud' (80cm/32in), 'Brookside' (60cm/2ft) and 'Nimbus' (90cm/3ft) are excellent, larger, long-flowering blues, while *G. pratense* 'Mrs Kendall Clarke' has lavender blue flowers attractively veined white (90cm/3ft). Long-flowering sprawlers for the front of the border include *G.* 'Jean Armour' and *G.* × *riversleai-anum* 'Mavis Simpson', both sugary pink with a satin sheen, and *G.* × *r.* 'Russell Prichard' in magenta.

***Gypsophila paniculata* 'Bristol Fairy'** A dainty airy plant, which everybody will know. 90cm/3ft. Summer.

***Hakonechloa macra* 'Alboaurea'** Gold tinged grass to set off yellow, orange and scarlet roses. 30cm/1 ft.

***Helenium* 'Moerheim Beauty'** Rich, bronze-red daisy-like flowers as companions for repeat-flowering yellow roses. 90cm/3ft. Late summer to autumn.

***Helichrysum petiolare*** Heart-shaped pale green felted leaves make attractive companions to roses in containers. 30cm/1 ft.

***Hemerocallis*** Like lilies and irises, these plants with their rush-like leaves and lily flowers, which range from clear yellow to orange,

apricot, buff and bronze, provide an excellent contrast to roses, but they can be thuggish. There are innumerable cultivars that are less invasive, the best of which flower before the end of the roses' first flush and continue into autumn. 80–110cm/32–42in. Summer. *H. lilioasphodelus* is pale yellow and flowers with late-spring and early-summer roses. 60–90cm/2–3ft. In 'Marion Vaughn' the clean lemon yellow flowers are borne over a long period. 'Corky' and 'Golden Chimes' both produce a profusion of dainty, well-shaped soft gold flowers with a brown stripe on the back of the petals, perhaps best with warm colours.

***Heuchera*** Some good new cultivars are available that are useful at the front of the border, many of them with purple foliage, such as *H. micrantha* var. *diversifolia* 'Palace Purple'.

***Hosta*** Plants with large, beautifully-sculptured leaves which vary greatly between species and variety, both in form and colour. They make an ideal contrast to the growth of roses. Bell-like flowers on tall elegant stems. For better foliage choose a shady position. 45–98cm/18–40in. Grey-leaved varieties cope better with sun and 'Halycon', with glaucous-blue leaves, is one of the best. 45cm/18in.

***Ipomoea*** Morning glory and other annual climbers, such as *I. lobata*, *Lathyrus grandiflorus*, *L. latifolius* and *L. rotundifolius*, are attractive scrambling into and over vigorous roses.

***Iris*** Bearded irises are often recommended for association with Shrub Roses. Spiky grey-green foliage forms a pleasing contrast, although this can become a little shabby towards the end of the season. The Intermediate Bearded cultivars coincide with early roses, while Tall Beardeds usually overlap with the first few weeks of the main rose season. They have the advantage that the majority of them flower before the roses, thus extending the flowering period of a rose border. Other irises that can be used include Spurias such as 'Monspur Cambridge Blue', *I. orientalis*, and *I. missouriensis* 'Tollong', which is good for a little later.

***Knautia macedonica*** Crimson pincushion flowers on slender, branched stems. 45cm/18in. mid and late summer.

***Lavandula*** There can be few more satisfactory subjects than lavender for planting with Old Roses, particularly in a formal setting. In growth, flower and leaf, cultivars of *L. angustifolia* and *L.* × *intermedia* are ideal and add to the old world effect where Old Roses are grown.

***Lilium*** Lilies are almost as important as roses in the history of garden plants and are ideal companions for Shrub Roses, their clean-cut elegance contrasting with the softness of the roses. *Lilium martagon*, *candidum* or *auratum* might be used, among others. It would probably be best to avoid some of the massive brightly-coloured hybrids.

***Lupinus*** Russell lupins make a good contrast of form with summer roses. Named clones are best, such as those raised by Woodfield Bros or West Country Lupins; named seed-raised sorts are a cheaper alternative, for example the Band of Nobles Series. Up to 90cm/3ft.

***Lychnis coronaria* 'Alba'.** Grey basal leaves, branching grey stems, simple white flowers. 90cm/3ft. Summer.

***Malva moschata* f. *alba*** One of our most beautiful native plants, with finely cut leaves. White flowers often with a suspicion of pink in the evening light. Seeds itself, but not a nuisance. 60–80cm/24–30in.

***Melica altissima* 'Atropurpurea'** Non-invasive grass that forms clumps of soft green foliage with flower tassels in mid summer. Up to 80cm/30in.

***Miscanthus sinensis* 'Strictus'** Upright grass with yellow cross-bands to the foliage. Narrow habit suitable for densely planted

*HARLOW CARR with lavender (Lavandula angustifolia 'Hidcote Blue')— a most effective combination*

*A mix of
perennials and
roses, LAVENDER
LASSIE towards
the back*

343

borders. Plumes in late autumn. 2m/78in. 'Flamingo' has a white midrib that turns golden in autumn and fluffy silver plumes. 1.6m/66in.

*Nepeta* × *faassenii* This dwarf catmint requires little description. It starts to flower in June and gives a good display well into the autumn. Use formally as an edging, or informally in a mixed border. 35cm/14in. Moisture-loving *N. govaniana* is taller with tiny pale yellow hooded flowers. 60cm/2ft. Summer.

*Nicotiana* Tall flowering tobaccos grown as annuals, including *N. sylvestris*, with large leaves and lily-like long white flowers in late summer, and *N. langsdorffii*, with greenish-yellow flowers, are elegant companions for roses.

*Nigella damascena* 'Miss Jekyll' A good selection of the much loved annual with clear blue flowers and delicate grass-like foliage. Sow seed in situ for summer flowering. 45cm/18in.

*Onopordum nervosum* A dramatic, tall biennial silver-leaved thistle that will sow itself not too invasively from year to year. 2.5m/8ft.

*Paeonia* In larger borders peonies may be used. Like the irises, they come before the roses, and later their large foliage forms an ideal foil, often turning to autumn tints later in the year.

*Pennisetum villosum* Arching grass with mid-green leaves, with feathery panicles in late summer. 60cm/2ft. Summer into autumn.

*Penstemon* Lovely colours and a long flowering season but may not survive cold, wet winters. 'Apple Blossom' (blush pink), 'Burgundy', 'Chester Scarlet', 'Evelyn' (rose pink), 'Andenken an Friedrich Hahn' (claret-coloured), 'Sour Grapes' (greyish blue, suffused with purple and tinged with green), *P. heterophyllus* (a lovely soft blue), 'White Bedder' (pink-tinged white). 45cm/18in. Mid summer to mid autumn.

*Phlox* Colour for a long season: *P. divaricata* (light blue in spring); *P. maculata* (mauve from late summer on); *P. paniculata* (violet-blues to reds, summer).

*Phygelius* Sun-loving subshrubs that will grow as shrubs in mild districts but can be cut back each spring and used like herbaceous perennials. Derived from the Cape fuchsia, *P. capensis* (up to 3m/10ft or more if trained against a wall), and/or *P. aequalis*, a more compact species with a one-sided inflorescence, there are some exceptionally showy and long-flowering cultivars in white, cream, pale yellow, orange, coral, scarlet and magenta such as the Somerford Funfair Series and Candy Drops Series, making an effective contrast of floral form when planted with roses. 40–75cm/16–30in. Mid summer to mid autumn.

*Polemonium foliosissimum* 'Bressingham' (syn. *P. archibaldiae*) Lavender blue flowers. No seed is produced, so propagated by division. 60cm/2ft. Early summer to early autumn.

*Rosmarinus* Rosemary deserves a place in every garden and there is a wide choice. One of the best, although not very hardy, is *R. officinalis* var. *angustissimus* 'Benenden Blue' with narrow, dark green leaves and vivid blue flowers. For cooler areas choose *R.o.* 'Miss Jessopp's Upright'.

*Ruta graveolens* 'Jackman's Blue' A most attractive blue-green dainty leaf. Cut this plant hard back in mid-spring as the leaves are so much more glaucous when young. 60cm/2ft. Ideal for the front of a border.

*Salvia* Both herbaceous and sub-shrub types are good companions for roses. The choice is wide, some are tender but many are hardy.

*S. argentea*, basal leaves woolly and almost white, branching stems with white flowers, 90cm/3ft. *S. nemorosa* 'Ostfriesland', a bushy plant with numerous erect spikes of violet flowers and crimson bracts over a long period, 90cm/3ft. Summer.

*Senecio viravira* Silvery white foliage, useful as a companion to alliums to disguise their untidy leaves. 60cm/2ft.

*Stachys byzantina* 'Silver Carpet' The well known silver lambs' ears goes well with Old Roses, making an ideal edging or ground-cover plant for roses, especially in cooler areas. 10cm/4in. 'Big Ears' is slightly taller (15cm/6in). Mid summer. They lose all their foliage in hot, humid weather, so can be without leaves in summer, though the leaves reappear in autumn.

*Stachys macrantha* Dark green indented leaves clothe erect stems with mauve flowers. 90cm/3ft. Summer.

*Thalictrum aquilegiifolium* 'Thundercloud' Glaucous green leaves and tall panicles of fluffy lilac-purple flowers. 1.2m/4ft. *T. a.* var. *album* is a white variety. 90–150cm/3–5ft. Early summer.

*Thalictrum delavayi* Dainty foliage with sprays of tiny, pinkish-mauve flowers. Delightful with pink and white roses. 'Hewitt's Double' flowers for a much longer period. 1.5m/5ft. Mid summer to early autumn.

*Thalictrum flavum* subsp. *glaucum* A very striking see-through plant. Although often reaching 1.5m/5ft in summer, when planted as a single specimen, it will not overwhelm the roses due to the nature of its growth. Glaucous blue-green divided leaves and complementary stems. Heads of fluffy lemon-yellow flowers which some gardeners prefer to remove.

*Verbascum* (mullein) Most species of verbascum associate well with roses, their long spikes shooting up between Shrub Roses. The tall silver-felted sorts with yellow flowers are dramatic, such as *V. bombyciferum* 'Polarsommer' and *V. olympicum*, 1.8m/6ft, also pale yellow *V.* 'Gainsborough' (Cotswold Group), 1.5m/5ft, and 'Pink Domino' 1.2m/4ft. Summer.

*Verbena bonariensis* A see-through plant. Tall square stems bear clusters of tiny lilac-purple flowers. Up to 1.5m/5ft in fertile soil. Self seeds and can be nuisance in some climates. Mid summer.

*Verbena corymbosa* Bears clusters of red-purple star-shaped flowers on tall, branched stems. 90cm–2m/3–6ft. *V. c.* 'Gravetye' is a reliable, reasonably hardy selection. Early to later summer.

*Viola* There are many beautiful violas to choose from; I am particularly fond of the species *V. cornuta* and its forms. All are evergreen, with small green leaves which form a complete ground cover. They flower in early summer and last well into the autumn. 30cm/12in. Planted at the base of a rose, they are capable of hoisting themselves to as much as 90cm/3ft. This can be attractive when the rose is tall enough not to be swamped. The type plant is a rich deep violet. The following two varieties are my favourites: *V. cornuta* Lilacina Group (a cool slate blue) and *V. cornuta* Alba Group, which is one of the cleanest whites. All violas need summer moisture to thrive. Watch for aphids in late spring/early summer which will cripple them with virus disease if not treated. Those classed as Violas in the florists' sense are also very good with roses, especially early roses, and even small-flowered, so-called winter violas (raised from seed, so relatively cheap) will continue blooming prolifically into the summer if prevented from getting too dry.

*Yucca* Good for focal points/exclamation marks towards the front of the border, including *Y. filamentosa*, *Y. gloriosa*, *Y. flaccida*.

*The silver leaved lamb's ears go well with roses right at the front of the border. Here we have the English Rose GEOFF HAMILTON with Stachys byzantina 'Big Ears'*

# 11

# ROSES IN
# THE HOUSE

O NE OF THE GREAT pleasures of roses is to cut and arrange them for the house. Whether a single bloom in a narrow-stemmed jar or a bowl full of blooms, roses bring life to a room as few things can. We are able to enjoy them in a more intimate and quite different way, and get to know them better.

No other flower is quite so beautiful at close quarters. Here is yet another field in which roses can be used for the most beautiful effects.

Almost all roses are suitable as cut flowers, particularly the Old Roses and the English Roses. The English Roses have the advantage of providing a wider range of colour than the Old Roses. They also last longer in water and, of course, unlike most of the Old Roses, they flower throughout the summer. The Hybrid Teas, with their rather angular flowers, are a little more difficult to arrange successfully but can, with a little extra skill, be very beautiful. These are the main groups of roses for use as cut flowers, but others can play an important auxiliary role. Most of these produce numerous small flowers in sprays, such as the Polyantha Roses, the Ground-cover Roses and many of the Rambler Roses. These can be used alone, but are particularly good for mixing with larger-flowered varieties, where they help to reduce the rather 'blobby' effect we sometimes get.

Single-flowered roses can enhance an arrangement, playing much the same role as the small-flowered ones, but they are not really practical as they often have a very short vase life. Where single roses come into their own is in the colourful hips that follow the flowers. These can form a delightful addition to an autumn bowl of roses or any other flowers. The hips of Species Roses vary widely in shape, all the way from the large, heavy fruit of *Rosa rugosa* to the long, elegant hips of *Rosa moyesii*—or, again, to the small black hips of the Scots Roses (*Rosa spinossisima*). There are also many single or semi-double flowered shrub roses that produce fine hips —the Shrub Rose 'Scintillation' is a fine example.

As a rose breeder and nurseryman, I frequently cut blooms and bring them indoors in order to study them more closely, but I cannot claim to be any kind of expert or to have any particular theories on flower arrangement. In the main, I prefer a simple and seemingly casual effect. Achieving this is not as easy as it may seem, for roses are not the most obedient of flowers. They have a habit of flopping over and looking in quite the wrong direction, and it is hard to get them to stand just as one would wish. Nearly always, you need something to hold them. Various holders are available on the market. Oasis or crumpled wire netting may also be used. I sometimes place a small jar within a larger bowl to act as support. There is room for considerable ingenuity here. Alternatively, if we go out into the garden and pick a large bunch of roses and simply dump them in an upright bowl, with a little adjustment, this often results in a beautiful chance effect.

Roses are not only beautiful in a bowl of their own; they can also associate very well with other flowers. In fact, it is easier to arrange them in this way, and it is often possible to create beautiful pictures. A few flowers we might use include: *Alchemilla mollis* with its yellow-green starry flowers and rounded soft green leaves; the large shapely leaves of any of the hostas; gypsophila for its dainty, many-flowered sprays of small pale flowers. Larkspur, particularly the paler blue, can give a pretty effect and looks especially well with roses of pink shades, as do nigella and cornflower. Copper beech can be very useful as a foil, particularly for red roses. Honeysuckles are lovely in combination with Old Roses. Ferns also might be used, as well as ivies.

Choosing bowls and vases for roses is a matter worthy of

*A wonderfully rich arrangement with the English Roses WILLIAM SHAKESPEARE 2000 and CHARLES RENNIE MACKINTOSH with the rampant weed, rosebay willow herb, and marjoram,* Origanum laevigatum 'Hopleys'

346

some thought. If the roses are to last well in an arrangement, their stems must be placed as deeply as possible in the water. Deep containers, whether small or large, rounded or straight sided, are generally more suitable than shallow ones. You can use jugs, old tea-pots, buckets and all manner of other receptacles. You might even consider collecting such objects when the chance arises. Glass vases can be flattering for roses, particularly when the light shines through them to show their stems. There is no reason why you should be restricted to the use of a single container. A group of bowls can often be effective, such as one large bowl with one or two smaller bowls around it. Small bowls can be useful. Blooms can be picked with short stems and placed in them, or even floated in them. These will show off the individual flowers to perfection.

*The upright stems of* SOPHY'S ROSE *make it an easy rose to arrange. Here it is with the exotic flowers of the glory lily,* Gloriosa superba 'Rothschildiana', *and a few pieces of a* Clematis viticella.

## THE ENGLISH CUT ROSES

At David Austin Roses we have developed a range of roses especially for the cut-flower trade. These are similar in form of flower to English Roses for the garden, except that they are bred to be grown under glass. They are the result of crossing English Rose varieties with cut-flower varieties of the Hybrid Teas. Instead of the pointed bud of the Hybrid Tea, they have the typical rosette flower of an Old Rose or an English Rose.

Unlike the vast majority of Hybrid Teas bred especially for cutting, which have no fragrance, the English Cut Roses have a strong fragrance. Unfortunately this fragrance comes at the cost of their ability to last long in water. The English Rose will last two or three days less than a typical Cut Hybrid Tea. The reason for this is that the chemicals that give us the wonderful rose scent also have the effect of hastening the decay of the petals of a rose. In other words, fragrance and lasting power are not compatible. This is true of all kinds of roses —not just English Roses. So we have to

349

*A very simple but charming little arrangement of the strongly fragrant JUBILEE CELEBRATION with a pulmonaria*

make a choice between the beautiful Old Rose flowers and rich fragrance of the English type and the rather mechanical flower and absence of fragrance of a typical Cut Hybrid Tea. We have taken the view that many people would prefer to have the fragrance at the expense of a slightly longer vase life.

The varieties of Cut Hybrid Tea are too numerous to include here and, in any case, are for specialist growers. At the time of writing, we have six varieties of English Cut Rose. We have been developing these roses since 1992 and are constantly improving them. They are, in fact, very difficult to breed, but we feel sure that we can have even more beautiful flowers with a variety of delicious fragrances in the years to come.

**Emily** (syn. Cymbeline) (*Ausglade*) The large, pure rose pink blooms have many folded petals arranged in a traditional Old Rose quartered style. As they open, the backs of the outer petals develop hints of lilac. The fragrance begins as the classic English myrrh, later developing aspects of heliotrope, vanilla and fruit.

**Juliet** (*Ausjameson*) Large, elegant flowers are a rich, creamy apricot-yellow. When fully open, they reveal many neatly-arranged petals nestling in folds at the heart of the bloom. Light Tea Rose fragrance.

**Miranda** (*Ausimmon*) This rose is remarkable for the giant blooms made up of many wavy petals, perfectly arranged to form beautiful, almost flat rosettes. When fully open, the heart of the rose is a pure rose pink while the outer petals turn back slightly and pale to the softest shades of pink. The outer petals of the huge buds have a lovely streaked green effect, which adds to the garden style, creating a look reminiscent of a parrot tulip. The outer petals become gradually hidden as the bloom opens.

**Patience** (*Auspastor*) The creamy-yellow buds gradually open out fully to form perfect, flat medium-sized frilled rosettes. The central petals stay folded in a classic button eye while the outer, frilled petals reflex and are reminiscent of fine lace. Over time, the buttermilk colour may pale almost to white, especially when placed in bright sunlight. There is an Old Rose fragrance with elements of fruit, lilac and myrrh. The fragrance is initially fairly strong, but tends to fade as the bloom ages.

**Phoebe** (originally 'Olivia Austin') (*Ausnotice*) This was in the first group of introductions in 2004 and is now only available in the United States of America. It has large, full-petalled blooms of pure rose-pink, the petals being arranged in a perfect rosette. The fragrance is deliciously fruity.

**Rosalind** (*Austew*) The small blush-pink buds open slowly into beautiful, peony-like blooms with a very natural and delicate appearance. There is a fruity fragrance.

*An informal arrangement of English Roses with the apricot JUBILEE CELEBRATION, strong pink GERTRUDE JEKYLL and HARLOW CARR, pale pink SCEPTER'D ISLE and EGLANTYNE and mid pink JAMES GALWAY in the lower right corner, making a rich and wonderfully fragrant mixture of blossoms*

# 12

# ROSE CULTIVATION

WHEN I AM ASKED FOR MY OPINION on the cultivation of roses, I usually start by saying that this need not be arduous. If you do no more than work the soil to a reasonable tilth and then plant your roses, firming them in gently, you can be sure of reasonable results. If you then prune them each year to a height of about two-thirds in the case of English Roses and Old Roses, and Bush Roses to about 20cm/8in, you will have good results every year. How good these will be depends, in some degree, on the soil being of at least average quality.

Having said this, there is no doubt that if you go into the subject in a little more detail, and are prepared to do a little more work, this will not only give you much better results, but also a great deal more satisfaction. Rose growing is an art and it is a pleasure to create the most beautiful pictures that you can. The following notes are intended for those who wish to make the most of their roses. Before I go further, I should say that my advice is for gardeners in the British Isles and other temperate regions in the northern hemisphere. Gardeners in other climates will need to consult books on rose growing in their area.

Most of the ancestors of the garden rose are natives of more fertile areas of the world and it is worth giving them a prime position. However, I should say that even the poorest soils can be made suitable by the addition of generous quantities of humus. Again, roses will not thrive in a position where there is too much shade. Avoid any area that has overhanging trees. South-facing sites are entirely satisfactory. West-facing is no problem. East-facing sites are not very good and a north-facing site is not really suitable at all. The problem is not only a question of shade; roses do not like competition from the roots of trees and shrubs. It is better to plant well away from these.

Then there is the question of rose re-plant disease, a disease which, not everyone agrees, exists. It is more likely that this is a collection of diseases which vary according to the area chosen. However this may be, it is certain that if a rose is planted in soil where roses have been before, they seldom thrive, even when the roses you have removed have been doing well. The simple answer to this problem is to move on and plant in fresh ground. Unfortunately this is not always possible—particularly in a carefully planned formal garden

*The rose borders either side of a sinuous grass path in the Renaissance Garden at David Austin Roses: in February (near right), with the roses pruned, tidied and mulched, through to full flower in late June (opposite, far right)*

352

and in a position where you specifically desire to have roses. The choice in such cases is to either replace the soil with high quality new soil from a different area before you plant the new ones or to treat the soil where they have been growing with ample quanitites of humus and Root Grow.

## Preparing the Soil

It is advisable to prepare the soil thoroughly before you plant. Dig to a depth of about 30cm/1ft. This should be done by trench digging: as you move the top soil, break up the subsoil in the trench with a fork to give good drainage and enable the long tap roots to go down deep. Give the top soil a liberal dressing of either well-rotted compost or well-rotted manure. This should be carefully mixed with the soil. Alternatively, you may find it convenient to buy proprietary planting compost from your Garden Centre.

## Planting

Planting of bare-rooted roses can be done at any time from autumn to late spring (mid October to the end of April in the UK). If you purchase container-grown roses, these can be planted at any time of year. In my opinion, bare-rooted roses are marginally superior to those grown in pots. They are able to develop their root system according to where they are planted. In any case, after a year or two, there is likely to be very little difference.

I would like, once again, to emphasise the advantages of growing roses in groups of three or more bushes of one variety, except where they are likely to form very large shrubs. See Chapter 10 for further observations on this point.

## Pruning

People are often baffled by the whole question of pruning. This is usually because they think it is more difficult than it really is. I believe it is as much an art as a craft. A lot depends on the end you wish to achieve. There is, in fact, a lot of latitude that can be taken. The following instructions on pruning should not be taken too literally. Much will depend on the size and even the shape of the shrub you require.

We have English Roses in the centre of our Renaissance Garden which are pruned much more severely than I suggest below and make the most beautiful small shrubs, whereas they could in another place be allowed to grow into much larger shrubs. Pruning may also depend, in some degree, on whether you require large individual flowers or a mass of smaller flowers. If you require the former, you will take away more wood; if you require the latter, you will leave more growth.

I will take the various forms of roses one at a time.

In the UK and elsewhere with relatively mild winters, pruning may be carried out at any time between the beginning of December and the end of March. Later pruning avoids any chance of the new shoots being caught by a late frost. I prefer earlier pruning for repeat-flowering roses, as they then get an earlier start, ensuring a longer season of flowering. It is always disappointing to see the last flush of bloom cut off by an early frost, but I would rather take this risk. In regions with cold winters, delay pruning until spring growth is just starting.

### Old Roses

On the whole, these roses require minimal pruning. When you receive your plants from your nurseryman, they will probably have been cut back sufficiently for the first year. If not, cut them down to about half their height. Very little pruning will be required in the second year. After that you should cut back any long main shoots by about one third of their length. The side shoots should be shortened to about 8cm/3in. In future, as the plant continues to mature, some of the growth will age and become unproductive—and other branches will die. These should be cut hard back to encourage new growth. Dead shoots must, of course, be removed completely.

Repeat-flowering Old Roses should receive very much the same treatment as the once-flowering roses. Many of the Bourbons and Hybrid Perpetuals will make tall and perhaps rather upright shrubs and in such cases it may suit your requirements to prune down to half their size.

### Hybrid Teas and Floribundas

Being bushes rather than shrubs, Hybrid Teas and Floribundas should be pruned to about 12cm/5in from the ground in the first year. From then onwards, stronger shoots should be pruned back to half their length and thinner side shoots, to 5 or 8cm/2 or 3in.

### English Roses

The English Roses are a diverse group bred from a wide variety of different parents. This makes it difficult to lay down hard and fast rules for pruning. Since we have done our best to breed roses of natural, bushy or arching growth, it is important to encourage and retain this rather than change it by over-pruning. If the growth is naturally bushy, insofar as is possible, try to help the rose to express itself.

As a rule, as with the Old Roses, it is usually best to first reduce the growth by one third. This may vary in accordance with the kind of shrub you require for any particular position. It is quite possible to prune a quite large English Rose very severely and get a quite small shrub. Having done the initial pruning, go over the plant again and cut back the short side shoots to about 8 or 10cm/3 or 4in. As the years go by, it will be necessary to occasionally take out dying and unproductive growth.

### Species Roses

The Species and their hybrids require little or no pruning except perhaps for the removal of dead wood. If they outgrow the position in which they are planted, try not to spoil the natural growth of the shrub. Take out whole branches insofar as this is possible, rather than cutting back branches in the manner of a hedge.

### Modern Shrub Roses

Most Modern Shrub Roses should be treated in the same way as the Species, as these roses are generally close to them in their breeding. With Modern Shrubs that are truly repeat-flowering, more pruning will be required. They can be treated in very much the same way as English Roses. Cut back the main shoots by about one third, then cut the short side shoots to about 8 or 10cm/3 or 4in and remove old wood.

### Ground Cover Roses

These require little pruning except for the removal of old and spent wood. Other than this, it is simply necessary to keep them within bounds.

### Miniature Roses

Miniature Roses need little pruning other than to cut out the oldest stems after a few years. Some varieties tend to have a desire to grow too tall and cease to be miniature. Such roses benefit from some cutting back.

### Standards and Weeping Standards

Pruning Standards is very much the same as for their bushy or shrubby brethren. If a variety is grown as a Standard, try to make as broad a head as possible. With Weeping Standards, the aim should be to build up growth, rather than reduce it: it is good to see this reach to the ground. Sometimes the shoots tend to grow upwards rather than down. These can be tied into position, or the whole shoot might be taken away, if this is not going to spoil the balance of the plant.

### Climbers and Ramblers

Repeat-flowering Climbing Roses of all kinds should have the side shoots that have borne the flowers in the previous season, shortened to about 8 or 10cm/3 or 4in. The main long growth needs to be tied into position, in order to bear further flowering growth for the coming seasons. When these become old and unproductive, they can be removed altogether to make way for further growth. Exactly when this will be depends on how well the rose is doing as a whole and whether growth can be spared, although it is of little use to keep old growth beyond a certain point.

The Rambler Roses require very little attention in the way of pruning. They can be left, to some extent, to their own devices. In this way we can achieve a natural, billowing effect, which often results in a beautiful display. Simply remove some of the growth when this becomes out of hand. If, however, you want something more neat and trim, as for example when the Ramblers are trained on an arch or a pergola, you should—as with the Climbing Roses—take out such main shoots as you can spare and cut back the side shoots to about 8 or 10cm/3 or 4in.

### Removing Suckers

Most roses are grown on root stocks and from time to time these may send up their own shoots which are generally known as 'suckers'. It is vital that these should be removed as soon as possible; otherwise they will soon take over the whole plant. Cut them as hard back as you can. It is advisable to take a little bark of the stock as you do this, thus eliminating all possibilities of it shooting again from the same point. Before doing this, however, you should take care that it is truly a sucker. The vigorous young growth of some shrub roses and especially the Albas is sometimes mistaken for suckers and so must not be removed. Suckers coming from the rootstocks have seven leaflets but then so do many other roses and this should not be used as a means of identification.

## Maintenance

Having completed the pruning of our roses, it is now necessary to consider the question of maintenance. By pruning time the soil will have become rather compacted and a light pricking over of the soil with a fork to a depth of 2 or 5cm/1 or 2in will help to aerate it. This is not entirely necessary, but I think it is beneficial. It also gives a chance to remove any weeds that may have appeared.

At this time it will be desirable to give the soil a feed in the form of a long-term fertilizer. Such rose fertilizers are available and they are nearly all good.

This done, it is a good idea to lay down a mulch of rotted compost or farmyard manure. This is not essential, but there is nothing better you can do in order to provide a good show of blooms in the coming summer. It will keep the soil cool and retain moisture—and at the same time help the life in the soil and provide an additional source of nutrition. During the flowering season, further dressings of fertilizers can be given at intervals. These should be high in nitrogen and should be applied towards the end of a flush of bloom in order to encourage further growth and flowers for the next flush.

During the summer, dead-heading will be necessary. This will stop the formation of hips, which use up the energy of the plant, thus inhibiting further bloom. This also gives us the opportunity to tidy up the shrub generally. If a rose is single flowered, it will often produce decorative hips and you may prefer to retain these rather than have further bloom. The vast majority of Species do not repeat flower, but often have the most beautiful hips.

### Watering
Watering is not essential in the British climate, but there can be no doubt that it will ensure much better flowering and continuity of flowering. Most garden plants flower only once in a season, but the rose has been bred to flower throughout the summer. It can do this well only if it is provided with moisture. This is not an unpleasant job—if you use a hosepipe, you have a good opportunity to enjoy your roses at the same time.

### Diseases and Pests
Disease in roses is perhaps their greatest drawback as a garden plant, yet I do not think it is as bad as some people think. There are some roses in all classes that are susceptible to disease and this is true especially of the Hybrid Teas and Floribundas.

It is possible to grow roses without spraying, if they are scattered around the garden rather than planted close to each other. If you have a rose border or a rose garden it is almost always necessary to spray, unless you confine yourself to a rather restricted number of disease-free varieties. The more recent English Roses come into this category and nearly all the Ground Cover Roses are highly resistant to disease.

There are a number of excellent sprays on the market and they can be obtained from any garden centre. They should be used in accordance with the makers' instructions. Spraying should be done as soon as the disease appears and repeated at intervals throughout the summer.

There are four main diseases of roses:
- POWDERY MILDEW This looks rather like a white powder. It is encouraged by dryness at the roots and so can be prevented by deep watering before the soil dries out. It is often variety specific.
- BLACKSPOT Usually occurs in midsummer (July or August in the UK) and spreads rapidly if not controlled. The spores only germinate if the leaves stay wet for at least seven hours when the weather is warm. Therefore, if you are watering, do so at a time when the leaves can dry out relatively quickly—usually in the morning. There is a great deal of variability in resistance between varieties although most have the potential to blackspot.
- RUST This appears as bright orange and later black pustules on the undersides of the leaves and occasionally stems. It occurs in cool weather, early or more likely late in the season. It is more difficult to eradicate but spraying will at least hold it back.
- DOWNY MILDEW Is not so common as the other three and is rather hard to detect. One sure sign is when the leaves begin to drop prematurely. Downy mildew tends to occur when you have low night temperatures and high humidity in the day. Because of that, you tend to get it earlier and later in the season. It is a disease that is found only on certain varieties.

Insect pests are less of a problem than disease. They are easily controlled by spraying with a proprietary insecticide. Alternatively encourage as many beneficial insects into your garden as possible, they can be most effective.

## The Life-Span of a Rose
Finally, there is the question of 'How long does a rose actually live?' This is rather like asking 'How long is a piece of string?' Some roses live for a very long time. On the walls of my house I have the Climbing version of the Hybrid Tea 'Madame Caroline Testout' which is, I know for a fact, over one hundred years old. Admittedly, it is only just alive now.

Generally, Hybrid Teas and Floribundas do not live as long as Shrub Roses but there is no doubt that there comes a point when any rose will begin to deteriorate. There is often a gradual decline. Before this becomes too steep, it is probably best to dig the rose up and replace it. So often we go around a garden and find a rose that consists of no more than two or three dying sticks. On the whole, it is repeat-flowering roses that tend to die earliest; they are under greater strain to produce flowers throughout the summer. The once-flowering Old Roses can go on living for a very long time indeed; this is perhaps the reason why they have remained with us to the present day.

# Glossary

**Anther** The part of the flower which produces pollen; the upper section of the stamen.

**Arching shrub** A shrub in which the long main branches bend down towards the soil, usually in a graceful manner.

**Balled, balling** The clinging together of petals due to damp, so that the bloom fails to open.

**Bare-root roses** Roses bought without soil, not in a container.

**Basal shoot** The strong main shoot that arises from the base of the rose.

**Bicolour** A rose bloom with two distinct shades of colour.

**Boss** The bunch of stamens at the centre of a flower.

**Bract** A modified leaf at the base of a flower stalk.

**Break** New growth from a branch.

**Budding** The usual method for the propagation of roses by the grafting of a leaf bud on to the neck of a root stock.

**Bud-shaped flower** I have coined this term to describe rose blooms that are in the form of a Hybrid Tea, i.e. flowers that are of high-centred bud formation and mainly beautiful in the bud (as opposed to those of Old Rose formation).

**Bud Union** The point where the rose stems join the root stock.

**Bush** I use this word to describe a closely pruned bedding rose, as for example a Hybrid Tea.

**Bushy shrub** A rose of dense, rounded growth.

**Button Eye** A button-like fold of petals in the centre of a rose bloom.

**Calyx** The green protective cover over the flower bud which opens into five sepals.

**Cane** A long rose stem, from the base of the plant, particularly as in a Rambling Rose.

**Chromosomes** Chains of linked genes contained in the cells of plants and animals.

**Climbing sport** See SPORT; the climbing form of this phenomenon.

**Corymb** A flower cluster that is flat-topped, or nearly so.

**Cross** See HYBRID.

**Cultivar** Plant raised or selected in cultivation.

**Denomination** The intellectual nomenclature recognised world wide under the auspices of plant breeders' rights and patents.

**Die back** The progressive dying back of a shoot from the tip.

**Diploid** A plant with two sets of chromosomes.

**Flore Pleno** Double flower.

**Flush** A period of blooming.

**Gene** A unit of heredity controlling inherited characteristics of a plant.

**Genus, genera** A group or groups of plants having common characteristics, e.g. *Rosa*.

**Group** The name for cultivars that have similar characteristics

**Heeling-in** Temporary planting of roses when conditions are not suitable for permanent planting.

**Height** The heights given for individual varieties are only approximate. Much will depend on soil, site, season and geographic area. The breadth of a rose bush or shrub will usually be slightly less than the height.

**Hips, heps** Seed pods of a rose.

**Hybrid** A rose resulting from crossing two different species or varieties.

**Leaflets** The individual section of a leaf.

**Modern appearance, rose of** Rose that usually has high-pointed buds and smooth foliage, similar to a Hybrid Tea Rose.

**Mutation** See SPORT.

**Old appearance, rose of** Rose with bloom of cupped or rosette shape, rather than the pointed bud and informal flower of a Modern Rose; the plant usually having rough textured leaves, i.e. Gallica, Centifolia, etc.

**Organic fertilizer** A fertilizer made from natural materials rather than chemicals.

**Patent appellation** The variety denomination which is protected by Plant Breeders' Rights worldwide

**Perpetual flowering** A rose that continues to flower in the same year after the first flush of bloom, though not necessarily continually.

**Pistil** Female organ of a flower consisting of the stigma, style and ovary.

**Pollen parent** The male parent of a variety.

**Pompon** A small rounded bloom with regular short petals.

**Quartered** A flower in which the centre petals are folded into four.

**Quilled petals** Petals folded in the form of a quill.

**Rambler-like** I use this term to describe roses bearing large sprays of small blooms similar to those of a small-flowered Rambling Rose, particularly a Multiflora Rambler.

**Recessive gene** A gene that is dominated by another, rendering it ineffective unless two copies of the gene are present.

**Recurrent flowering** See PERPETUAL FLOWERING.

**Remontant** See PERPETUAL FLOWERING.

**Repeat flowering** See PERPETUAL FLOWERING.

**Roots, roses on their own** Not budded on to a stock; grown from cuttings.

**Root stock** The host plant on to which a cultivated variety is budded.

**Rugose** Leaves with a wrinkled surface.

**Scion** A shoot or bud used for grafting on to a root stock.

**Seedling** A rose grown from seed. In the context of this book, the offspring of a variety.

**Sepal** One of the five green divisions of the calyx.

**Shrub** A rose that is normally pruned lightly and allowed to grow in a more natural form, as opposed to a bush which is pruned close to the ground.

**Species** A wild rose.

**Sport** A change in the genetic make up of the plant, as for example when a pink rose suddenly produces a white flower.

**Spreading shrub** A shrub on which the branches tend to extend outwards rather than vertically.

**Stamen** The male organ of a flower, consisting of the filament and anther, which produces pollen.

**Stigma** The end of the pistil or female flower organ.

**Stock** See ROOT-STOCK

**Style** The stem of the pistil which joins the stigma to the ovary.

**Sucker** A shoot growing from the root stock instead of from the budded variety.

**Tetraploid** A plant with four sets of chromosomes.

**Trade designation** See DENOMINATION.

**Triploid** A plant with three sets of chromosomes.

**Upright shrub** A rose in which the growth tends to be vertical.

**Variety** Strictly speaking, a naturally occurring variation of a species. The popular meaning, so far as roses are concerned, is a distinct type of cultivated rose.

× A cross (multiplication sign) that indicates a hybrid

# Bibliography

American Rose Society's *Annuals*, from 1917.

AUSTIN, David *The English Roses*, Conran Octopus, 2005.

BEAN, W.J., *Trees and Shrubs Hardy in the British Isles*, Murray, 8th edn. revised.

BOIS, Eric and TRECHSLIN, Anne-Marie, *Roses*, 1962.

BUNYARD, A.E., *Old Garden Roses*, Collingridge, 1936.

DOBSON, B.R., *Combined Rose List. Hard to Find Roses and Where to Find Them*, Beverly R. Dobson, Irvington, New York 10533, 1985.

EDWARDS, G., *Wild and Old Garden Roses*, David & Charles, Newton Abbot, 1975; Hafner, New York, 1975.

ELLWANGER, H.B., *The Rose*, Dodd-Mead, New York, 1822; 1914.

FISHER, John, *The Companion to Roses*, Viking, 1986

FLETCHER, H.L.V., *The Rose Anthology*, Newnes, 1963.

FOSTER-MELLIAR, Rev. A., *The Book of the Rose*, Macmillan, 1894; 1910.

GAULT S.M. and SYNGE P.M., *The Dictionary of Roses in Colour*, Michael Joseph and Ebury Press, 1970.

GORE, C.F., *The Book of Roses or The Rose Fancier's Manual*, 1838; Heyden, 1978.

GRIFFITHS, Trevor, *The Book of Old Roses*, Michael Joseph, 1984.

GRIFFITHS, Trevor, *The Book of Classic Old Roses*, Michael Joseph, 1986.

HARKNESS, Jack, *Roses,* Dent, 1978.

*Hillier Manual of Trees and Shrubs, The*, 3rd rev edn, David & Charles 2007.

HOLE, S. Reynolds, *A Book about Roses*, William Blackwood, 1896.

HOLLIS, L., *Roses*, Collingridge, 1969; 2nd edn. with new illustrations, 1974.

JEKYLL, G. and MAWLEY, E., *Roses for English Gardens,* Country Life, 1902; reprinted by Antique Collectors' Club, Woodbridge, 1982.

KEAYS, F.L., *Old Roses*, Macmillan, New York, 1935; facsimile edn. Heyden, Philadelphia and London, 1978.

KORDES, Wilhelm, *Roses*, Studio Vista, 1964.

KRUSSMAN, G., *Roses*, English edn, Batsford, 1982.

LAWRENCE, Mary, *A Collection of Roses from Nature*, 1799.

LE GRICE, E.B., *Rose Growing Complete*, Faber & Faber, 1965.

LORD, Tony, *Designing with Roses*, Frances Lincoln, 1999.

McFARLAND, J.H., *Modern Roses*, 8th edn, McFarland Co., USA, 1980.

McFARLAND, J.H., *Roses of the World in Colour*, Cassell, 1936.

MANSFIELD, T.C., *Roses in Colour and Cultivation*, Collins, 1947.

NOTTLE, T., *Growing Old Fashioned Roses in Australia and New Zealand*, Kangaroo Press, 1983.

OLSON, Jerry and John Whitman, *Growing Roses in Cold Climates*, Contemporary Books, 1998.

PAUL, William, *The Rose Garden*, 10th edn, Simpkin, Marshall, Hamilton, Kent & Co., 1903.

PEMBERTON, Rev. J.H., *Roses, Their History, Development and Cultivation*, Longmans Green 1908; rev. edn. 1920.

PHILLIPS, Roger and RIX, Martyn, *The Ultimate Guide to Roses,* Macmillan, 2004.

QUEST-RITSON, Charles and Brigid, *The Royal Horticultural Society Encyclopaedia of Roses*, Dorling Kindersely, 2005.

REDOUTÉ, P.J., *Les Roses*, 1817–24, reprinted by Taschen, 2001.

*RHS Plantfinder* **2007**–**2008**, Dorling Kindersely, 2007.

RIDGE, A., *For the Love of a Rose*, Faber & Faber, 1965.

RIVERS, T., *The Rose Amateur's Guide*, Longmans Green, 1837.

ROSS, D., *Shrub Roses in Australia*, Deane Ross, 1981.

Royal National Rose Society's *Annuals*, from 1911.

SHEPHERD, R., *History of the Rose*, Macmillan, New York, 1966.

STEEN, N., *The Charm of Old Roses*, Herbert Jenkins, 1966.

THOMAS, G.S., *The Old Shrub Roses*, Phoenix House, 1955.

THOMAS, G.S., *Shrub Roses of Today*, Phoenix House, 1962.

THOMAS, G.S., *Climbing Roses Old and New*, Phoenix House, 1965.

THOMPSON, Richard, *Old Roses for Modern Gardens*, Van Nostrand, New York, 1959.

WARNER, C., *Climbing Roses*, Tiptree Books.

WILLMOTT, Ellen, *The Genus Rosa*, Murray, issued in parts 1910–14.

YOUNG, Norman, *The Complete Rosarian*, Hodder & Stoughton, 1971.

# General Index

# Index of Plants Suitable for Growing with Roses

## Intellectual Property Rights

Throughout this book I have referred to each variety by its commercial name. David Austin Roses Ltd reserves all Intellectual Property Rights on their rose varieties and trade marks are listed below. Throughout this book each variety is referred to by its commercial name (eg Heritage). The variety denomination (eg AUSBLUSH) of all varieties protected by Plant Breeders' Rights worldwide is clearly stated in Part Two on each variety's main descriptive page, but have been omitted elsewhere for clarity.

## Trade Marks

This book will be read in many countries, so below is a list of David Austin trade marks that have Trade Mark rights somewhere in the world. For a definitive list for a specific country, contact the Licensing Department, David Austin Roses Limited, on +44 1902 376327.

A Shropshire Lad
Abraham Darby
Admired Miranda
Alan Titchmarsh
Ambridge Rose
Anne Boleyn
Austins Buttercup
Austins Herbalist
Austins Windflower
Barbara Austin
Benjamin Britten
Blythe Spirit
Bredon
Brother Cadfael
Cariad
Charity
Charles Austin
Charles Darwin
Charles Rennie
    Mackintosh
Charlotte
Charmian
Christopher Marlowe
Claire Austin
Claire Rose
Comte de Champagne
    (syn. Coniston)
Coniston (syn. Comte de
    Champagne)
Constance Spry
Corvedale
Cottage Rose
Country Living
Crocus Rose
Crown Princess
    Margareta
Darcey Bussell
Eglantyne
Ellen
Emanuel
England's Rose
English Elegance
English Garden

Evelyn
Fair Bianca
Falstaff
Fighting Temeraire
Fisherman's Friend
Francine Austin
Gentle Hermione
Geoff Hamilton
Gertrude Jekyll
Glamis Castle
Golden Celebration
Grace
Graham Thomas
Happy Child
Harlow Carr
Heather Austin
Heritage
Hyde Hall
James Galway
Janet
Jayne Austin
John Clare
Jubilee Celebration
Jude The Obscure
Kathryn Morley
Kew Gardens
Lady Emma Hamilton
Lady of Megginch
Lady of Shalott
Lady Salisbury
L.D. Braithwaite
Leander
Lichfield Angel
Lilian Austin
Lucetta
Maid Marion
Malvern Hills
Marinette
Mary Magdalene
Mary Rose
Mary Webb
Mayor of Casterbridge
Miss Alice

Mistress Quickly
Molineux
Mortimer Sackler
Mrs Doreen Pike
Munstead Wood
Noble Antony
Othello
Pat Austin
Peach Blossom
Pegasus
Perdita
Portmeirion
Port Sunlight
Princess Alexandra
    of Kent
Princess Anne
Prospero
Queen Anne
Queen Nefertiti
Radio Times
Redouté
Rose-Marie
Rosemoor
Rushing Stream
Scarborough Fair
Scepter'd Isle
Sharifa Asma
Shropshire Lass
Sir Edward Elgar
Sir John Betjeman
Sister Elizabeth
Skylark
Snow Goose
Sophy's Rose
Spirit of Freedom
St Alban
St Cecilia
St Swithun
Summer Song
Susan Williams-Ellis
Sweet Juliet
Symphony

Tam o'Shanter
Tea Clipper
Teasing Georgia
Tess of the d'Urbervilles
The Alexandra Rose
The Alnwick® Rose
The Countryman
The Dark Lady
The Generous Gardener
The Ingenious
    Mr Fairchild
The Lady's Blush
The Mayflower
The Pilgrim
The Prince
The Shepherdess
The Squire
The Wedgwood Rose
The Yeoman
Tradescant
Trevor Griffiths
Warwick Castle
Wenlock
Wife of Bath
Wild Edric
Wildeve
William and Catherine
William Morris
William Shakespeare
William Shakespeare
    2000
Winchester Cathedral
Windrush
Wisley 2008
Wollerton Old Hall
Yellow Charles Austin
Young Lycidas

Austin
David Austin
David Austin Roses

## David Austin Roses

Bowling Green Lane,
Albrighton,
Wolverhampton WV7 3HB
*Telephone* +44 (0)1902 376300
*Fax* +44 (0)1902 375177
*Email* retail@davidaustinroses.com
www.davidaustinroses.com